The Perilous Frontier

Studies in Social Discontinuity

General Editor   *Charles Tilly, The New School for Social Research*

Studies in Social Discontinuity began in 1972 under the imprint of Academic Press. In its first 15 years, 53 titles were published in the series, including important volumes in the areas of historical sociology, political economy, and social history.

Revived in 1989 by Basil Blackwell, the series will continue to include volumes emphasizing social changes and non-Western historical experience as well as translations of major works.

Titles now in preparation include:

Regents and Rebels
The Revolutionary World of an Eighteenth-Century Dutch City
Wayne Ph. Te Brake

Nascent Proletarians
Class Formation in Post-Revolutionary France
Michael P. Hanagan

Modern French Anti-Semitism
A Political History
Pierre Birnbaum

Coffee and Contention
Political Change in Modern Brazil
Mauricio Font

Rites of Revolt
The War of the Demoiselles in Ariège, France (1829–1831)
Peter Sahlins

The Perilous Frontier

Nomadic Empires and China

Thomas J. Barfield

Basil Blackwell

Basil Blackwell Inc.
3 Cambridge Center
Cambridge, Massachusetts 02142, USA

Basil Blackwell Ltd
108 Cowley Road, Oxford, OX4 1JF, UK

Library of Congress Cataloging in Publication Data

Barfield, Thomas J. (Thomas Jefferson), 1950–
The perilous frontier.
(Studies in social discontinuity)
Bibliography: p.
Includes index.
1. Asia, Central–Relations–China.
2. China–Relations–Asia, Central.
3. Nomads–Asia, Central–History.   I. Title.
II. Series: Studies in social discontinuity
(Basil Blackwell Publisher)
DS329.4.B37 1989   958   88–7746
ISBN 1–55786043–2

British Library Cataloguing in Publication Data

Barfield, Thomas J. (Thomas
Jefferson), 1950–
The perilous frontier: nomadic empires
and China. – (Studies in social
discontinuity).
1. Asia. Inner Asia. Nomadic tribes. Social
change, history
I. Title II. Series
951

ISBN 1–55786–043–2

Typeset in 10 on 11 pt Ehrhardt
by Vera-Reyes, Inc.
Printed in Great Britain by T.J. Press Ltd., Padstow, Cornwall

Contents

Editor's Preface

Charles Tilly, New School for Social Research

THIS SERIES

Studies in Social Discontinuity present historically grounded analyses of important social transformations, ruptures, conflicts, and contradictions. Although we of Basil Blackwell interpret that mission broadly, leave room for many points of view, and absolve authors of any responsibility for propaganda on behalf of our intellectual program, the series as a whole demonstrates the relevance of well-crafted historical work for the understanding of contemporary social structures and processes. Books in the series pursue one or more of four varieties of historical analysis: (1) using evidence from past times and places systematically to identify regularities in processes and structures that transcend those particular times and places; (2) reconstructing critical episodes in the past for the light they shed on important eras, peoples, or social phenomena; (3) tracing the origins or previous phases of significant social processes that continue into our own time; (4) examining the ways that social action at a given point in time lays down residues that limit the possibilities of subsequent social action.

The fourth theme is at once the least familiar and the most general. Social analysts have trouble seeing that history matters precisely because social interaction takes place in well-defined times and places, and occurs within constraints offered by those times and places, producing social relations and artifacts that are themselves located in space-time and whose existence and distribution constrain subsequent social interaction. The construction of a city in a given place and time affects urban growth in adjacent areas and subsequent times. Where and when industrialization occurs affects how it occurs. Initial visions of victory announce a war's likely outcomes. A person's successive migrations have cumulative effects on his or her subsequent mobility through such simple matters as the presence or absence of information about new opportunities in different places and the presence or absence of social ties to possible destinations. A population's previous experience with wars, Baby Booms, and migrations haunts it in the form of bulging or empty cohorts and unequal numbers of the sexes. All these are profoundly historical matters, even when they occur in the present; time and place are of their essence. They form the essential subject matter of *Studies in Social Discontinuity*.

Edward Shorter, Stanley Holwitz, and I plotted the Studies in Social Discontinuity in 1970–1; the first book, William Christian's *Person and God in a Spanish Valley*, appeared in 1972. Over the years, Academic Press published more than 50 titles in the series. But during the early 1980s publication slowed, and then ceased. In 1988, happily, Basil Blackwell agreed to revive the Studies under my editorship. The appearance of Thomas Barfield's *Perilous Frontier* begins the new enterprise.

THIS BOOK

The new beginning is auspicious. In a bold, sweeping analysis, Barfield reanalyzes the interaction between successive Chinese mainland empires and the various nomadic empires that formed in the steppe to their north, preying upon the Chinese with great effectiveness. For almost two millennia nomadic empires formed and reformed in the steppe; from the thirteenth to seventeenth centuries the Eurasian Mongol empire was arguably the world's most extensive and powerful. The thriving of such a vast empire on a nomadic base has always seemed peculiar, even a contradiction in terms, so much that analysts have often denied that anything resembling a real empire ever lived for long on the steppe. As a consequence, relations between imperial nomads and imperially organized Chinese, including the frequent conquests of China from the north and the existence of a Mongol-run Chinese empire, have likewise remained troubling.

Historians have customarily treated that interaction as a peripheral feature of Chinese experience, as part of the biography of particular nomadic groups, or as a feature of Asia's frontier regions. It took an anthropologist to turn the problem around, and treat the interaction itself as the focus of a long, long history. While reflecting on his field work with nomads of Afghanistan, Barfield began to see that their diverse social organizations depended heavily not on their mode of production but on their relations to other powerful groups in their environments. That led him to examine the surprising durability of imperial organization in the Eurasian steppe, and to investigate the possibility that the empires of Mongols and other predatory nomads thrived not because of their ability to extract resources from their own people, but because of tribute they drew from their neighbors. Barfield pursued that possibility across 2,000 years of Asian history.

The possibility became a probability, even a near-certainty, and a new perspective opened upon a very old history. What had seemed to be ceremonies in which Mongols submitted themselves to Chinese overlordship, for example, turned out to be the occasions of exchanges in which nomad chiefs profited handsomely. Chinese rulers paid protection to their northern neighbors, and with that support the northerners maintained control over their own people and predation over a vast hinterland. Mongol power, however, generally contracted when Manchurian groups were conquering China, because ruling Manchurians maintained a separate military and political structure which fought the Mongols on their own terrain. "No nomadic state ever emerged from Mongolia," remarks Barfield, "during periods when north China was torn apart by warlord struggles following the collapse of a long-lived native dynasty" (p. 14). The farther the story goes, the more fascinating it becomes.

The story matters to more than sinologists. Predatory steppe nomads – Huns, Turks, Tatars, Mongols, and others – battered Europe's eastern states for centuries, formed their own strong states along that frontier, and deeply influenced the formation of other states in Eastern Europe, not to mention the Middle East. Barfield's analysis helps explain how they maintained their surprising power. Chinggis and Khubilai Khan become more than mighty warriors, and come to exemplify the system of control in a peculiar and potent sort of empire. *The Perilous Frontier* challenges, furthermore, our common presumption that empires build their strength on internal hierarchies ultimately dependent on the labor of subjugated peasants in a landlord-dominated agrarian economy. The imperial process illuminated by Barfield illustrates, finally, the ways in which past history constrains the operation of present social structure. Over enormously long periods the efficient practice of economic predation built organizations of kinship and politics that endured beyond the ready availability of the prey, and affected the behavior of nomads who had nothing but their flocks to control and each other to battle. Barfield tells this complex, crucial story with consummate skill.

Preface

Until the advent of modern times the nomads of the Eurasian steppe periodically established powerful empires and then invaded bordering sedentary
civilizations. Though their numbers were few, their economies underdevel-
oped, and their cultural sophistication limited, these nomads had an undeniable
impact on world history. In the eyes of their neighbors they were the archetypi-
cal barbarians, alien, yet potentially powerful and dangerous. Historians, both
ancient and modern, have attempted to explain the nature of these societies and
their relations with the outside world, yet satisfactory answers, like the nomads
themselves, seem to appear only fleetingly on the intellectual horizon before
vanishing out of reach.

In large measure this difficulty has arisen because the nomadic peoples of
Inner Asia were organized in a very different fashion from their sedentary
neighbors. Tribal in political structure and raising livestock for a living, the
dynamics of steppe nomadic culture were not readily apparent to their eth-
nocentric neighbors. Although a surprisingly large number of descriptions
written by sedentary historians (particularly by the Chinese) have survived, they
rarely treat the nomads on their own terms. The nomads, of course, took their
own customs for granted. The few inscriptions and texts produced by the tribes
themselves assume the reader is intimately familiar with steppe life and values.

This book is an attempt to unravel some of the history of Inner Asia by
applying anthropological models of tribal and state development to the available
historical data on the tribal peoples who bordered China's northern frontier.
The Chinese frontier was chosen because it was here that the largest and most
complex nomadic polities, such as those of the Hsiung-nu, Turks, and Mongols
arose. The Chinese historical records of their northern neighbors were also of
unparalleled richness. Although this work draws very heavily on these original
sources, it attempts to use them to define the sphere of interaction between
Inner Asia and China from the perspective of the steppe. Historians who find
the description of Chinese events and policies a bit too sketchy should realize

that only enough is included to understand what problems the Inner Asians faced, the very opposite of the usual approach in Chinese studies which relegates Inner Asia to a few summary paragraphs. Similarly, the anthropological models of political and economic organization are applied to the historical data in order to show how they can make sense of the seemingly endless series of wars, empires, and invasions which have traditionally made Inner Asian history a subject to be avoided.

Anthropologists are fond of proposing general models, but then ignoring the details. In this work I wish to demonstrate that models of interaction can be tested against historical data to explain major changes within specific time frames. The anthropology throws light on the events, while the events more clearly define how the rules of these interactions were played out in the real world. Working in this way produces a general history of the steppe tribal frontier in East Asia over the course of 2,000 years, but this is a byproduct of the analysis. It is by no means a complete history. The considerable secondary literature on Inner Asia is only briefly discussed, for example, and some of the lesser known periods receive a greater treatment than is usually found in standard histories. For the specialist, the issue will be whether the proposed hypotheses hold up under more detailed scrutiny. For the general reader, the major question will be whether it is possible to come away with a clear idea of Inner Asia as a dynamic part of world history with its own distinct cultural patterns.

My interest in the relationship between nomadic and sedentary peoples grew out of ethnographic research in Central Asia. For two years I conducted fieldwork among the Central Asian Arab nomads of northern Afghanistan. They migrated annually from the lowland marshes of the Oxus River to the high mountain pastures of Badakhshan. Specializing in raising sheep for urban meat markets, they were thoroughly integrated into the local economy in spite of their nomadic ways. Their social organization followed the lines of a modified conical clan, more typical of Inner Asia than the Middle East. In researching their history I found that nomadic tribes in central Asia had developed distinctively different relationships with their sedentary neighbors. Although patterns of domestic life and livestock production were quite similar (with differences attributable largely to ecological conditions), each tribe's political organization, economic ties with the outside world, and degree of centralization varied widely. These differences appeared to have less to do with internal developments than external relations. Since nomadic pastoral peoples today are entirely encapsulated by sedentary states, history rather than ethnography seemed to be the place to investigate this question for the broad range of nomadic societies that once dominated Inner Asia.

It was after my anthropological fieldwork that I discovered that classic dynastic histories of imperial China normally contained extensive accounts of the foreign peoples along its borders. Because the nomads of the northern frontier traditionally constituted a major foreign policy problem for China, they were treated in some detail. I am not a sinologist, but for over a century there has been a tradition of translating these histories of foreign peoples into

Western languages, sometimes derisively referred to as "translating the bar-barians." In almost all these works the authors' stated purpose was to make these records available to those who worked outside of Chinese studies, although in practice few non-sinologists were aware of the depth of this record. For an anthropologist interested in frontier relations they are extremely reveal-ing, providing more long-term historical information on tribal politics and economics than is found anywhere else in the world. However, the translations vary in quality and are not adequate for investigating some of the more complex problems of linguistics or geography. To avoid drawing unwarranted con-clusions, the translations quoted in the book have been compared against the original sources by more competent scholars for basic accuracy and changes made to apply a unified transcription system to names and places. Dual citation has been employed so that sinologists can more easily verify the original source.

I was encouraged in undertaking this research by the late Professor Joseph Fletcher, the premier historian of Inner Asia, whose own work ranged over a variety of cross-cultural approaches. He was enthusiastic about applying an-thropology, with its rich ethnographic tradition, to the historical study of people whose culture, economy, and social organization were not well understood. As an anthropologist more familiar with nomadic migrations than historical sources I expressed some trepidation, but he offered to guide me past scholarly pitfalls more numerous and deadly than the feigned retreats of Chinggis Khan. He gave freely of his unrivaled knowledge of Inner Asian history, both of the original sources and the secondary literature. We would meet to discuss the draft chapters as I produced them and no author could ask for a more challenging, yet sympathetic, critic. His untimely death has left a great void in the discipline and taken a good friend from me. This book is dedicated to his memory.

I would like to express my gratitude to the Fairbank Center for East Asian Research at Harvard for facilitating a study outside the usual canons of East Asian history. There I had both access to the necessary library resources and the opportunity to consult with scholars whose intimate knowledge of Inner Asian history and linguistics was much greater than my own. Among the scholars who commented directly on the manuscript I am particularly indebted to Francis Cleaves, Elizabeth Endicott-West, Chin-fu Hung, Anatoly Khaza-nov, Michael Khodarkovsky, Ho-dong Kim, Beatrice Manz, Nancy Park, Omeljan Pritsak, and Lothar von Faulkenhausen, for their suggestions as to how I might correct and improve various versions of the draft manuscript. I am for my own part, of course, fully responsible for the errors in fact and interpretation inevitably contained in the monograph presented here.

I also feel a strong sense of gratitude to those scholars whom I know only through their writings, and upon whose critical foundation this work depends. It is said that books and articles these days have a half-life of only a few years or decades before becoming completely obsolete. This is not true of the relatively few works about Inner Asia. One shares in the excitement of fresh discovery and passionate debate coming through the sometimes yellowing pages of volumes relegated to the quiet recesses of great research libraries. These scholars, whose works have too often lain fallow for long periods (if library circulation cards are a reliable indicator), have been my colleagues in an extremely long-running international seminar. Like many of them, my interest in the topic has been more personal than practical. No grants were requested or received to support the research or writing.

Thomas J. Barfield

Acknowledgements

The author would like to thank the authors and publishers of the following books for permission to reproduce material from them:

The History of the Mongol Conquests, by J. J. Saunders (Routledge); *History of Chinese Society: Liao*, by Karl Wittfogel and Feng Chia-Sheng (Harvard University Press); *Records of the Grand Historian of China*, by Burton Watson (© 1961 Columbia University Press, New York); *The Successors of Genghis Khan*, by John Boyle (© 1971 Columbia University Press, New York).

Notes on Transliterations

Chinese The Wade–Giles system of romanization is used except for those spellings (particularly geographical ones such as Peking) which have been accepted into English and for which the usual idiosyncratic style is retained.

Mongolian and Turkish I have used the system found in A. Mostaert, *Diction-naire Ordos* (Peking, 1941) as modified by Francis Cleaves in his articles in the *Harvard Journal of Asiatic Studies* with the following changes:

č is ch	q is kh
š is sh	ǰ is j
γ is gh	

Because Inner Asia was the meeting place of a wide variety of linguistic and cultural groups, some with writing systems, some without, the normal problems associated with the transcribing of foreign names and terms into an English text are compounded. Should the Chinese, Mongol, Turkish, Manchu, or Persian version be accepted as the standard? Because this is not a study in linguistics, I have tried to use common sense and maintain consistency where possible at the cost of neglecting the issues surrounding the definition and development of language and writing in Inner Asia.

It should be noted from the outset that foreign names and places derived from Chinese ideographs, whose original pronunciation is now unknown and which often did violence to the original even when it was known, are less than satisfactory but are often the only renderings we have for early periods. The reader should realize that the transcriptions of foreign words extracted from Chinese characters often produce awkward strings of linked syllables which bear about as much relation to their original pronunciation as an attempt to pronounce the written score of a Mozart sonata rather than play it. Lacking the music, we transcribe the notes.

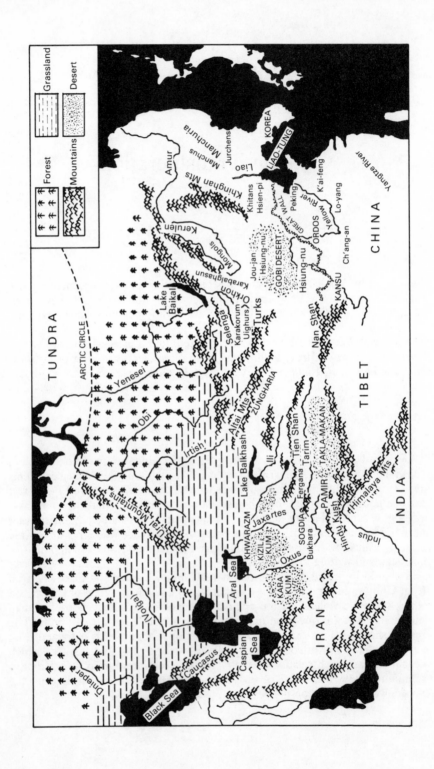

1

Introduction

The Steppe Nomadic World

Around 800 BC, the Eurasian steppe underwent a profound cultural transformation that was to shape world history for the next 2,500 years. For the first
time the literate civilizations to the south began encountering nomadic horse-
riding peoples who migrated with their herds of grazing animals across the
grasslands of Inner Asia. What set these people apart from their predecessors
was their invention of cavalry: fast-moving men on horseback using compound
bows to direct a withering barrage of arrows at their enemies from a distance. In
spite of their relatively small numbers, within a few centuries they came to
dominate the steppe, establishing great empires which periodically terrorized
their sedentary neighbors. The apogee of nomad power was reached in the
thirteenth century when the armies of Chinggis Khan and his descendants
conquered most of Eurasia. By the middle of the eighteenth century revolutions
in technology and transportation had shifted the military balance of power
decisively in favor of their sedentary neighbors and the nomads were incorporated into the expanding empires of Russia and China.

The nomads of Inner Asia have remained a subject of fascination and
controversy into modern times: the stereotype of barbarians who were both
feared and despised, or romantically portrayed as wild and free by those who
admired them. However, most histories fail to make the region and its people
comprehensible. These accounts consist of seemingly random events presented
chronologically, with one obscure tribe following another. When the nomads
did make an appearance on the stage of world history by invading their
neighbors, such events were often treated as a form of natural history, like a
plague of locusts. Many Han dynasty scholars, for example, argued that China
could never have proper relations with people who moved to and fro like birds
and beasts. Later Christian and Muslim commentators explained that invasions
by nomadic peoples such as the Huns or Mongols were simply God's punishment for sinful societies. In more recent times it was believed that nomads

invaded sedentary areas in response to drought. However, the main obstacle to creating a coherent Inner Asian history has always been the lack of an appropriate analytical framework which made sense of events there. Even those scholars who take Inner Asia as the focus of their studies (and not just an adjunct to the history of Iran, Russia, or China) are often at a loss when addressing fundamental problems of historical development. The bulk of the specialist literature on Inner Asia is narrowly focused, almost untouched by modern methods of history or social science, restricting itself to translations of historical texts or inscriptions, questions of linguistics, art history, and identifying the locations of historically known tribes.

This narrow focus is unfortunate, for the study of Inner Asia has the potential to illuminate many more significant questions of historical and anthropological concern. Inner Asia was a zone of long-term interaction between two opposing cultures with powerfully fixed ideas of themselves and others. For more than 2,000 years the nomadic peoples of the steppe confronted the world's largest agrarian state without being politically incorporated by it or adopting its culture. On one side was imperial China, which had a deeply rooted cultural tradition that viewed itself as historically superior to other peoples and states. Its very name *Chung-kuo* (Middle Kingdom) designated the center of all civilization. Over time China had absorbed many neighboring foreign peoples directly into its cultural domain as it expanded south to the borders of Southeast Asia. Throughout East Asia even fiercely independent neighbors such as Korea, Japan, and Viet-nam all adopted Chinese models of state organization and foreign relations, ideographic literacy, cuisine, clothes, and calendars. All of East Asia that is except for China's great opponents on the steppelands in the north. There horse-riding nomads not only rejected Chinese culture and ideology, worse, they obstinately refused to see any value in it except in terms of the material goods the Chinese could offer. With an economy based on mobile nomadic pastoralism that scattered people across a vast landscape, living under the sky's great blue dome in tents of felt, consuming milk and meat as the central part of their diet, glorifying military adventure and heroic personal achievement, these horse-riding peoples stood in stark contrast to their Chinese neighbors.

Both the nomads and Chinese of course maintained the superiority of their own cultural values and way of life, hardly a surprise to anthropologists who take ethnocentrism as a historical fact of life. Yet along Inner Asia's China frontier both societies were in constant contact and must have had considerable influence upon one another. Recent anthropological theory has stressed the importance of analyzing the changing structural developments in social and political relations as the product of interactions between societies rather than as products of purely indigenous origin. From earliest times varieties of "world systems" have directly impinged on even seemingly remote peoples.[1] The relationship between Inner Asia and China provides a classic, if little known, example of the usefulness of this broad perspective. Viewed in isolation, Inner Asian polities appear to rise and fall almost randomly, but when put in a regional context over a long duration they reveal a number of striking regularities that are related to cycles of centralization in China.

The question of interaction also raises the more difficult issue of cultural

communication. When different cultures encountered one another the significance of the events that resulted was often interpreted in radically different
ways. On what common ground could two alien societies meet, and to what
degree could they come to understand each other's strengths and weaknesses?
Differences between the worldview of the nomads and the Chinese made their
relationship particularly problematic. The dynamics of a tribal society whose
ideal leader was a heroic warrior blessed by heaven with luck and charisma, who
showered his followers with gifts, was entirely at odds with the Chinese
conception of the emperor of all under heaven, secluded in his palace administering a complex bureaucracy by reading memorials. Although keeping good
accounts of the events that occurred on the border, Chinese officials were more
at home dealing with interchangeable institutional representatives than with the
charismatic personalities central to steppe politics. They were usually at loss to
explain the sudden rise and fall of a particular leader or his group because they
failed to understand the political dynamics that produced change among the
nomads. As Sahlins has noted in his analysis of structurally similar Polynesian
kingdoms, "for societies of certain types, the stories of kings and battles are
with good reason privileged historiographically. The reason is a structure that
generalizes the action of the king as the form and destiny of the society."[2]

Over time the issue of cultural relations probably troubled court scholars
more than nomad military attacks, for the nomads' refusal to accept Chinese
values struck at China's own definition of itself as the center of world order.
This was true even during the times when the Chinese were successful in
employing their own ideological framework of foreign relations. Frontier
peoples became quite skillful at manipulating this system, often accepting
Chinese forms while rejecting their content, thereby developing reputations as
insolent or insincere "barbarians." Of course the reverse was also true – there
was perhaps no greater example of cultural miscommunication than the destruction wrought over much of Eurasia by Chinggis Khan and his immediate
successors who saw little value in maintaining farms and cities that had no place
in a world of yurts and horses.

It is possible to conduct a study of the long-term relations between China
and its northern neighbors because of the availability of original source material
dating from the first appearance of the nomads. It consists largely of official
Chinese records, supplemented by inscriptions and historical texts left by the
nomads themselves after the sixth century. The Chinese material is unique in
that it presents a continuous sequence of accounts for the entire imperial
period, as it was customary for each new dynasty to commission an official
history of its predecessor. There was always a detailed chapter on the foreign
peoples along China's northern frontier because they presented military and
political problems that engaged the close attention of every dynasty. The record
was biased by the negative attitudes about non-Chinese peoples held by the
Confucian scholars who compiled the histories. However, because history was
viewed as a tool for instructing current rulers, frontier politics could not be
ignored and the historians justified their own positions by extensive excerpts
from earlier policy debates. The histories of foreign dynasties in China often
provide even more information, since they originated in the frontier areas.

The full value of these records has not been exploited because for scholars of

Chinese civilization they represented a marginal history of little intrinsic value. In addition, the true nature of frontier relationships was usually obscured by attempts to present tribal peoples as perpetually subservient to China. Thus we hear of nomads coming to "pay tribute," "present homage," or "sending hostages," when in fact this was usually a diplomatic smoke screen which disguised the payment of large bribes to the frontier peoples in order to appease them. While the biases in the sources are fairly transparent, they have often been uncritically perpetuated in modern scholarship through a process of secondary ethnocentrism. Scholars who devoted their lives to exploring the history of imperial China, for example, so immersed themselves in the classical literature of that culture that they often unconsciously absorbed and accepted its values and worldview. Careful and critical about interpretations within the Chinese cultural sphere, when they wrote of those other people, "barbarians," who threatened their civilization, it was usually from the Chinese perspective, with all the sympathy of a report by court scholars recounting the reception of a smelly envoy from the steppe come to insult the empire with an outrageous demand.

Yet even with the best of intentions it has always been difficult for the historians of sedentary societies to understand the cultural values and social structures of tribal nomadic peoples whose ways were so different from their own. However, by combining anthropology and history it is possible to create a fuller picture of the relationship between these different cultures, a confrontation of 2,000 years' duration which played a key role in the development of cultural and political history in Eurasia.

The history of nomadic pastoral societies in Inner Asia and their relationship with the outside world centers on five basic issues that will reoccur throughout this book.

1   Political organization: On what basis did the nomads form and maintain states that united regional socio-political organizations?
2   Spheres of interaction: What was the relationship between the nomads of Inner Asia and their sedentary neighbors, particularly China, and why were the nomads powerful in some historical periods but not in others?
3   Conquest dynasties in China: Was there a cycle of frontier relationships that would explain why it was peoples of Manchurian origin who established most of the foreign dynasties that ruled in north China for about half of the imperial period?
4   The Mongol world conquests: Did the Mongol empire represent the culmination of political development on the steppe or a deviation from it?
5   The development of pastoral nomadic societies: Were there significant differences among nomadic pastoral societies through time that would justify making analytical distinctions among ancient, medieval, and modern periods?

The historical data, though often biased, are extensive enough to answer these questions and allow us to interpret the societies of Inner Asia on their own terms. But the test of any hypothesis is in its application. Those presented here should explain the data in a coherent fashion so that a non-specialist can understand the flow of events and changing social formations, while allowing the specialist to test them further against the total body of historical information in any given period.

STEPPE POLITICAL ORGANIZATION AND FRONTIER RELATIONS

The emergence of nomadic states in Inner Asia has been the subject of considerable debate because it appears to be a contradiction in terms. At the head of a nomadic empire there is an organized state led by an autocrat, yet most of the tribesmen within the nomadic polity seem to retain their traditional political organization, which is based on kinship groups of various sizes – lineages, clans, tribes. In the economic sphere there is a similar paradox – a state based on an economy that is both extensive and relatively undifferentiated. To resolve this dilemma theorists have generally tried to show that either the state exists and that the tribal sub-structure is just a hollow shell, or that the tribal structure exists but that it never forms a true state.

Based on his extensive observations of the Kazakh and Kirghiz in the nineteenth century, the Russian ethnographer Radloff interpreted political organization among nomads as the replication of local level politics at ever-higher levels of incorporation. The basic herding unit was at the core of both pastoral production and politics. Differences in wealth and power within these small groups enabled certain men to claim leadership positions; they regulated conflict within the group and organized it for defense or aggression against external enemies. Radloff saw the growth of larger units as an attempt by ambitious strongmen to combine ever-greater numbers of nomads under their control. This process could eventually result in the creation of a nomadic empire, but the power of a steppe autocrat was purely personal. It stemmed from his own skillful manipulation of force and wealth within an elaborate tribal network. Such a ruler was a usurper of power, and at his death his personal empire dissolved back into its component parts.[3] Barthold, the great historian of medieval Turkestan, modified Radloff's model by proposing that a nomadic leader could also be the popular choice of a political movement within a nomadic society, as had occurred during the rise of the second Turkish empire in the seventh century. Choice, he argued, was a complement to coercion in any nomadic empire because rising leaders attracted voluntary followers by their success in war and raiding.[4] Both theories stressed that nomadic states were inherently ephemeral, the state organization disappearing upon the death of its founder. Nomadic states, therefore, only temporarily dominated a tribal political organization which remained the basis for social and economic life on the steppe.

An alternate set of theories resolved the paradox of a state based on tribal political organization by positing that tribal organizations were destroyed in creating the state, even if this new relationship was disguised by the use of the older tribal terminology. In a study of the Huns, the Hungarian historian Harmatta argued that a nomadic state could only emerge from a process in which the tribal basis of a nomadic society was first destroyed and then replaced by class relations. The focus of his analysis was not on great leaders, but on the profound changes within a socio-economic order that made the rise of autocrats like Attila possible.[5] Although the evidence of this process was hard to demonstrate, Krader, an anthropologist writing about nomads and state formation, claimed that because states could not exist without class relations – direct producers supporting non-producers – the historical existence of nomadic states presupposed such relations.[6] If these states lacked stability, it was because the resource base on the steppe was too narrow for any degree of permanency.

The existence of nomadic states was a more troubling issue for some Marxist interpretations, both because pastoral nomads did not fit readily into any unilinear historical stages very well, and because when these states collapsed the nomads appeared to revert to their traditional tribal organization, an impossibility if these institutions had truly been destroyed during state creation. Soviet writings have been particularly concerned with this problem, generally debating the concept of "nomadic feudalism" first proposed by Vladimirtsov in his analysis of the Mongols which achieved wide usage in part because he never explicitly defined it.[7] This form of "feudalism" was grounded on the assumption that classes existed within the nomadic community based on the ownership of pasture. Support for this proposition was derived from the organization of Mongolian banners during the eighteenth and nineteenth centuries under the Ch'ing dynasty rule where banner princes were set apart from ordinary tribesmen who were not permitted to leave the boundaries of their districts. Similarly the archaeological excavations at the old Mongol capital city of Karakorum, which revealed extensive development of farming communities in the surrounding area, appeared to mark the development of a class of settled nomads supporting a feudal nobility. However, other Soviet theorists pointed out that ownership of animals rather than land *per se* was the crucial element, and these remained under the control of ordinary tribesmen, and that the development of craft production or farming could quite easily be incorporated into the existing kinship structures so that such economic specialists never formed a separate class of people.[8] In addition, examples cited from Mongolia under the Ch'ing or the Kazakhs under Czarist administration had only limited value in understanding earlier nomadic polities. Following a policy of indirect rule, such sedentary empires protected an elite class of indigenous rulers whose economic and political power was a product of a colonial system.

Whether viewing political leadership of nomadic society as class-based or the product of the accumulation of power by charismatic leaders, both sets of theories had in common the assumption that the creation of a nomadic state was the result of internal development. Yet historically known nomadic states were organized at a level of complexity far beyond the needs of simple nomadic pastoralism. Radloff and Barthold stressed the nomadic state's ephemeral nature, but many nomadic empires long outlived their founders, notably those of the Hsiung-nu, Turks, Uighurs, and Mongols, and compared favorably in dynastic stability with their sedentary neighbors. With the exception of the Mongols, all remained steppe empires employing state political structures without conquering any significant sedentary territory. Those theorists like

Harmatta and Krader who accepted the existence of the state, but denied the continuity of tribal social organization, were forced to argue the necessity of class structure on the steppe without being able to produce the evidence of how it emerged in a relatively undifferentiated and extensive pastoral economy. While nomadic aristocracies were commonly found in steppe societies, such a hierarchical social division was not based on the control of the means of production, for access to key pastoral resources was obtained on the basis of tribal affiliation. Class relations were of little consequence in Inner Asia until the nomads became incorporated into sedentary states during the past few hundred years, or when they left the steppe and became part of a pre-existing class structure.

A potential solution to this dilemma has emerged from comparisons of recent anthropological research on nomadic pastoral societies in Africa and southwestern Asia. It throws doubt on the assumption that nomadic states were the result of any sort of internal evolution. In a comparison of African nomadic pastoralists, Burnham concluded that low population density and ease of geographic mobility made the indigenous development of any institutionalized hierarchy in such societies improbable. Under these conditions segmentary opposition would provide the most efficient and advantageous model for political organization. The development of the state among nomadic pastoralists, therefore, was not a response to internal needs; rather it developed when they were forced to deal with more highly organized sedentary state societies on a continual basis.[9] Drawing on cases from southwestern Asia, Irons came to the same conclusion and reduced it to a hypothesis: "Among pastoral nomadic societies hierarchical political institutions are generated only by external relations with state societies and never develop purely as a result of internal dynamics in such societies."[10]

This argument has a number of far-reaching implications for the understanding of nomadic states in Inner Asia. It is not a diffusionist explanation. The nomads did not "borrow" the state; rather, they were forced to develop their own peculiar form of state organization in order to deal effectively with their larger and more highly organized sedentary neighbors. These relations required a far higher level of organization than was necessary to handle livestock problems and political disputes within a nomadic society. It was no accident that the least formally organized nomads were found in sub-Saharan Africa where they encountered few state societies until the colonial period, and that the most formally organized nomadic societies emerged facing China, the world's largest and most centralized traditional sedentary state.

In his wide-ranging anthropological survey of pastoral nomadic political organizations, Khazanov has argued that nomadic states were the product of asymmetrical relationships between nomadic and sedentary societies which benefited the nomads. For Inner Asia he focused primarily on those relationships created by nomadic peoples' conquest of sedentary areas where they became the ruling elite of a mixed society.[11] However, many nomadic states established and maintained such asymmetrical relationships without conquering sedentary regions. Taking advantage of their military power, these nomadic states extorted subsidies from neighboring states, taxed and controlled international overland trade, and let loose organized raiders who specialized in "direct appropriation" (looting), all without leaving the protected refuge of the steppe.

In northern Asia it was this relationship between China and the steppe that supported a state hierarchy among nomads. The nomadic state maintained itself by exploiting China's economy, and not by exploiting the production of scattered sheep herders who were effectively organized by the nomadic state to make this extortion possible. Therefore it is not necessary to posit the development of class relations on the steppe to explain the existence of the state among nomads, nor was the nomadic state necessarily just the personal creation of a nomadic autocrat, doomed to disintegration at his death. However, because a state on the steppe was structured by its external relations, it differed significantly from sedentary states, simultaneously containing both a tribal and state hierarchy, each with separate functions.

Inner Asian nomadic states were organized as "imperial confederacies," autocratic and statelike in foreign affairs, but consultative and federally structured internally. They consisted of an administrative hierarchy with at least three levels: the imperial leader and his court, imperial governors appointed to oversee the component tribes within the empire, and indigenous tribal leaders. At the local level the tribal structure remained intact, under the rule of chieftains whose power was derived from their own people's support, not imperial appointment. Thus the state structure changed little at the local level, except to ensure an end to raiding and murders endemic to the steppe in the absence of unity. The component tribes were linked into the empire by their subservience to appointed governors, often members of the imperial lineage. The imperial appointees handled regional problems, organized levies of troops, and suppressed opposition generated by local tribal leaders. The imperial government monopolized foreign affairs and warfare, negotiating with other powers for the empire as a whole.

The stability of this structure was maintained by extracting resources from outside the steppe to fund the state. Loot from raids, trading rights, and subsidies were obtained for the nomads by the imperial government. Although local tribal leaders lost their autonomy, they received material benefits from the imperial system in return, benefits individual tribes were not powerful enough to obtain on their own. The tribal organization never disappeared at the local level, but its role during periods of centralization was restricted to domestic affairs. When the system collapsed and local tribal leaders became autonomous, the steppe reverted to anarchy.

CYCLES OF POWER

The imperial confederacy was the most stable form of nomadic state. First employed by the Hsiung-nu between about 200 BC and AD 150, it was the model later adopted by the Jou-jan (fifth century), Turks and Uighurs (sixth to ninth centuries), Oirats, Eastern Mongols, and Zunghars (fifteenth to eighteenth centuries). The Mongol Empire of Chinggis Khan (thirteenth and fourteenth centuries) was based on a far more centralized organization that destroyed the existing tribal links and made all leaders imperial appointees. The short-lived Hsien-pi empire during the latter half of the second century AD was a simple confederacy which dissolved on the death of its leaders. During other periods, particularly between 200 to 400 and 900 to 1200, the steppe tribes were under no central authority.

Nomadic imperial confederacies came into existence only in periods when it was possible to link themselves to the Chinese economy. The nomads employed a strategy of extortion to gain trade rights and subsidies from China. They raided the frontier and then negotiated a peace treaty with the Chinese court. Native dynasties in China were willing to pay the nomads off because this was cheaper than going to war with people who could avoid retaliation by moving out of range. During these periods the entire northern frontier was split between the two great powers.

Extortion demanded quite a different strategy than conquest. While it is conventional wisdom that the nomads of Mongolia prowled like wolves beyond the Great Wall waiting for China to weaken so that they could conquer it, the facts are that the nomads from the central steppe avoided conquering Chinese territory. Wealth from Chinese trade and subsidies stabilized the imperial government on the steppe and they had no desire to destroy this resource. The Uighurs, for example, were so dependent on this revenue that they even sent troops to put down internal rebellions in China to maintain a compliant dynasty in power. With the exception of the Mongols, "nomad conquest" occurred only after the collapse of central authority within China left no government to extort. Powerful nomadic empires rose and fell in tandem with native dynasties in China. The Han and Hsiung-nu empires appeared within a decade of one another, while the empire of the Turks emerged just as China reunified under the Sui/T'ang dynasties. Similarly both the steppe and China entered periods of anarchy within decades of one another. When China fell into severe disorder and economic decline it was no longer possible to maintain this relationship and the steppe devolved into its component tribes, unable to reunify until order was restored in north China.

The conquest of China by foreign dynasties was the work of Manchurian peoples, either nomads or forest tribes from the Liao River region. The contemporaneous political collapse of centralized rule in both China and Mongolia freed these border peoples from domination by either great power. Unlike the tribes of the central steppe, they had an egalitarian political structure and close contact with sedentary regions within Manchuria. In times of disunion they established small kingdoms along the frontier that combined both Chinese and tribal traditions within a single administration. Islands of stability, they waited in the wings as short-lived dynasties founded by Chinese warlords or steppe tribal leaders destroyed one another in north China. When these dynasties collapsed, the Manchurians moved to conquer first a small part of north China, and then, usually under a second Manchurian dynasty, to conquer all of it. While the unification of north China under foreign rule created favorable economic conditions for the rise of a nomadic state in Mongolia, such states rarely emerged because foreign dynasties employed a strikingly different frontier policy than did native Chinese administrations. The Manchurians practiced a policy of political and military disruption, and they actively campaigned against the nomads to prevent their unification. The nomads from the central steppe, with the exception of the Mongols under Chinggis Khan, were never able to establish powerful empires when their cousins from Manchuria ruled in China. Only when the foreign dynasties abandoned their aggressive frontier defenses to deal with rebels within China were the nomads able to unify. By the time Chinese rebels had ousted the foreigners and founded a new native dynasty, the steppe was also unified and prepared to begin its campaign of extortion.

There was a cyclical pattern to this relationship, which repeated itself three times over the over the course of two thousand years. Working from a different perspective, Ledyard, in his study of the relationships among Manchuria, Korea, and China, has observed a similar three-cycle pattern in international relations which he divided into *"yin* and *yang"* phases based on whether China was expansive (*yang*) or defensive (*yin*). His *yang* phases correspond to our native dynasties ruling all of China, his *yin* phases to the rule of conquest dynasties. Interestingly, he too found the Mongol Yüan dynasty to be anomalous, though his analysis excluded the role of other nomadic empires in Mongolia.[12] However, his observations do not account for how and why such relationships developed.

To understand how such a cyclical pattern could emerge we must focus our analysis on the changing nature of the frontier political environment over long periods of time. A type of political ecology was at work in which one brand of dynasty succeeded another in a predictable fashion because under one set of conditions a particular socio-political organization had significant advantages over rivals whose structures were based on different principles. Yet as conditions changed the very advantages that brought about a dynasty's political success laid the groundwork for its own replacement. The process was analogous to ecological succession following a fire in an old climax forest. In a climax forest a small number of large established tress dominate the landscape, excluding other species which could not survive their natural herbicides and shade. When destroyed by fire or other disaster, the dead trees are quickly replaced by a succession of more varied but unstable species which invade the burnt over area. Fast-growing short-lived weed and bush species with high rates of reproduction first establish themselves, creating a new ground cover until they are replaced in turn by more stable species of fast-growing trees. Eventually these trees create a mixed forest that lasts for many decades, until one or two species of trees again become completely dominant, exclude other species from the area and return the forest to a stable climax state, bringing the cycle full circle.

The bipolar world of a unified China and unified steppe which split the frontier between them was a stable climax state. No alternative political structures could emerge while they existed. The dual collapse of order within China and the steppe produced a highly unstable environment. Dynasties that arose during this period were numerous, poorly organized, unstable and short-lived – the target of attack by any rising warlord or tribal chieftain who could raise an army. They were replaced by better organized dynasties which restored order and successfully administered large areas. Native dynasties in the south and foreign dynasties from the northeast and northwest divided China's territory among themselves. During the wars of unification which destroyed the foreign dynasties and brought about a united China under native rule, the steppe reunited unimpeded, bringing the cycle full circle. The lag time between the fall of a major native dynasty and the re-establishment of order under stable foreign rule decreased with each cycle: centuries of instability followed the collapse of the Han empire, decades after the fall of T'ang, and hardly any time upon the overthrow of the Ming. The duration of foreign dynasties showed a similar pattern – shortest in the first cycle, longest in the third.

In essence my contention is that the steppe tribes of Mongolia played a key role in frontier politics without becoming conquerors of China, and that Manchuria, for political and ecological reasons, was the breeding ground for foreign dynasties when native dynasties collapsed in the face of internal rebellions. This framework departs significantly from a number of previous theories offered to explain the relationship between China and its northern neighbors.

Wittfogel's influential study of "conquest dynasties" in Chinese history ignored the importance of steppe empires like those of the Hsiung-nu, Turks and Uighurs – dividing foreign dynasties into subcategories of pastoral nomads and agricultural tribes, with both in opposition to typically Chinese dynasties. This emphasis on economic rather than political organization obscured the striking fact that, with the exception of the Mongol Yüan, all of Wittfogel's conquest dynasties were of Manchurian origin. He also failed to distinguish between the nomads of Mongolia who established steppe empires that ruled the frontier successfully in tandem with China for centuries, and the nomads from Manchuria who established dynasties within China but never created powerful empires on the steppe.[13]

Perhaps the most significant work on the relationship between China and tribal people to the north is Lattimore's classic *Inner Asian Frontiers of China*. His personal familiarity with Mongolia, Manchuria, and Turkestan gave his analysis a richness found nowhere else, and after fifty years it still stands as a landmark contribution. Particularly influential was his "geographical approach" (which today we would be more likely to label cultural ecology) that divided Inner Asia into key regions, each with its own dynamic of cultural development. Lattimore's basic concern was with the emergence of steppe pastoralism on China's frontier and he devoted only a brief section to the development of frontier relations during the imperial period. While the present analysis is firmly rooted in Lattimore's tradition it does take issue with a number of hypotheses he proposed concerning cycles of nomadic rule and the establishment of conquest dynasties.

Lattimore described a cycle of nomadic rule which he claimed gave nomadic states a lifespan of only three or four generations, citing the Hsiung-nu as an example. At first the polity included only nomads, then expanded during a second stage in which nomad warriors maintained a mixed state drawing tribute from their non-nomad subjects. Such a mixed state produced a third stage in which the sedentarized garrison troops of nomadic origin eventually obtained the lion's share of the revenue at the expense of their less sophisticated cousins who remained on the steppe. Such conditions created a fourth and final stage and brought about the states's collapse because the "difference between real wealth and nominal power on one side and real or potential power and relative poverty on the other side had become intolerable, [beginning] a breakup of the composite state and a 'return to nomadism' – politically – among the outlying the nomads."[14] In fact the Hsiung-nu empire displayed no such pattern. The Hsiung-nu leaders established their rule over other nomads and then stayed on the steppe without ever conquering sedentary regions that required garrisons. It was a state whose ruling dynasty lasted unbroken not for four generations, but for 400 years. When, after the fall of the Han dynasty, a Hsiung-nu ruler did establish a short-lived dynasty along the border of China, the outlying nomads did not run back to the steppe when they felt cheated of revenue, they seized the state for themselves instead.

In terms of conquest dynasties Lattimore recognized that there was a distinction between the nomadic peoples of the open steppe and the marginal frontier zones occupied by peoples of mixed cultures. He noted that it was the marginal zone that was the source of conquest dynasties and not the open steppe.[15] However, like Wittfogel, he failed to point out that the vast majority of successful conquest dynasties originated in the Manchurian marginal zone and not elsewhere. Also, by including Chinggis Khan as a major example of such a frontier margin leader, he muddied his own distinction between open steppe societies and culturally mixed border communities, for Chinggis was as far from the frontier as any Hsiung-nu or Turkish leader that preceded him in Mongolia. The reason for this seeming geographical contradiction was that the very definition of the frontier changed radically depending on whether a native or foreign dynasty ruled north China. Northern Mongolia became part of a "mixed frontier zone" only when foreign dynasties implemented policies designed to disrupt the political organization of the steppe. When native dynasties and steppe empires split the frontier between them there were no politically autonomous mixed societies.

These criticisms point both to the complexity of developments in Inner Asia and the need to study them as the products of changing relationships through time. The Mongolian steppe, north China, and Manchuria must be analyzed as parts of a single historical system. A comparative outline of the major native and conquest dynasties and steppe empires makes a start at providing such a model (table 1.1). It provides a gross representation of the three cycles of dynastic replacement (with only the Mongols appearing out of phase) which set the parameters for frontier relations. The description below only briefly describes the basic flow of frontier relations, and the issues raised in each period will be examined at greater length in succeeding chapters.

The Han and Hsiung-nu were closely linked as part of a bipolar frontier that developed at the close of the third century BC. When the Hsiung-nu empire lost its hegemony on the steppe around AD 150, it was replaced by the Hsien-pi who maintained a loosely structured empire by constantly raiding China until the death of their leader in 180, the same year that a major rebellion broke out in China. Within twenty years the Later Han dynasty existed in name

Table 1.1   Cycles of rule: major dynasties in China and steppe empires in Mongolia

		Chinese dynasties		Steppe empires
		Native	Foreign	
CYCLE 1	(1)	Ch'in and Han (221 BC–AD 220)		HSIUNG-NU (209 BC–AD 155)
	(2)	Chinese dynasties during the Period of Disruption (220–581)		Hsien-pi (130–180)
	(3)		T'o-pa Wei (386–556) and the other foreign dynasties directly before and after	Jou-jan
CYCLE 2	(4)	Sui and T'ang (581–907)		FIRST TURKISH (552–630) SECOND TURKISH (683–734) UIGHUR (745–840)
	(5)	Sung (960–1279)		
	(6)		Liao (Khitan) (907–1125)	
	(7)		Chin (Jurchen) (1115–1234)	
	(8)		Yüan (Mongol) --------MONGOL (1206–1368)	
CYCLE 3	(9)	Ming (1368–1644)		Oirats Eastern Mongols
	(10)		Ch'ing (Manchu) (1616–1912)	Zunghars

Note: The official dates traditionally assigned to each dynasty's origin and demise are often misleading. For native dynasties the dates of establishment are generally correct, but dates of their end are overstated because established Chinese dynasties had so much prestige that they were usually maintained as facades by ruling warlords for decades before their formal abolition. For most foreign dynasties the reverse was true. Dates of their establishment extended back to the founders of small frontier states which later became powerful, but their dates of demise are accurate.

Adapted from Wittfogel and Feng, *History of Chinese Society: Liao*, pp. 24–5
Upper case denotes strong steppe empires.

only and both its population and economy declined precipitously. It should be noted that it was not the nomads, but Chinese rebels, who destroyed the Han. For the next century and a half, while warlords of all sorts fought over China, the Manchurian descendants of the Hsien-pi established small states. Of these the Mu-jung Yen state proved the most viable, establishing control over the northeast during the middle of the fourth century. They created the framework which was adopted wholesale by the T'o-pa Wei, another Hsien-pi tribe, which overthrew Yen and unified north China. It was only with unification of north China that the nomads in Mongolia again established a centralized state under the leadership of the Jou-jan tribe. However, the Jou-jan never really controlled the steppe because the T'o-pa maintained huge garrisons along the frontier and invaded Mongolia with the aim of capturing as many people and livestock as possible. They succeeded so well that the Jou-jan were unable to threaten China until the end of the dynasty's history, when the T'o-pa had become sinicized and began employing the appeasement policies similar to those of the Han.

Internal rebellion brought down the Wei and began a period of reunification in China under the Western Wei and Sui dynasties at the close of the sixth century. The Jou-jan were overthrown by their vassals the Turks, who were so feared by the leaders of China that they were paid large subsidies in silk to remain at peace. The frontier again became bipolar and the Turks began a policy of extortion similar to that practiced by the Hsiung-nu. During the fall of Sui and the rise of T'ang, the Turks made no attempt to conquer China, but instead backed Chinese contenders for the throne. As the T'ang dynasty declined it became dependent on the nomads to curb domestic rebellions, calling on the aid of the Uighurs who proved decisive in putting down the An Lu-shan Rebellion in the middle of the eighth century, probably prolonging the life of that dynasty for another century. After the Uighurs fell victim to an assault by the Kirghiz in 840, the central steppe entered a period of anarchy. The T'ang was destroyed by the next major rebellion in China.

The fall of the T'ang provided an opportunity for the development of mixed states in Manchuria. The most important of these was the Liao dynasty which was established by the nomadic Khitans. They picked up the pieces after the demise of a series of short-lived dynasties that succeeded the T'ang in the middle of the tenth century. Kansu became a Tangut kingdom while the rest of China was in the hands of the native Sung dynasty. Like the Mu-jung state of Yen centuries earlier, the Liao employed a dual administration to accommodate both Chinese and tribal organization. Like Yen, Liao also fell victim to another Manchurian group, the Jurchen, forest tribes who overthrew the Liao in the early twelfth century to establish the Chin dynasty and went on to conquer all of north China, confining the Sung to the south. To this point, the first two cycles were remarkably similar in structure, but the rise of the Mongols created a major disruption that was to have profound consequences not only for China, but for the world.

No nomadic state ever emerged from Mongolia during periods when north China was torn apart by warlord struggles following the collapse of a long-lived native dynasty. The re-establishment of order by foreign dynasties from

Manchuria solidified the frontier and presented a single target which favored the creation of centralized states on the steppe. These foreign dynasties were aware of the danger from Mongolia and played tribal politics to disrupt them, employing strategies of divide and rule, conducting massive invasions which removed large numbers of people and animals from the steppe, and maintaining a system of alliances through the use of reciprocal marriage ties to link some of the tribes to them. The strategy worked fairly well: the Jou-jan were never able to deal effectively with the T'o-pa Wei, and during the Liao and Chin dynasties the tribes in Mongolia failed to unite at all before Chinggis Khan. Chinggis Khan's later success should not blind us to the difficulties he faced in uniting the steppe against Jurchen opposition – it consumed most of his adult life and he came very close to failure on a number of occasions. His state was unlike any other. Highly centralized and with a disciplined army, it did away with the power of autonomous tribal leaders. However, like previous unifiers from Mongolia, Chinggis's aim was initially to extort China, not to conquer. Although highly sinicized culturally, the Jurchen court rejected appeasement and refused to cut a deal with the Mongols. The ensuing wars over the next three decades destroyed most of north China and left the Mongols in charge. Their lack of interest and preparation to rule (rather than extort) was reflected by their failure to declare a dynastic name or establish a regular administration until the reign of Khubilai Khan, Chinggis's grandson.

Chinggis Khan's victory demonstrates that the model we have presented is probabilistic, not deterministic. There were always tribal leaders like Chinggis in times of disorder, but their chances of unifying the steppe against determined opposition from established Manchurian states, which drew on the wealth of China, were low. Thus, while the Jou-jan were notably unsuccessful, the Turks who followed them created an empire greater than the Hsiung-nu, not because the Turks were necessarily more talented, but because they were able to exploit the new Chinese states which paid generously not to be disturbed. Chinggis overcame massive odds – the Jurchen were powerful, Mongolia had not been united since the fall of the Uighurs more than three centuries earlier, and the Mongols were one of the weaker tribes on the steppe. The encounter between a powerful nomadic state and a strong foreign dynasty was unique and highly destructive. The Mongols employed the traditional strategy of savage attacks with the aim of inducing a lucrative peace, but it failed when the Jurchen rejected a treaty approach and caused the Mongols to increase their pressure until the victim was destroyed.

The Mongols were the only nomads from the central steppe to conquer China, but that experience colored Chinese attitudes toward the nomads from that time forward. The sequence of political succession described earlier would have predicted the rise of a steppe empire when the Jurchen succumbed to domestic rebellion and China unified under a dynasty like the Ming. During the Ming such empires did arise, led first by the Oirats and later by the Eastern Mongols, but they were unstable because until the mid-sixteenth century the nomads were unable to gain a system of regular trade and subsidies from China. With the memory of the Mongol invasion still fresh, the Ming ignored the Han and T'ang precedents and adopted a policy of non-intercourse, fearing the nomads wished to replace the Ming in China. The nomads responded by continually raiding the frontier, subjecting the Ming to more attacks than any other Chinese dynasty. When the Ming finally changed its policy to accommodate the nomads, the attacks largely ceased and the frontier remained at peace. After the Ming was toppled by Chinese rebels in the mid-seventeenth century, it was the Manchus, and not the Mongols, who conquered China and established the Ch'ing dynasty. Like earlier Manchurian rulers, the Ch'ing employed a dual administrative structure and effectively prevented the political unification of the steppe by co-opting the Mongol leaders and dividing their tribes into small units under Manchu control. The cycle of traditional relationships between China and Inner Asia ended when modern weapons, transportation systems, and new forms of international political relations destroyed the sinocentric East Asian world order.

CULTURAL ECOLOGY

The relationship between Inner Asia and China was played out along a vast frontier that could be divided into four key ecological and cultural areas: Mongolia, north China, Manchuria, and Turkestan.[16] Mongolia was the home of the nomads who raised vast herds of animals on the steppes and mountain slopes of Inner Asia. With their seasonal migrations, an extensive economy, low population density, and tribal political organization the nomads were in almost every respect the opposite of the Chinese whose society was organized around intensive irrigated agriculture with high population densities ruled over by a centralized bureaucratic government. The cleavage between the two societies was also sharp geographically, for the frontier between them was linear, and at its center ran the Great Wall – an enormously ambitious construction originally completed by the Ch'in dynasty at the end of the third century BC to physically demarcate and separate China from the world of the nomads. While Mongolia and China could be easily categorized, the geographical areas to the east and West were more complex. Both Manchuria and Turkestan incorporated a number of different ecological zones inhabited by a variety of peoples, both nomadic and sedentary. When China and Mongolia were powerful, control of these regions was split between these two great powers, but when China and the steppe periodically fell into anarchy, border regions formed their own states which incorporated elements of both Chinese and nomadic culture.

The geographic region of Mongolia occupies a plateau encompassing 2,700,000 square kilometers in central Eurasia. It is continental in climate with severely cold winters, hot summers, and relatively low rainfall. The land is mostly steppe, for Mongolia forms the eastern half of the great Eurasian steppes, those rolling plains of grass and scrubland punctuated by high mountain ranges, extending from the borders of Manchuria westward to the Black Sea and the plains of Hungary. The Mongolian steppe is much higher in elevation, averaging 1,500 meters or more, than the Turkic steppes to the west which lie at around sea level. This altitude change marks the ecological boundary of Mongolia in the west and has also traditionally marked the limit of its political and cultural influence.

The Gobi Desert accounts for two-thirds of Mongolia's area. As many geographers have noted, the Gobi is not really a desert but rather a dry steppe. It divides the main northern and southern grazing areas, traditionally called inner and outer Mongolia on the basis of their geographical proximity to China. The Gobi is most arid at its center, where it supports relatively few people or livestock, but precipitation rises as one moves toward the margins of the plateau which supports the bulk of Mongolia's nomadic population. The best pasturage is located on the northern margin, in the regions drained by tributaries of Lake Baikal and the Amur River, and along the slopes of the Altai Mountains. The steppe bordering China, particularly the Ordos Plains, the Jehol Mountains, and western Manchuria, traditionally supported large numbers of nomads, although Chinese farming settlements have largely displaced them today.[17]

The Mongolian plateau borders strikingly different ecological zones. On the north and northeast it abuts the Siberian forests. This territory was inhabited by small tribes of hunters and reindeer herders. The nomads, who were better organized and militarily more powerful than the forest tribes, sought to control Siberia in order to extract furs and other forest products. The interaction was not one-way, for those tribes which became familiar with pastoral nomadism had the option of adopting a new way of life by migrating south to enter the world of the steppe. However, the Siberian forest was not suitable for extensive sheep or horse raising, and reindeer could not eat grass, so the regions remained culturally distinct. The historic relationship among the peoples and cultures along the Mongolian-Siberian interface is still obscure because of the lack of written records and archaeological research.[18]

The edge of the Mongolian plateau to the south, which overlooked China, was demarcated by the Great Wall. While the frontier here was linear, it was hardly fixed, for it straddled a transitional zone that could support either nomads or farmers. Yet it was not pasture which attracted the nomads, but the riches of China, making the border a magnet for tribes from all over the steppe. To the nomads, China was a storehouse of wealth, a land of lively border markets and the object of raids for grain, cloth, and captives. It was also the source of luxury goods like silk and wine which could be extorted as gifts from the Chinese government. Throughout Chinese history this frontier line remained surprisingly constant, as did China's attempts to keep their own border populations isolated from the independent nomads of the north.

China's frontier with the Mongolian plateau occupied the center of its northern border. Although from Mongolia agricultural China appeared to be a single unit occupying the drainage basin of the mighty Yellow River, from the Chinese perspective there were at least four distinct regions. To the east lay the flat, low-lying floodplain of the Yellow River where most of China's imperial capital cities, such as Lo-yang, K'ai-feng, and Peking were located. The hills and mountains of Jehol separated it from Mongolia, while in the northwest it was linked by a narrow corridor to the Manchurian plain of the lower Liao River valley. Because the eastern plain was so flat, once an enemy pierced the frontier defenses there were few natural barriers to prevent movement across the whole region. Farther to the west were the loess highlands, an area of complex drainage and severe erosion which, nevertheless, was quite productive and contained the imperial capital city of Ch'ang-an (modern Sian) during Former Han and T'ang times. Directly north of the loess highlands, the horseshoe bend of the Yellow River ran through the Ordos steppe and desert. This was an anomalous and perennially troublesome border region, for China defined its "natural" political frontier as the bend of the river, even though it passed squarely through steppe territory where it was subject to nomad occupation. The arid Kansu corridor was China's northwestern extension. It was largely Chinese in population and culture, although Turkestan had a strong cultural influence there. It was hemmed in by nomads from Mongolia to the north and from Koko-nor in the southwest, while bordering Tibetan peoples in the mountains to the southeast.[19]

Another key Chinese ecological region with important but indirect effects on the northern frontier was the drainage of the lower Yangtze River which marked the beginning of southern China. North China was the dry land of wheat and millet, cold winters and hot summers, a place where foot soldiers and cavalry marched swiftly from one region to another. Upon moving south of the Fei River into the Yangtze River region, China became a different country, set in a region of lakes, rivers, and fens with a warm humid climate supporting wet rice agriculture. Foreign dynasties found the south difficult to conquer because their horses got stuck in the mud and they were unfamiliar with naval warfare vital for controlling the region's strategic waterways. During the Han dynasties the Yangtze was at the empire's limit, often used as a place of exile. Yet following the collapse of the Later Han the region grew in economic and political importance. By the T'ang period the south had become the most heavily populated and productive region in China but, because the north was the cradle of Chinese civilization, it was never willingly abandoned even after it stopped being self-supporting. Defense of the northern frontier was always an imperial rather than a local responsibility. When later dynasties chose northern imperial capitals and maintained large standing armies along the Mongolian frontier, most of the food and revenue to support them was extracted from the south.

Bracketing north China and Mongolia to the east and west were Manchuria and Turkestan, two regions which did not fit neatly into either camp because both supported mixed economies. When China and the steppe were united into strong empires, these territories became pawns in a larger frontier struggle, but when centralized rule broke down, they formed their own states. These kingdoms had great historical significance, for most of China's successful foreign rulers came not from the Mongolian steppes, but from the borderlands of Manchuria.

The Mongolian steppe was separated from Manchuria by the Khinghan Mountains in the north and the Jehol Mountains to the south. Nomadic peoples from Mongolia occupied the western slopes of the Khinghan Mountains, which were extensions of the steppe ecological zone, but they made relatively little use of the far steeper slopes of the range's eastern flank that descended into the

Manchurian Basin. Between the Khinghan and the Jehol mountains lay a large gap where rolling grasslands extended beyond the plateau into Manchuria, forming the Liao-hsi steppe. This was the home of an important nomadic population similar in culture to those found on the Mongolian plateau, but with a distinct political history and tradition.

Manchuria itself was divided into four major zones. The first consisted of the lower Liao River plain and the Liao-tung peninsula, a region suitable for agriculture which had been Chinese in culture at least since the Warring States period. It was linked to the north China plain by a narrow pass that ran between the mountains and the sea at Shan-hai-kuan. The Liao-tung peninsula closely resembled Shan-tung which it faced across a short stretch of sea. Yet because the Manchurian plain and Liao-tung were physically isolated from China, they were vulnerable to attacks by pastoral nomads or forest tribes; and in times of disunion in China these districts fell under their control. The second ecological zone of Manchuria was the western steppe of Liao-hsi and the Jehol Mountains, the home of pastoral nomads. Somewhat removed from Mongolia proper, they maintained their political independence when possible and their close proximity to the farmers of the Manchurian plain provided them with a sedentary economic base that was richer and more easily exploited than other parts of the frontier. Manchuria's largest ecological zone consisted of heavy forests that bordered Korea and Siberia. The forests were settled by villagers who had a mixed economy of stockraising and agriculture. Unlike the steppe tribes of the west, they raised pigs, an animal never found among pastoral nomads. The Pacific current created a fourth maritime coastal zone located in the far north. It was inhabited by hunters and fishers who were isolated from the rest of region and of little historical significance. A rich land, but with severe winters, Manchuria supported a variety of different cultures within a relatively small area.

Turkestan encompassed an extensive region of arid lands consisting of deserts, oases, and dry steppe stretching from the Kansu corridor to the Aral Sea, bounded on the south by the mountains of Tibet, the Pamirs, and the Hindu Kush, while on the north it was bordered by the Tien-shan Mountains and the great Eurasian steppe. Turkestan's eastern border with Mongolia was not distinct, for the plains of Mongolia gradually merged into it through regions of dry steppe which became progressively more arid until they no longer supported nomadic pastoralism. Turkestan itself was divided into eastern and western sections separated by the Pamir mountains. Settlement in eastern Turkestan was confined to oases, strung like beads on a necklace encircling the Tarim Basin. While each was supported by a snowfed river from the nearby mountains which permitted irrigation, none was much more than self-sufficient in food production. The vast interior of the basin was virtually uninhabited. Western Turkestan occupied the drainage of the Amu Darya and Syr Darya (also known as the Oxus and Jaxartes rivers) which defined the area traditionally known as Transoxiana. These rivers carried much more water than those in eastern Turkestan and the climate was less severe. The west was therefore more densely populated than the east, supporting major cities of international importance such as Bukhara and Samarkand. Large in territory, small in population, Turkestan traditionally linked eastern and western Asia by means of caravan routes handling luxury goods. The division between eastern and western Turkestan at a line along the Altai, Tien-shan, and Pamir mountains also marked a great Eurasian cultural divide between those nomads who looked east toward China and those who looked west towards Iran and Europe.

NOMADIC PASTORALISM IN INNER ASIA

Pastoral nomadism was the dominant way of life on the Inner Asian steppe throughout most of its known history. While often denigrated as primitive by outside observers, it was in fact a sophisticated economic specialization for exploiting the resources of the steppe. Yet this way of life was so alien to the surrounding sedentary civilizations that misunderstandings and misinterpretations were unavoidable. The history of the nomads and their relationships with surrounding regions was predicated on what the nomads themselves took for granted: their cycles of movement, the demands of stockraising, economic constraints, and basic political organization.

Pastoral nomadism is the commonly used term for a form of mobile stock-raising in which families migrate with their animals from one seasonal pasture to another through a yearly cycle. The most distinctive cultural feature of this economic adaptation is that nomadic pastoral societies are adapted to the demands of mobility and the needs of their livestock. It should be immediately noted, however, that nomadism, pastoralism, and culture are analytically separate. There are pastoralists who are not nomadic (such as modern dairy farmers), and nomads who are not pastoral (such as hunting peoples). There are also societies in which mobile forms of pastoralism are only an economic specialization in which individual shepherds or cowboys are hired to look after the animals (as occurred throughout western Europe or Australia with sheep breeding and in the Americas with cattle). When raising livestock is an occupational specialty firmly embedded in the surrounding sedentary culture, no separate society of pastoralists ever comes into existence.

Inner Asian pastoralism traditionally depended on exploiting the extensive but seasonal grassland of the steppes and mountains. Since humans could not digest grass, raising livestock that could was an efficient way of exploiting the energy of a steppe ecosystem. The herds consisted of a mix of grazing animals including sheep, goats, horses, cattle, camels, and sometimes yaks. There was no specialization in the production of a single species, which developed among the camel-raising Bedouin of the Near East and the reindeer herders of Siberia. The Inner Asian ideal was to have all the types of animals necessary for subsistence and transportation, so that a family or tribe could approach self-sufficiency in pastoral production. The actual distribution of animals within a herd reflected both ecological variables and cultural preferences but their composition was basically similar whether the nomads were using the open steppe or mountain pasture. Variations in herd composition were most frequent among pastoralists who exploited more marginal regions where, for example, goats survived better than sheep or where aridity favored camel production over horse-raising.

Sheep were by far the most important subsistence animal raised and the mainstay of Inner Asia pastoralism. They provided milk and meat for food, wool and hides for clothing or housing, and dung which could be dried and used as fuel. Sheep reproduced rapidly and ate the most varied diet of plants on the steppe. On the Mongolian plateau they accounted for between 50 and 60 percent of all animals raised, although their numbers declined in those parts of Mongolia where the pasture was poor in grasses, such as in the arid deserts, at high altitudes, or in the forest margins. The percentage of sheep reached its maximum among the tribes of nomads which raised sheep for the lambskin trade or sold meat animals to urban markets. For example, under the same ecological conditions in nineteenth-century Kuldja (Ili Valley), sheep constituted 76 percent of the flocks among the Turkic Kazakhs, who were involved in the lambskin trade, as compared with 54 percent of the herds among the more subsistence oriented Mongol Kalmuks.[20]

Although sheep were more important economically, it was the horse which held pride of place among the steppe nomads. From its beginnings, traditional Inner Asian pastoralism has been defined by the importance of horse riding. Horses were vital to the success of nomadic societies in Inner Asia because they permitted rapid movement across vast distances, allowing communication and cooperation among peoples and tribes that were by necessity highly dispersed. Steppe horses were small and hardy, living on the open range throughout the winter, usually without fodder. They provided a secondary source of meat and fermented mare's milk (*kumiss*) was the favorite drink of the steppe. The horse figured most prominently in the military exploits of the nomads, giving their small numbers a mobility and power in battle that allowed them to defeat much larger opponents. The oral histories of Inner Asia sang their praises and horse sacrifice was an important ritual in their traditional religions. The man on horseback became the very symbol of steppe nomadism, and as a metaphor for power passed into the cultures of neighboring sedentary societies. However, while some anthropologists have defined them as horse cultures, horse-raising was never the exclusive focus of any steppe tribe, in spite of the animal's cultural and military importance. Although there were no great sheep epics, the small stock were the foundation of the steppe economy, with horse-raising an important adjunct to this more essential task.[21]

Large stock like horses and cattle required wetter regions in order to thrive. For this reason, their numbers were higher in those parts of the steppe with streams and good pasture. They also had to be pastured separately from the small stock because of their feeding habits. Sheep and goats crop the grass too closely for large stock to be able to graze after them. Therefore special pastures must be reserved for the large stock, or they must be pastured ahead of the sheep and goats if a single area is used. In arid regions, where horses and cattle are hardest to raise, the number of camels greatly increases. Camels in Inner Asia are generally of the two-humped variety known as Bactrian. Unlike their Near Eastern relatives, Bactrian camels have a thick wool coat that enables them to survive the cold winters. They were the mainstay of the overland caravan route for more than 2,000 years and their hair is still a highly valued export for making cloth. Yaks are relatively rare in Inner Asia, found mostly near the Tibetan frontier. They do well only in high altitudes, but they can be crossed with a cow to produce a hybrid (*dzo*, Tibetan; *khainak*, Mongolian) that has more tolerance for lower elevations, is more tractable, and gives better milk.

A nomadic life is based on the ability of people to move with their animals throughout the seasonal migration. Shelter and household goods must be portable. In this respect nothing is more striking than the yurt used throughout the Eurasian steppe. It consists of a series of folding wooden lattice frameworks that are set in a circle around a doorframe. Curved or straight wooden spokes are tied onto the top of the lattice frame and linked to a round wooden crown to form a hemispherical or conical dome, depending on the angle at which they are bent. The resulting framework is lightweight yet exceptionally strong and cannot be easily blown down. In the winter the yurt is covered by thick mats of wool felt which provide insulation against even bitter cold. In the summer the side felts are removed and replaced by reed matting that allows air to circulate. In ancient times, yurts were erected on large carts and moved around as a unit, but by the Middle Ages this practice had become relatively rare. However, the use of wheeled carts pulled by oxen or horses to transport goods has always been characteristic of nomadic life in Inner Asia, whereas in the Near East nomads used no wheeled vehicles.[22]

In most pastoral societies pasture was held in common by extended kinship groups while animals were private property. Nomadic migrations to these pastures were not random, but within a defined range of pastures to which a group had access. Where pasture was dependable, nomads tended to have only a few fixed camps to which they returned each year. If only marginal pastures were available then the migratory cycle displayed both more frequent movement and greater variation in the location of camps. In the absence of an outside power, a pastoralist's range was also defined by the power of his kinship group. The strongest tribes and clans laid claim to the best pastures at the best time of year, weaker groups could use them only after they had moved on. For nomads, time and space were linked units: they were concerned with the right to use a pasture at a particular time or maintain proprietary rights over fixed investments like wells; exclusive land ownership per se had little intrinsic value.[23]

The migratory cycle of Inner Asian pastoralists had four seasonal components, each with its own characteristics. The region's continental climate is characterized by temperature extremes, and winter is the harshest season of the year. The location of winter camp sites was therefore critical for survival because they had to provide both shelter from the wind and sufficient pasture. Once chosen, winter camps tended to remain fixed for the season. Favored sites include lower-lying mountain valleys, river flood plains, and depressions on the steppe. The yurt's felt insulation and smooth round shape provided adequate protection against high winds even at extremely low temperatures. Because the use of stored fodder was rare or non-existent, the availability of winter pasture set a limit on the total number of animals that could be raised. Windswept areas free of snow were preferred when available, but if the ground had snow cover, horses would be let loose to paw through the icy surface to uncover the pasture below. The area could then be used by other animals which could not graze through the snow. Winter pastures provided a bare minimum of subsistence and, under open range conditions, the livestock lost considerable weight.

Aided by spring rains, new pastures bloomed after the winter snows melted. Although at other seasons of the year much of the steppe was brown and waterless, in the spring vast stretches became soft green carpets enameled with red poppies. Camping groups dispersed widely to take advantage of the abundant pasture. Moving deep into these grasslands, the nomads drew on seasonally available pools of melted snow in low lying areas to water their cattle and horses. In such pasture the sheep did not have to be watered at all, getting the moisture they needed from the grass and dew. Animals weak from the winter's cold and hunger began to recover their weight and vitality. Lambing commenced in the spring and the fresh milk became available. Adult animals were sheared of wool. Although normally considered one of the best of times, there was always the possibility of disaster if unseasonal snowstorms struck the steppe and covered it with ice. Under these conditions much of the livestock, particularly the newborn young, would quickly die. Such an event might occur but once a generation, but it could cripple the pastoral economy for years thereafter.

Movement to the summer pastures began when the spring grasses dried and the pools of water evaporated. Nomads using the flat steppe would move north to higher latitudes, while those near mountains would move higher in altitude where pastoralists found a "second spring." In the summer camps animals rapidly gained weight. Mares were milked to produce *kumiss*, a mildly intoxicating drink favored by the nomads of Inner Asia. (Stronger alcoholic beverages were obtained in trade from sedentary societies.) Surplus milk from other animals, mostly sheep, was processed into yoghurt and then dried into rock-like balls which were stored for winter use. Wool from sheep and hair from goats or camels was cleaned and spun into thread that was used to make rope, or dyed and woven into rugs, saddle bags, or knotted carpets. Much of the sheep wool was reserved for making felt which was produced by first beating the wool, pouring boiling water on it, then rolling it back and forth until the fibers locked to create the fabric. Felts could be decorated by applying a layer of dyed wool to the surface before rolling. Heavy felt panels made of coarse wool were used to cover yurts, while the more delicate wool sheared from the lambs was used to make cloaks, winter boots, or saddle blankets.

The summer camp was abandoned at the onset of cold weather when the nomads began their return to winter quarters. Autumn was the time to breed the sheep for a spring lambing, for lambs dropped out of season had a high mortality rate. Those nomads who employed stored fodder would cut it at this time, but the more common strategy was to graze the animals away from the winter encampment to preserve the nearby pasture for the hardest times. In areas where nomads could not sell their animals to sedentary markets, they were slaughtered and smoked for a winter meat supply, particularly when winter pasture was limited. In general nomads attempted to maintain as many live animals as possible, for in the event of a disaster where half the herd was lost to frost, drought, or disease, the herdowner with 100 animals would recover far more quickly than one with fifty. Autumn was also traditionally the time nomads preferred to raid China and other sedentary areas because their horses were strong, the work of the pastoral cycle was largely done, and the farmers had their harvests completed. These raids provided grain to help the nomads through the winter.

The annual migratory cycle required mobility, but the movement was within a fixed ranged. However, the ability to readily transport herds and families had considerable political importance. When the nomads were threatened with attack by sedentary armies they disappeared, so that an invader found nothing but an empty plain with dust on the horizon. When the invader left, the nomads returned. In more extreme cases, nomads used their mobility to emigrate from a region entirely rather than remain subject to the control of another nomadic tribe. Whole peoples relocated themselves hundreds, even thousands, of miles away where they established new migratory ranges. Such mass movements necessarily displaced other tribes, leading to invasions of sedentary areas by those nomads on the margin of the steppe. Such large-scale emigrations were exceptional, however, the results of political decisions by a tribe to find a new home range rather than fight for their old one. They were not the product of hungry sheep seeking new pasture.

TRIBAL ORGANIZATION

Throughout Inner Asia historically known pastoralists shared similar principles of organization alien to sedentary societies. While the details are known to have varied, it is still useful to briefly examine the social world of the steppe to explain some of the concepts the nomads took for granted in their daily lives.

The basic social unit on the steppe was the household, usually measured in number of tents. Patrilineal relatives shared common pasture and camped together when possible. Aberle's description of the Kalmuk pattern was typical of the Inner Asian ideal:

An extended family may consist of several generations of consanguine male relatives, connected more or less closely by patrilineal descent, together with wives and immature children, and headed by the senior male of the senior family. After marriage a son may demand his livestock and move away, but ideally he should remain with his father and brothers. Moving away is a sign of trouble between kin. There is a tendency for extended family herds to be held in common as long as possible.[24]

Camping groups consisting of extended families were well adapted to pastoral production. A single man could not manage separate herds of large and small stock without assistance. Because pasture was held in common and a herdsman could efficiently look after hundreds of animals, individually owned livestock were combined to create a single large herd. Similarly, extended families made it easier for the women to carry out cooperative tasks like milk processing or felt making. But a man was always responsible for his livestock, and if he disagreed with their management he had the right to remove them and go elsewhere. Large groups of kin also provided protection against theft and allies in disputes with other groups.

The composition of camping groups reflected stages in a household's development. An independent household came into existence upon marriage when a man generally received his share of the herd and a woman got her own tent, but it lacked the necessary livestock and labor to be fully autonomous. During the engagement period, young men sometimes did brideservice and lived with their in-laws, but it was customary for the couple to live in the husband's father's camp upon marriage. As children were born and the family's herd increased, it became increasingly self-sufficient, but when the children were ready for marriage, a significant percentage of the household's livestock was consumed by bridewealth payments and anticipatory inheritance. Each son received his share of the herd based on the total number of brothers with a one share reserved for the parents. The youngest son eventually inherited the paternal household along with his own share, a form of social security for his parents. The senior household thereby increased its authority, because a man could rely on the support and labor of his adult sons and their families. The development of a household cycle was normally restricted to a set of brothers and their sons, the death of the brothers bringing about the dissolution of the group.[25]

The extended family was a cultural ideal and had many economic advantages, but it was not easy to maintain because large groups were inherently unstable. Because individuals owned their own animals and could break away from the group if dissatisfied, cooperation was voluntary. While sets of brothers usually maintained enough solidarity to herd collectively, their own sons, sets of cousins, rarely could. It was also difficult to maintain extended families intact if the number of animals they owned rose above the carrying capacity of the local pasture. Nomadic pastoralism's adaptability was based on flexibility of movement and attempting to maintain too many people or animals in one place reduced its viability. When local pasture was insufficient, some families would migrate to other areas, maintaining political and social ties, but no longer residing together.

Women had more authority and autonomy than their sisters in neighboring sedentary societies. Among political elites polygyny was common, but each wife had her own yurt. It was not possible to practice the forms of seclusion so common in many sedentary Asian societies. Day-to-day life required women to take on a more public role in economic activities. Although the details cannot be confirmed for the entire history of Inner Asia, most visitors made comments similar to those of Johann de Plano Carpini, the Pope's envoy to the Mongols in the thirteenth century.

The men do nothing but occupy themselves with their arrows and to a small extent look after their herds; for the rest they go hunting and practice archery . . . Both men and women stay in the saddle for a long time. . . . All the work rests on the shoulders of the women; they make the fur coats, clothes, shoes, bootlegs, and everything else made from leather. They also drive the carts and mend them, load the camels, and are very quick and efficient in all their work. All the women wear trousers, and some of them shoot with the bow as accurately as the men.[26]

Even though the formal social structure was strongly patrilineal, women also participated in tribal politics. Reciprocal alliance patterns among clans gave women an important structural role linking tribes together. So daughters, while lost to their natal family, still bound them to other groups. For example the Unggirad people, the clan of Chinggis Khan's wife, were fond of proclaiming that their political power lay in the strength of their marriage alliances and not their military power: "They are our daughters and daughters of our daughters, who, become princesses by their marriage, serve as shields against our enemies and by the petitions they present to their husbands obtain favors for us."[27] Even after the death of her husband a woman maintained considerable influence through her sons, and if they were young she often acted as the legal head of household. From the time of the Hsiung-nu in the second century BC, Chinese political accounts regularly depicted elite women in critical positions during conflicts over succession to the leadership. The best example of this was seen in the early Mongol empire when the senior wife of the "Great Khan" was the normal choice for regent during the inter-regnum.

The household and camp group were the most important units in the daily life of the Inner Asian nomad, but to deal with the world beyond herding it was necessary to organize into larger units. Tribal political and social organization was based on a model of nested kinship groups, the conical clan. The conical clan was an extensive patrilineal kinship organization in which members of a common descent group were ranked and segmented along genealogical lines. Elder generations were superior in rank to younger generations, just as elder brothers were superior in rank to younger brothers. By extension, lineages and clans were hierarchically ranked on the basis of seniority. Political leadership was restricted to members of senior clans in many groups, but from the lowest to highest, all members of the tribe claimed common descent. This genealogical charter was important because it justified rights to pasture, created social or military obligations between kinship groups, and established the legitimacy of local political authority. When nomads lost their autonomy to sedentary governments, the political importance of this extensive genealogical system disappeared and kinship links remained important only at the local level.[28]

Yet this ideal concept of tribe was less easy to precisely define at higher levels of organization. The conical clan structure relied on a set of principles that were subject to considerable alteration and manipulation. Ideal explanations assigned leadership by seniority and stressed the solidarity of patrilineal kin against outsiders, but, in the world of steppe politics, these rules were often ignored or abused in the pursuit of power. Tribal chieftains recruited personal followers who renounced their own kinship ties by swearing exclusive loyalty to their patron. Junior lines promoted themselves by murdering more senior rivals, a practice that was common in many steppe dynasties. Similarly, the simple principles of patrilineality by which tribesmen claimed descent from a common ancestor were frequently modified to attach non-related people. For example, some groups justified their inclusion because their founder had been adopted into the tribe, or as a result of a matrilineal tie, or even because their kin-group had a historical client relationship with a dominant lineage. Patrilineal kinship groups were also cross-cut by marriage ties which created long-term relationships with other clans or tribes with which they would ally even against more directly related kinsmen. For these reasons the question of whether tribes or tribal confederations were ever truly genealogical has led to a particularly sharp debate among historians.[29]

Part of the problem has stemmed from the failure to make a distinction between a tribe, which was the largest unit of incorporation based on a genealogical model and a tribal confederation, which combined many tribes to create a supratribal political entity. Because Inner Asian tribal systems employed segmentary building blocks at the local level, with successively larger units of incorporation bringing in more people, it has been assumed that each higher level was simply the product of the same principles applied to an ever-expanding number of people. Yet this was rarely true. "Actual" kinship relations (based on principles of descent and affiliations by marriage or adoption) were empirically evident only within the tribe's smaller units: nuclear families, extended households, and local lineages. At higher levels of incorporation clans and tribes maintained relationships of a more political origin in which genealogical relationships played only a minor role. In powerful nomadic empires the organization of component tribal groups was generally a product of reorganization enforced by division from the top down rather than the result of alliance from the bottom up.

It was of course possible for a political structure based on kinship to exist only in the minds of the participants. For example, among the Nuer of East Africa there were no permanent leaders. Factions organized on the basis of segmentary opposition in which an individual supports more closely related groups against more distantly related groups. Sets of brothers in opposition to their cousins in family disputes would unite with them in fights against outsiders. When faced with invasion by another tribe, feuding lineages and clans would unite to defeat the aggressor, only to resume their internal disputes when the enemy was repulsed. Segmentary opposition was particularly well suited to pastoralists because it directed expansion against outsiders to the benefit of the whole tribe. Among Inner Asian nomads, however, the segmentary structure was more than a mental construct, it was reinforced by permanent chieftains who provided leadership and internal order for lineages, clans, and whole tribes. Such a hierarchy of leadership positions went far beyond the needs of simple pastoralism. It was a centralized political structure which, though still based on a kinship idiom, was much more complex and powerful than those observed among nomads in other regions.[30]

In summary, kinship played its most important role at the level of the family, lineage, and clan. Units of organization at the tribal level, or supratribal level, were more political in nature. Tribal confederations formed through alliance or conquest always contained unrelated tribes. The idiom of kinship, however, remained the common currency for determining legitimacy of leadership within the ruling elite of an established nomadic empire because there was a long cultural tradition among the tribes of the central steppe of drawing leadership from a single dynastic lineage. Deviations from this ideal were disguised by manipulating, distorting or even inventing genealogies that justified changes in the status quo. Powerful individuals saw ancestors retroactively promoted at the expense of declining elites and "structural amnesia" relegated genealogically senior, but politically weak, lines of descent to oblivion. This tradition produced dynasties of unparalleled duration. The direct descendants of the Hsiung-nu founder Mao-tun ruled over the steppe for 600 years in greater and lesser capacities, as did the direct descendants of Chinggis Khan for 700 years, and a single unbroken Turkish dynasty (of Inner Asian heritage) ruled over the Ottoman Empire for more than 600 years. However, this hierarchical tradition was not shared by all Inner Asian nomads; those in Manchuria traditionally rejected hereditary succession and elected their leaders based on talent and ability. Even in the central steppe, conquering tribes could wipe the slate clean by promoting themselves to power after they eliminated their rivals or reduced them to marginal territories.

THE RISE OF STEPPE PASTORALISM

We tend to assume that because horse riding appears so natural it must be very ancient; but it really developed only within the period of written historical accounts. From archaeological evidence, the horse was domesticated in the southern Russian steppe around 3,200 BC, but it was not until 1,700 BC that the horse chariot, with its complex harnessing and spoked wheels, made its appearance in western Asia. The chariot revolutionized warfare. The Hittite and the Assyrian empires, which arose on the southern margin of the steppe, both depended on chariots to overwhelm enemy foot soldiers. This technology spread quickly, even to regions where horses had to be imported. Although the transmission links are not yet fully known, chariot technology had been adopted in China by 1,200 BC and became an integral part of the military organization.[31] In all these societies chariots were not only weapons of war, but also key symbols of power for their ruling aristocracies. Surprisingly, chariot using seems to have preceded horse riding, for there is no evidence of riding technology like saddles or bits, and while surviving illustrations show many chariots, horsemen are shown mounted on the rump as if they were riding a donkey.[32]

Horse-riding cultures developed on the western steppe between 900 to 800 BC and began to displace the semi-nomadic riverine agricultural settlements there. The first historically known nomads were the Cimmerians and Scythians who descended on the kingdoms of the Near East at the end of eighth century BC. The Scythians initially allied themselves with the Assyrians, making a marriage alliance with them in 674 BC, but they later helped destroy them and raided throughout the region. The Medes eventually pushed them back onto the Pontic steppe around 600 BC. In 514 BC, the Scythians destroyed a Persian expeditionary force led by Darius the Great.

Herodotus visited the Scythians in the middle of the fifth century BC and left a classic account of their culture, verified by later archaeological excavation of tombs. They were heavy drinkers of imported wine, smoked hemp, worshiped a pantheon of gods, and built elaborate tombs stocked with rich goods and sacrifices (some human) for their dead. The famous "animal style" of art with its leaping stags and fighting animals, done in gold, carved wood, or felt appliqué in bold colors displayed a cultural ethos strikingly different from their sedentary neighbors.[33] But it was in war that they were most feared:

In what concerns war, their customs are the following. The Scythian soldier drinks the blood of the first man he overthrows in battle. Whatever the number he slays, he cuts off all their heads and carries them to the king; since he is thus entitled to a share of the booty, whereto he forfeits all claim if he does not produce a head. . . . The skulls of their enemies, not indeed of all, but of those they most detest, they treat as follows. Having sawn off the portion below the eyebrows, and cleaned out the inside, they cover the outside with leather. When a man is poor, this is all that he does; but if he is rich, he also lines the inside with gold: in either case the skull is used as a drinking cup.[34]

These characteristics in warfare were also noted specifically by later Chinese accounts, while the material culture described by Herodotus was confirmed by discoveries of frozen tombs in the Siberian borderlands.[35] The uniformity in material culture and other customs was the result of the rapid spread of horse riding across the Eurasian steppes. Lattimore has argued that this spread was not the result of migrations of people bearing a new culture, but of the adoption of a new technology and way of life by people on the fringes of the steppe. Marginal farmers from China, forest hunters from Siberia, and the older inhabitants of the steppe could now make fuller use of the Inner Asian grasslands and adopted a fully nomadic style of life.[36] That such profound changes could occur rapidly was seen much later in history when the horse was introduced to the plains of North America by the Spaniards. Plains Indian culture, based on horse riding and bison hunting, was taken up within a century of the introduction of the horse on the plains by a wide variety of tribes which adopted similar cultural practices despite their heterogeneous origins.[37] So natural did this style of life appear to outsiders that it became the stereotype for all North American Indian cultures in the popular imagination, even though it did not exist in the pre-contact period.

Horse-riding nomadic pastoralists appeared along the Chinese frontier some time after the beginning of the fourth century BC. Before that time Chinese accounts of frontier affairs recorded in the *Tso Chuan* speak only of loosely organized tribes like the Jung and Ti, who fought in small groups on foot.[38] The *Shih-chi* described the frontier peoples during this period as troublesome but ill-organized. "All of them were scattered about in their own valleys, each with their own chieftains. From time to time they would have gatherings of a hundred or more men, but no one tribe was capable of unifying the others under a single rule."[39]

Sun Tzu's classic *The Art of War*, dating from the middle of the fourth century BC, devotes considerable attention to the use of chariots in battle, but makes not a single mention of cavalry.[40] The first indicators of a major change are references to the Hu, tribes of horse-riding nomads that came into contact with the Chinese states along the northern frontier. The Jung and Ti, the "old barbarians," quickly disappeared from Chinese accounts, replaced by these horse-riding "new barbarians," probably the same tribes with a radically different culture. The Chinese states along the northern frontier were the first to adopt cavalry troops into their armies. " . . . King Wu-ling of Chao (325–299 BC) changed the customs of his people, ordering them to adopt the barbarian dress and practice riding and shooting, and led them north in a successful attack on the forest barbarians and the Lou-fan."[41]

This innovation accelerated the ongoing consolidation of China into a single state by changing the rules of warfare. The chariot-riding aristocracies of old with their gentlemanly code of conduct fell before states employing large armies of foot soldiers and cavalry.[42] Both the steppe and China had entered a new period of history.

NOTES

1   Wolf, *Europe and the People without History*.
2   Sahlins, *Islands of History*, p. xi.
3   Radloff, *Aus Siberien*, vol. 1, pp. 513–17.
4   Barthold, *Zwölf Vorlesungen über die Geschichte der Türken Mittelasiens*, pp. 11–13.
5   Harmatta, "The dissolution of the Hun Empire."
6   Krader, "The origin of the state among nomads."
7   Vladimirtsov, *Le régime social des Mongols: le féodalisme nomade*; see also Khazanov, *Nomads and the Outside World*, pp. 228ff for a summary of Soviet interpretations.
8   Caroline Humphrey, "Editor's introduction," in Vainshtein, *Nomads of South Siberia*, pp. 13–31.
9   Burnham, "Spatial mobility and political centralization in pastoral societies."
10 Irons, "Political stratification among pastoral nomads," p. 362.
11 Khazanov, *Nomads and the Outside World*.
12 Ledyard, "Yin and Yang in the China–Manchuria–Korea Triangle."
13 Wittfogel and Feng, *The History of Chinese Society: Liao*, pp. 1–26.
14 Lattimore, *Inner Asian Frontiers of China*, pp. 521–3.
15 Ibid., pp. 542–52.
16 These terms are used to define geographical regions and do not imply a continuity of occupation by the ethnic or linguistic groups that now inhabit them. It is not clear, for example, what the historical relationship is between the Mongols of medieval and modern times and the Hsiung-nu who occupied the same territory a thousand years earlier. Similarly, for the first half of its history, Turkestan was Iranian in culture and language, while the term Manchuria is a creation of Western geographers.
17 Murazaev, *Die mongolische Volksrepublik, physisch-geographische*.
18 Vainshtein, *Nomads of South Siberia*.
19 Cf. Lattimore, *Inner Asian Frontiers*, pp. 21–5.
20 Krader, "The ecology of central Asian pastoralism," p. 313.
21 Bacon, "Types of pastoral nomadism in Central and Southwest Asia," on culture area; Eberhardt in *Conquerors and Rulers* provides an example of a typology drawn from a small set of examples with little ethnographic justification.
22 Andrews, "The white house of Khuransan: The felt tents of the Iranian Yomut and Goklen;" Bulliet, *The Camel and the Wheel* for details.
23 Barth, "The land use patterns of migratory tribes of South Persia."
24 Aberle, *The Kinship System of the Kalmuk Mongols*, p. 9.

25 Stenning, *Savannah Nomads*, on Fulani for more detailed analysis of the developmental cycle in a pastoral society.
26 Spuler, *History of the Mongols*, pp. 80–1.
27 Mostaert, *Sur quelques passages de l'Histoire secrète des Mongols*, p. 10 (cited in Cleaves, *The Secret History of the Mongols*, p. 16, n. 48).
28 Krader, *Social Organization of the Mongol–Turkic Pastoral Nomads*. Lindholm, "Kinship structure and political authority: The Middle East and Central Asia."
29 Tapper, "Your tribe or mine? Anthropologists, historians and tribespeople on the concept of tribe in the Middle East," in Joseph Kostiner and Phillip Khoury (eds), *Tribe and State in the Middle East*.
30 Sahlins, "The segmentary lineage: an organization for predatory expansion."
31 Chang, Archaeology of Ancient China, pp. 279–80; Shaughnessy, "Historical perspectives on the introduction of the chariot in China."
32 Downs, "The domestication of the horse."
33 Cf. Jettmar, *The Art of the Steppes*.
34 Herodotus, *The History*, Book IV, ch. 64–5.
35 Rudenko, *Frozen Tombs of Siberia*.
36 Lattimore, *Inner Asian Frontiers*, pp. 58–66.
37 Holder, *The Hoe and the Horse on the Plains*.
38 Prušek attempts to prove that horse riding appeared much earlier along the Chinese frontier, but while he finds evidence for the existence of horses he is unable to present a unambiguous example of their use as cavalry among the Jung and Ti (*Chinese Statelets and the Northern Barbarians in the Period 1400–300 BC*).
39 *Shih-chi* (SC) 110:5; Watson, *Records of the Grand Historian of China*, vol. 2, p. 158.
40 Griffith (trans.), *Sun Tzu: The Art of War*.
41 SC 110:6; Watson, *Records*, vol. 2, p. 159.
42 Hsu, *Ancient China in Transition*, pp. 68–71; Kierman, "Phases and modes of combat in early China," in Frank Kierman and John Fairbank (eds), *Chinese Ways in Warfare*, pp. 27–66.

2

The Steppe Tribes United

The Hsiung-nu Empire

The mounted nomads of the northern steppe enter the Chinese historical record in the fourth century BC under the generic name Hu. With the founding of the short-lived Ch'in dynasty in 221 BC the Hu became differentiated in the Chinese records, reflecting a new and more specific interest in the northern frontier. At this time three major nomadic groups occupied positions along China's frontier: the Yüeh-chih in the west, the Hsiung-nu in the Ordos region, and the Tung-hu on the eastern flank.

After Shih-huang-ti, the first Ch'in emperor, crushed the old warring states of China to create a unified empire, he turned his attention and his armies to the north. Using corvée labor the Ch'in government linked the frontier walls built by older states to establish what became known as the "Great Wall" to separate China from the steppe. This building project, though massive in scope, was not prompted by any immediate threat of nomadic invasion, as the nomads stayed clear of the powerful Ch'in armies during this period. Instead it represented the culmination of an older tradition in which each state had surrounded itself by walls, both along the northern frontier with the nomads and inside of China to delineate boundaries with other states. The Ch'in conquest had rendered the internal walls superfluous and they were abandoned to decay. The walls along the northern frontier, however, were strengthened and linked together to mark the frontier of the empire. In this sense they were as much political as military constructions. In the eyes of all subsequent Chinese rulers the Great Wall marked the edge of Chinese civilization and the beginning of barbarian territory. Its purpose was as much to keep the frontier population of China separate from any potential allies on the steppe as it was to keep the nomads out of China. Only after the completion of the Wall and the fall of the Ch'in dynasty did it become associated with the threat of nomadic invasion. In retrospect the aggressive Ch'in frontier policy of which wall construction was a part was reinterpreted as a purely defensive action.[1]

The expansion of Ch'in power onto the edge of the steppe had immediate consequences for the Hsiung-nu who bore the brunt of the new Chinese attacks. Shih-huang-ti expelled them from their homeland in the Ordos in order to construct a more defensible frontier. The Hsiung-nu retreated to the north where they remained in exile for ten years until the sudden fall of the Ch'in dynasty led to a civil war and the abandonment of its frontier defenses. Taking advantage of the turmoil in China, the Hsiung-nu reoccupied the Ordos.

At the fall of the Ch'in dynasty the Hsiung-nu were the weakest of the nomadic confederations on the steppe. They had lost territory to China, had sent a hostage to the Yüeh-chih – a sure sign of subservience on the steppe – and were treated with contempt by their eastern neighbors, the Tung-hu. The sudden rise of the Hsiung-nu empire under the leadership of Mao-tun, who created an empire that proved to be the dominant force on the steppe for many centuries, therefore demands some explanation.[2]

Mao-tun was the son of T'ou-man – the *Shan-yü*, or supratribal leader, of the Hsiung-nu – who had led the Hsiung-nu into exile and later brought them back to the Ordos. Although Mao-tun was officially the heir-apparent, when T'ou-man had a son by a second wife he schemed to remove Mao-tun from the line of succession. He sent Mao-tun as a hostage to the Yüeh-chih and then attacked them, expecting that Mao-tun would be killed in retaliation. But Mao-tun stole a fast horse, escaped the Yüeh-chih, and returned home to the Hsiung-nu as a hero. Mao-tun's bravery was greatly admired and his father was obliged to appoint him commander of 10,000 horsemen, a high Hsiung-nu rank.

Mao-tun soon attracted a band of loyal followers whom he trained to obey his every command without question. Mao-tun's method included the use of stern tests. On the signal of his whistling arrow each follower was to fire at whatever Mao-tun pointed. After practicing in hunting Mao-tun took aim at one of his favorite horses. Those who failed to fire were put to death. Next he took aim at one of his consorts; and again those who had failed to fire were put to death. Finally he took aim at one of his father's valuable horses and saw his command had been obeyed by all. Now satisfied with the loyalty of his men, Mao-tun seized the next opportunity to aim his whistling arrow at his father, T'ou-man, who met his death in a hail of arrows. Mao-tun proclaimed himself *Shan-yü* and proceeded to execute his rival half-brother, his step-mother, and those Hsiung-nu officials who refused to support him.[3]

When Mao-tun assumed power in 209 BC any ambitions he had to rule over the steppe were tempered by the knowledge that the Hsiung-nu were not powerful enough to win an open contest of arms with either of their nomadic neighbors. Mao-tun's conquest of the steppe therefore relied as much on cleverness as it did on military strength. He even used the perceived weakness of the Hsiung-nu to his advantage.

News of Mao-tun's violent accession to power soon reached the Tung-hu. Hoping to benefit from the turmoil, they dispatched an envoy to demand one of T'ou-man's best horses, a Hsiung-nu treasure. Such a demand was an insult to the Hsiung-nu and as such was a test of strength. Mao-tun had the choice of complying and admitting Hsiung-nu subordination or refusing and risking open warfare in which the Hsiung-nu might well be beaten. Over the objections of his ministers Mao-tun complied with the Tung-hu demand. The Tung-hu interpreted this as a sign of weakness based on fear; so they sent another envoy to Mao-tun and demanded one of his consorts. Again over the objections of his ministers, Mao-tun yielded. The Tung-hu now regarded the Hsiung-nu with contempt and set about raiding their territory. They also sent a third envoy to claim title to the desert wasteland that separated them from the Hsiung-nu. Although many considered this demand meaningless, Mao-tun refused declaring, "Land is the basis of a nation" and he executed those ministers who favored giving it up.[4] Mao-tun immediately mounted an attack on the Tung-hu, who, in their overconfidence, had posted neither scouts nor prepared defenses. They were caught completely by surprise and were utterly defeated. The whole Tung-hu people and their livestock fell into Mao-tun's hands. The Tung-hu ruler who had insulted the Hsiung-nu lost his life and had his skull made into a drinking cup.

To at least some of the Hsiung-nu ministers the concrete demands for a horse and a woman had appeared more serious than the issue of sovereignty over some wasteland that neither people used; yet Mao-tun's war against the Tung-hu has been interpreted as centering on the importance of land even among nomadic people because it was the demand for land which triggered the war. This explanation is incomplete, however, because it overlooks the political context in which the demands were made, confusing the pretext for beginning the war with its underlying cause.

The Tung-hu demands were tests of power and Mao-tun's response was part of a larger design to enable the militarily weaker Hsiung-nu to win a victory over a mobile opponent. Mao-tun employed one of the classic steppe tactics – the feigned retreat. The attacker is led to believe that he is pursuing a defeated enemy only to fall unprepared into an ambush. Mao-tun feigned a diplomatic retreat before the ever-increasing Tung-hu demands. The disagreements in the Hsiung-nu court about yielding reinforced the image of a new leader who was on the defensive and unable to rule. The Tung-hu's last demand for Hsiung-nu land indicated their overconfidence and triggered a war Mao-tun must have long planned as the only way to catch his enemy off guard. To be successful the attack had to be both sudden and unexpected. A nomadic people could not be easily defeated if they were given an opportunity to move their people and livestock to safety. Mao-tun was able to strike swiftly because nomads on the steppe were always prepared for war and were extremely mobile. The Hsiung-nu had an army in the field within days of Mao-tun's command.

Having swallowed the Tung-hu, Mao-tun turned west and inflicted the first of many defeats on the Yüeh-chih who had formerly dominated the Hsiung-nu. During the course of this operation he seized all the remaining land south of the Yellow River that the Ch'in armies had previously taken from the Hsiung-nu. From here he mounted raids on China in districts left undefended because of the civil war there. In campaigns to the north in Mongolia he conquered five tribes. "Thus the nobles and high ministers of the Hsiung-nu were won over by Mao-tun, considering him a truly worthy leader."[5] Mao-tun now faced south and presented a newly reunited China with a steppe imperium of great military strength.

Mao-tun's establishment of a steppe empire was contemporaneous with the re-establishment of a unified China under the rule of Kao-tsu, the first emperor of the Han dynasty. Although the nomads on the steppe took no part in China's civil war struggles that followed the collapse of the Ch'in dynasty, the new Han rulers looked upon the Hsiung-nu as a major threat to China. The most obvious threat they posed was that of invasion. The Hsiung-nu had the power to devastate border regions, wreaking havoc and stealing anything that could be carried off. A less obvious but more potent threat to the dynasty was the danger that the empire might start to unravel along the northern frontier if rulers in the border areas allied themselves with the Hsiung-nu against the central government.

The first conflict between Han China and the Hsiung-nu occurred over this issue in 201–200 BC. The war began with a Hsiung-nu attack on the border city of Mai-i in Tai province where Han Hsin, a civil war ally of Kao-tsu, was enfeoffed as king. He defected with his troops to the Hsiung-nu. The loss of a border region was a minor problem to the empire, but the defection of a disloyal king was a more dangerous matter. Kao-tsu had been forced to create a number of autonomous kingdoms as rewards to civil war allies. Against the central authority of the emperor and his control of the imperial armies these kings had little chance of breaking away from Han control. However, if a king, or even a provincial governor, could ally himself with the Hsiung-nu, then the chances of becoming independent of China were good, albeit within the Hsiung-nu orbit. All the kings feared they would lose their kingdoms when the dynasty became more established. They were thus ripe for subversion.

Kao-tsu could not allow Han Hsin's defection to go unpunished. The emperor called up the Han forces and personally led them to the frontier. The campaign went poorly from the start. Severe cold and snow struck the army while on march and frostbite caused the loss of 20–30 percent of the troops. When the army finally made contact with the Hsiung-nu they pursued what they took to be a weak cavalry force. Kao-tsu led the advance column himself. Unfamiliar with steppe warfare, the Chinese vanguard hurried after the re-treating nomads only to fall into an ambush at P'ing-ch'eng. Fooled by the Hsiung-nu feigned retreat, Kao-tsu found himself separated from the main Han army and surrounded by the whole Hsiung-nu cavalry.

The main Han army was unable to break the siege and for seven days the emperor remained trapped by the nomads. In desperation he sent an envoy to the *Shan-yü*'s wife and struck a secret bargain with her to help gain his release. She convinced the *Shan-yü* that the capture of the Han emperor would not be in the best interests of the Hsiung-nu because the nomads could never occupy China. According to later reports, Kao-tsu had gained her cooperation by threatening that if she did not work out a settlement he would send the *Shan-yü* a number of beautiful Chinese consorts to win away his affection.[6] However, Mao-tun also had strong practical reasons for ending the siege: his ally Han Hsin had failed to make the planned rendezvous with the Hsiung-nu and if he had switched sides again the nomads would have been put in a difficult position.

In any event a small hole opened up in the Hsiung-nu line and Kao-tsu fled with his troops.

This was the most humiliating defeat that the Chinese were ever to suffer at the hands of the Hsiung-nu. For centuries to come the very mention of P'ing-ch'eng was enough to make the court think twice before going to war against the Hsiung-nu. Hsiung-nu military power was now viewed with respect and the "Hsiung-nu problem" became the dominant foreign policy issue in the Han court.

Mao-tun's strength was further enhanced when, during the early part of the reign of Han Wen-ti (r. 179–157 BC), the Hsiung-nu again routed the Yüeh-chih who fled to the west. As a consequence of this victory, the Hsiung-nu also took control of the small oasis kingdoms in Turkestan. Mao-tun sent word of these victories to the Han court announcing that,

All the people who live by drawing the bow are now united into one family and the entire region of the north is at peace. Thus I wish to lay down my weapons, rest my soldiers, and turn my horses to pasture, and forget the recent affair [of raiding China] and restore the old pact, that the peoples of the border may have the peace that they enjoyed in former times, that the young may grow to manhood, the old live out their lives in security, and generation after generation enjoy peace and comfort.[7]

The Han court decided the Hsiung-nu were far too powerful to attack and so agreed to renew the treaty and open border markets. Mao-tun died peacefully in 174 BC leaving his huge empire to his son.

THE IMPERIAL CONFEDERACY

Internal organization

Mao-tun created the Hsiung-nu empire with his great conquests. More remarkable than the extent of these conquests, however, was the structure and stability he established in the Hsiung-nu state, which lasted longer than any steppe empire in history. For the first 250 years of its existence the Hsiung-nu empire completely dominated the steppe and for over 500 years the Hsiung-nu *Shan-yü* remained a major political actor in Chinese frontier affairs. *Shan-yü* followed *Shan-yü* for ten peaceful successions until civil war broke out in 57 BC, after which another ten successions followed without trouble until the empire was again split in civil war after AD 48. As rulers of a united empire the single dynasty of *Shan-yü*s outlasted the Former Han and, as rulers of a smaller state, they outlived the Later Han as well. The roots of this stability are to be found in the special nature of the Hsiung-nu state and the relationship it established with China. It was an "imperial confederacy," autocratic and statelike in foreign and military affairs but consultative and federally structured for dealing with internal problems. The *Shan-yü*'s power derived from his dual role as a war leader and sole intermediary between China and the tribes on the steppe. The Hsiung-nu strategy for dealing with Han China in both diplomacy and war was based on the fact that the Hsiung-nu imperial government owed its financial and political stability to its exploitation of resources from outside the steppe. Rather than being the result of indigenous evolution, the Hsiung-nu state was a structural response by the nomads to the problems of organizing themselves so that they could effectively manipulate China. The organizing principles of the Hsiung-nu state and its foreign policy can be summarized as follows:

1   The power of the supratribal *Shan-yü* was limited internally by indigenous tribal leaders and succession to imperial office was strictly regulated.

2   The *Shan-yü* acted as the sole intermediary between the Han government and the tribes in the empire both as a negotiator and war leader in order to obtain subsidies and trade benefits from China.

3   The Hsiung-nu state established a deliberately predatory policy in its relationship with China and cultivated a particularly violent reputation in order to maximize its bargaining position with the Han government.

4   The Hsiung-nu state was organized such that it was relatively impervious to Han countermeasures aided in part by the failure of the Han government to grasp the difference between the Hsiung-nu state and its own.

The Chinese were familiar with the organization of the Hsiung-nu state and recorded a description of it in the *Shih-chi*.

Under the *Shan-yü* are the Wise Kings of the Left and Right, the left and right Luli kings, left and right generals, left and right commandants, left and right household administrators, and the left and right Ku-tu marquises. The Hsiung-nu word for "wise" is "t'u-ch'i", so that the heir of the *Shan-yü* is customarily called the "T'u-ch'i King of the Left". Among the other leaders, from the wise kings on down to the household administrators, the more important ones command 10,000 horsemen and the lesser ones several thousand, numbering twenty-four leaders in all, although all are known by the title of "10,000 Horsemen". The high ministerial offices are hereditary, being filled from generation to generation by the members of the Hu-yën and Lan families, and in more recent times by the Hsü-pu family. These three families constitute the aristocracy of the nation. The kings and other members of the left live in the eastern sector, the region from Shang-ku east to the lands of the Hui-mo and Ch'ao-hsien peoples. The kings and the leaders of the right live in the west, the area from Shang-ku west to the territories of the Yüeh-chih and the Ch'iang tribes. The *Shan-yü* has his court in the region of Tai and Yün-chung. Each group has its own area, within which it moves about from place to place looking for water and pasture. The Left and Right Wise Kings and the Luli kings are the most powerful, while the Ku-tu marquises assist the *Shan-yü* in the administration of the nation. Each of the twenty-four leaders in turn appoints his own "chiefs of a thousand," "chiefs of a hundred," and "chiefs of ten," as well as his subordinate kings, prime ministers, chief commandants, household administrators, *chü-ch'ü* officials, and so forth.[8]

According to this account, the Hsiung-nu administrative hierarchy had three levels. At the top the *Shan-yü* and the Ku-tu marquises ran the imperial government and coordinated the affairs of the empire at large. At the second level the twenty-four imperial leaders, each with the title "Ten Thousand

Horsemen" were distributed east and west over the whole empire. They acted as imperial governors for the major regions of the empire and were usually close relatives of the *Shan-yü* or members of the Hsiung-nu aristocracy. Because the *Shan-yü* appointed his own chosen successor to the post of Wise King of the Left, an individual might hold a number of different imperial ranks during his lifetime. These positions owed their power and their authority to the strength of the Hsiung-nu state. It is striking to note that (unlike Chinggis Khan's later Mongol empire) the *Shan-yü*'s personal bodyguard, so prominent in aiding Mao-tun's rise to power, was not institutionalized and is not mentioned in any other context by the Han histories of the Hsiung-nu.

At the third level of administration was a large class of indigenous tribal leaders (subordinate kings, prime ministers, chief commandants, household administrators, *chü-ch'ü* officials, etc.) who were officially under the command of the twenty-four imperial governors. However, in practice they drew their support from their own tribal groups, each of which had its own territory. The total number of these tribal groups within the empire is not known. Han records list at least a dozen but this was an underestimate since the Chinese were unaware of those groups, even sizable ones, with whom they had no direct contact.

The use of such titles such as "Ten Thousand Horsemen," "chiefs of a thousand," and "chiefs of ten," implies a far more rigid Hsiung-nu administrative hierarchy than actually existed. The *Shih-chi* account explicitly states that only the most important men among those who held a Ten Thousand Horsemen title actually commanded 10,000 troops. Less important men with the same rank commanded only a few thousand troops. The same was likely to have been true of their subordinate commanders of a thousand, of a hundred, and of ten. In addition the list of decimal ranks is followed immediately by a parallel set of political ranks (subordinate kings, prime ministers, chief commandants, etc.). Since the twenty-four imperial Ten Thousand Horsemen held separate political titles, it may be concluded that their subordinates also held such dual titles. This gave the Hsiung-nu empire two systems of ranking, each with a separate function. The system of named non-decimal ranks was used for the political administration of tribes and territories which included groups of many different sizes. The system of decimal ranks was used in time of war when large numbers of troops from many parts of the steppe were brought together under a single military command structure.

The *Shan-yü* and his court were the indigenous leaders of the Hsiung-nu core tribes; although in other respects the core tribes consisted of ordinary tribesmen, they therefore had double ties to the *Shan-yü*, who could rely on their consistent support. The indigenous leaders of the tribes incorporated into the empire by conquest or alliance were linked into the imperial administration under the control of one of the twenty-four Ten Thousand Horsemen who acted as the *Shan-yü*'s agents. Structurally the weakest part of the system was the link between the leaders of the incorporated tribes and the imperial commanders. Although the leader of an incorporated tribe held a position within the Hsiung-nu imperial hierarchy, his power derived from the support of his own people. Such leaders retained a great deal of autonomy at the local level. Trouble within the empire usually broke out at this level over issues concerning the amount of independence granted to the leaders of the incorporated tribes. The power of the *Shan-yü* to rule in absolute fashion, though unlimited in theory, was constrained in practice.

Three options were open to a dissatisfied tribal leader: to secede by moving west, to defect to China in the south, or to rebel. None of these strategies was without cost and were only employed when a tribal leader was under severe pressure. The three cases that follow illustrate the use of such strategies and demonstrate the degree to which the *Shan-yü* and the Hsiung-nu state were forced to recognize the power of local tribal elites.

Tribal groups on the western edge of the empire could become independent by moving beyond the *Shan-yü*'s sphere of control. However this option usually necessitated displacing an existing tribe from the territory and set up a domino effect where each tribe pushed its neighbor further to the west or south. This occurred on a large scale after the Hsiung-nu defeated the Yüeh-chih. Rather than remain as a subordinate part of the expanding Hsiung-nu empire, the Yüeh-chih moved west to a new home along the Oxus River beyond the reach of the Hsiung-nu, displacing the Sai nomads who moved into Afghanistan.

The displacement of the Yüeh-chih opened their territory to the Wu-sun who had been incorporated into the Hsiung-nu empire around 176 BC. According to the *Shih-chi* account, the leader of the Wu-sun was killed and his son K'un-mo (actually a title) was reared at the Hsiung-nu court.

When K'un-mo had grown to manhood, the *Shan-yü* put him in command of a band of troops and he several times won merit in battle. The *Shan-yü* then made him leader of the people whom his father had ruled in former times and ordered him to guard the western forts. K'un-mo gathered together his people, looked after them and led them in attacks on small settlements in the neighborhood. Soon he had twenty or thirty thousand skilled archers who were trained in aggressive warfare. When the *Shan-yü* died, K'un-mo led his people far away, declared himself an independent ruler, and refused to journey to the meetings of the Hsiung-nu court. The Hsiung-nu sent surprise parties of troops to attach him but they were unable to win a victory. In the end the Hsiung-nu decided he must be a god and left him alone, still claiming he was a subject of theirs but no longer making large-scale attacks on him.[9]

In spite of their success the Wu-sun still feared Hsiung-nu power and even many years later (circa 121 BC) K'un-mo rejected a Chinese proposal that he return east to his old homeland to act as a Han ally in the territory abandoned by the Hun-yeh king.

Most tribal groups in the Hsiung-nu empire were not in a position to move west. In times of trouble they looked south to China as a place of refuge. It was Han policy to offer substantial sums of money and titles to Hsiung-nu leaders who defected, but surrender to China under such circumstances meant a loss of autonomy. While an individual leader might do well in China, incorporation into the Han empire nevertheless meant loss of his influence on the steppe. Such surrenders therefore were not undertaken lightly. In 121 BC two tribal kings were defeated in a surprise attack by a Han expeditionary force which inflicted great losses on them, thereby incurring the displeasure of the *Shan-yü*.

The *Shan-yü* was angry at the Hun-yeh and Hsiu-t'u kings who lived in the western part of his domain because they allowed the Han to capture or kill twenty or thirty thousand of their men; in the autumn he sent them a summons, intending to execute them. The Hun-yeh and Hsiu-t'u kings, terrified, sent word to the Han that they were willing to surrender. The Han dispatched Huo Ch'ü-ping to go and meet them, but on the way the Hun-yeh king murdered the Hsiu-t'u king and combined the latter's forces with his own.[10]

At the border subordinate generals who were opposed to surrender tried to desert but were killed in their escape attempt by the Han force that had come to receive the Hun-yeh king. In all, a force of between thirty and forty thousand crossed the frontier and were resettled in Chinese controlled areas where they were permitted to follow their own customs. The surrender of these two groups left a gaping hole in the Hsiung-nu frontier because a full tribal component, and not just a military unit, had left the empire. It was this land the Han court tried unsuccessfully to get the Wu-sun to reoccupy.[11]

Movement out of the *Shan-yü*'s control was the preferred strategy used by nomads seeking to escape imperial rule. Rebellions were relatively rare. It is significant that the first major rebellion within the empire was directed at a *Shan-yü* who attempted to restructure the Hsiung-nu empire by creating a more centralized government. This occurred in 60 BC, when the *Shan-yü* Hsü-lü-ch'üan-ch'ü died and his throne was usurped by a lesser noble at the expense of the old *Shan-yü*'s son who was the rightful heir. Having provoked opposition, the new *Shan-yü*, Wu-yen-ch'ü-ti, quickly responded by executing the relatives and close supporters of the old *Shan-yü* and replacing the twenty-four Ten Thousand Horsemen with his own relatives. This bloody succession struggle was unusual for the Hsiung-nu who had handled the ten previous successions with a minimum trouble. After gaining control of the imperial level of government, Wu-yen-ch'ü-ti turned his attention to the tribes within the confederation.

Upon the death of the Yü-chien tribal king, Wu-yen-ch'ü-ti broke custom and appointed his own son to the post instead of granting it to the dead man's son. Outraged, the Yü-chien nobles rejected the *Shan-yü*'s decision and pronounced the dead man's son their king. They then defeated an army sent by the *Shan-yü* to punish them.

The Wise King of the Left, who was heir apparent and son of the new *Shan-yü*, also exceeded his authority as imperial overseer of the eastern tribes. He alienated them with his overbearing manner and "having several times reviled the nobles of the Left hand land he succeeded in exciting a spirit of indignation against himself." The eastern tribes revolted and marched against the *Shan-yü* with 50,000 troops, defeating Wu-yen-ch'ü-ti, who was forced to send a plea for help to his brother, the Wise King of the Right. The reply was cold: "He who has no love for his people and puts to death his brothers and the nobles of the nation must die in his own place. Do not come to harass me." The defeated Wu-yen-ch'ü-ti committed suicide. He had ruled for less than three years.[12]

These cases demonstrate that a tribal group's loyalty rested first with its own tribal leadership and only secondarily with the *Shan-yü* and his court. The Hun-yeh king was able to command loyalty of his own people even when fleeing an imperial summons. Although only his life was in danger, the Hun-yeh king did not defect to China as an individual but took his entire tribe with him. The Wu-sun likewise followed their own leadership and left the empire. One of the difficulties of ruling a nomadic empire was that its component parts could quite literally walk away, and the ability of the *Shan-yü* to punish tribes was severely limited once they left his territory.

In theory the *Shan-yü* could command complete obedience and impose any sanctions on the tribes within the empire. In practice he was constrained by the knowledge that tribal kings were political actors in their own right and not simple appointees. Thus the links between the tribes and the imperial government were more federal than autocratic. Wu-yen-ch'ü-ti's attempt to create a more centralized state in which tribal leaders would be kinsmen of the *Shan-yü* provoked revolt rather than flight because all the tribal elites at the local level felt threatened. In the long run the *Shan-yü's* supratribal power was accepted only as long as he observed certain limits. The most basic of these was tribal autonomy within the confederation. The Hsiung-nu remained in control of the steppe for a longer period of time than any other nomadic group because their political system was flexible. A steppe empire that was thoroughly autocratic or centralized was inherently brittle because local leaders had only the choice of absolute obedience or rebellion. At the first sign of weakness they would rebel. On the other hand, if relations between the tribes were completely voluntary, then each leader would try to act for himself in all areas and refuse to take orders he did not like. The Hsiung-nu empire plotted a course between these two extremes. Tribal leaders had autonomy to run their own local affairs, but they were obliged to accept imperial order in foreign relations and intertribal affairs. As we will see, in addition to the strong military sanctions if they failed to obey, there were substantial material benefits for tribal leaders who cooperated.

Succession to leadership

The Hsiung-nu empire showed remarkable political stability over a period of several centuries. In part this stability was due to a system of succession that avoided civil wars, a feature fatally characteristic of the later Turco-Mongolian steppe empires. Although Mao-tun murdered his father and killed his opponents to become *Shan-yü*, Hsiung-nu leadership thereafter was passed on with a minimum of discord. For 150 years ten successions moved smoothly until 59 BC when the peaceful pattern was broken, beginning a period of civil war that divided the Hsiung-nu for the next fifteen years. When order was re-established the old dynasty continued and the office of *Shan-yü* was passed on for another century until a second civil war split the Hsiung-nu in AD 48 and ended their hegemony on the steppe. In both cases, a combination of economic disaster and deep-seated rivalries disrupted the usual succession to office. In later times, as rulers of smaller states, the Hsiung-nu *Shan-yüs* could claim an unbroken lineage from Mao-tun until well into the fifth century.

The two most important features of Hsiung-nu political structure were the existence of a system of fixed imperial ranks (the twenty-four Ten Thousand Horsemen and the Ku-tu marquises) and an accepted set of rules governing the appointment of a new *Shan-yü*.

The *Shan-yü*'s sons and brothers held the most important ranks while three aristocratic clans – the Hsü-pu, Hu-yen, and Lan clans – held hereditary claims to lesser ranks in the imperial system.[13] Each *Shan-yü* appointed his own successor to the post of Wise King of the Left, who controlled the eastern part of the empire. At the *Shan-yü*'s death the Wise King of the Left could use the influence of his position to enforce his claim to the throne, provided of course he was old enough to take command. The Hsiung-nu did not favor the succession of child rulers and, if the heir was too young, custom held that the *Shan-yü*'s brother should take the post. Over the course of centuries the pattern of succession changed. Initially it was lineal, from father to son; with lateral succession, elder brother to younger brother, used in unusual situations. As a result of political compromises following the first civil war, the system became explicitly lateral with elder brother following younger brother until a generation was exhausted. In both systems the *Shan-yü* had to be a member of the imperial lineage.

The aristocratic Hsiung-nu clans outside the imperial line played an important role in preventing conflict caused by rivalries among Mao-tun's descendants. The aristocratic clans traditionally intermarried with the imperial lineage, producing strong affinal and matrilineal kinship ties between them. Barred from becoming *Shan-yü*, but benefiting from the imperial system, the members of the non-imperial Hsiung-nu clans had a vested interest in preserving the system intact regardless of who became *Shan-yü*. At the death of the *Shan-yü* they played a major role as electors of a successor by proclaiming the new *Shan-yü* and, in exceptional circumstances, they could and did ignore the claims of the Wise King of the Left in favor of another heir. Because all potential heirs to the throne competed for the support of the same Hsiung-nu elite, a loser usually had no base of support to fall back on when his claim to the throne was ignored. The Hsiung-nu aristocracy rarely allowed the squabbles within the imperial lineage to degenerate into civil war, which was only possible if the Hsiung-nu elite was itself seriously divided.

The list of Hsiung-nu *Shan-yüs* in table 2.1 shows that most of the successions followed the prescribed pattern without major incident. Three exceptions provide some details of the politics and mechanics at the imperial level of government.

The first recorded succession dispute took place in 126 BC when "the *Shan-yü* Chün-ch'en died and his younger brother, the Luli King of the Left, I-chih-hsieh, set himself up as *Shan-yü*. He attacked and defeated Chün-ch'en's heir, Yü-tan, who fled and surrendered to the Han. The Han enfeoffed

Table 2.1   Succession of Hsiung-nu *Shan-yüs* down to the first civil war

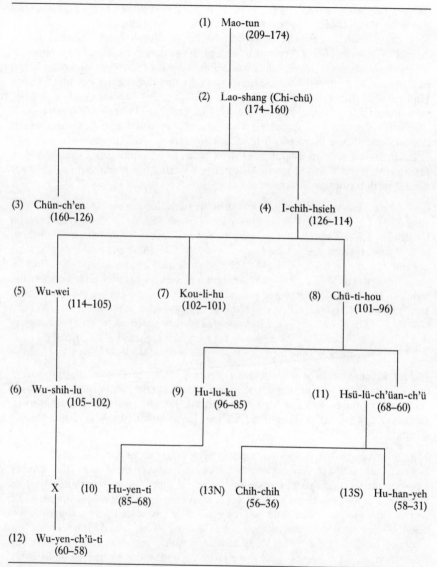

The Chinese records for this period list the *Shan-yüs* by referring to their titles rather than their personal names, which were provided only for Mao-tun and his son Chi-chü, thus Chün-ch'en Shan-yü, Wu-wei Shan-yü, etc.

Yü-tan as Marquis of She-an but he died several months later."[14] This coup showed that without support from the imperial hierarchy an heir could not take the throne. Because Yü-tan and his uncle were competing for the same base of support, when that support shifted to I-chih-hsieh, Yü-tan found himself alone with no choice but to accept the situation or leave the steppe. In sharp contrast to the tribal kings who defected with their own people, Yü-tan fled to China as an individual. The reasons for this dispute are not given in the Han records, but it was probably no coincidence that this succession was the first after China began large-scale attacks on the Hsiung-nu. Under such conditions the nomads probably preferred a proven warrior to an untried youth and in time of war there was a tendency towards lateral succession.

In 96 BC, a second dispute, resolved peacefully, highlighted the details of Hsiung-nu politics and illustrates the active role that the Hsiung-nu aristocracy played in determining succession.

Chü-ti-hou *Shan-yü* died in the fifth year of his reign, leaving his eldest son the Wise King of the Left to succeed him as Hu-lu-ku *Shan-yü*. The old chieftain named him on his deathbed as his successor but being absent at the time, the nobles of the nation, believing he was sick, elected his brother, the Left Great General to the dignity. The news of this occurrence reaching the Wise King of the Left, he would not venture to come forward. His brother, however, sent him a messenger to invite him to assume the throne. The elder brother excused himself on account of sickness but the other would accept no refusal saying, "unless you transmit the succession to me at your death, I will not take it." The Wise King of the Left acceded and appointed his brother to the dignity that he thereby vacated [i.e. Wise King of the Left, heir apparent]. The latter fell sick in a few years and died. . . . The [new] *Shan-yü* made his own son Wise King of the Left.[15]

The agreement between the two brothers to succeed one another was a common political compromise when both men had support. The problem with such compromises was that they often pitted the *Shan-yü*'s sons (or his sons' mothers) against his brothers. In 85 BC, Hu-lu-ku's death set off just such a struggle.

Now the *Shan-yü* had a younger brother by a different mother who was the Left Commandant and was very popular with the best men of the nation. The Mother Consort, fearing that the *Shan-yü* would supplant their son by appointing the Left Commandant his successor, had secretly caused the latter to be assassinated. The uterine elder brother of the victim felt resentful of this act of treachery and never again made his appearance at the palace of the *Shan-yü*. When the *Shan-yü* lay on his deathbed he said to the nobles: "My son being young and unable to undertake the government of the nation, I appoint my younger brother the Right Luli King as my successor." When the *Shan-yü* was dead Wei Lü and others formed a plot with the Chuan-ch'ü Consort, the widow, to falsify his dying commands. She then raised her son the Left Luli King to the succession with the style of Hu-yen-ti *Shan-yü*.[16]

The Right Luli King and the Wise King of the Left were unhappy with this situation and began plotting their own defection to China. When this became known they abandoned the strategy but never again went to the *Shan-yü*'s court.

In spite of their discontent it was quite difficult to instigate a civil war once an election of a new *Shan-yü* had occurred. In part this was because the *Shan-yü* held a real office with an independent economic and political base. He was not just the charismatic leader of a loose confederation, but a vital key in the relationship between China and the steppe. Disputes centered on who should become *Shan-yü*, not whether there should be one.

FOREIGN AFFAIRS – THE HAN CONNECTION

A state formed by nomadic pastoralists in Inner Asia faced different problems in maintaining itself than those found in states based on intensive agriculture. In an agricultural society, a ruler's power ultimately rested on the control of accumulated grain surpluses. By means of annual taxation, the sedentary state took a percentage of all grain produced, stored it with low maintenance costs at strategic locations, and called upon these reserves for a variety of purposes with little risk of loss.

The steppe ruler was in a far more precarious position because the steppe economy was based on extensive and highly mobile pastoralism. Pastoral wealth could not be effectively concentrated or stored. Animals had to be dispersed to take advantage of available grass and water, required constant care and eventually died. Even if a ruler did amass a large number of animals, his store of wealth was vulnerable and could be wiped out overnight by disease, a blizzard, or theft.[17] As long as the animals could not be converted into some more stable and diversified range of products, a nomadic ruler could not usefully engage in annual taxation, and he was forced to rely on irregular exactions to meet his immediate needs. Even this power was limited by the inherent fluidity of the nomadic polity; if the exactions were viewed as too heavy, then nomads had the alternative of deserting their leader and taking their animals with them.[18]

These internal weaknesses compelled the rulers of successful nomadic states to develop a more secure economic base. In Inner Asia this was accomplished by financing the nomadic state with resources from outside the steppe. The Hsiung-nu imperial government organized the nomadic tribes into a unified force that was then used by the *Shan-yü* to extract goods and trade benefits from China. The *Shan-yü* retained the exclusive right to conduct foreign affairs and used this power to control the distribution of Chinese goods to the various Hsiung-nu tribes. In time of war the *Shan-yü* organized raids that provided loot for his followers and the Hsiung-nu state. In time of peace the *Shan-yü* acted as the sole intermediary between China and the steppe, bringing trade and subsidies for redistribution throughout the state hierarchy. By drawing on resources from outside the steppe the Hsiung-nu state gained a stability it could not otherwise have achieved.

The establishment of formal relations between the Han and the Hsiung-nu began after Han Kao-tsu's escape from the Hsiung-nu trap at P'ing-ch'eng in 200 BC. The emperor sent envoys to the *Shan-yü* to negotiate peace and establish the *ho-ch'in* policy as a framework for relations between the two states.

The *ho-ch'in* policy had four major provisions:

1 The Chinese made fixed annual payments of silk, wine, grain, and other foodstuffs to the Hsiung-nu.
2 The Han gave a princess in marriage to the *Shan-yü*.
3 The Hsiung-nu and Han were ranked as co-equal states.
4 The Great Wall was the official boundary between the two states.

These provisions demonstrate that the treaty was based on a strategy of appeasement since it was quite favorable to the Hsiung-nu. In exchange for these benefits the Hsiung-nu agreed to keep the peace.[19]

The *Shan-yü* used this treaty and the Han subsidies to fortify his own position on the steppe. The Han subsidies could be redistributed to the political elite of the empire to buy their support. In addition to the material benefits, the treaty provided the *Shan-yü* with prestige by ranking him as an equal of the Han emperor with a Han princess as a consort. From the perspective of the steppe, the *Shan-yü* was receiving tribute from China. Nevertheless, as generous as the treaty provisions seemed, the Hsiung-nu were not satisfied and soon returned to raiding the frontier. These raids were followed by Hsiung-nu envoys with peace proposals that demanded better terms, including an increase in the amount and types of subsidies as well as the opening of border trade. The new demand for border trade was incorporated into the peace agreement during the reign of Han Wen-ti (r. 179–157 BC).

Han accounts of the establishment of the *ho-ch'in* policy paint the Hsiung-nu as greedy barbarians who were never satisfied and who were unwilling to keep their treaty obligations. A closer look reveals a more complex situation. In negotiations the *Shan-yü* had two goals. The first, and initially the most pressing, was to win direct subsidies which could be used to entertain and reward the political elite of the empire. Once the Han had provided these goods, the *Shan-yü* changed his emphasis and began demanding that the Han court meet the needs of the ordinary nomads by permitting them to trade at border markets.

The sequence of Hsiung-nu demands was part of the *Shan-yü*'s strategy to preserve his own position on the steppe in peace or war by manipulating China. This required that he integrate the newly conquered tribes into the empire, that he reward the political elites, and that he provide the average tribesmen with benefits not available without the imperial government. Each Hsiung-nu attack or demand was designed to meet one of these needs.

The raids on China provided loot for the numerous tribesmen who had recently been incorporated into the empire by conquest or alliance and who needed to be won over politically. The Hsiung-nu allowed all warriors who killed or captured an enemy to keep the spoils they seized in battle, and "therefore whenever they fight, each man strives for his own gain."[20] Raids on China were a profit-making enterprise that served to weld the Hsiung-nu into a single unit.

The *Shan-yü* agreed to halt the raids in exchange for subsidies from China. However, the amount and types of subsidies could have had only a minimal impact on the basic subsistence economy of the pastoral Hsiung-nu. At its maximum under the *ho-ch'in* agreement the annual Han subsidy amounted to less than 5,000 *hu* of grain, 10,000 *shih* of wine, and 10,000 *p'i* of silk.[21] The average annual grain ration supplied by the Han administration to an adult male serving on the frontier was around 36 *hu* (about 720 liters).[22] At this rate the Han grain subsidy to the Hsiung-nu could have supported only 140 men annually; if reduced to a fifth and combined with the Hsiung-nu diet it might have supported 700 men annually. From these figures, clearly, the food subsidy was designed merely to allow the *Shan-yü* to entertain his court in style, not to support a large part of the population.

The main value of the Han subsidy to the *Shan-yü* was as a source of valuable luxury items not available on the steppe. An annual wine subsidy of 10,000 *shih* (around 200,000 liters) provided the *Shan-yü* with the capacity to entertain his hard drinking followers on an immense scale. A silk subsidy approaching 10,000 *p'i* (92,400 meters) supplied a Han product greatly in demand on the steppe and in the West which the *Shan-yü* could redistribute to tribal leaders within the empire or trade elsewhere for other goods. The Han themselves used silk as a form of currency, and it is well represented in tombs found on the steppe. For example, tombs excavated at Noin Ula that date to a somewhat later period display a wealth of Chinese silk goods.[23] In addition to silk, the Han court also supplied the *Shan-yü* with gold, suits of clothing, and other miscellaneous items of value. These gifts and subsidies were the economic benefits the *Shan-yü* offered tribal leaders and which, in combination with a strong military threat, kept the nomadic imperium intact.

Direct subsidies from the Han government may have enabled the *Shan-yü* to reward the Hsiung-nu elite, but they were insufficient to meet the needs of the mass of Hsiung-nu tribesmen. The easiest way to meet their needs was to raid China. However, continuous raiding endangered the supply of luxury goods that were part of the peace treaty. Therefore as soon as the *Shan-yü* won subsidies from China, he pressed for the opening of border markets where the nomads could trade pastoral products for Han goods. If the *Shan-yü* were to remain at peace with China, trade at the frontier was a necessity. The pastoral economy produced large surpluses that could easily be exchanged for Chinese goods if the Han government would end its prohibition on trade with the nomads.

The right to trade at the frontier had to be wrung from an unwilling Han court because China opposed it for political reasons. Although the Hsiung-nu were a natural market for the grain surpluses and craft production of the northern areas, such trade would orientate the population away from the Han court and Chinese interests. The Han court attempted to tie the frontier regions to the center even if it meant hardship for the local population. Its policy was to create as much cleavage between the steppe and China as possible; the Great Wall was to be a barrier against all contact with the steppe. The *Shan-yü* was forced to overcome this reluctance by extorting trade rights the same way he extorted subsidies – by raiding, or threatening to raid – China. This served a double purpose. Loot from the raids kept the Hsiung-nu tribesmen supplied until China finally agreed to their demands and opened the border markets.

Once established, these markets quickly became important trade centers to which the Hsiung-nu flocked, exchanging pastoral products for Han goods. By Han law these markets were restricted to the sale of goods with no military value to the Hsiung-nu. In spite of the death penalty for violations of these restrictions, the border markets were also the bases for smugglers who provided the Hsiung-nu with prohibited goods such as iron.[24]

The establishment of regular trade with China stabilized the *Shan-yü*'s position. He could maintain his economic base without having to engage in continual wars with China. The *Shan-yü*'s role as intermediary in trade relations between the Han court and the steppe became as important as his position of supreme military commander of the Hsiung-nu. The whole relationship between China and the nomads became more stable. By the time of Han Ching-ti (r. 156–141 BC) the northern border had become peaceful, frontier communities suffered only minor raids, and old hostilities were forgotten. "From the *Shan-yü* on down all the Hsiung-nu grew friendly with the Han, coming and going along the Great Wall."[25] This situation lasted until 133 BC when, hoping to militarily defeat the Hsiung-nu, the Han court abruptly abandoned the *ho-ch'in* policy by mounting a surprise attack on the nomads, beginning more than a half century of frontier warfare.

Another economic resource was the production from Chinese farmers and artisans who had been captured during Hsiung-nu raids and taken back to the steppe. Little is known of these Chinese captives or their descendants. There is evidence, however, that the pastoral Hsiung-nu had very large quantities of grain at their disposal, probably produced by captive farmers. For example in 119 BC, when Han troops invaded Mongolia and overran the *Shan-yü*'s capital, the Han general Wei Ch'ing and his 50,000 troops feasted on captured Hsiung-nu grain, the remainder of which they burned before returning south.[28] Later during the reign of Hu-yen-ti (r. 85–68 BC), the Hsiung-nu were advised by a Han defector to protect their grain supply by building an elaborate stockade and a series of forts to be manned by Chinese captives. Soon after beginning the project the Hsiung-nu decided to abandon construction because as nomads they were unwilling to sacrifice their mobility.[29] In addition to grain supplies produced in Mongolia or acquired by trade along the Chinese frontier, the Hsiung-nu also had alternative sources in southern Siberia and eastern Turkestan. In this regard, it may be that after a generation of warfare with China the Hsiung-nu moved their capital further to the west in 105 BC in order to better exploit the Hsiung-nu empire's secondary resources areas.

While China was the most significant source of subsidies and trade, the Hsiung-nu also exploited the resources of other areas. The oasis states of Turkestan, particularly in the north, were vulnerable to Hsiung-nu pressure. They were small and had little defense against Hsiung-nu demands. Providing agricultural products and manufactured goods, they remained an important part of the Hsiung-nu empire until the first Hsiung-nu civil war (circa 60 BC) when the area fell under Han control. The Hsiung-nu did not rule this area directly, but depended on agents to extract revenue from local rulers, a practice that was particularly suitable to the nomadic way of life.

The states of the Western Regions for the most part [have inhabitants] who are settled on the soil, with walled cities, cultivated fields and domesticated animals. Their customs differ from those of the Hsiung-nu and the Wu-sun. Formerly they were all subject to the Hsiung-nu; at the western edge of the Hsiung-nu, the Jih-chu king established the post of Commandant of T'ung-pu (Slaves) with orders to direct the Western Regions. He was permanently situated in the areas of Yen[-tsai], Wei-su, and Wei-li, and acquired wealth and resources by levying taxes on the various states.[26]

Along its northern frontier the Hsiung-nu controlled a number of productive regions in Siberia. While known only indirectly from archaeological excavations, it appears that many regions which initially suffered from nomad attacks and lost population then recovered and prospered once under the control of nomadic empires like the Hsiung-nu and Wu-sun that could protect them in exchange for trade and revenue. In the Ob Valley, for example, tombs of the Bronze Age Karasuk culture (thirteenth to eighth centuries BC) were rich in grave goods and never included weapons. However with the coming of nomadic peoples to the neighboring Altai region the first phase of the succeeding Bolshaya Rechka culture (seventh to sixth centuries BC) showed evidence of decline. Their grave goods were poorer both in quantity and quality than in earlier periods while half the tombs discovered contained weapons. Excavated village sites also displayed signs of sudden abandonment. Around 200 BC the situation began to improve. Burials contained more elaborate grave goods, horse sacrifices and iron weapons. The Soviet archaeologist Gryaznov attributes this change to a less hostile relationship between the local sedentary population and their nomadic neighbors. Similarly the Minusinsk Basin, which was famous for its bronze production, showed a marked increase in the size of tombs and the quality of their furnishings during the Hsiung-nu period.[27]

The outer frontier strategy

The Hsiung-nu state owed its continued existence to its effectiveness in dealing with China in war and peace. The number of nomads was small, perhaps about a million people yet they confronted a Han state that rule over 54 million people.[30] Therefore they had to be organized in a way that compelled the Han court to recognize their interests. The *Shan-yü* had to influence decision-making at the highest levels of Han government because frontier policy was made at court and not by frontier governors or border officials. To this end the Hsiung-nu devised a predatory strategy of extortion aimed at impressing the Han court with their power. Their "outer frontier" strategy took full advantage of the nomads' ability to suddenly strike deep into China and then retreat before the Chinese had time to retaliate. It had three major elements: violent raiding to terrify the Han court, the alternation of war and peace to increase the amount of subsidies and trade privileges granted by the Chinese, and the deliberate refusal to occupy Chinese land even after great victories.

The Hsiung-nu used violent raiding, or the threat of it, as a tool in negotiations with the Han court. These intentionally destructive raids served a political purpose. The Han court feared that disruptions along the northern frontier might lead to an unraveling of the empire. Wanton violence and horrible reports from the border helped increase those fears. The greater the devastation, the greater the impact on the Han court. Even a small group of nomads could cause a great deal of disruption if they were well organized. Terror along the border was a weapon used by the *Shan-yü* to extract benefits from China as a whole. The Hsiung-nu were not concerned with the local consequences of their invasions or with establishing good relations with farmers and officials along the frontier. They looted provinces with the expectation that the Han central government would rebuild and resettle the areas so that they could be looted again. The Hsiung-nu were not naturally violent, but they did cultivate violence as a tactic in dealing with the Chinese. The Han court could never ignore the Hsiung-nu or their demands, and they were obliged to treat the *Shan-yü* as a ruler equal to the Han emperor, a status granted to no other foreign ruler.

The Hsiung-nu alternated periods of war with periods of peace in order to extract ever-increasing benefits from China. Plundering invasions were followed by envoys from the *Shan-yü* who always suggested that the current troubles could be resolved by a new treaty. Building upon each broken treaty as the foundation for new demands, the *Shan-yü* extracted larger subsidies and gained trade benefits in return for the promise of peace. The length of the peace was determined in part by the adequacy of the newly formed treaty. The initial agreements providing subsidies but not trade lasted only a few years. After trade was added the periods of peace became substantial. Nevertheless, behind even the most peaceful relations lay the implicit threat that the Hsiung-nu could cause the Han empire serious trouble if their demands were not satisfied, and that no peace treaty could bind them permanently. This was true even when the Hsiung-nu were later put on the defensive by Chinese attacks. They continued to ask for more benefits, not less, to end the war, because they knew that military campaigns were far more expensive and disruptive for the Han government to conduct than for the nomads. The Han court interpreted this alternation of hostility and requests for peace treaties as the height of "barbarian" gall and evidence of their incurable greed. As one Han official noted: "Now, the Hsiung-nu are arrogant and insolent on the one hand, and invade and plunder us on the other hand, which must be considered an act of extreme disrespect toward us. And the harm they are doing to the empire is extremely boundless. Yet each year Han provides them with money, silk floss, and fabrics."[31]

In defense of the nomads, it has been argued that they were usually peaceful and raided China only when they were denied trade. Neither of these interpretations fully explains Hsiung-nu policy, however. The alternation of war and peace was calculated to constantly remind the Han government that peace treaties were cheaper and less disruptive than border wars. Behind even the most peaceful relations lay a threat of violence, which was made explicit by a Chinese advisor, Chung-hang Yüeh, who had defected to the Hsiung-nu.

When Han envoys complained about the amount of subsidies and gifts the Hsiung-nu received he dismissed them saying:

Just make sure that the silks and grainstuffs you bring the Hsiung-nu are the right measure and quality, that's all. What's the need for talking? If the goods you deliver are up to measure and good quality, all right. But if there is any deficiency or the quality is no good, then when the autumn harvest comes we will take our horses and trample all over your crops![32]

The Hsiung-nu exploited China from a distance and avoided holding Chinese agricultural land. No match for China's large armies, the Hsiung-nu made it a point to retreat before they were attacked: "If the battle is going well for them they will advance, but if not, they will retreat, for they do not consider it a disgrace to run away. Their only concern is self-advantage, and they know nothing of propriety or righteousness."[33] When Han Wu-ti mounted a sustained offensive against them, the Hsiung-nu retreated across the Gobi Desert to make it difficult and expensive for Han troops to pursue them. In times of strength the Hsiung-nu raided deep into China, even to the outskirts of the Han capital Ch'ang-an on one occasion, but they never occupied Chinese land that they would have been obligated to defend. Although the Hsiung-nu posed the most dangerous foreign threat to the Former Han dynasty, none of the many debates in court about the Hsiung-nu problem ever expressed any fear that the Hsiung-nu might try to conquer China. The Hsiung-nu maintained a careful policy of keeping themselves from coming too close to China. In this way they were able to exploit China without exposing their own weakness in numbers or losing their mobility.

The Chinese response

Throughout the Former Han period, the Chinese attempts to destroy the Hsiung-nu state met with no success. The Han court's failure in this area was galling because the Hsiung-nu were supposed to be crude barbarians who could be outwitted in diplomacy or defeated by China's considerable military power. However, the Hsiung-nu state was well designed to meet pressure from China. It was prepared to counter, even take advantage of, Han strategies designed to overthrow it.

Originally, the Han government viewed the *ho-ch'in* policy of subsidies to and appeasement of the Hsiung-nu as a way to avoid costly disruptions on the northern frontier. They also hoped that the gifts and subsidies could be used as an economic weapon to weaken and perhaps eventually destroy the Hsiung-nu. This strategy was referred to as the "Five Baits":

1. elaborate clothes and carriages to corrupt their eyes;
2. fine food to corrupt their mouths;
3. music to corrupt their ears;
4. lofty buildings, granaries, and slaves to corrupt their stomachs;
5. gifts and favors for Hsiung-nu who surrendered.[34]

The Five Baits strategy also had the potential to weaken the Hsiung-nu as a whole by making them dependent on China. Chung-hang Yüeh warned the Hsiung-nu of this danger:

All the multitudes of the Hsiung-nu would not amount to one province in the Han empire. The strength of the Hsiung-nu lies in the very fact that their food and clothing are different from those of the Chinese, and they are therefore not dependent on the Han for any thing. Now the *Shan-yü* has this fondness for Chinese things and is trying to change the Hsiung-nu customs. Thus, although the Han sends no more than a fifth of its goods here, it will in the end succeed in winning over the whole Hsiung-nu nation. From now on, when you get any of the Han silks, put them on and try riding your horses through brush and brambles! In no time your robes and leggings will be torn to shreds and everyone will see that silks are no match for the utility and excellence of felt and leather garments. Likewise when you get any of the Han foodstuffs, throw them away so that people can see that they are not as practical or tasty as milk and kumiss![35]

Although in theory the Five Baits strategy appeared to threaten the Hsiung-nu, it failed because their subsistence economy was never put at risk. While trade was extremely valuable to the ordinary nomads who could exchange pastoral surpluses for Han manufactured goods like cloth and metal, or foodstuffs like grain and wine, they did not depend on this trade for survival. In fact the goods most in demand from the Han court were luxuries which the *Shan-yü* redistributed to the political elite. For the Hsiung-nu Han gifts, subsidies, trade, and loot provided a major source of wealth and as Lattimore has noted, "the only pure nomad is the poor nomad."[36] Therefore each *Shan-yü* carefully guarded his exclusive right to deal with China on behalf of the steppe tribes in order to preserve his own political power. While a tribal leader might defect to China, just as a Han traitor might defect to the Hsiung-nu, no local Hsiung-nu leader was allowed to negotiate for himself and remain in the empire. Frontier relations were never handled locally but through envoys from the *Shan-yü* to the Han emperor and vice versa. The Han government sometimes managed to entice large groups of nomads into China with lavish gifts and titles, but given the structure of the Hsiung-nu state they found it impossible to form alliances with Hsiung-nu leaders on the steppe and they were never able to circumvent the centralized power of the *Shan-yü*.

In 133 BC, Han Wu-ti tried to solve China's Hsiung-nu problem once and for all by abandoning the *ho-ch'in* policy in favor of a war of aggression. In radically altering Han foreign policy Wu-ti was responding to long-standing complaints against the *ho-ch'in* treaties and to a more activist philosophy now dominant among the court ministers.

Ideologues at court had long argued that these agreements forced China to pay tribute to the Hsiung-nu, and that they accorded the *Shan-yü* and the Hsiung-nu nation equal status with the Han emperor and China. These two features violated the very essence of a sinocentric world order in which all human relations were viewed as interrelated parts in a hierarchy of moral order. The emperor, in particular, could have no recognized equal as ruler of all under heaven. In theory foreign relations were only proper with nations or leaders that formally accepted this view in their dealings with China. Formal acceptance of a sinocentric world order was essential since Han court ministers believed that the symbolic order of the universe was a necessary prerequisite for, and a reflection of, temporal earthly order. In their minds a violation of the proper symbolic order, be it in the form of omens, natural disasters, or in the regulated aspects of human behavior, had direct political implications. They were acutely aware of threats against that symbolic order.

The most obvious and offensive violators of a sinocentric world order were the Hsiung-nu because they had demanded and received equal status with China. Initially the untutored Hsiung-nu did not realize that this official acknowledgment of their power was an acute embarrassment to the Han court. Until the situation was explained to them by the Chinese defector Chung-hang Yüeh, the Hsiung-nu took their relationship with the Han court for granted. However, with Chung-hang's help, the Hsiung-nu began to taunt the Han court by manipulating Chinese symbols of power and authority in a sophisticated fashion, a form of revenge on the Han court by one of its former officials.

The Han letters addressed to the *Shan-yü* were always written on wooden tablets one foot one inch in length and began, "The emperor respectfully inquires about the health of the great *Shan-yü* of the Hsiung-nu. We send you the following articles, etc., etc." Chung-hang Yüeh however, instructed the *Shan-yü* to use in replying to the Han a tablet measuring one foot two inches, decorated with broad stamps and great long seals, and worded in the following extravagant manner: "The great *Shan-yü* of the Hsiung-nu, born of Heaven and Earth, and ordained by the sun and the moon, respectfully inquires about the health of the Han emperor. We send you the following articles, etc., etc."[37]

These letters provoked the rage of Chia I, an official at the court of Han Wen-ti (r. 179–157 BC). He had long opposed the *ho-ch'in* policy, asserting it was in direct contradiction to fundamental Confucian principles.

The situation of the empire may be described just like a person hanging upside down. The Son of Heaven is at the head of the empire. Why? Because he should be placed at the top. The barbarians are at the feet of the empire. Why? Because they should be placed at the bottom. . . . To command the barbarian is a power vested in the Emperor at the top, and, to present tribute to the Son of Heaven is a ritual to be performed by vassals at the bottom. Now the feet are put on the top and the head at the bottom. Hanging upside down is something beyond comprehension.[38]

Chia I then proposed that troops should be called up to attack the Hsiung-nu and force them to recognize their proper role, advice that was ignored out of fear of the nomads.

In this and other criticisms of the *ho-ch'in* policy symbolic order rather than practical issues were at the heart of the debate. Initially these objections had little influence. Han Kao-tsu, who had established the policy, was not concerned with symbolic order. He had enough problems enforcing real order in the aftermath of the civil war that followed the collapse of Ch'in and the birth of the Han dynasty. As an underdog in that war Kao-tsu had been victorious in part because of his willingness to make expedient, but unseemly, bargains. Having almost been captured by Mao-tun, Kao-tsu had great respect for Hsiung-nu power. Gifts, a marriage alliance, and diplomatic recognition of the

Hsiung-nu as an equal state were the easiest ways to pacify the Hsiung-nu while the Han state took root in China. Indeed, Kao-tsu was prepared to send his own daughter as a wife to Mao-tun until he was blocked by an outraged Empress Lü. Quibbles about the improper form of such a relationship could have little impact on a man whose opinion of Confucian philosophers during the civil war was well known – he pissed into their distinctive hats every time they approached him with advice.[39]

The *ho-ch'in* policy was continued throughout the reigns of Empress Lü and Emperors Wen and Ching in spite of periodic Hsiung-nu attacks and insults. These included one earthy marriage proposal to Empress Lü from Mao-tun which infuriated her to the point of demanding war, but court ministers noted that Han troops had fared none too well against the Hsiung-nu during her husband's time and sent Mao-tun a gracious refusal. Putting up with Hsiung-nu demands was in accord with a basic Han *laissez faire* policy in which government exactions from the Chinese people were kept to a minimum. Emperor Wen in particular was noted for his conservative spending habits and modest style of life. In spite of its improper form and troubles, the *ho-ch'in* policy did accomplish its primary goal of avoiding continuous frontier warfare which would have imposed a heavy burden on the Han treasury.

By the time of Emperor Wu (r. 140–87 BC) China had long recovered from the ravages of the civil war in which the Han dynasty was founded. Accommodation with the Hsiung-nu was again revived as a political issue and criticized as inappropriate for a great power. In sharp debate, officials following Chia I's old advice argued that the time had come for Han to rid itself of the Hsiung-nu menace once and for all. Defenders of the *ho-ch'in* system responded that such a war would be extremely expensive and ultimately accomplish little because the Han could not occupy the steppe and displace the Hsiung-nu. Defenders of the old policy initially won out, but in 133 BC Han Wu-ti sided with the war faction. Over the next forty years of Wu-ti's reign, China made an immense effort to destroy the Hsiung-nu.[40].

The Han strategy for its Hsiung-nu wars had four major objectives. First, the Han frontier was pushed forward to the old Chi'in dynasty's borders and in some places beyond them. The whole frontier was garrisoned with conscripts, often convicts, who manned the walled defenses and who were expected to be partially self-supporting by establishing farming colonies. Second, the Han court attempted to create alliances with the nomadic neighbors of the Hsiung-nu – the Yüeh-chih and the Wu-sun. The Yüeh-chih had settled in the Oxus region and had no desire for further wars with the Hsiung-nu. They rejected a Chinese alliance. The Wu-sun were willing to accept a loose alliance, sealed by the marriage of K'un-mo to a Han princess, and occasionally aid the Han by attacking the Hsiung-nu from the west. Third, Han troops moved into the Tarim Basin and conquered the city states there. This move was an attempt to "cut off the right arm of the Hsiung-nu" by preventing them from linking up with the Ch'iang tribesmen in the Tibetan borderland and to stop the revenue the Hsiung-nu derived from the city states of Turkestan.[41] Finally, the Han military mounted huge punitive expeditions designed to destroy the Hsiung-nu on the steppe itself.

The Han strategy underestimated the resilience of the Hsiung-nu confederacy and the difficulties of winning a war on the steppe. The Chinese managed to seize and occupy only the marginal land along their linear frontier with the Hsiung-nu. They were not able to occupy the whole steppe nor to introduce a Chinese style agricultural economy there as they did in conquered areas in the south and west. Indeed, even fighting on the steppe was a considerable burden requiring huge baggage trains to keep the Han troops supplied since the Hsiung-nu had no rich cities to conquer or croplands to be seized. No matter how many victories they won, in the end the Han troops had to withdraw from the Hsiung-nu homeland and leave the steppe in the hands of the nomads.

The Hsiung-nu, meanwhile, revised their outer frontier strategy to cope with China's new policy of aggression. As before, it exploited the nomads' unsurpassed ability to move quickly and the inability of Han troops to remain on the steppe for more than a few months before their supplies ran out.

Hostilities opened when Han troops laid a trap for the Hsiung-nu at the border market city of Mai-i. The *Shan-yü* entered the region with his troops but grew suspicious when he saw animals in the fields without any shepherds. Suspecting a ruse, he uncovered the plot and the Hsiung-nu retreated unharmed. The Hsiung-nu then raided the frontier, forcing the Han court to commit the bulk of its military effort to manning and supplying the lengthy walled defenses that bordered the steppe. While these fortifications were vital to China's defense, they did nothing to destroy the Hsiung-nu. In such a war with China the Hsiung-nu had the advantage of the interior lines. From their central location on the steppe the Hsiung-nu forced the Han to invest heavily along all of the frontier while they could concentrate their entire force on the weakest points for an attack. While the Chinese held an advantage when fighting from fixed defenses, they found it difficult to both man the border in strength and send expeditionary forces onto the steppe. The task of maintaining the border defenses fell most heavily on the frontier population which also bore the brunt of Hsiung-nu raids. The Han court therefore had the additional worry that the Hsiung-nu might subvert the frontier population, which had always been considered politically unreliable.

When the military pressure on the Hsiung-nu began to build, the *Shan-yü* moved his people and headquarters away from the area near the frontier to a new territory in northern Mongolia. In order to reach the Hsiung-nu on the other side of the Gobi Desert, Han expeditionary forces had to travel hundreds of miles into the steppe. The Hsiung-nu generally had ample notice of Han troop movements and often avoided fighting simply by moving out of their way. As component parts of a single empire those tribes threatened by invasion could temporarily withdraw into territories normally occupied by their neighbors without opposition. Many Han armies never saw the enemy. Others exhausted themselves chasing the Hsiung-nu, only to be attacked and wiped out when they tried to return to China. The tactic of avoiding battle by continual retreat was part of an old nomad strategy designed to let the enemy defeat himself. Just as the Hsiung-nu refused to hold Chinese land they would have to defend against superior Han armies, on the steppe they avoided battle until chances for victory were in their favor. With no cities or villages to defend, the nomads were content to let the hard journey and difficult conditions on the steppe defeat Han armies. Major victories against the nomads could only be won when the Han armies adopted the fighting style of the Hsiung-nu by employing swift cavalry and surprise attacks. Most Han troops and generals were neither familiar nor comfortable with this type of fighting. Those at home with steppe warfare were men of frontier origin, often, to the Han court's displeasure, equally at home fighting on the side of the Hsiung-nu to whom they often surrendered rather than face Han military death penalties for failure.

The Hsiung-nu continued their policy of alternating fierce attacks with proposals for peace. The Hsiung-nu seem to have been aware that prolonged warfare was more difficult for the Han government to sustain than for the nomads. The Hsiung-nu peace proposals always asked for a resumption of the *ho-ch'in* policy with greater, not lesser, demands for gifts than the *Shan-yü* received before the war began. In spite of the loss of his subsidy, the *Shan-yü* remained secure on the steppe. If in time of peace the *Shan-yü* maintained his position by negotiating benefits for the nomads from China, in time of war he became military leader of the steppe as a whole and coordinated an organized defense against Han attacks which helped unify the tribes behind the *Shan-yü*'s leadership. In China, on the other hand, the prolonged war against the Hsiung-nu drained the treasury, disrupted the normal workings of government, and impoverished the people. If the *Shan-yü* could no longer use the direct damage done by Hsiung-nu raids to extort subsidies, he could use the indirect damage the Hsiung-nu wars caused to the Han government and economy as a tool to restore the trade and gifts the nomads expected from China.

A look at the details of the major Han campaigns and their costs shows that they placed a tremendous burden on China. It took ten years before the Han court could claim any significant success against the Hsiung-nu. Direct attacks first yielded victories in the Ordos in 124 BC. In 121 BC, the Hun-yeh king surrendered with 40,000 of his people. In 119 BC an expedition to northern Mongolia inflicted a major defeat on the Hsiung-nu. These losses put the Hsiung-nu out of action for about a decade, but by 110 BC Han troops began to be withdrawn from their most advanced frontiers. In the west Han expansion continued beyond this date. After one failed attempt the Han general Li Kuang-li conquered Ta-yüan in 102 BC, putting most of eastern Turkestan under Han control. Three years later when this great commander turned his attention to the Hsiung-nu, he lost between 60 and 70 percent of his troops in a steppe campaign. Li Kuang-li himself was captured by the Hsiung-nu in 90 BC during another disastrous expedition. Thus, after an initial series of victories against the Hsiung-nu, the Han empire suffered major reverses that put it on the defensive by the end of Wu-ti's reign.

Victories, as well as defeats, cost the Han heavily. The campaigns of 125–24 BC, in which 19,000 Hsiung-nu and a million sheep were reportedly captured, cost the government 200,000 *chin* of gold in rewards to the generals and troops, and the loss of 100,000 horses. The surrender of the Hun-yeh king was induced partially by an expenditure of 10 billion cash in gifts and food to the surrendered leader and his people. (One *chin* of gold = 244 g and was officially valued at 10,000 cash.) The great Han victory of 119 BC cost tens of thousands of Han dead, 100,000 lost horses, and 500,000 *chin* in gold as rewards. These figures did not include the enormous cost of supplying the army on the steppe with provisions. Li Kuang-li lost 80 percent of his men during the first abortive attack on Ta-yüan in 104 BC, mostly through mismanagement of supplies. In his successful second attempt, only 30,000 men reached Ta-yüan out of an initial force of 180,000.[42]

To understand what these figures meant in terms of Han finances, it has been estimated that the empire's annual revenue amounted to 10 billion cash for the government administration and 8.3 billion cash for the emperor's purse.[43] In bounty money alone the 119 BC campaign must have devoured half the treasury's annual receipts. The ten billion cash used to finance the Hun-yeh king's surrender forced the imperial court and staff to drastically cut their expenses. These figures were inserted into the records of victories by the court historian Ssu-ma Ch'ien who opposed the war policy. They show that it was not without reason that Han Wu-ti was later criticized for bankrupting China in pursuit of glory. The loss of huge numbers of horses in each campaign and the necessity of amassing supplies to support the troops also meant that the Han court could not follow up on its victories. The Hsiung-nu thereby always had time to recover their own strength before the next Han attack. Even on the defensive the Hsiung-nu damaged the Han economy by forcing China to find ever-increasing amounts of revenue to pay for the continuing wars.

From its inception, the war policy split the Han court. The more aggressive ministers justified their actions as necessary to bring the Hsiung-nu in line with a sinocentric world order based on Confucian moral principles. Implementation of this policy, however, required actions like building up the military, centralizing the economy by the establishment of state monopolies, heavy taxation, and widespread conscription that were the hallmarks of the rapacious Legalist philosophy which guided the defunct Ch'in dynasty.[44]

The similarity between Han Wu-ti's policies and those of the hated Ch'in was a common theme cited by critics in court memorials. The powerful court minister Chu-fu Yen delivered an extremely long memorial which in part observed,

It is not only our generation which finds the Hsiung-nu difficult to conquer and control. They make a business of pillage and plunder, and indeed it would seem to be their inborn nature. Ever since the time of Emperor Shun and the rulers of the Hsia, Shang, and Chou dynasties, no attempt has been made to control them, rather they have been regarded as beasts to be pastured, not as members of the human race.

Now your majesty does not observe how Emperor Shun and the Hsia, Shang, and Chou dynasties managed to preserve their rule for so long, but imitates only the mistakes of the recent past [i. e. Ch'in] which is a source of great concern to me and tribulation and trial to the common people.

Moreover, warfare prolonged over a long period often gives rise to rebellion, and the burden of military service is apt to lead to disaffection, for the people along the border are subject to great strain and hardship until they think only of breaking away, while generals and officers grow suspicious of each other and begin to bargain with the enemy.[45]

Prolonged warfare also had consequences within the Han government which went against the interests of the civilian bureaucrats who traditionally controlled the state administration. War increased the importance of both the military and merchant classes who represented the only real rivals to the monopoly on government positions held by the civilian bureaucrats. In times of peace these officials could restrict entry into the government to their own class through a system of examinations and recommendations based on ideal models of talent and virtue as demonstrated by a sound knowledge of the literary classics. Merchants were legally excluded from the examination system because their occupation was deemed disreputable, while soldiers traditionally lacked the required virtue. In time of war the civilian bureaucrats' ability to exclude these groups broke down and military commanders could expect money, noble rank and government positions if they succeeded in war. Merchants could buy offices and noble rank when the emperor's wars created an empty treasury. With the introduction of outside advisors and the need to conduct a war, the emperor himself was less likely to accept limits on his own power and more likely to take a direct hand in running the government. In contrast to his virtue-minded predecessors (particularly Emperor Wen), Emperor Wu earned the reputation of a tyrannical autocrat. For these reasons there was always a powerful faction at court determined to put an end to the military adventures on the steppe. Following the series of defeats ending in the capture of Li Kuang-li and a number of court intrigues, these ministers succeeded in ending further aggressive campaigns and Wu-ti's successor abandoned the policy entirely.

The Hsiung-nu were able to resist Han pressure because their imperial government was exceptionally stable. The loss of the Ordos, the surrender of the Hun-yeh king, and the defeat of the *Shan-yü* in 119 BC appear to have done nothing to reduce the Hsiung-nu control of the steppe. Not until Han attacks began to fail and its forward policy was abandoned did the Hsiung-nu encounter serious difficulties.

The Han government changed its policy to one of pure defense with no active campaigning while refusing to make peace. This policy unintentionally proved to be most damaging to the Hsiung-nu. They could defeat Han troops on the steppe but they could not easily penetrate the reinforced defense lines where the Chinese held the military advantage. This put the *Shan-yü* in a predicament. When Han troops invaded the steppe his position as defender of the nomads was secure. Even in defeat they rallied to his banner in order to defend themselves, or left him and surrendered to China where they were no longer part of the Hsiung-nu polity. When the Chinese withdrew from their forward positions and the Hsiung-nu went on the offensive, the nomads expected that once again the rewards would soon follow. The *Shan-yü* had to provide them with booty from raids on China or restore the lucrative peace treaty which provided trade and subsidies from the Han court. Against the Han's strong but passive defense the *Shan-yü* could do neither. Consequently it was no accident that the Hsiung-nu claimed that their decline began during the reign of Chü-ti-hu *Shan-yü* (101–96 BC), the very time in which the Hsiung-nu pushed China back from the steppe.[46] All of the four successions following Chü-ti-hou were plagued by ever greater and more bitter disputes. For the first time the Hsiung-nu elite became divided into factions. Disputes that had arisen over succession in the past and had been resolved peacefully now led to fragmentation. Other tribes on the steppe soon tested the limits of Hsiung-nu power.

The Hsiung-nu defense against Han attacks had always rested on the knowledge that Han troops could not permanently occupy the steppe. This was not the case for the other nomadic tribes on the steppe. They had the potential to force the Hsiung-nu out of the region or to rule over them, just as the Hsiung-nu had expelled the Yüeh-chih and incorporated the Tung-hu to establish their own hegemony on the steppe. Attacks on the Hsiung-nu by other nomads were therefore qualitatively different from the Han attacks. For this reason the Hsiung-nu watched over subject tribes with care. It was a measure of imperial disorder that disputes over succession became opportunities for attack by tribes who had previously avoided offending the Hsiung-nu.

The first nomad attack on the Hsiung-nu was conducted by the Wu-huan around 78 BC, when they pillaged the tombs of the *Shan-yü*s. This act of sacrilege and contempt infuriated the Hsiung-nu who mounted a punitive raid in retaliation and easily defeated the Wu-huan. A few years later conflict broke out in the west when the Hsiung-nu seized border territory in Turkestan and threatened the Wu-sun. Invoking their alliance with the Han court, for which they had done little previously, the Wu-sun received military aid for an attack on the Hsiung-nu in 71 BC. This attack was only partially successful, but the Hsiung-nu suffered three major disasters. First, to avoid Chinese attacks they had been forced to move their people and animals at unseasonable times of the year, resulting in the loss of large numbers of both. Second, after a successful winter counterattack on the Wu-sun, the Hsiung-nu army was struck by a blizzard and almost wiped out. Word of this calamity provoked attacks from all sides against the Hsiung-nu: the Ting-ling from the north, the Wu-sun from the west, and the Wu-huan from the East. In 68 BC, the Hsiung-nu suffered from a famine and the death of a *Shan-yü* in the same year. Yet in spite of these disasters the Hsiung-nu maintained their grip on the steppe. Not until 60 BC, during another succession crisis, did the Hsiung-nu empire break up in civil war. It was this war which forced the Hsiung-nu to negotiate a peace with China. The Hsiung-nu had long refused to accept any peace treaty with China because the Han court had insisted that the *ho-ch'in* system could not be restored and that the Hsiung-nu must enter the tributary system as part of any new agreement.

A new peace

One of the major aims of Han Wu-ti's military policy was to establish the tributary system as the sole framework for China's foreign relations. Under such a framework each foreign nation or people was expected to accept a subservient status. Following their defeat in 119 BC, the Hsiung-nu requested a resumption of the old peace treaty based on the *ho-ch'in* policy. The Han court informed them that peace was only possible if the *Shan-yü* would agree to send a hostage to China, pay homage to the emperor, and offer him tribute. The

Shan-yü I-chih-hsieh angrily rejected these demands. In 107 BC, his successor rejected a similar proposal with this complaint:

"That is not the way things were done under the old alliance," the *Shan-yü* objected, "Under the old alliance the Han always sent us an imperial princess, as well as allotments of silks, foodstuffs, and other goods, in order to secure peace along the border, while we for our part refrained from making trouble at the border. Now you want to go against old ways and make me send my son as hostage. I have no use for such proposals."[47]

The Hsiung-nu continued to reject these new Chinese demands for another half century. Then, in 54 BC, long after the death of Wu-ti and the abandonment of his aggressive policies, the Hsiung-nu accepted China's terms. From that time onward no nomadic power on the steppe ever seriously objected to the tributary framework. The reason for this sharp change was the discovery that the tributary system was a sham – demanding mere tokens of submission in exchange for huge benefits. Once the Hsiung-nu understood its operation, they actively supported the tributary system, which allowed them to rebuild their power on the steppe.

The *Shan-yü's* original rejection of the tributary system was based on a sound understanding of his own political position on the steppe. The *Shan-yü* and the Hsiung-nu state were dependent on exploiting China's economy for the benefit of the steppe as a whole. The Hsiung-nu political structure could not survive a reversal of that role: if the *Shan-yü* were to pay tribute to China he would destroy a key pillar maintaining his own power. The Hsiung-nu did not see the tributary system as an ideological construct for conducting foreign relations. From their own experience as imperial rulers of the steppe they interpreted China's offer as an attempt to force their submission. The Hsiung-nu demanded hostages and tribute from neighboring tribes to insure the continuation of an exploitative relationship that directly benefited the Hsiung-nu. It was beyond their imagination that China might only be dealing in the symbols of formal submission that had little real meaning. To the pragmatic Hsiung-nu, the world of symbols was confined largely to burning towns and taking heads as a sign of hostility. That China might be demanding only token submission in exchange for a huge increase in gifts, regular subsidies and trade was, to quote Chia I's phrase in a very different context, "something beyond comprehension – like hanging upside down." The Hsiung-nu thus continued to fight for the restoration of the *ho-ch'in* treaty provisions as the only basis for peace. It would take a civil war among the Hsiung-nu and the desperate actions of a losing leader to discover the true nature of the Han tributary system.

THE HSIUNG-NU CIVIL WAR

The first Hsiung-nu civil war was the culmination of ever more divisive contests for the position of *Shan-yü* described earlier. The death of Hsü-lü-ch'üan-ch'ü in 60 BC set off a civil war because the imperial elite was divided over which of two lineages should inherit.

On the death of the *Shan-yü* the Hao-su king Hsing-wei-yang sent messengers to assemble all the kings. Before they arrived, however, the Lady Chuan-ch'ü and her younger brother the Left Great Chü-ch'ü Tu-lung-chi formed a plot, and set up the Wise King of the Right with the style of Wu-yen-ch'ü-ti *Shan-yü*. The latter had succeeded his father as Wise King of the Right, being the great-grandson of Wu-wei *Shan-yü*.[48]

Previous disputes had involved only claimants from a single extended family, the question usually hinging on whether a brother or son should inherit. This plot set two powerful lineages within the royal line at each other's throats. As Wu-wei's great grandson, Wu-yen-ch'ü-ti actually represented a line of senior descendants of Mao-tun who had lost control of the throne to the descendants of Wu-wei's younger brother. Wu-yen-ch'ü-ti's coup not only took the throne from the appointed heir but from his whole line, for to secure his own power Wu-yen-ch'ü-ti executed his predecessor's close advisors and removed all of Hsü-lü-ch'üan-ch'ü's sons and brothers from the ranks of the Ten Thousand Horsemen, replacing them with his own relations. This action divided the Hsiung-nu elite into rival lineages and, to compensate for the insecurity of his support at the elite level, Wu-yen-ch'ü-ti attempted to expand his power base by extending his network of personnel appointments to the level of local tribal organization.

It was this action (as we noted earlier) which provoked the revolt of the tribes within the confederation because it threatened the traditional autonomy of the local tribal elites. The Yü-chien tribal elite refused to accept the *Shan-yü*'s appointment of his own son to the post of tribal king which rightfully belonged to their own chiefly lineage. Aided in their opposition by the disinherited members of the imperial lineage, the tribes within the confederation revolted and brought about Wu-yen-ch'ü-ti's death in 58 BC. However, once the matter of seniority and the questionable successions of the past had been raised, it was not immediately possible to restore unity. Anyone with even a remote claim to the throne gathered troops in an effort to seize it. At one time there were as many as five self-proclaimed *Shan-yüs* battling for power. In the end the contest fell to two brothers (or half-brothers), Chih-chih and Hu-han-yeh, both sons of Hsü-lü-ch'üan-ch'ü.

In the Chinese records Chih-chih, who drove his rival out of the Hsiung-nu capital, was known as the northern *Shan-yü*. Hu-han-yeh, who fled towards the Han frontier, was known as the southern *Shan-yü*. Neither had full control over the tribes on the steppe, but Chih-chih appears to have been the stronger of the two, capable of destroying the southern *Shan-yü* in battle. In desperation, one of Hu-han-yeh's advisors recommended that they become subjects of China in order to obtain protection from Chih-chih.

At a council called to discuss the proposal, a majority opposed submission to China, stating:

By no means! It is the character of the Hsiung-nu to value independence and disparage submission. By mounting our horses and fighting for the national cause, we have gained renown for courage among all nations whose sturdy warriors fight to the death. Now we have brothers striving together for supremacy, and if the elder is unsuccessful it falls to the younger. Although both may die in the contest, they leave an unsullied reputation for courage to their children and descendants, excelling all other nations. Although China is strong there is no reason why the Hsiung-nu should be annexed to it. How can we thus subvert the institutes of our ancients, becoming subjects of the Chinese, disgracing former *Shan-yü*s and being the laughingstock of all nations? Although we might obtain peace at this price, how could we any more be looked upon as the head of nations?[49]

In favor of submission one minister pointed out that,

Ever since the time of Chü-ti-hou *Shan-yü* the Hsiung-nu have gradually been whittled down and can never gain their former status. Although we exhaust ourselves in that endeavor we can never find a day's repose. Now if we submit to China, our nation will be preserved in peace; but if we refuse to submit we are running into perdition. We cannot avert this by our plans.[50]

Hu-han-yeh's dilemma was this: if, as most of the Hsiung-nu believed, submission to China meant surrender and annexation then he could save his life only at the cost of giving up any hopes of returning to the steppe. When his allies reminded him in council that the civil war was a struggle between two brothers, they meant that the fate of the Hsiung-nu nation was not tied to Hu-han-yeh's personal fate. Many of them would undoubtedly defect to Chih-chih rather than be annexed by China. Hu-han-yeh also had the examples of earlier Hsiung-nu defections. The Hun-yeh king had surrendered to the Han and had been lavishly rewarded with gifts and titles, but his people had been divided up and placed under Han supervision. A more immediate example was the surrender of the Jih-chu king around 59 BC with a large number of followers. He too had been personally well received and given a Han title, but he had disappeared as an actor in steppe politics. Chih-chih himself believed that if Hu-han-yeh submitted to China his brother would then lose all the power and influence he had previously acquired on the steppe. In view of Chih-chih's military superiority, however, Hu-han-yeh felt he had no choice but to submit to China and sent the required hostage in 53 BC.

The demands of the tributary system proved to be largely ceremonial. Because he was a *Shan-yü*, Hu-han-yeh was treated with special respect, ranked above all the Han nobility, and showered with gifts, but no attempt was made to annex his people. Upon word of this news Chih-chih reversed his own policy and also sent a hostage to the Han court to compete for tributary benefits. The Hsiung-nu now realized that the Chinese were primarily interested in symbolic submission and were willing to pay lavishly to get it. From this time forward the tributary system, with its vocabulary of "submission," "homage," and "tribute" became the norm. Tribes on the steppe never again voiced strong objections to it once its operational nature became clear. Instead they regarded the tributary system as a new framework within which they could manipulate China as before. Chinese critics often objected to this very fact, noting that the nomads were not sincere in their motivation as tributaries, but were guided solely by greed. To the steppe tribes words were cheap, and if China was willing to pay for flattery they would willingly sell it along with horses and sheep. Both the Han court and the Hsiung-nu knew that beneath the new professions of goodwill lay the nomads' ability to disrupt China by means of raids or blackmail.

The inner frontier strategy

The discovery of the true nature of the Han tributary system allowed Hu-han-yeh to implement a new strategy in steppe politics. In essence the southern *Shan-yü* used Han wealth and military protection to win a civil war on the steppe. The strategy, which was repeated in later times, consisted of one party (usually the weaker) in a tribal civil war obtaining China's aid to destroy his steppe enemy. This strategy differed from outright surrender to China in which a tribal leader accepted Chinese titles and entered the Han administrative framework. The "inner frontier" strategy called on a leader to maintain his autonomy and keep free of direct Chinese control. Such a course was possible only when a united steppe confederation broke up, because when it remained intact there was no room for a rump state on the frontier. The Chinese were eager to support contenders in a civil war, thereby "using barbarians to fight barbarians," a policy always popular at the Han court.[51] They also expected that aiding the winning side would lay the basis for friendly relations in the future. While in the short term both these goals could be realized, in the long term Chinese aid enabled the nomads to rebuild their empire.

From the nomads' point of view, China was financing the rebuilding of a shattered confederation. As has been noted, the *Shan-yü* owed much of his influence to his ability to reward the federated tribal components of the empire. Whichever contender for the throne gained China's support had access to a huge store of wealth that could be used to attract new followers and build an army. By creating an alliance with China a nomad chieftain also received military protection from his rival as he rebuilt his coalition. This position could be used offensively to blockade rivals on the steppe by denying them access to trade or gifts from the Han court, making it difficult to maintain control over the tribes remaining on the steppe. In the best of circumstances, an allied leader might convince China to finance a tribal army, or, better yet, to send a Chinese army to fight his opponent. Indeed, once the Chinese got involved in civil war conflicts on the steppe, they could often be coerced into doing more out of fear that their "allies" might turn hostile and start raiding. With these assets the side allied with China almost invariably won a civil war, at which point a leader had two possible options. He could move back on to the steppe, unite it under his rule, and return to the outer frontier strategy in his dealings with China; or he could leave the steppe fragmented and maintain control only around the immediate frontier (often in the role of China's "protector") in order to dominate the flow of goods to the steppe and keep the less organized nomads from gaining access to the system. The reunification of the Hsiung-nu under Hu-han-yeh demonstrated the inner frontier strategy in action. Within ten years he restored the Hsiung-nu empire to its former greatness by using Chinese resources.

The southern *Shan-yü*'s visit to the Chinese capital in 51 BC was one of the great events of Han history. It immediately raised the question of what type of protocol was appropriate in order to establish Chinese superiority without alienating the *Shan-yü*. Some Han ministers demanded that he be ranked below all grades of Han nobility to illustrate to the world that he was just a barbarian who had surrendered. The emperor vetoed this idea. For more than eighty years the Han and Hsiung-nu had been at war because a continous series of *Shan-yü*s had refused to accept the principles of a tributary structure and none of the earlier Han military campaigns had succeeded in forcing a change in their attitude.[52] Emperor Hsüan had no intention of scaring the Hsiung-nu off now that they were willing to accept the formal structure of tributary relations. "Extraordinary rites were decreed in honor of the occasion, and his rank was fixed above all the lords and princes of the empire." As a legitimate *Shan-yü*, even with a rival, he was now ranked almost equal to the Chinese emperor himself, a barely perceptible change from the full equality granted under the *ho-ch'in* treaties. He was neither forced to kowtow before the throne nor was he granted any Han titles, demonstrating that the *Shan-yü* was not part of the Han administrative structure. In exchange for the visit to court, Hu-han-yeh received twenty *chin* of gold, 200,000 cash, seventy-seven suits of clothes, 8,000 pieces of silk, and 6,000 *chin* of silk floss; his followers were supplied with 34,000 *hu* of rice. The next year both he and Chih-chih sent envoys to collect gifts, but Hu-han-yeh got more from the Han in return. In 49 BC, Hu-han-yeh returned for a second personal visit and received greater gifts – including 9,000 pieces of silk and 8,000 *chin* of silk floss. The next year Hu-han-yeh complained that his people were in distress and the Han court forwarded 20,000 *hu* of rice to feed them, although famine was raging in parts of China itself. These gifts, grain, and trade with China helped Hu-han-yeh unite the Hsiung-nu.[53]

Chih-chih was the loser in this new competition for tributary benefits. In 45 BC he requested that the Han court return his hostage. Unsure of how to handle this problem, the Han court delayed almost two years before sending him back with an official escort. Chih-chih murdered the Han envoy and then abandoned the old Hsiung-nu territory, moving far to the northwest where he fought with the Wu-sun and came to dominate the Fergana region. Hu-han-yeh had won the civil war by virtue of his superior economic resources without ever meeting his brother on the battlefield. Later, in 35 BC, Chih-chih would meet his death at the hands of Han troops on campaign in western Turkestan.[54]

Although the southern *Shan-yü*'s return visits to the Chinese emperor's court and the requests for grain made it appear that the Hsiung-nu were quite weak, in fact they were rapidly gaining power. Two Han envoys sent to investigate the loss of the mission to Chih-chih were astonished to see the extent to which the Hsiung-nu had recovered from their civil war losses.

[The envoys] observed from the flourishing and populous condition of the Hsiung-nu settlement, that they had more than regained their former prosperity; and that the territory outside the stockades was no longer tenanted by beasts of the forest and desert. Confident in his strength, the *Shan-yü* was now free from apprehension in reference to

Chih-chih, and it was rumored that he had strongly been urged by his principal ministers to move north.[55]

In 43 BC, Hu-han-yeh did return north to his homeland, "and his people all gradually came together from various quarters, so that the old country again became settled and tranquil."[56]

Back on the steppe, Hu-han-yeh was free to employ a modified form of the outer frontier strategy. The threat remained the same. The Hsiung-nu were beyond the control of the Han government and could raid the frontier if they desired. The significant difference during this period was that under the tributary system the Hsiung-nu used implied threats rather than the direct language of a century earlier. In their messages to the Han court they wrote in polite terms, confident that the Han court was able to calculate the cost of refusing Hsiung-nu requests.

Having obtained a peace treaty with the Hsiung-nu by offering aid and trade as part of the tributary system, the Han court constantly worried that offending the Hsiung-nu might provoke an expensive and unwanted frontier war. By examining just the official allocations of silk made to successive tributary missions it is clear that the longer the peace lasted the more expensive it became, with a steady increase in the value of gifts allocated to each *Shan-yü* who visited the Han court:[57]

Year of visit	Silk floss	Silk fabric
51 BC	6,000 *chin*	8,000 pieces
49 BC	8,000 *chin*	9,000 pieces
33 BC	16,000 *chin*	16,000 pieces
25 BC	20,000 *chin*	20,000 pieces
1 BC	30,000 *chin*	30,000 pieces

The initial three visits were by Hu-han-yeh, who used the first two to finance the rebuilding of the Hsiung-nu confederation. The large increase in gifts during his last visit in 33 BC was indicative of the restored power of the Hsiung-nu. After Hu-han-yeh's death it became customary for a *Shan-yü* to make a court visit once during his reign, usually after he had been on the throne a number of years. The only *Shan-yü* who failed to visit the Han court during this period died in 12 BC while en route. The Hsiung-nu, not the Han court, requested these visits and, far from being welcomed, the Han dreaded them because of their vast expense to the state and because they were thought to bring bad luck. Fear of witchcraft was widespread at the Han court and Hsiung-nu shamans were known to lay curses on gifts for the emperor.[58] In both 49 BC and 33 BC, visits by a *Shan-yü* had been immediately followed by the death of the Han emperor. In 3 BC, the Han court initially rejected a proposed homage visit as too expensive and ill omened, but fear of Hsiung-nu displeasure forced a reconsideration after one minister pointed out the dangers.

Now the *Shan-yü*, reverting to right feeling and cherishing an unfeignedly sincere heart, wishes to leave his palace and take his place at the audience before the august presence; this is a custom that has been handed down from early ages and is regarded favorably by spiritual intelligences. Although it may be costly to the state, it is a thing that must not be dispensed with. . . . To quarrel with those who have good intentions is to engender heartfelt hatred.

Repudiating their former expressions of good will, they will look upon our declarations of the past, and imbibing a bitter hatred of China, will sever every connecting bond, and never more will they respect the imperial presence. It will be impossible to overawe them, it will be useless to address them. . . . Now in governing the Hsiung-nu, if the laborious efforts of a hundred years are to be lost in a day – if one is to be secured at the expense of ten – it is your servant's humble opinion that this will not tend to the peace of the country. May your Majesty reflect a little on the subject, so that calamities may be averted from the peoples of the borders, ere turbulence has broken out, or war has been declared.[59]

The *Shan-yü* arrived for his state visit in 1 BC and was highly rewarded. That same year the Han emperor died.

A close look at the tributary system during the last fifty years of the Former Han dynasty shows that it was still firmly rooted in the old *ho-ch'in* tradition in spite of the veneer of tributary language. Hostage, homage, and tribute were largely symbolic requirements. A hostage at court counted for little because the Han risked war if they harmed one. At most they could hope to influence the Hsiung-nu, but not constrain them. From the nomads' point of view, the tributary system was a charade.

The Han records do not record the details of the treaties signed between Hu-han-yeh and Emperors Hsüan and Yuan, perhaps because they too closely resembled the *ho-ch'in* treaties. Until the time of Wang Mang, when negotiations were reopened, the treaties appeared to have had the same structure. The *ho-ch'in* agreements had four provisions.

1 Annual payments of silk, grain, and wine were made to the *Shan-yü*.
2 The Han court provided the *Shan-yü* with a princess in marriage.
3 The Han and Hsiung-nu states were ranked as equals with each ruler sovereign in his own realm.
4 Both parties accepted the Great Wall as the boundary between the two states.

The tributary system made very few changes in these provisions. Pan Ku, in a critique of frontier policy, noted that "gifts consequent upon the treaty did not exceed a thousand *chin*," which would indicate that the *Shan-yü* continued to get an annual subsidy, though in comparison to the gifts obtained during tributary visits this was of minor importance.[60] The Han court also provided Hu-han-yeh with an imperial consort who, following Hsiung-nu custom, later remarried his successor. In all but tributary ceremonies, the Hsiung-nu state was treated as China's equal and the legitimate ruler of all peoples north of the Wall. The *Shan-yü* retained the explicit right to take hostages and levy tribute (real taxes in the Hsiung-nu case) from the area. Later, when Wang Mang complained of Hsiung-nu actions in the west, the *Shan-yü* pointed out that they were in accord with the treaty provisions signed by Hu-han-yeh. The special seal granted to the *Shan-yü* did not imply a subordinate status because it was unlike any other in the Han empire, similar only to the emperor's own. Neither Hu-han-yeh nor his successors accepted Han titles. Finally, the Great Wall remained the boundary between the two states, China recognizing its lack of sovereignty on the steppe.

In effect, the tributary system was an addition to the old *ho-ch'in* treaties and not a replacement of them. In exchange for accepting new ceremonial demands, the Hsiung-nu received new benefits. The focus of both the Han court and Hsiung-nu *Shan-yü* was now on this new and vastly more expensive part of the system which far eclipsed the value of the regular subsidies. Having accepted the framework of the tributary system, the Hsiung-nu immediately set about exploiting it, often showing great sophistication in manipulating Han values to serve their own ends. It was the *Shan-yü* who controlled the time and frequency of tributary visits, it was he who requested and received special grants of grain, and it was he who received lavish gifts from the Han court with each embassy, while providing his own envoys with only token gifts. Near the end of his reign Hu-han-yeh generously offered to relieve China of the task of guarding the frontier by having the Hsiung-nu take over the responsibility. This proposal was rejected after one Han critic noted that it would give the Hsiung-nu even more power than they already had to hold China hostage in the future.

The tributary system provided sixty years of frontier peace. Like the earlier period of peace under the *ho-ch'in* treaties, this peace was possible because gifts financed the Hsiung-nu state. The *Shan-yü* received a steady supply of silk and other goods which he could sell or redistribute within the empire. With no rivals anywhere near as powerful as the *Shan-yü*, Hsiung-nu hegemony on the steppe was restored. Ordinary tribesmen again had access to frontier markets where they could trade for Chinese goods. The fear that the Hsiung-nu might go to war was sufficient to keep the Han court increasing the amount of gifts. This long period of peace was finally broken when Wang Mang, like Han Wu-ti, attempted to change the status quo and provoked the Hsiung-nu. However, as a result of their experience in the tributary system, the Hsiung-nu response was now a much more sophisticated version of the outer frontier strategy – they raided China's frontier while using humble words to collect as many tributary gifts as possible.

WANG MANG: CHINA TRIES A NEW APPROACH

Wang Mang was an important imperial in-law who became the dominant court minister at the end of the Former Han dynasty. He came to control the government and then established his own short-lived Hsin dynasty (AD 9–23). An arch-Confucianist, Wang Mang was determined to create a single, ideologically consistent order that would guide both foreign and domestic policy. He disapproved of the compromises that had allowed the Hsiung-nu to become tributaries without acknowledging China's sovereignty. He therefore sought to revise the treaty and redefine Han–Hsiung-nu relations more in China's favor. To implement his policy, Wang Mang employed two strategies. He initially demanded changes from the Hsiung-nu while bribing them with lavish gifts, but when the Hsiung-nu proved insincere, accepting the gifts and ignoring the demands, Wang Mang undertook an offensive policy of raising troops and appointing his own *Shan-yü* to break the Hsiung-nu confederation. In almost clockwork fashion, Wang Mang shifted his approach about every five years until he met his death at the hands of Chinese rebels in AD 23.[61]

The Hsiung-nu response to Wang Mang's policies showed that they had grown far more sophisticated in conducting foreign relations since entering the tributary system. Throughout the reigns of three *Shan-yü*s the Hsiung-nu put pressure on Wang Mang to continue the lucrative tributary system. During this period, it was China rather than the Hsiung-nu who broke relations. This is best illustrated by examining the four alternating periods of peace and war along the frontier under Wang Mang.

In AD 5, the first dispute arose when the *Shan-yü* accepted a group of refugees from Turkestan who were fleeing Han control. Wang Mang demanded their return. The *Shan-yü* referred Wang Mang to the Hu-han-yeh treaty, which gave him the right to accept subjects from all areas beyond the Great Wall, excluding only refugees from China itself. As a goodwill gesture, however, he returned them with a request that they be pardoned. Wang Mang had them beheaded and sent envoys to the *Shan-yü* demanding that the treaty be revised to specifically exclude refugees and hostages from the Wu-sun and Wu-huan tribes, and from China's dependencies in eastern Turkestan. At about the same time he also asked the *Shan-yü* to take a Chinese surname, to replace his own "barbaric" multisyllabic one, in exchange for lavish gifts. The *Shan-yü* picked a name, took the gifts, and formally agreed to the treaty changes.

In point of fact, the *Shan-yü* had no intention of changing the nature of his relationship with China, nor did he feel bound by the new treaty provisions. Hsiung-nu tax collectors proceeded as usual to mulct the Wu-huan. When they resisted, on the grounds that they were now exempt from the *Shan-yü*'s control, the Hsiung-nu attacked them and seized many prisoners as hostages for ransom. The *Shan-yü*'s policy was to agree with as many of Wang Mang's demands as were necessary to continue the supply of gifts, while doing essentially what he pleased. The *Shan-yü* acted in a such a fashion in AD 9, when Wang Mang sent him a new Hsin dynasty seal to replace the one granted by the Han. Unlike the old seal, the new seal implied that the *Shan-yü* was an official of the new dynasty – and a low ranking one. Unfortunately, the *Shan-yü* discovered the change only after the Han seal had been destroyed. Enraged, he insisted that Wang Mang restore the old format. Wang Mang refused, but did send the *Shan-yü* another large load of gifts. Instead of declaring war on China, the *Shan-yü* simply became disruptive, organizing unofficial raids on the frontier.

Soon after the business with the seal, the *Shan-yü* received a second set of deserters from Turkestan and raided China's outposts in that region. Wang Mang responded by trying to break-up the Hsiung-nu empire. Announcing his intention to appoint fifteen new *Shan-yü*s to rule over the steppe, envoys were dispatched to the border in AD 11 to lure the descendants of Hu-han-yeh with gifts of gold. Two brothers, Teng and Ch'u, were attracted by the offer and defected to Wang Mang, followed later by their father Hsien, one of Hu-han-yeh's sons and a half-brother of the ruling *Shan-yü*. Hsien received 1,000 *chin* of gold (1000 *chin* = 244 kg, $3.5 million in modern terms) and the title "Filial *Shan-yü*." Ch'u was named "Obedient *Shan-yü*" and got 500 *chin* of gold, while his brother was made a Han duke and a general in the imperial guard. Both brothers were sent to Ch'ang-an where, after Ch'u died of natural causes, his title was given to Teng. The *Shan-yü*, furious at this direct interference in Hsiung-nu politics, ordered his subordinates to raid the frontier and for the first time in generations China's border felt the sting of large-scale Hsiung-nu attacks. Hsien quickly deserted Wang Mang, leaving his son Teng behind, and returned to the *Shan-yü*'s court to explain his actions. The *Shan-yü* degraded his greedy half-brother to a minor Hsiung-nu rank, thereby removing him from the line of succession. Wang Mang, meanwhile, held Hsien responsible for some of the frontier raids and had Teng publicly executed in retaliation. He also began assembling an army of 300,000 troops with 300 days' provisions to be used to drive the Hsiung-nu off the steppe. Although a large army of uncertain size was sent to the frontier, it never left the cover of its frontier defenses.

Wang Mang's plan for dividing the Hsiung-nu was based on the expectation that, as with Hu-han-yeh, China's support would give its candidate the ability to win a civil war. However, this historical analogy was not correct. Chinese aid was critical only when the Hsiung-nu themselves were divided. When they were united, a Chinese-picked *Shan-yü* had no base of support on the steppe. Hsien had recognized this fact by returning to the steppe as soon as hostilities began. Unfortunately for Wang Mang, the more appropriate example was Han Wu-ti, whose grand plans had also gone awry and embroiled China in an expensive and unwinnable war with the Hsiung-nu.

Throughout this period the raids mounted by the *Shan-yü* Nang-chih-ya-szu were not of great intensity, rather they were designed to demonstrate to Wang Mang that the cost of a frontier war was greater than the cost of a Hsiung-nu peace. The Hsiung-nu policy was not aimed at continuing full-scale hostilities, but at re-establishing the flow of tributary benefits. At Nang-chih-ya-szu's death in AD 13, the Hsiung-nu chose the previously disgraced Hsien to be *Shan-yü* over other rivals on the grounds that he would be the most capable of convincing Wang Mang to restore gift diplomacy. To this end, Hsien's first act was to return the defectors from Turkestan to Wang Mang (who had them burned alive) in exchange for gold, silk, and clothes. These good relations quickly soured after Hsien learned of his son's execution.

The *Shan-yü* coveted Wang Mang's gifts, and hence outwardly conformed to the old Chinese institutions; but he secretly profited from raids and seizures. On the return of his envoys, becoming aware that his son Teng had been formally put to death, he was filled with rage and hatred, and the raids and captures were carried out unceasingly from the left hand land. The envoys heard the *Shan-yü* invariably stating, "The Wu-huan with some disreputable Hsiung-nu have carried out raids on the stockades – just as thieves and robbers in China. When I first acceded to the supreme power, I found the national dignity and good faith at low ebb, and I have exerted all my strength to put a stop to the disorder, not daring to act with duplicity."[62]

Hsien died in AD 18, and his successor Yü attempted to continue the peace policy. Wang Mang, however, had again decided to disrupt the Hsiung-nu by creating a puppet *Shan-yü*, whereupon the Hsiung-nu resumed open attacks on the border. Wang Mang's attempts to bring the Hsiung-nu into true tributary subservience to China resulted in a series of unsuccessful wars, but it was his unpopular domestic policies which led to his downfall. Rebel armies besieged the capital and Wang Mang met his death at their hands in AD 23. China's new rulers tried to pacify the *Shan-yü* by returning the old style seals to him and giving up the prisoners they had taken. The *Shan-yü* noted their weak position:

Now a state of anarchy is present in China. Wang Mang had usurped the supreme power, thus when the Hsiung-nu also sent troops to attack him, devastating his border land, this caused great consternation throughout the empire and the thoughts of the people reverted to the Han. Wang Mang has been killed, his cause overthrown, and thus through our means the Han has been re-established. Now we ought to be treated with greater honors.[63]

THE OUTER FRONTIER STRATEGY IN TIMES OF TURMOIL

China fell into a long civil war following the death of Wang Mang. During this period, the Hsiung-nu were at the height of their military power and united under the rule of a *Shan-yü* who was hostile to China. Yet they did not take a very active role in the civil war, despite their many opportunities to determine China's future. As during the Ch'in-Han interregnum (and later the Sui-T'ang disorders) the nomads stayed neutral. This restraint belies the common notion that disorder in China always invited an immediate attempt at conquest by the steppe nomads.

An explanation of this restraint can be found by reviewing the dynamics of the relationship between China and the Hsiung-nu. The Hsiung-nu state was supported in large part by resources extracted from China. To this end the Hsiung-nu required a stable government in China to extort. Theoretically, the Hsiung-nu could conquer China and rule it themselves, but the nomads possessed no administrative structure capable of such a task, nor were they willing to expose their limited number of troops to the series of fixed battles needed to hold rather than raid China. The outer frontier strategy, successfully employed by the Hsiung-nu for 200 years, called for the *Shan-yü* to avoid holding Chinese land. Raids could supply the necessary revenue until the civil war ended, when the old extortion relationship could be re-established with a new dynasty. It was in the *Shan-yü's* interest to see China reunited. A China divided into small warring states would destroy the resources and the political structure to which the Hsiung-nu state was parasitically attached. With this in mind, the Hsiung-nu policy at the start of the Later Han becomes clearer.

Following Wang Mang's death, Chinese rebels on the border sought Hsiung-nu aid, but the nomads were more interested in dealing with the existing central power in China than in establishing a candidate of their own. They appear to have supported frontier rebels merely to generate additional problems for China. For example, when P'eng Ching revolted in AD 26, he gave the *Shan-yü* his daughter in marriage and gifts of silk, but received little aid in return and was defeated within two years. At the same time Lu Fang, an adventurer in the northwest, declared himself emperor while among the Hsiung-nu, and gained the support of petty warlords in the region. He too received little assistance from the Hsiung-nu, eventually surrendering to the Later Han dynasty.[64]

Kuang-wu, the first Later Han emperor (r. AD 25–57), found these rivals posed little problem, but constant Hsiung-nu raids forced him to abandon many frontier regions and create a new series of defenses. For their part, the Hsiung-nu simply looted the border and expanded south into territory abandoned by the Chinese during the civil war. As early as AD 30, Kuang-wu had sent envoys with gifts to the Hsiung-nu, but the *Shan-yü* remained hostile, consistent with the Hsiung-nu strategy of using savage raids to induce a new dynasty to renegotiate the terms of the tributary system. A new treaty was inevitable because Kuang-wu engaged in purely defensive border policies; at no time during his reign did he contemplate direct attacks on the Hsiung-nu. As in the time of Han Kao-tsu, the Hsiung-nu were in such a strong position that they aspired to restore the formal diplomatic equality accepted by China in the *ho-ch'in* treaties. But, at the height of their power and with China on the defensive, the Hsiung-nu were suddenly engulfed by a civil war that left them permanently divided.

THE SECOND HSIUNG-NU CIVIL WAR

The second Hsiung-nu civil war came as a surprise to China. On two occasions Wang Mang's attempts to disrupt the Hsiung-nu political structure had met with failure. Now after more than 100 years of stability and following seven peaceful successions, the Hsiung-nu empire split over who should become *Shan-yü*. Yet this war was the predictable and perhaps inevitable result of the political compromise that had provided the Hsiung-nu with stability after the first civil war. Following Hu-han-yeh's reign, the Hsiung-nu had shifted from a modified lineal system to a lateral system of succession.

Until the end of the first Hsiung-nu civil war, lineal succession, from father to son, had been the traditional Hsiung-nu pattern. The major modification to this rule was that when an heir was considered too young the Hsiung-nu relied on lateral succession, from elder brother to younger brother, as an alternative. The lineal pattern then reasserted itself, for the younger brother passed the throne on to his own son rather than returning it to the son of his elder brother. Lateral successions increased during the times of wars because the Hsiung-nu valued mature leaders as battle commanders. This advantage was offset, however, by the creation of multiple lines of succession. Each son of a former *Shan-yü* could lay some claim to the office, although the traditional position of Wise King of the Left as heir apparent generally gave one candidate a superior political advantage. In times of turmoil, as during the first civil war, rival contenders from dispossessed lineages were the focus of opposition.

The coexistence of both lineal and lateral principles were uneasy. In most lineal succession systems, a younger brother was forbidden from taking the throne so long as a son still lived. The problem of youthful heirs was handled through a regency, often headed by a younger brother. Occasionally these uncles murdered nephews who stood between them and the throne, as the rule made the existence of a son an absolute bar to the succession of collateral heirs. A lineal system of this kind avoided a multiplicity of heirs, but created tension between a ruler and his brothers who were excluded from power. A pure lateral system produced harmony among brothers, each of whom had a chance to succeed, but created a multiplicity of heirs in the next generation. In a society where polygyny was the norm for the supreme ruler, the number of sons could be quite large. Ideally, the solution to this problem was to exclude the descendants of the younger brothers from future succession. Succession would pass from elder brother to younger brother until a generation was exhausted, and then in the next generation the eldest son of the eldest brother would inherit.

Having the two systems in tandem produced situations in which younger brothers asserted lateral principles to take the throne and lineal principles to pass it on to their own sons. This produced an explosive situation when power had to be passed from one generation to the next after a long series of brothers had held power. Their sons, all sets of cousins, refused to be excluded and often pressed their cause through violent struggles until opposing lines were eliminated. This produced the seeming paradox of many years of peaceful rule by brothers followed by a large-scale civil war.

At the time of Hu-han-yeh's death in 31 BC, he had two chief wives who were sisters from the Hu-yen clan. The elder sister, who was the Chuan-ch'ü Consort, had two sons: Chü-mo-chü and Nang-chih-ya-szu. The younger sister, styled the Great Consort, had four sons: Tiao-t'ao-mo-kao and Ch'ü-mi-hsu, who were older than her sister's sons, and Hsien and Le, who were younger. Hu-han-yeh also had at least ten other sons by lesser wives. On his deathbed, Hu-han-yeh wanted to appoint Chü-mo-chü as his heir because he was eldest son of his senior wife, but she raised some practical objections to this choice.

For more than ten years the Hsiung-nu have been in a state of turbulence and within a hair of being exterminated. Thanks to the power of China, peace has been restored; but now when we are scarcely settled, and are still smarting from our wounds, there is again quarreling and fighting. My son is but young and the people being not attached to him, I fear it would bring the nation into great danger. The Great Consort and I are both sisters of the same parents and it would be better to appoint his senior, Tiao-t'ao-mo-kao.[65]

The succession question hinged on whether the son who had the senior lineage should be given the throne over a half-brother who was mature enough to hold the position securely. A compromise was reached whereby the sons of the two sisters would inherit the throne laterally in order of age. Such cooperation between wives was extremely rare, in previous disputes consorts had fought furiously for the right of exclusive succession. In this case, however, the consorts were sisters and in terms of kinship their sons could be considered full brothers since they had the same maternal and paternal relatives. This agreement led to an extremely long rule of seventy-seven years by the sons of Hu-han-yeh before the last of their generation died. It also permanently altered the principles of Hsiung-nu succession, making the lateral principle primary and the lineal principle secondary. While this reversed a long-standing tradition, the question of how power was to pass once the sons of Hu-han-yeh were gone was not clear.

Lateral succession was insured by having each *Shan-yü* appoint his younger brother to the post of Wise King of the Left, through a system of ranks called the "Four and Six Horns."

Of the great offices the noblest was Wise King of the Left, the next was the Left Luli King, then the Wise King of the Right and the Right Luli King: the above were styled the "four horns." Next came the Left and Right Jih-chu Kings, and the Left and Right Wen-yü-ti, and the Left and Right Chien-chiang Kings. These were the six horns. All the above were the *Shan-yü*'s sons and younger brothers, and might become *Shan-yü* in due succession.[66]

The system worked smoothly through the reigns of three *Shan-yü*s, and when Nang-chih-ya-szu took the throne in 8 BC, he continued the pattern by choosing his younger half-brother Le to be Wise King of the Left. Sometime later Le died, but Nang-chih-ya-szu then appointed his own son Su-ti-hou to fill the vacant post instead of picking Hsien or any other of his surviving half-brothers. This change, forty years after the death of Hu-han-yeh, was an attempt by Nang-chih-ya-szu to use the power he had gained during his long rule to restrict the inheritance of the throne to his own heirs, thereby removing his younger half-brothers from the direct line of succession. This exclusionary policy was undoubtedly the motivating factor in Hsien's decision to temporarily defect to Wang Mang, for by seniority he should have preceded his brother Le as Wise King of the Left. Ironically, when Nang-chih-ya-szu died in AD 13, the Hsiung-nu nobles ignored his son Su-ti-hou and selected Hsien to be *Shan-yü* because they believed he was in the best position to revive the lucrative tributary system.

Hsien reinforced the lateral system by appointing his younger half-brother Yü as Wise King of the Left. Su-ti-hou was degraded in rank and removed from the line of succession. By the time Hsien died in AD 18, only two of Hu-han-yeh's sons survived: Yü, by then a man in his mid-fifties, who was named *Shan-yü*, and his half brother Chih-ya-shih, the son of a Han consort. The question of passing power to a new generation seemed near at hand. Yü had Chih-ya-shih assassinated to remove the last collateral rival for the throne, and then appointed his own son Wise King of the Left. As a set of brothers aged and died off, the pressure mounted in the next generation over which heirs would assume power. Even as a *Shan-yü* defended his own right to the throne on the basis of fraternal succession, he schemed to ensure that his own sons replaced him. But the expected generational shift of power was long postponed, for Yü proved to be the longest ruling of any of Hu-han-yeh's sons, dying around the age of eighty in AD 46.

For the hundred years following their first civil war, the Hsiung-nu empire remained stable under the leadership of Hu-han-yeh and his sons, even as

Table 2.2 Hsiung-nu *Shan-yüs* to AD 140

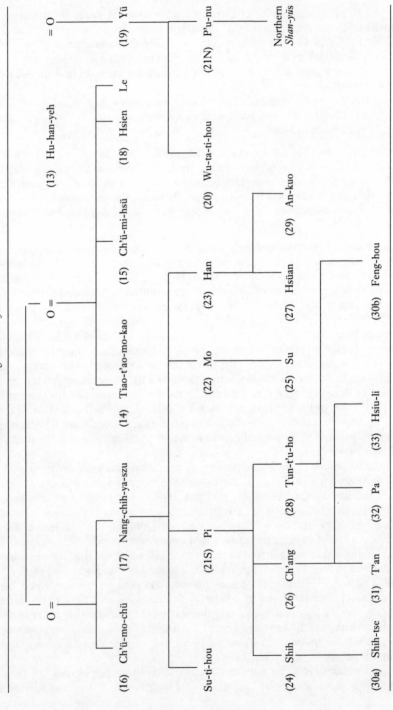

Table 2.3   Titles and dates of reigns of the *Shan-yü*s 58 BC to AD 140

---

(13)   Hu-han-yeh Shan-yü (58–31 BC)

(14)   Fu-chu-lei Shan-yü (31–20 BC)

(15)   Sou-hsieh-jo-t'i Shan-yü (20–12 BC)   .

(16)   Chü-ya-jo-t'i Shan-yü (12–8 BC)

(17)   Wu-chu-liu-jo-t'i Shan-yü (8 BC–AD 13)

(18)   Wu-lei-jo-t'i Shan-yü (13–18)

(19)   Hu-tu-erh-shih-tao-kao-jo-t'i Shan-yü (18–24)

(20)   ? Shan-yü (46)

(21N)   ? Northern Shan-yü (46–?83)

(21S)   Hsi-lo-shih-chu-t'i Shan-yü (48–56)

(22)   Ch'iu-fou-yu-t'i Shan-yü (56–7)

(23)   I-fa-yü-lu-t'i Shan-yü (57–9)

(24)   Hsi-t'ung-shih-chu-hou-t'i Shan-yü (59–63)

(25)   Ch'iu-ch'u-chü-lin-t'i Shan-yü (63)

(26)   Hu-yeh-shih-chu-hou-t'i Shan-yü (63–85)

(27)   I-t'u-yü-lü-t'i Shan-yü (85–8)

(28)   Hsiu-lan-shih-shu-hou-t'i Shan-yü (88–93)

(29)   ? Shan-yü (93–4)

(30a)   T'ing-tu-shih-chu-hou-t'i Shan-yü (94–8)

(30b)   ? Shan-yü (94–118)

(31)   Wan-shih-shih-chu-t'i Shan-yü (98–124)

(32)   Wu-chi-hou-shih-chu Shan-yü (124–8)

(33)   Ch'ü-ch'ih-jo-shih-chu-chiu Shan-yü (128–40)

? Shan-yü = title unknown.
Source: Eberhard, *Türk Tarih Kurumu Belleten*, 1940: 387–435

China collapsed. Such stability had a price. While the lateral principle reinforced the unity of brothers and the continuity of rule, it prepared the ground
for the enmity of cousins. The sons of each *Shan-yü* could lay some claim to the
throne, so without a firm rule excluding heirs in the next generation such a
situation was explosive. Disputes over succession had broken out as early as AD
13, when Su-ti-hou was removed from office, and provided the motive for
Chih-ya-shih's murder, but none of these events was serious enough to create a
split within the Hsiung-nu elite. Nevertheless, there was discontent like that
expressed by Nang-chih-ya-szu's eldest surviving son Pi, who represented the
senior line of descent, upon the elevation of Yü and the murder of Chih-ya-
shih,

"From the point of view of brothers, the Right Luli King [Chih-ya-shih] was the next
successor. From the point of view of sons I am the last *Shan-yü*'s eldest son and I ought
to have succeeded." So he nourished suspicion and dread within himself and seldom
presented himself at court functions.[67]

Two factions developed. The first, represented by Pi, upheld the rights of the
senior line to whom the throne should have returned after the last of Hu-han-
yeh's sons had died. The second, represented by Yü's heirs, argued that the
throne should be inherited by the sons of the last *Shan-yü*. This dispute
fractured the seemingly solid Hsiung-nu state, yet without understanding the
dynamics of tribal politics and lateral succession it is impossible to understand
why, after a hundred years of stability, the Hsiung-nu state divided at Yü's
death and entered a long period of civil war. To the Chinese, for whom these
principles were alien, the breakup of the Hsiung-nu empire came as a welcome
relief, but one which was mysterious, as were "barbarian" affairs in general.
    In cause and result the two Hsiung-nu civil wars were very similar. Both
resulted from political difficulties revolving around lateral succession, and both
were exacerbated by economic hardship on the steppe. Political stability was
usually insured by appointing an heir apparent, the Wise King of the Left,
although other heirs could be elected *Shan-yü*. Unsuccessful rivals for the
throne had little recourse when the Hsiung-nu elite moved solidly behind the
new *Shan-yü*. If the choice was within an extended family network of brothers,
uncles, or sons, the Hsiung-nu elite had little incentive to divide over the issue.
The case was more complex when the choice was between two or more groups
of cousins. The choice of one inevitably meant the exclusion of the rest, pitting
one lineage and its supporters against another. In the first civil war, which broke
out around 60 BC, it was the usurpation of the throne by just such an excluded
lineage that began the fighting. The second civil war began when Yü's son
became *Shan-yü* at the expense of the descendants of Nang-chih-ya-szu. In
both cases the political struggle was intensified by severe drought which
weakened the pastoral economy.
    Wu-ta-ti-hou succeeded his father Yü in AD 46, but he died within months,
and his brother P'u-nu became *Shan-yü*. His rival Pi immediately began
plotting with China, offering an alliance in AD 47, and war between the two
Hsiung-nu leaders broke out soon thereafter. Pi, along with tribes who had

proclaimed him *Shan-yü*, then moved south of the Wall into Han territory which had been largely abandoned by the Chinese during their civil war. He offered to guard the frontier and, in a reversal of earlier policy, the Later Han dynasty accepted. To emphasize his Chinese alliance, Pi proclaimed himself Hu-han-yeh II. The Hsiung-nu were now divided into northern and southern factions.

As in the first civil war, the southern *Shan-yü* was initially at a disadvantage. By force of circumstance, the weaker party in a struggle on the steppe sought out a Chinese alliance. The southern *Shan-yü* was thus protected from his rival by his proximity to Chinese military aid, and, more important in the long run, had access to Chinese economic aid. Relying on this alone, Hu-han-yeh had united the Hsiung-nu and returned to the steppe. The southern *Shan-yü* Pi and his successors utilized the same "inner frontier strategy." Unlike Chih-chih, P'u-nu was well aware of the consequences of this policy and he attempted to interfere with its implementation, first by raiding China to keep his own people supplied with loot, and then by negotiation with the Han to establish his own trade and tributary links.

The southern *Shan-yü*'s war strategy had three components. First, he established a blockade to stop Chinese trade from reaching his rival, thereby weakening the northern *Shan-yü* whose power rested on his ability to provide such goods. Second, the southern *Shan-yü* maintained exclusive control of the lucrative tributary system, which both prevented the Han court from offering tributary benefits to the northern *Shan-yü* as well as providing the southern *Shan-yü* with the wealth to attract more allies. Finally, the southern *Shan-yü* induced the Chinese to provide military aid with which to destroy the northern nomads. Under the Later Han Emperor Kuang-wu military aid initially consisted largely of payments to the Wu-huan and Hsien-pi for attacks on the northern Hsiung-nu. Under Emperors Ming (r. 58–75) and Chang (r. 76–88), the Chinese increased their support, supplying troops and financing invasions of northern Hsiung-nu territory.

The division of the Hsiung-nu left the steppe fragmented for the first time in 250 years. Previously, when the Hsiung-nu were united and controlled all of Mongolia, foreign relations were a monopoly of the *Shan-yü*. No tribal leader could act on his own, except to flee the steppe or surrender to China. The second civil war opened new alternatives. The Wu-huan and then the Hsien-pi threw off Hsiung-nu control. They had an undeveloped supratribal organization because they had been component parts of the Hsiung-nu state since the time of Mao-tun. Now they came directly to China and entered the tributary system as small autonomous tribes. This had the effect of encouraging fragmentation, since the Later Han tributary system was open to everyone, permitting any petty chieftain, even a leader of just a hundred men, to act for himself. The Hsien-pi, in particular, took advantage of the situation and received payments for Hsiung-nu heads.

China could not easily control the system, and its great cost often seemed to benefit the southern Hsiung-nu more than the Han. When the subsidies were regularized between AD 50 and 100 they amounted to the following:[68]

Hsien-pi	270,000,000 cash
Hsiung-nu	100,900,000 cash
Western Region	74,800,000 cash
Total	445,700,000 cash

Similar amounts were also paid to the Wu-huan and Ch'iang tribes, although the totals were not recorded. It has been estimated that the annual subsidy amounted to one-third of the government payroll or 7 percent of all the empire's revenue.[69] Using the traditional Han exchange rate of 10,000 cash equaling one *chin* (244 grams) of gold, this would have amounted to about $130 million dollars a year in modern terms. Of course, these figures mostly represented the value of goods provided, not cash payments.

The northern Hsiung-nu first responded to their exclusion from this system by raids on the south. In AD 52, P'u-nu shifted his approach to a diplomatic offensive, offering peace in return for being allowed to join the tributary system. Acceptance of this proposal could have benefited the Han, for it would have produced a fragmented steppe unable to unify and dependent on Chinese aid. But China was not able to act freely in her own interests, for any relationship with the northern *Shan-yü* threatened the wrath of the southern *Shan-yü* who was "protecting" China's frontier. The Han heir apparent, the future Emperor Ming, expressed this fear:

The southern *Shan-yü* has but lately joined us, and the northern pillagers are afraid of being attacked, they therefore lend a ready ear [to our proposals], and vie with the others in expression of their eagerness to act rightly. As we do not presently have the power to send out a military force, if we open relations with the northern Hsiung-nu, I fear that the southern *Shan-yü* may waver in his allegiance and those who have already submitted will be the last we shall ever see come in.[70]

The next year, AD 53, another peace proposal by P'u-nu was rebuffed but, in a letter to the northern *Shan-yü*, the Chinese expressed their own concerns about being manipulated by the southern *Shan-yü*:

Recently the southern *Shan-yü* has faced south and presented himself at the Wall with his horde to receive our commands. As he is the oldest direct descendant of Hu-han-yeh we have held the succession is his due. But in failure of his duty he has extended his conquests and has made attacks in a suspicious spirit, craving troops with a view to securing the disappearance of the northern horde, causing no end of trouble. We cannot confine ourselves to considering only his side of the question, for we must take into account that the northern *Shan-yü* has for successive years offered tribute and expressed a desire to improve relations. Consequently, we have rejected the southern *Shan-yü*'s propositions, to give effect to the [northern] *Shan-yü*'s loyal and filial sentiments.[71]

Pi died in AD 56, but his successors continued his policies. Their inheritance of the title *Shan-yü* was strictly lateral because the Chinese, having learned how the Hsiung-nu determined seniority,would support the candidate who had the best legal claim to the position. Since Chinese support was vital to the southern Hsiung-nu, such recognition was tantamount to election to the throne. Over the course of about eighty years, through three generations, a dozen successions occurred, moving from elder brothers to younger brothers and even through multiple sets of cousins, producing the very complicated genealogical record in table 2.2 above. There was some irony in this, for the Chinese themselves did not recognize the legitimacy of lateral inheritance, except in the absence of sons. Under the traditional conditions of steppe politics, it is unlikely that such an extreme example of lateral succession could have been maintained without periodic wars to reduce the number of claimants.

The northern Hsiung-nu remained strong under P'u-nu leadership, raiding China for what they needed, while periodically making attempts to establish more normal relations with the Han court. After negotiating a trade agreement with China in AD 66, P'u-nu was almost able to bring about a revolt among some southern Hsiung-nu clans, but he was thwarted by Chinese troops. In AD 73, China mounted an attack on the northern Hsiung-nu in the steppe, but it failed when they retreated out of range. For the next decade there was a stalemate and, in spite of the south's strategic advantages, the north remained intact.

The north managed to remain strong because of its success in raiding the Chinese frontier and because of P'u-nu's long reign. Although Chinese records refer only to the "northern *Shan-yü*," P'u-nu appears to have outlived a large number of southern *Shan-yü*s, and as long as he was alive tribal leaders in the north remained loyal. Evidence for this supposition can be drawn from the stability of the northern Hsiung-nu state until AD 83, when he probably died. The decade before that had been relatively uneventful following the defeat of a Han expeditionary force. The years immediately following P'u-nu's death were filled with reports of large-scale defections of northern Hsiung-nu to the south, massive invasions by neighboring tribes, and a civil war over the throne. These actions destroyed the northern Hsiung-nu state.

Without P'u-nu's personal leadership, many tribes quickly defected to the south. Thirty-eight thousand tribesmen moved south with their animals in AD 83. Attempting to stabilize his position, the new northern *Shan-yü* immediately began negotiations with the Han court to open trade along the frontier. The proposal was accepted by the Chinese, border markets organized and, in AD 84, the northern Hsiung-nu brought 10,000 sheep to sell. The Han court also sent gifts to the northern Hsiung-nu. This promising relationship was cut short by the southern *Shan-yü*, who organized a raid to capture and rob the visitors. In response, the northern *Shan-yü* threatened to raid China if he did not get redress. The Han, caught in the middle of this conflict, tried to please both sides. They ordered the prisoners seized by the southern Hsiung-nu returned, but agreed to continue paying them the going rate for northern captives and heads.

Meanwhile, the northern Hsiung-nu were suffering from attacks on every side: from the Hsien-pi in the east, the Ting-ling in the north, the southern Hsiung-nu on the Chinese frontier, and tribes from the Turkestan area in the west. The situation reached a climax in AD 87 when the Hsien-pi beheaded the northern *Shan-yü*. Large numbers of northerners thereupon defected south, altogether fifty-eight tribes amounting to 200,000 people according to Han reports. Those who remained behind were divided into two factions, each supporting a brother of the dead *Shan-yü*. They also moved further northwest to escape raids by their neighbors. The southern *Shan-yü* pushed the Han court to provide him with an expeditionary force to wipe out the crumbling northern horde. Many Han ministers agreed and argued that this would be using barbarians to fight barbarians for China's interest. In fact, the chief beneficiary was the southern *Shan-yü* who used China to fight his tribal foes. In AD 89, a force of Hsien-pi, Hsiung-nu, and Han troops routed the northern Hsiung-nu. The northern *Shan-yü* fled even further to the north while the majority of the northern Hsiung-nu, 100,000 tents according to Han reports, declared themselves Hsien-pi and abandoned the northern *Shan-yü*. Although the northern Hsiung-nu court appeared in Han diplomatic records as late as AD 155, it was finished as a power.[72]

The inner frontier strategy had again prevailed as the south defeated the north. Unlike the first civil war, however, this war left the steppe fragmented. The Hsiung-nu and Wu-huan now lived along the frontier with the Hsien-pi in loose control of the northern steppe. For China, the victory it helped bring about was hollow. The defeat of the northern Hsiung-nu soon opened a period of new raids by its former allies.

NOTES

1 Lattimore, *Studies in Frontier History*, pp. 97–118.
2 The history of the Hsiung-nu during the Former Han period is found in the *Shih-chi* (SC), chapter 110, of Ssu-ma Ch'ien and the *Han-shu* (HS), chapters 94 A & B, by Pan Ku. Other material relating directly to the nomads of this period may be found in the chapters on the Western Region (SC 123 and HS 96 A & B). Parts of this chapter first appeared in Barfield "Hsiung-nu imperial confederacy" for the *Journal of Asian Studies*, vol. 41, pp. 45–61.
3 SC 110:7b–8a; Watson, *Records of the Grand Historian of China*, 2:161.
4 SC 110:7b–8a; Watson, *Records*, 2:161.
5 SC 110:8b; Watson, *Records*, 2:162.
6 Cf. Dubs, *History of the Former Han Dynasty* (HFHD), 1:116–17.
7 SC 110:14a; Watson, *Records*, 2:168.
8 SC 110:9b–10b; Watson, *Records*, 2:163–4.
9 SC 123:9b–10a; Watson, *Records*, 2:271–2. A different version of this story more favorable to the Wu-sun is to be found in HS 61:4a–b. It also makes it clear that K'un-mo was the title of the Wu-sun king and not a proper name. Cf. Hulsewé, *China and Central Asia, The Early Stage: 125 BC–AD 23*, nn. 803–7.
10 SC 110:25; Watson, *Records*, 2:181.
11 SC 111:10b–11b; Watson, *Records*, 2:204–5.
12 HS 94A:35a–38b; Wylie, "History of the Heung-noo in their relations with China," 3:450–1.
13 See n. 8 above.
14 SC 110:22b; Watson, *Records*, 2:179.
15 HS 94A:27b; Wylie, "History," 3:438.

16 HS 94A:30b–31a; Wylie, "History," 3:442.
17 Lattimore, *Inner Asian Frontiers of China*, pp. 325–40.
18 Smith, "Mongol and nomadic taxation."
19 Yü, *Trade and Expansion in Han China*, pp. 41–2.
20 SC 110:11a; Watson, *Records*, 2:165.
21 HS 94A:29b; Wylie, "History," 3:440. Han measurements (cf. Loewe, *Records of the Han Administration*, vol. 1, p. 161) translate into modern equivalents as follows:

Length:	1 *p'i* = 9.24 meters	
Capacity:	1 *hu* or *shih* = 19.986 liters	
Weight:	1 *chin* = 244 grams	

22 Loewe, *Records of the Han Administration*, vol. 2, pp. 65–75.
23 Rudenko, *Die Kultur der Hsiung-nu*.
24 Yü, *Trade and Expansion*, pp. 101, 117–22.
25 SC 110:21a; Watson, *Records*, 2:176.
26 HS 96B:5b; Hulsewé, *China and Central Asia*, p. 73.
27 Gryaznov, *The Ancient Civilization of Southern Siberia*, pp. 199–219.
28 SC 111:12b–13a; Watson, *Records*, 2:207.
29 HS 94A:31b–32a; Parker, "The Turko-Scythian Tribes," 20:118–19.
30 Loewe, "The Campaigns of Han Wu-ti," pp. 80–1. The Chinese estimated the Hsiung-nu population at less than a province, or even a large district, of the Han state. Cf. HS 48:13b, SC 110:16a.
31 HS 48:12b; Yü, *Trade and Expansion*, p. 11.
32 SC 110:17b; Watson, *Records*, 2:172.
33 SC 110:2a; Watson, *Records*, 2:155.
34 Yü, *Trade and Expansion*, pp. 36–7.
35 SC 110:16a; Watson, *Records*, 2:170.
36 Lattimore, *Inner Asian Frontiers*, p. 522.
37 SC 110:16a–16b; Watson, *Records*, 2:170–1.
38 HS 48:12b–13a; Yü, *Trade and Expansion*, p. 11.
39 Cf. SC 97:1b; Watson, *Records*, 1:270.
40 Drawing on the *Han-shu* accounts, Loewe, "Campaigns," provides a detailed description and analysis of this war from which the summary account below is drawn, particularly Appendix A: "Summary of principal military events (138–90 BC)."
41 HS 61:4b; Hulsewé, *China and Central Asia*, p. 217.
42 Loewe, "Campaigns," pp. 96–101.
43 Yü, *Trade and Expansion*, pp. 61–4.
44 Cf. Yang, "Historical notes on the Chinese world order."
45 SC 112:7a; Watson, *Records*, 2:228–9.
46 HS 94B:3a–3b; Wylie, "History," 5:44.
47 SC 110:28b; Watson, *Records*, 2:186.
48 HS 94A:37a–37b; Wylie, "History," 3:450.
49 HS 94A:37a–37b; Wylie, "History," 3:450.
50 HS 94B:3a–3b; Wylie, "History," 5:44.
51 Yü, *Trade and Expansion*, pp. 14–16.
52 Dubs, *History of the Former Han Dynasty*, 1:305.
53 HS 94B:3b–5a; Wylie, "History," 5:44–7.

54 See Loewe, *Crisis and Conflict in Han China*, pp. 211–43; Hulsewé, *China and Central Asia*.
55 HS 94B:6a–6b; Wylie, "History," 5:47–8.
56 Ibid.
57 Yü, *Trade and Expansion*, p. 47.
58 Loewe, *Crisis and Conflict in Han China*, p. 90.
59 HS 94B:17a–18a; Wylie, "History," 5:62–3.
60 HS 94B:32b; Wylie, "History," 5:79. If the units referred to mean *chin* of gold it would have amounted to about 15 kg in weight or about $200,000.
61 Although Wang Mang declared a new dynasty, its history is related simply as a coda to the *Han-shu* which brings the story of the Former Han dynasty to a close.
62 HS 94B:27a; Wylie, "History," 5:74.
63 HS 94B:28b; Wylie, "History," 5:76.
64 The history of the Hsiung-nu in the Later Han period is found in the *Hou Han-shu* (HHS), chapter 89 (or 119 in those editions that place it after the biographies). Bielenstein, "The restoration of the Han dynasty," pp. 92ff covers the dynasty's foreign policy during its formative period.
65 HS 94B:10b–11a; Wylie, "History," 5:55.
66 HHS 89:7b; Parker, "The Turko-Scythian Tribes," 21:257–8. There is considerable debate about the meaning of the differences in this description of Hsiung-nu offices and those found in the *Shih-chi*. Pritsak in "Die 24 Ta-ch'en" has argued that the Chinese came to better understand the Hsiung-nu in the later Han and so revised their original description to correct it. Mori ("Reconsideration of the Hsiung-nu state") on the other hand, argues that the Later Han record is evidence of a change in the Hsiung-nu government. Much of the debate has centered on the meanings of various Chinese and Hsiung-nu titles. Without entering the morass about titles, I would side with Mori because it is clear that from the description of the "Four and Six Horns" system that it was designed to accommodate the explicitly lateral succession system that developed following the death of Hu-han-yeh (see table 2.2).
67 HHS 89:3b–4a; Parker, "Turko-Scythian Tribes," 21:255.
68 Yü, *Trade and Expansion*, p. 61.
69 Ibid., pp. 61–4.
70 HHS 89:9a; Parker, "Turko-Scythian Tribes," 21:259.
71 HHS 89:10b; Parker, ibid.
72 HHS 89:11b–18a, HHS 90:9b; Parker, "Turko-Scythian Tribes," 21:264–7; ibid., 20:93.

GLOSSARY OF KEY NAMES

MAIN TRIBES ON THE STEPPE FRONTIER

CH'IANG
proto-Tibetan tribal peoples on western border of China
little involvement with Hsiung-nu empire

HSIEN-PI
  formerly Tung-hu tribe of Manchuria ruled by Hsiung-nu empire
  became autonomous during second Hsiung-nu civil war
HSIUNG-NU
  originally from Ordos region
  united all nomads of Mongolia in single empire (210 BC–AD 48)
  split steppe between northern and southern branches (48–155)
TING-LING
  nomads north of the Hsiung-nu in the Lake Baikal area
TUNG-HU
  Eastern nomads of Manchurian steppe
  incorporated by Hsiung-nu empire
WU-HUAN
  formerly Tung-hu tribe in Liao-hsi steppe
  abused by Hsiung-nu and China
WU-SUN
  broke from Hsiung-nu empire during middle of second century BC
  established autonomous state in land abandoned by Yüeh-chih
YÜEH-CHIH
  Western nomads of the Altai region
  displaced by Hsiung-nu
  Greater Yüeh-chih move west to trans-Oxus
  Lesser Yüeh-chih move southeast to Tibetan borderland

KEY TRIBAL FIGURES

CHIH-CHIH
  northern *Shan-yü* of Hsiung-nu (r. 56–36 BC)
  loser of first civil war
HU-HAN-YEH
  southern *Shan-yü* of Hsiung-nu (r. 58–31 BC)
  winner of first civil war who reunited Hsiung-nu
  accepted "tributary system" of foreign relations with China
K'UN-MO
  founder of Wu-sun state (circa 150 BC)
LAO-SHANG (Chi-Chü)
  son of Mao-tun, *Shan-yü* of Hsiung-nu (r. 174–160 BC)
  completed expansion of Hsiung-nu empire
MAO-TUN
  founder of the Hsiung-nu empire
  Shan-yü of the Hsiung-nu (r. 209–174 BC)
PI
  first Hsiung-nu southern *Shan-yü* (r. 48–56) in second civil war
  created military alliance with China
P'U-NU
  first Hsiung-nu northern *Shan-yü* (r. 46–?83) in second civil war

WU-YEN-CH'Ü-TI
Hsiung-nu *Shan-yü* (r. 60–58 BC) who provoked first civil war

DYNASTIES IN CHINA

CH'IN (221–207 BC)
united China in single empire for first time
completed Great Wall to keep out nomads
expelled Hsiung-nu from border,

FORMER HAN (206 BC–AD 8)
reunited China after civil war following collapse of Ch'in
Hsiung-nu nomads most powerful external threat
foreign policy oscillated between appeasement and aggression

HSIN (9–23)
short dynasty of Wang Mang
attempt to make the Hsiung-nu true tributaries failed

LATER HAN (25–220)
restored Han line
allied itself with border nomad tribes

KEY CHINESE FIGURES

HSÜAN
Former Han emperor (r. 73–49 BC)
established "tributary system" for dealing with nomads

KAO-TSU
Former Han dynastic founder (r. 206–195 BC)
established treaty and marriage relations with Hsiung-nu

KUANG-WU
first emperor of restored Later Han dynasty (r. 25–57)
re-established tributary relations with nomads
ceded control of border to nomads
allied China with southern Hsiung-nu

WU-TI
Former Han emperor (r. 140–87 BC)
launched series of wars in failed attempt to destroy Hsiung-nu

SHIH-HUANG-TI
first unifier of China
founder of Ch'in dynasty (r. 221–210 BC)

WANG MANG
founder of Hsin dynasty (r. 9–23)
renewed hostility with nomads

3

The Collapse of Central Order

The Rise of Foreign Dynasties

The Hsien-pi took control of the northern steppe after the defeat of the northern Hsiung-nu, but in almost every respect their empire was a secondary phenomenon. They inherited a position they were incapable of creating themselves. From China's point of view the Hsien-pi appeared similar to the Hsiung-nu with whom the Han had long dealt. Yet in many ways the Hsien-pi were different, and these differences had a profound effect on their relationship with China. Unlike the Hsiung-nu, the Hsien-pi had a weak confederacy with little supratribal leadership. In the Hsien-pi political structure authority was vested in petty chieftains, who only occasionally united under a charismatic leader. This occurred but once, under T'an-shih-huai (r. 156–80), and even he never institutionalized his power, so central control ended at his death.[1]

The radically different political structures of the Hsiung-nu and Hsien-pi stemmed from two sources. The Hsien-pi had been dominated by the Hsiung-nu since the destruction of the Tung-hu. They were unknown to Former Han historians, though they were the northern neighbors of the Wu-huan, a tribe the Han knew well. As part of the Hsiung-nu empire, where supratribal leadership rested with the *Shan-yü* and his twenty-four "Ten Thousand Horsemen" officials, Hsien-pi leadership was confined to the chieftain level. Some supratribal leadership might have developed had the Hsien-pi been forced to fight to overthrow Hsiung-nu hegemony, but this was not the case. The Hsien-pi gained autonomy by default at the outbreak of the second Hsiung-nu civil war. When the imperial Hsiung-nu leadership withdrew, the remaining political organization was a loose confederation of petty chieftains. Within the tributary system, Han records of AD 108 counted 120 such small Hsien-pi tribes as compared to one or two dozen tribal groups whose names appeared in Han reports for the whole steppe under the Hsiung-nu. This does not mean that there was a proliferation of new tribes following the breakup of the Hsiung-nu empire, rather that power to conduct foreign relations had devolved onto the petty chieftains, who had previously handled only local affairs.

The Hsien-pi showed no inclination toward centralization even after they won freedom and increased their power. They retained a radically different concept of government than the Hsiung-nu and other steppe tribes to the west, like the Wu-sun and Yüeh-chih. This eastern, or Manchurian pattern, stressed an egalitarian political system with no hereditary succession or hierarchical clan structure, in sharp contrast to the ranked clans, strictly hereditary leadership, and central authority of the Hsiung-nu. While the basic political structure of the Tung-hu is not recorded, the tribes who succeeded them in the region all followed this pattern. Han descriptions of the Wu-huan and Hsien-pi note that they had both a common origin and language, as well as a similar political organization:

They always elected the bravest and the sturdiest of chieftains and those who could best decide between litigants, trespassers, and disputants. Each settlement had a petty chieftain, but the position was not hereditary. Several hundred or a thousand home-steads might form a community; and whenever the head chieftain had any orders, a piece of carved wood served as evidence of authority, although there was no writing system to convey messages from place to place. They had no continuous family names, but the personal names of their most valiant chieftains were used as family names. From the chieftain on down, each man had his own flocks and herds and managed his own property: no man served another. . . . If there were mutual murders the tribes were told to avenge themselves and if vengeance went on indefinitely, they would apply to the head chief to arrange matters.[2]

The Hsien-pi could not have extracted huge benefits from China, being in such a disorganized state, without the previous work of the Hsiung-nu. The Han had the ability to turn away or defeat petty chieftains who, alone, could do little for or against China. It was the unified military and diplomatic pressure exerted by the Hsiung-nu in the Former Han period that established the *ho-ch'in* subsidy system, gained trade privileges, and ultimately instituted the funding of the lucrative tributary system. As long as the Hsiung-nu ran the system, petty Hsien-pi chieftains could participate only through the Hsiung-nu government, which prevented them from negotiating directly with China. Gifts and trade were all controlled by the *Shan-yü*, who then redistributed them to the steppe tribes. The collapse of the Hsiung-nu empire gave the Wu-huan and Hsien-pi a chance to negotiate for themselves. The tributary system shifted from a closed system, in which the *Shan-yü* controlled the benefits, to an open one, in which any chieftain who came to the Han court was rewarded. Because Hsien-pi political organization was so different from that of the Hsiung-nu, a new pattern of relations, more hostile to China, eventually evolved.

The Later Han established contact with the Hsien-pi in AD 49. Five years later, two chieftains presented themselves at court and received gifts. Soon these and other Hsien-pi chieftains agreed to attack the northern Hsiung-nu in return for a bounty paid on heads delivered to the Han frontier. This became a profitable business, with Hsien-pi flocking to markets in Liao-tung to exchange heads, receive gifts, and trade for Chinese goods. The annual subsidy to the

Hsien-pi was 270 million cash, almost three times the amount provided to the southern Hsiung-nu. This did not mean that the Hsien-pi were the most powerful tribe at this time. Until 87, the northern Hsiung-nu, although not part of the tributary system, remained the major power on the steppe. As late as 130, some Hsien-pi tribes were still performing military service for the Hsiung-nu. It was the continuing civil war that made the Hsien-pi valuable strategic allies for China and the southern Hsiung-nu against the northern Hsiung-nu.

The fragmentation of Hsien-pi leadership itself caused their help to be so expensive. If the Han wished to hire the Hsien-pi it had to provide gifts and subsidies to hundreds of petty chieftains. In dealing with the Hsiung-nu tributary benefits had been a wholesale affair, with the *Shan-yü* taking responsibility for the entire steppe; the subsidies to the Hsien-pi were at the retail level. The cost was also higher because the Han administration was not just buying border peace, but financing Hsien-pi attacks against the northern Hsiung-nu.

The open tributary system tended to preserve and encourage continued fragmentation of the Hsien-pi. If the Han court was willing to deal directly with chieftains of a hundred or a thousand households, why would any petty leader feel it necessary to subordinate himself permanently to another ruler? The Hsien-pi confederation was normally voluntary and supervised by an elected leader, but this leader did not have a monopoly on tributary benefits. Lacking control over his nominal subordinates in external affairs, such chieftains also had little internal power, as illustrated by the fact that murders were normally resolved by resorting to blood feud, in sharp contrast to the stern Hsiung-nu law which demanded the death penalty for anyone who drew his sword in peacetime. This fragmented structure was attractive to war-weary northern Hsiung-nu tribal leaders. After the defeat of the northern *Shan-yü* it was a simple matter to declare themselves Hsien-pi. As the Hsien-pi lacked any strong supratribal government, such a declaration freed the northern Hsiung-nu leaders from any further obligations to either northern or southern *Shan-yü* and at the same time increased their own autonomy and authority. The mass defection of the northern Hsiung-nu to the Hsien-pi in 89 prevented the southern *Shan-yü* from uniting the steppe.

During the reigns of Emperor Ming and Chang (58–88) they [the Hsien-pi] kept to the line of the Great Wall and there was no trouble. During the time of the Emperor Ho (89–105) . . . the Hsiung-nu were routed. The northern *Shan-yü* took flight and the Hsien-pi moved in and occupied his land. The remainder of the Hsiung-nu who did not go with him still numbered over 100,000 tents and all styled themselves Hsien-pi. The Hsien-pi gradually grew in power from this time.[3]

The fall of the northern Hsiung-nu was not the result of the rise of a Hsien-pi empire. On the contrary, the demise of the northern Hsiung-nu gave rise to Hsien-pi power.

THE OUTER FRONTIER STRATEGY RETURNS

"To make use of barbarians to attack barbarians is to the advantage of the state."[4] So said a military advisor to the Han court in 88 after approving a campaign to destroy the northern Hsiung-nu. The war was a military success, but soon brought trouble to China, for it radically changed the balance of power on the steppe, which had directed nomads' attention at each other rather than at China. The major proponent of the war had been the southern *Shan-yü*, who had hoped to reunify the steppe. He failed in his aim. Instead, large numbers of northern Hsiung-nu joined the Hsien-pi, creating a new and volatile situation among the nomads. Those northern Hsiung-nu who had surrendered or had been captured by the southerners were not easy to control. They immediately began to participate in southern Hsiung-nu succession politics, inciting raids on China in 93. As long as the southern *Shan-yü* received Han help in the civil war, the tribes under his command were peaceful and cooperative. By using the inner frontier strategy he gained material wealth and military aid from China throughout the course of the forty-year war with the north. The reversion to hostility by the southern *Shan-yü* toward China marked a return to the outer frontier strategy of raiding China and alternating peace or war to increase Han benefits to the Hsiung-nu. When the civil war ended, an alliance with China had far less to offer the *Shan-yü* than a policy of extortion.

The Hsien-pi also opened hostilities with China. The large payments from the Han tributary system had been conditioned on their strategic importance in the steppe civil war. With the war's end, the Hsien-pi lost their lucrative head-hunting contracts. In addition, the defecting Hsiung-nu had swelled their ranks and increased the need for Han trade and subsidies. After aiding the Chinese in a postwar attack on the southern Hsiung-nu, the Hsien-pi took to raiding, first in Liao-tung in 97, and then throughout the frontier area. Han peace offers and expanded tributary benefits brought about a short-lived peace in 108, but "after this they sometimes submitted or revolted, or were again at war with the Hsiung-nu and Wu-huan."[5]

The Hsien-pi adopted the outer frontier strategy developed by the Hsiung-nu: violently raiding for loot to terrify the Han court, alternating peace and war to increase subsidies or trade, and refusing to occupy Han land. There was a significant difference in the implementation of the policy, however. The Hsiung-nu *Shan-yü* used raids as a means to get new and better treaty terms. Raids and then envoys from the *Shan-yü* calling for peace came in rapid succession. Once the treaty benefits were provided, the number of raids declined substantially and the years of peace between China and the Hsiung-nu eventually outnumbered those of war. As the Hsien-pi gained power, they relied far more on raids than on treaty benefits and were more often at war with China than at peace. Around 167, they even turned down a generous peace offer proposed by the Han, something the Hsiung-nu would never have done. For the Hsien-pi, raids were an end in themselves.

The more violent policy toward China was a consequence of the lack of strong central leadership and the fragmented political structure among the Hsien-pi. Their paramount chieftain held a non-hereditary rank with little inherent power – the strength or weakness of the position was dependent largely on the personality of its occupant. The clearest way to achieve power was by displaying military and political talent, and, once having gained supremacy, Hsien-pi rulers found that the best strategy for preserving unity was to raid

China. This provided instant rewards for the participants and served to dampen internal divisions. The Hsien-pi's first attacks on China were prompted by the need to integrate the newly arrived Hsiung-nu. There was no better way to do this than by combined military action.

Warfare against China also increased the power and importance of the head chieftain, who organized and led large-scale attacks. Peace treaties, on the other hand, tended to work against his interests for, unlike the Hsiung-nu *Shan-yü*, he had no monopoly on the redistribution of tributary benefits. From the start of their relationship with the Han court, each petty Hsien-pi chief had been entitled to establish his own direct link with China and in times of peace benefits flowed directly into their hands. This naturally undermined the ability of the head chieftain to enforce his authority by controlling access to Chinese goods. In times of war, however, a strong leader could dominate his subordinates by determining who would get to take part in the most lucrative raids, and by using his military power to threaten those who were recalcitrant. Hence, Chinese peace proposals offering to reopen the tributary system were rejected by powerful Hsien-pi leaders. Whereas tributary benefits increased the central power of the Hsiung-nu, they had the opposite impact among the Hsien-pi. The Hsien-pi were therefore most receptive to China's peace proposals when they lacked a strong leader and, not surprisingly, were most hostile during the twenty-year rule of T'an-shih-huai, who united the steppe and became the most powerful Hsien-pi ruler in their history.

The rise of T'an-shih-huai exemplifies the importance of individual achievement in the Hsien-pi system of elected leadership. Though of illegitimate birth, while still a youth he impressed his fellow tribesmen by his strength and ability. In 156, at the age of twenty-three, he was elected overall chief of the Hsien-pi. Within a year he mounted a major raid on China and returned almost every year thereafter, employing an organized strategy of intensive pillage and withdrawal to the steppe. During one six-month period in 177, T'an-shih-huai mounted thirty raids along the entire length of the Han frontier. Between raids on China he attacked other nomadic tribes until the Hsien-pi controlled all of the steppe territory formerly ruled by Mao-tun.

T'an-shih-huai organized the empire into eastern, western, and central sectors. Each tribe or group of tribes had its own leaders who owed their personal allegiance to T'an-shih-huai. There was no imperial state structure resembling that of the Hsiung-nu, with its ranked kings and Ku-tu marquises who helped administer the Hsiung-nu state and who were loyal to the office of the *Shan-yü*, not just its current occupant.

Even at the height of his power, T'an-shih-huai never attempted to negotiate a peace treaty with China. He exterminated all the Han armies sent against him.

The court was in great distress at this, but was powerless to check it, so an envoy was sent to carry a seal and sash to T'an-shih-huai who was created a king [the highest Han rank] and to whom offers of a treaty relationship were made. T'an-shih-huai declined all these offers and raided more vigorously than ever.[6]

Lucrative tributary benefits had previously induced the Hsiung-nu to settle on peace terms, but now this policy failed because the Han did not realize that

Hsien-pi leaders relied on war to maintain themselves in power. T'an-shih-huai control of the Hsien-pi was personal. Successful warfare reinforced his charismatic aura and discouraged rivals from challenging his preeminence. The fragile nature of such a political system became evident when T'an-shih-huai died around 180. His son immediately claimed his father's position, but was deserted by half the tribes. They refused to accept his leadership, so "from T'an-shih-huai's death the different chieftains were always at war with each other."[7]

China seems to have learned something about Hsien-pi politics from this experience. When another Hsien-pi leader, K'o-pi-neng, rose to power, China eventually sent an assassin instead of an army or envoys. K'o-pi-neng was murdered in 235 and the Hsien-pi were again divided.

THE FALL OF HAN – AN END OF TWO IMPERIAL TRADITIONS

That the unification of the nomads and the unification of China occurred almost simultaneously is unlikely to have been coincidental. Likewise the destruction of China's economy and its fragmentation could not but have direct repercussions on the steppe. A nomadic chieftain might by his military prowess unite the steppe, but keeping a steppe empire intact demanded resources that only China could supply. The Hsiung-nu civil wars showed that when the nomads were forced to depend on their own resources their large-scale political structures collapsed. Even T'an-shih-huai's empire depended on continuous raiding to keep it supplied and the steppe fragmented following his death.

In the period before the fall of Han (circa 190) the nomads relied on an inner or outer frontier strategy to exploit China's wealth. Thus after 190 there could be no unity on the steppe until north China was again stable. This was so because nomad strategy required certain preconditions in order to function properly:

1   A prosperous and populous north China.
2   An effective administrative system within China.
3   A government policy dominated by civilian Chinese bureaucrats.

These conditions were best met when China was united, internally at peace, and under native Chinese rule. Over the course of imperial history disintegration or unification in China was simultaneous with a similar phenomenon on the steppe.

Let us examine the preconditions for stability more closely.

1 *A prosperous and populous north China*   The nomads' relationship with China occurred along the northern frontier. By raiding this region, or by exploiting the tributary system, they extracted wealth to support their empires. The goods they obtained were produced by the farmers and artisans within the Han empire. No such surplus wealth could be extracted if the economic base of north China was destroyed and its population greatly reduced. Try as they

might, the nomads would soon discover there was very little to extort from a region of abandoned villages or from a population racked by famine.

2 *An effective administrative system in China* The outer frontier strategy required that the nomads not occupy Chinese land because it would expose the weakness of their numbers. Throughout the Han period the Hsiung-nu, and later the Hsien-pi, depended on the Chinese government to organize the production of needed goods. In general steppe nomads avoided responsibility for any type of sedentary administration. The whole outer frontier strategy was based on terrifying or wooing the Chinese imperial government to extract the wealth of the land and deliver its fruits to the nomads. Even nomads like the Hsien-pi indirectly depended on the Han administration – for unless the Chinese government provided aid and relief to the invaded territories, there would not be enough to support annual attacks. When China was united the nomads accepted its administration as a natural condition, for the nomads had no real conception of the labor involved in producing the massive quantities of goods they demanded, nor did they understand the mechanics of the Han government that produced such revenue. When the empire broke down and Chinese rulers were unable to support themselves, let alone frontier parasites, the stream of wealth dried up and no amount of threats or raids could change the situation.

3 *A government dominated by civilian Chinese bureaucrats* The outer frontier strategy's success depended on eliciting a predictable and favorable response to the nomads' demands. The Chinese government had to be willing to provide for the nomads' needs in preference to declaring war on them. As we noted earlier, civilian officials trained in the Confucian tradition generally were opposed to offensive military schemes because they disrupted the state and generated opportunities for the advancement of merchants and soldiers. These advisors preferred static defenses and liberal benefits in order to avoid war on the steppe. They cited the wars of Ch'in Shih Huang-ti and Han Wu-ti as examples of bad policy for dealing with an area China could never incorporate or easily pacify. Supporters of more aggressive military policies were usually accused of oppressing the population, wasting China's wealth, and allowing the rise of unvirtuous men. These were all things to be avoided in maintaining a stable government, and if stability could be maintained by a policy of appeasement under the cloak of the tributary system, then paying off the nomads was a cheaper and better strategy than constantly fighting them. Hence when the nomads made demands on the Han court, they could expect favorable results. The policies of foreign dynasties that succeeded Han were quite different in approach and, as we will see, created great difficulties for the nomads. However, traditional Chinese histories written by Confucian-trained scholars provided models of proper conduct and policy in government; for such scholars the histories of foreign dynasties simply provided negative examples of how a government and foreign policy should be conducted.

It has often been assumed that the fall of the Han dynasty, like the fall of Rome, was the product of barbarian invasion. In both cases, alien kingdoms were founded on the ruins of a formerly unified empire. For China, however, this assumption is not valid. The nomads on the steppe did not play a key role and showed remarkably little intervention in the Chinese civil wars that followed the collapse of Ch'in, the fall of Wang Mang, or dissolution of Later Han. The rebellions themselves were the results of internal problems and the revolts erupted inside China, not along the frontier. The foreign dynasties that are associated with the collapse of Han did not appear until around 300, more than a hundred years after Chinese warlords had shattered China's unity themselves. Only after these warlord states themselves collapsed did the "barbarians" move to pick up the pieces in north China.[8]

The fall of the Later Han dynasty started with the Yellow Turban rebellion of 184, which was an internal affair, beginning in eastern China where it drew its support.[9] Mismanagement of the Han government fell more strongly on the central Chinese provinces than it did on the frontier because the Han government had traditionally funneled resources to the frontier in the form of subsidies and trade to prevent unrest. Imperial armies put down the rebellion but more revolts soon broke out. It soon became clear to many military commanders that the dynasty was finished and that they held the keys to power. Keeping merely the fig leaf of imperial commissions, these men became regional warlords. After the death of Emperor Ling in 188, the Han ruler was just a puppet of his warlord keepers. The dynasty continued in name only until 220 when it was formally abolished, beginning the period known as the Three Kingdoms.

The collapse of order in China was no boon to the nomads. Civil war in China destroyed the agrarian economy so that little was left for the nomads to extract. The constant wars beginning with the Yellow Turban rebellion reduced China's population substantially. From a high of 56 million in the Later Han period, postwar accounts lamented that only a tenth survived. While this assertion is undoubtedly an exaggeration, it was nevertheless true that within a single lifetime China experienced a severe economic and population collapse. From stable political order and prosperity China fell into anarchy and poverty. Formerly wealthy cities like Ch'ang-an were deserted. Famine and disease ravaged the land in the wake of roving armies. Even the emperor's own court was at times reduced to gathering wild plants for lack of grain. This was truly a dark age, but it was one of Chinese – not barbarian – origin.[10]

At the onset of the Yellow Turban rebellion the Hsien-pi were dominant on the steppe, although recently fragmented into a number of small groups which struggled for supremacy in the wake of the death of T'an-shih-huai in 180. The southern Hsiung-nu and the Wu-huan, both of whom were closely allied with the Han government, had suffered from T'an-shih-huai's raids in their capacity as "frontier guarding barbarians," buffers between China proper and the steppe. When revolts arose inside China, the Han government saw the nomads as both a danger to the dynasty and as an important defense. This contradictory attitude stemmed from fear that the nomads would join in a general attack on China combined with a dependency on foreign frontier troops to aid the dynasty in putting down trouble.

For this reason the northern frontier remained relatively better off than other parts of China. The Wu-huan and Hsiung-nu benefited from direct aid while the Hsien-pi were active smugglers, when they were not engaged in raiding. In 177, an official complained that the border had become so porous that iron, a traditionally prohibited item, was being illegally sold to the Hsien-pi. Indeed, when the Hsien-pi were later hired as mercenaries to fight against Ch'iang rebels in the west, they demanded large payments in contraband goods. When conditions were not to their liking, they turned to looting.[11]

The unrest in central China increased the importance of the northern frontier. Prosperity there had been supported by a program of subsidies. The cost of this program was immense and it had been financed by taxing the very provinces of central China that were caught up in the rebellion. When the central government was no longer able to get subsidies to the border, local officials drained their own provincial resources to maintain the peace. The border regions therefore remained areas of surplus in the midst of growing famine in China proper and began to attract immigrants. This process was seen most vividly in the northeastern frontier province of Yu where the governor, Liu Yü, reorganized the local economy to cope with the growing anarchy to his south.

In the past, Yu province had to deal with people from outside the frontiers. The expenses were extremely great, and every year more than two hundred million cash was taken from the taxation of Ch'ing and Chi provinces to make up [the deficit of Yu province]. At this time [circa 190] all communications were cut off, the grain transport could not arrive, so Yü wore old clothes and rope sandals, had only a single dish of meat at any meal, and held it essential to maintain a lenient administration. He encouraged the farming of mulberries and he opened a prosperous trading market with the barbarians of Shang-ku, and brought surplus salt and iron from Yü-yang. The people enjoyed the harvest . . . and more than a million gentry and commoners of Ch'ing and the Hsü fled from the troubles and came to Yü. He took them in and looked to them with warm sympathy, settled them and set them in a livelihood. All the refugees forgot their exile.[12]

Pursuing their usual policy, the nomads initially remained aloof from the civil war. Yet both the Hsiung-nu and the Wu-huan had for some time provided auxiliary troops to the Later Han government, and the Hsien-pi were also informally recruited. As its troubles grew, the dynasty was forced to seek significant amounts of unreliable tribal military aid. For example, when a rebellion began in the northwestern frontier province of Liang in 184, the Han administration sent 3,000 Wu-huan to fight there. These troops were not adequately supplied for the long journey and they revolted, looting Chi province before returning home. The Han government turned to the Hsiung-nu for troops to fight in central China in 188, but when the *Shan-yü* tried to raise this levy the Hsiung-nu became "afraid that the demand for troops would never end." They killed their *Shan-yü* and placed his son on the throne. After these revolts, both the Hsiung-nu and Wu-huan leaders opened negotiations with rival warlords in the north.[13]

In terms of frontier relations the most noteworthy aspect of the nomads' involvement with various Chinese warlords was that they always acted as junior partners. In theory the nomads could have built their own coalitions in which they were politically dominant. In practice they preferred a secondary role in which they sought alliances with strong frontier leaders who could act as new patrons, and provide the nomads with the benefits of luxury goods, grain, and manufactured products formerly distributed by the central government. This attitude can be traced back to the old outer frontier strategy which had left the nomads deliberately free of sedentary governmental responsibilities. The warlords needed all the military force they could muster, especially fast-moving cavalry, and they were more than willing to offer handsome rewards.

As the war developed, the Wu-huan and the Hsiung-nu allied themselves with Yüan Shao, a major frontier warlord. Yüan Shao had long been familiar with the tribal leaders of the nomads and he put his connections to good use in building his army. Yüan Shao's major rival was Ts'ao Ts'ao who controlled the puppet Han court. Both recognized that a nomad alliance could tip the balance in the battle for north China. However Yüan Shao died in 203 and his forces were divided among his relatives, greatly weakening the Yüan political position.

The Wu-huan were of critical importance to the Yüan family, and Ts'ao Ts'ao used every means possible to neutralize them. When the Wu-huan assembled 5,000 cavalry troops for the Yüan army, Ts'ao Ts'ao sent an envoy to the Wu-huan king in an attempt to persuade him that such support would be unwise. During the formal audience with Ts'ao's ambassador, the Wu-huan leader, Su-p'u-yen, asked him to explain the confusing pattern of authority in China, noting that:

Once before Lord Yüan said that he had received the command of the Son of Heaven to make me *Shan-yü*. Now Lord Ts'ao says that he will tell the Son of Heaven and have me made *Shan-yü* properly. And besides all this, there is an envoy with insignia from Liao-tung. Which is the right one?[14]

As the Han emperor and his seals fell captive to one warlord or another the question of the legitimacy of new titles was constantly debated, but such issues of arcane protocol appeared mysterious to the frontier tribes. Why, the Wu-huan wondered, should their leader need to be twice declared *Shan-yü* by the Han government? Ts'ao's envoy had a ready, albeit complex, answer that involved the question of using the imperial seal to grant titles. He claimed the Yüan grant was invalid, but, in recognition of the importance of the Wu-huan, Ts'ao Ts'ao would now bestow a proper title on their leader. The envoy from Liao-tung (a representative of the Kung-sun family of warlords), had no business granting titles to anyone, Ts'ao's ambassador claimed, because it was just a "miserable commandery." When the Liao-tung envoy raised objections to this slur, Ts'ao's ambassador attempted to behead him. Su-p'u-yen intervened to prevent bloodshed and then heard Ts'ao's real message, "telling them who would win and who would lose and the right course to follow." Impressed, the Wu-huan king temporarily discharged the troops he had raised.[15]

This incident revealed much about the disorder in the crumbling Han state and the changing character of China's foreign relations. Civilian ministers in the Confucian tradition, when dominant in the court, had prided themselves on maintaining a proper decorum in dealing with foreigners to impress them with the sophistication of the Han civilization. The new warlords were men of a very different stamp – "men of talent rather than virtue," was the historical cliché used to describe them. Attempting to behead another envoy in a formal audience was ill bred, to say the least. It was also significant that Su-p'u-yen was offered the title of *Shan-yü*, a Hsiung-nu rather than Han rank. Moreover competing for Wu-huan support went beyond the Later Han policy of "using barbarians to fight barbarians." Barbarian support was now needed to help Chinese fight other Chinese.

Ts'ao Ts'ao recognized that the Wu-huan were the military bulwark of the Yüan cause. In order to eliminate them as a threat, he marched against the Wu-huan in 207, planning to ambush them in their grazing grounds far to the north. This was a risky venture in which Ts'ao's lightly armed and mobile army had to rely on the speed and unexpectedness of their attack to catch the nomads by surprise. If it failed, his senior advisors warned, this isolated force would be completely destroyed. When Ts'ao's attack was prematurely discovered, he engaged the Wu-huan in a pitched battle at Po-lang Mountain. The nomads suffered a great defeat, including the loss of T'a-tun and their other major chiefs, and Ts'ao Ts'ao incorporated the remaining Wu-huan into his army. He also gained control of a large number of Chinese families, previously under Yüan control. The power of the Yüan house was broken, and, after its leaders sought refuge in Liao-tung, the Kung-sun warlord sent their heads as presents to Ts'ao Ts'ao. The nomads had picked the losing side in the battle for the north.[16]

The warlords of this period provided the nomads with examples of a new type of Chinese leader, one who was aggressive and who put military affairs ahead of civil administration. These warlords were field commanders leading their own troops in the battle. In this respect they were more similar to tribal leaders of the steppe, who were expected to take an active public leadership role, than they were to the traditional Han emperors, who rarely left the confines of the court and who relied on officials to develop policy. Even their tactics smacked of the frontier. Ts'ao Ts'ao's attack on the Wu-huan violated practically every norm of classical Chinese military thinking. His emphasis on surprise, fast-moving troops, and seeking a vulnerable time to strike at the enemy, incorporated the same tactics employed by the nomads themselves. Warlords like Ts'ao Ts'ao were even greater risk-takers than the nomad chieftains. Few nomad leaders would have risked their whole fortune on the uncertainty of a pitched battle if it could be avoided by a strategic retreat. Ts'ao Ts'ao himself later admitted it had been foolhardy to risk both life and state on a battle so far from China's frontier. That he took the risk is evidence that the nomads were faced with Chinese leaders more dangerous than any since the Ch'in dynasty. In these chaotic times, the gap between the militaristic Chinese warlords and nomadic tribal leaders was narrowed. For once communications between the two worlds was direct and based on similar principles of military power and economic aggrandizement.

After Ts'ao Ts'ao had taken control of north China he imposed more discipline on the Hsiung-nu and Wu-huan. In 216, there was concern about a renewed threat from the Hsiung-nu:

Before this the southern Hsiung-nu had lived a long time within the borders. They were much the same as the registered [Chinese] inhabitants, but they did not send in tribute or tax. Many people were afraid that their numbers were becoming too great and that it would be increasingly difficult to keep them under control.[17]

Ts'ao Ts'ao's solution was a policy of indirect rule. The *Shan-yü* was held hostage at court while his brother, the Wise King of the Right, looked after local affairs. The tribes were further separated into five divisions, each with its own tribal leader under the supervision of a Chinese political agent.

This policy could be implemented because the Hsiung-nu had such a deeply ingrained system of hereditary rulers and a fixed pattern of succession. By holding the *Shan-yü* hostage, dividing the tribes, and providing the *Shan-yü* and other members of the Hsiung-nu elite with annual allotments of silk, cash, and grain, Ts'ao Ts'ao's new Wei dynasty hoped to control the Hsiung-nu with a minimum of expense. He could also then depend on their loyalty to China and use tribal troops for his own wars. Of course, the Hsiung-nu were no longer the supreme power of the steppe as they had been in earlier days; they were now merely border tribes. Nevertheless, both the core tribes of the Hsiung-nu and their imperial organization still existed. This, and the fact they were on Chinese land, made them a constant concern to China. No other people had a continuous lineage of leaders going back to Ch'in times, and the ability of the Hsiung-nu to rise from defeat was legendary.

Ts'ao Ts'ao's policy toward the Wu-huan was different. Unlike the Hsiung-nu they lacked a tradition of hereditary leadership and were prone to division. In 216, for example, the Wu-huan in Tai were split into three groups, each with a chieftain who styled himself "*Shan-yü*." They caused considerable trouble until an experienced frontier administrator, P'ei Ch'ien, arrived. Refusing to use military force, he relied on political manipulation to quiet the frontier. This posed a far more complicated task than controlling the Hsiung-nu through their own developed political organization. It required skill to pacify such a large number of petty rulers. In particular P'ei Ch'ien warned that oscillations in policy, such as loosening up and then suddenly reimposing authority, would generate rebellion. His successor did just that and threw the northeast into war. Ts'ao Ch'ang, the Wei founder's son, then led an army that defeated the Wu-huan in 218 and destroyed the last remnants of their power.

Present at the destruction of the Wu-huan was K'o-pi-neng, a new and powerful Hsien-pi chieftain. As usual the Hsien-pi were not united, but because K'o-pi-neng's territory was close to the frontier he was the most significant leader for China. Impressed by the Wei army, K'o-pi-neng negotiated trade relations with the Wei administration which was in need of horses for its southern campaigns. In 222, 3,000 Hsien-pi drove 70,000 head of cattle and horses to the frontier to trade. The Wei also wanted to avoid trouble with the other Hsien-pi and so gave all their leaders kingly titles.[18]

Trouble with the Hsien-pi was probably inevitable given the history of their relationship with China. Wei policies to recruit Hsien-pi tribal leaders to man the northern frontier created tension, as well as the periodic desertion of their frontier guards from one side to another, involved the dynasty in tribal rivalries.

In 233, for example, K'o-pi-neng incited one of these tribes to rebel and join him in the north. Wei troops chased them onto the steppe where the Chinese force was destroyed. This defeat induced all the border Hsien-pi tribes to defect to K'o-pi-neng and they attacked the very settlements they had formerly defended. The main army of Wei was rushed to the frontier but K'o-pi-neng retreated north of the Gobi Desert and avoided battle.

In the end, the Hsien-pi chieftains refusal to accept K'o-pi-neng's authority broke up the coalition. After bestowing gifts upon them, the Wei welcomed its returning frontier guards back to the very provinces they had so recently looted. The Wei feared that if K'o-pi-neng's strength grew it would lose control over the frontier. With an astute understanding of Hsien-pi political structure the Wei did not again employ an army on the steppe. Instead it sent an assassin: K'o-pi-neng was murdered in 235 and the Hsien-pi dissolved into their component tribes. Unlike the Hsiung-nu who had loyalty to a line of *Shan-yüs*, a Hsien-pi ruler's power was personal and charismatic. His followers' loyalty, therefore, ended at his death.

This lack of unity among the Hsien-pi would have been a distinct liability facing a strong and united China. In those times, small tribes either fell under the influence of a central authority on the steppe or defected to China. Independent frontier states could not exist without being crushed by one side or the other. The small-scale Hsien-pi political organization, however, now became an asset because in the Three Kingdoms period a weakened China was unable to police its own frontier, let alone wipe out rivals, and the steppe was also fragmented. Small tribes struck their own bargains with China, laid claim to various frontier districts and, for the first time, began to assume administrative responsibilities. For reasons to be examined in the next section, these new hybrid states along the northern frontier became seed beds for the foreign dynasties that were to rule north China for the next three centuries and drastically alter the relationship between the nomads and China.

SYSTEMIC COLLAPSE: THE SIXTEEN KINGDOMS PERIOD

The era of the Sixteen Kingdoms (301–439) was a watershed in China's relations with its northern frontier neighbors because, for the first time, foreign dynasties founded states in north China. Yet this period has traditionally been one of the most neglected areas of study, for "barbarian" kingdoms held little significance for Chinese scholars except as a dark night separating the sunset of Han from the sunrise of T'ang, two of China's most glorious periods. This bias is compounded, however, by the very real problems involved in attempting to bring any analytical order to the seemingly endless series of China's foreign dynasties and their conflicts. The major requirement for such an analysis is the acceptance of the foreign dynasties on their own terms, and not as mere deviations from Chinese norms. In this time of anarchy, a new type of political structure emerged which was quite different from the imperial confederacies of the central steppe. It was a type of dual organization that could accommodate both the organization of tribal peoples and a Chinese style government within a single state. Although not fully developed in this period, it became the model for the successively more powerful foreign dynasties, such as the Khitan Liao and Jurchen Chin which followed the collapse of the T'ang, and the Manchu Ch'ing dynasty which controlled China after the collapse of the Ming.[19]

The traditional view of the fall of the Han dynasty assumes that it was overrun by tribal peoples pressing at its frontiers. It portrays the border tribes as merely waiting for China's defenses to weaken before beginning wars of conquest that would establish their direct control over north China. Almost by default, the century between the fall of Han and the first foreign conquests has been encapsulated to give the impression of an immediate cause and effect. Yet we noted earlier that the nomads had refused to play a primary role in the civil wars that established the Three Kingdoms.

The nomads sought out new patrons as the Han collapsed. They had no intention of running China themselves, although tribes like the Hsiung-nu had lived within Chinese frontiers since the middle of the Later Han period. During the Three Kingdoms period, the Wei government replaced the Han as the source of trade goods and direct aid. The Wei attempted to keep China's frontier secure by employing a policy of indirect rule over tribal peoples settled inside its borders, and provided liberal subsidies and access to trade for those nomads living beyond its control. When a coup took place within China, creating a (Western) Chin dynasty in 265, there were few ripples in the north where the new dynasty maintained Wei's old policies. Indeed the presence of the Hsiung-nu *Shan-yü* at the Chin coronation ceremony was deemed a signal honor, for he, though a barbarian, was the only participant with a direct and unbroken lineage that dated back to before the beginning of the Han.

In 280 Chin forces reduced the southern state of Wu to unite China for the first time since the fall of the Later Han. Internal problems led to its swift decline from this high point. The most difficult problem was produced by an attempt to disband much of the military after the country was unified. Soldiers found themselves unemployed and many sold weapons to border tribes. More important, the extensive network of Chin princes in the provinces refused to disband their personal armies.

The northern frontier was still fairly stable but potentially quite dangerous. Foreign groups, though under Chinese administration to one degree or another, were settled in much of north China. In Kuan-chung, the old capital area of Ch'ang-an, the Ti people of Tibetan stock predominated. Around T'ai-yüan were nineteen tribes of Hsuing-nu, which still maintained their own political organization and lifestyle within China's borders. In the northeast there were a large number of Hsien-pi tribes straddling the Manchurian frontier, including the T'o-pa, Yü-wen, Tuan, T'u-fe, Ch'i-fu, and Mu-jung. In the northwest territory of Kansu towards Turkestan there was a polyglot population of diverse origins.

The Hsien-pi were the most actively hostile. They were no longer purely nomadic, but had carved territories out of the Manchurian frontier where they ruled farmers and established cities. In 281 they mounted a major attack on China, but were defeated the next year by the Chin army. Soon thereafter twenty-nine clans of Hsien-pi agreed to make peace with China, but independent groups still raided the frontier when an opportunity presented itself.

The Hsiung-nu also remained a potential threat to China because the Wei reorganization of 216 had not proved effective. Holding the *Shan-yü* hostage had merely increased the power of local leaders. In 251, a Chin official explained:

Since the *Shan-yü* came to the interior of China, the barbarians have lost their leader and need a ruler to control their unity or disunity. At present, the dynasty of the *Shan-yü* declines daily while the power of the outer territory increases daily. We must take deep seated precautions against the barbarians. . . . Clear their territory and weaken their forces, give them posthumous honors, this is the best plan for the defense of the frontier.[20]

Ultimately, the best protection of the dynasty was its position as a patron. As long as it could supply gifts and trade to the frontier, the nomad tribes would attempt to extort the dynasty but would not try to destroy it.

Beginning around 292, the Western Chin government was racked by internal conflict. Factions at court used assassination to clear away rivals. Provincial princes began to vie for power, negotiating for support from frontier tribes. These conflicts reached a climax in the decade around 300 as fratricidal battles destroyed Chin cohesion. Rather than support a Chinese warlord, the Hsiung-nu revolted in 304 and established their own state.

The decision of the Hsiung-nu to abandon their strategy of 500 years was the result of two factors. First, as the Chin state dissolved into civil war it was clear that the successors of the Han could not fulfill their roles as reliable patrons able to meet the needs of the nomads. Second, the Wei/Chin policy of keeping the *Shan-yü* as a hostage at court had produced a new type of sinicized Hsiung-nu leader who had ambitions to rule China himself.

The Hsiung-nu *Shan-yü* Liu Yüan was of the royal lineage, a descendant of Mao-tun. As a hostage at the Chin court, he had picked up a classical Chinese education. The Hsiung-nu royal lineage had long used the surname Liu, which was also the surname of the house of Han. Periodically in their history, the Hsiung-nu *Shan-yü*s had argued that as distaff relations to the old imperial house, they were in fact more entitled to the throne than the usurpers of Wei and Chin. With 50,000 troops at his disposal Liu Yüan was a formidable enemy after he declared his Latter Han dynasty (subsequently renamed Chao). Once again, the Hsiung-nu had proved to be innovators. If there were to be a foreign ruler in north China, it was appropriate to begin with a Hsiung-nu *Shan-yü*.

It is important to understand both why the Hsiung-nu established the first foreign state within China and why it was so short-lived. Previously, the Han/Hsiung-nu relationship had been relatively easy to understand because the two created a bipolar world. Marginal areas were forced to be part of the Han state or the Hsiung-nu state, each of which represented an opposite type of economy and society. We have previously shown that there was a close relationship between unity on the steppe and unity in China, the latter encouraging the former. When unity broke down, it broke down in tandem. In these unsettled times border peoples who had previously been ground between the steppe and China now had the opportunity for autonomous development.

Depending on their history and location these developments took different routes.

The developmental cycle of frontier dynasties

The succession of foreign dynasties was not the result of random conflict but a system of socio-political succession. There was direction in this process from less stable to more stable forms, but each conquest dynasty laid the groundwork for its own replacement. The cycle, which was repeated later in frontier history, had the following outline:

1 When internal order collapsed in China, the frontier people with the best opportunity of moving in were those from the central steppe, like the Hsiung-nu, who had a powerful military force organized along the lines of an imperial confederacy. Their superior military organization cleared north China of rivals, but, because they traditionally avoided holding Chinese territory in favor of extorting existing dynasties, they had little administrative experience in ruling sedentary peoples. Such dynasties could conquer, but could not effectively rule.

2 These military dynasties, though often powerful, proved short-lived and were replaced by more sophisticated frontier states that had developed a system of government which combined tribal armies with a Chinese-style bureaucracy. Such a development was the product of a couple of generations and took place in marginal regions, like Manchuria or Kansu, which were geographically isolated and not caught up in the constant warfare between rival warlord states attempting to hold north China. These "Manchurian dynasties," established by various Hsien-pi tribes, were not predators like the militaristic Hsiung-nu states, but scavengers. They had enough power to defend themselves against invasions, but demonstrated little success in conquest against the warlords to the south. It was only after the Hsiung-nu dynasties collapsed because of poor organization that the Manchurians moved in to pick up the pieces.

3 These first Manchurian dynasties survived the initial period of anarchy because they were well-organized and conservative. However, once in control of territory in north China this conservatism became a liability. Their military forces and civil bureaucracy were too large to be supported within limited boundaries without expansion, and when this type of dynasty proved unable to conquer the remaining states in north China, it eventually fell victim to a fiscal crisis that greatly weakened its defensive capabilities. This provided an opportunity for the creation of a new dynasty, which was founded by frontier clients of the first Manchurian dynasty. Militaristic, and often the most uncultured of the lot, they invaded and destroyed the top level of the reigning dynasty but were careful to maintain its dual military/bureaucratic organization. Indeed they were often welcomed by officials from the old dynasty who were attracted by the promise of expanded wealth and new jobs that would result from an aggressive policy of expansion. This third wave of invasions produced the most powerful foreign dynasties that quickly extended their rule to all of north China.

However, they were necessarily heirs to the first two types. They could not have created the dual system on their own.

The conditions favoring these different developments occurred at specific points along the frontier. The steppe tribes in the center already had their military organization in place. Used to combining into confederations under established tribal leaders, the steppe tribes could quickly recruit allies and put a formidable force in the field. In times of anarchy they were the strongest contenders for power. The heritage of their nomadic past gave them a ready made strategy of attacking weak spots, supporting themselves by pillage, and fighting to destroy their opponents rather than to induce retreat. Government under such conditions was an afterthought.

The more complex states developed in regions that were outside the main area of conflict where, in a single territory, it was possible to combine Chinese and tribal peoples. In these areas, rulers learned through experience and experimentation how to organize and run a dual system on a small scale where mistakes in policy were not fatal. The most fruitful area for such development was the Manchurian borderland in the Liao River Basin. Here, in one reasonably sized kingdom, nomadic pastoralists on the Liao-hsi steppe, Chinese farmers and cities in the Liao-tung peninsula, and forest peoples living at the Liao River head waters, could all be contained in a single state. This area was the cradle of almost all of China's stable foreign dynasties. The northwestern Kansu corridor offered a similar area for developing a mixed state, combining oasis farmers, steppe tribes, and Chinese colonists. However, the northwestern states were historically less important because they were too distant to be able to easily capture the Chinese heartland. The Manchurian frontier, though off the beaten trail, bordered on the populous north Chinese plain. When Manchurian forces moved into the heart of China, their source of support was nearby. The third wave dynasty was also from the northeast, a client group of the second. Of either steppe or forest origin they had to be within striking distance of Manchuria to seize the center of power from their rivals without having a developed political organization of their own. Ironically, their very backwardness encouraged them to adopt their rivals' political/military structure intact, which was preadapted to their needs.

HSIUNG-NU MILITARY STATES

The Hsiung-nu overwhelmed the Chin dynasty in a series of military actions. The most significant was the fall of Lo-yang and the capture of the Chin emperor in 311. The fall of Lo-yang was a shocking loss, for the great metropolis was reduced to ashes, and for the first time a capital city and an emperor were both in foreign hands. The Hsiung-nu first kept the emperor as a servant, but later executed him because they feared he might become the focus of anti-foreign plots. In 316, Ch'ang-an and a second Chin emperor fell to the Hsiung-nu. This monarch met the same fate as his predecessor. The Hsiung-nu now ruled all of north China, with the exception of the Liang state in the northwest and the Hsien-pi states in the northeast. The Chin court and much of China's elite fled south. By 325 from 60–70 percent of the Chinese upper classes had moved south.[21] They continued to proclaim themselves the only legitimate rulers of China, known as the Eastern Chin dynasty.

The Hsiung-nu conquests were extensive but their state structure did not approach the effectiveness of their military organization. Almost from the beginning they were seriously divided on the approach to take toward the conquest of China. One faction favored the establishment of a Chinese-style government, while the other pushed, in effect, for simple domination of China with as little administration as possible. At the root of this conflict was the usefulness of employing the outer frontier strategy once China's defenses had collapsed.

Liu Yüan (r. 304–10), the *Shan-yü* of the Hsiung-nu, had been educated at the Chin court, which became his model of government for the new dynasty. To this end, he established a replica of the Chin court at his capital at P'ing-ch'eng. Liu Yüan appears to have believed that by declaring himself a Chinese-style emperor he could eventually win the acceptance of the Chinese elite. In any event, his court was an island of stability that attracted many refugees, including officials, who were fleeing turmoil in other parts China. Liu Yüan's control of his tribal supporters was based on his position as *Shan-yü*. Liu Yüan had the experience and charisma to carry out this dual role, but his son and successor, Liu Ts'ung (r. 310–18) did not. Even as the Hsiung-nu conquests reached their peak during his reign, the Chin court model proved inadequate for organizing the state.

The creation of a Chinese-style state was not popular among the Hsiung-nu. While the positions of *Shan-yü* and emperor were superficially alike, in fundamental ways they were quite different. The emperor proclaimed universal rule over all subjects, while the *Shan-yü* was at the apex of a tribal system in which his people's welfare was his exclusive interest. To the Hsiung-nu, a Chinese-style court with its Chinese staff was both useless and a danger to tribal supremacy. This opposition was personified by a Hsiung-nu leader of a more old fashioned stamp, Shih Le.

Shih Le's career began after he escaped from capture by the Chinese to become a famous bandit. Times being what they were, it was an easy step from that position to a generalship under Liu Yüan. Liu Yüan's policy of conquest in China was to preserve the population intact, with an eye to its future production. Shih Le's campaigns violated this norm. He was an advocate of the traditional outer frontier strategy – the use of extreme violence, rewarding followers with loot, and supporting the army by the extortion of local populations. In 310 he raided across China, reportedly killing 100,000 Chinese. He exterminated a party of forty-eight Chin princes who fell into his hands and the next year, during the conquest of Lo-yang, he was instrumental in the city's destruction. Shih Le's further campaigns in 314–15 covered even larger amounts of territory, but like his ancestors he chose to withdraw rather than defend it.

Shih Le's methods were those of the steppe. His success generated more followers, who deserted Liu Ts'ung. Liu found it difficult to compete with Shih

Le because he was concerned with maintaining the productivity of China in the long term while Shih Le was interested only in the short term. If under Shih Le north China were reduced to pasture, so much the better for Hsiung-nu horses. Shih Le's traditional approach to warfare had great appeal. Liu Ts'ung's control was soon confined largely to western China. Shih Le hesitated to remove his rival and establish his own dynasty because Shih was not only not a member of the royal Hsiung-nu clan, but from Chieh, a western tribe of the Hsiung-nu confederacy. Like the Wu-sun, they were described as having heavy beards and light-colored hair.[22] For over 500 years, the Hsiung-nu leadership had always been drawn from the descendants of Mao-tun. Yet by establishing a Chinese-style court, the Chao rulers had diluted their strength as tribal leaders and made themselves vulnerable to challenges by figures like Shih Le. In spite of his great power, however, Shih Le moved very cautiously in replacing the old ruling lineage. At Liu Ts'ung's death in 319 Shih first refused to recognize the succession of Liu Yao, and then established his own Later Chao dynasty. Ten years later, he annexed Liu Yao's remaining territory and then murdered as many members of the Liu clan as he could find to dispose of any future rivals.

Shih Le's victory ended any chance for the Hsiung-nu to establish stable rule in China. Their military power had made them paramount, but the desire to employ destructive raiding and ignore administration was a fatal flaw. Liu Yüan had seen the need for a governmental organization, but he was unable to forge a single state that integrated the necessary bureaucracy with his tribal armies. Rivals like Shih Le were concerned only with the support of the tribal part of the state. Shih Le's death led to a brief struggle from which Shih Hu (r. 334–49) emerged victorious. He was similar to his predecessor in attitude, but now that most of north China was in his hands, administration became an acute problem. Shih Hu put huge armies in the field which were the terror of all China. The success of the Later Chao state, however, could no longer depend on the outer frontier strategy, which had required an intermediary state to rule China. Now the long running civil wars in China and the Hsiung-nu conquests had destroyed that intermediary. The nomads' extortionary tactics had killed the victim.

In order to continue ruling China, Shih Hu had to pattern together an ad hoc administration. He could not trust the Chinese who were the victims of his policies, nor was the tribal organization fit for the task. His solution was to hire foreigners: men without their own power bases and with a loyalty to himself alone, motivated by self interest. It was a regime in which order was imposed from the top. When Shih Hu died, a bloody struggle broke out and the Chao state shattered. Jan Min, a Chinese adopted son of Shih Hu and a rabid sinophile, took power. In 349 he led a pogrom against the foreign inhabitants of the capital region, in which 200,000 were reported slain. Though this figure is probably highly exaggerated, it did demonstrate a basic weakness in the Chao state. Without some support among the majority Chinese population, the small number of foreign rulers risked being swamped by revolt as soon as their coercive grip loosened. Scavenger dynasties like the Mu-jung Hsien-pi moved in to take control with a more successful state structure designed to overcome these handicaps.

MANCHURIAN BORDERLANDS – THE RISE OF DUAL ORGANIZATION

When both China and the steppe were united, the Manchurian frontier had little independent identity. The steppe border of Liao-hsi was the eastern wing of the nomadic imperium. Liao-tung, although only narrowly connected to China proper, was always Chinese in culture and organization. The forests to the north were inhabited by various clans, organized into small villages, which looked as much to Korea as they did to China. Within a relatively confined area one could find forest villages, nomadic camps, and Chinese farming villages and cities. As long as the northern frontier was bipolar these diverse groups could not be part of a single political unit. It is clear from Han descriptions of trade and frontier administration that economically this division was not so sharp. Both the Wu-huan and Hsien-pi engaged in major frontier trade, and Chinese administrators had close ties to the tribes with whom they dealt.

When the bipolar world of the frontier collapsed, these separate peoples combined to form a new "mixed state." Which group would be dominant in such a mix was not predetermined. Over the course of history, steppe nomads, forest tribes, and frontier Chinese, have each formed the dominant stratum. In general, though, it was forest or steppe tribes which took command because the border Chinese were usually willing to attach themselves to a new state rather than create their own kingdoms, which would have had to compete with an established dynasty in China.

The development of such a state took time. Time was available because the northeast was marginal to the main battles in China or on the steppe. In times of anarchy rulers in China, native or foreign, gave the northeastern frontier low priority and left the people who lived there considerable autonomy. It was during this interregnum that a new type of state structure developed. It took the form of a dual organization with separate administration for tribal peoples and Chinese. The dynasty controlled the tribes by creating a military organization in which discipline and centralization replaced the loose tribal confederation with an autocratic leadership. The dynasty also ruled over Chinese subjects, employing Chinese bureaucrats and institutions. The integration of these spheres was the task of the ruling dynasty and by means of separate administration they attempted to combine the strengths of Chinese civil administration with the power of a tribally based military elite. Such a combination was not as powerful militarily as a centralized steppe confederacy nor administratively as well organized as a native Chinese dynasty. In times of trouble, however, it was a potent combination – steppe tribes were unable to organize their conquests and Chinese bureaucrats lacked military power. When both Chinese warlords and militaristic steppe tribes had destroyed one another, and most of north China, the Manchurian state offered the best hope of stability.

To build such a structure took generations and changes were made slowly. The pattern was for a tribal group first to fix a territory and then expand its local area to include Chinese subjects. The next step was to provide separate administration using Chinese bureaucrats for agricultural areas, and tribal leaders for the military. This was done for both ease of administration and because the tribal leader who made the conquests realized that a separate

Chinese sphere would provide him with an exclusive power base outside the tribal structure. Using this power base, he, or his successor, would gradually reduce tribal autonomy until its members had become a disciplined and centralized military arm under the dynasty's control. In the final stage the dynasty would abandon its tribal roots entirely and claim rights of universal rule. When the tribal army conquered Chinese territory, it was not divided up as booty but was administered by a Chinese staffed bureaucracy. Though reduced to subservience, the tribal component was not under the control of the bureaucracy. It remained segregated with its own rules, privileges, and responsibilities. This provided the dynasty with a coercive arm to suppress Chinese rebellion as well as protect the state. The separate civil and military commands were combined in the hands of an emperor who theoretically had absolute power over both sectors.

It was in the period of the Sixteen Kingdoms and the north–south division that this process took place for the first time. It may be argued that from this alone no theoretical explanation could be derived, especially because the process lurched along in an uncertain fashion. But it was this confused period of anarchy that first provided a model which was later to be employed when other dynasties collapsed. The process became clearer then because the time lag was shorter. It took 150 years from the fall of Han to the first Manchurian state, about 75 years from the fall of T'ang, and it occurred simultaneously with the fall of Ming. The time got shorter, but the pattern remained the same.

THE HSIEN-PI STATES

The potential of an autonomous Manchurian borderland was first apparent during the establishment of Ts'ao Ts'ao's Wei dynasty. His rival Yüan Shao had been heavily dependent on the Wu-huan, and his family's downfall was sealed by their defeat in the Manchurian borderland. A more important example from the same period was the persistence of the Kung-sun warlords in Liao-tung. They were never as strong as their opponents but their location was favorable for defense. Not until 253, long after the rest of north China was in the Wei grip, did Liao-tung fall, and then only to a combined Korean-Chinese attack.[23] Liao-tung and the surrounding area provided the resources to support a Chinese style state, yet was geographically separated from China. In times of anarchy Liao-tung was always the first Chinese provincial area to break away. Conversely, when China was united Liao-tung was always incorporated in it.

It was the Hsien-pi tribes who became the dominant force in the Manchurian borderland during Wei/Chin times. Their small size and disunity had always prevented them from becoming a stable power like the Hsiung-nu. Under the new conditions along the frontier small-scale organization had its advantages. Each group laid claim to a specific territory which they were willing to defend and develop, beginning their transformation into a mixed state. The process occurred among many of the Hsien-pi tribes who periodically gained and lost power. The most successful of these tribes was the Mu-jung who established the first Hsien-pi dynasty in China following the collapse of the Hsiung-nu

Chao state. The organization that the Mu-jung created was the base on which their cousins the T'o-pa built to unite north China.[24]

In the northern Wei period the Mu-jung were just one of many nomadic tribes in the northeast. They acted both as allies of China and as raiders, following the Hsien-pi variation of the outer frontier strategy outlined above. After the death of K'o-pi-neng there was little supratribal organization to unite them and local tribal leaders negotiated for themselves. In 237, Wei Hsüan-ti employed the Mu-jung against the Kung-sun warlords in Liao-tung. For this help they received gifts and titles from the Wei court. They received more honors in 246 for a similar campaign. Chin policy basically followed the same course set by Wei. In 281 they recognized the Mu-jung leader She-kuei as *"Shan-yü* of the Hsien-pi" in an attempt to win his support. Although by that time the title *Shan-yü* had become devalued, it was still highly coveted by the frontier tribes. This was an indication that the Hsien-pi were still part of the steppe tradition and that their leaders valued a Hsiung-nu title over a Chinese one. When the nomad leaders began to take more interest in China the reverse was true. She-kuei felt powerful enough to desert his Chinese patrons only a few months after receiving his title. He moved his people to Liao-tung and raided his old territory in Liao-hsi. The next year a Chinese punitive expedition inflicted a severe defeat on the Mu-jung. They were presumably one of the twenty-nine northeastern tribes which returned to a Chinese alliance six months later.

Cooperation with border officials along the frontier gave all the Hsien-pi tribes familiarity with Chinese ways. They became less nomadic and claimed exclusive territories. She-kuei was the first Mu-jung leader to provide his sons with a Chinese education and adopt some Chinese customs himself. The next generation of Mu-jung leaders, therefore, took a very different view of their political role and began to organize recognizable state structures. Unlike Liu Yüan, the Hsiung-nu founder of Chao, who was their contemporary, the Mu-jung leaders never attempted to adopt the Chinese court structure in a wholesale fashion. Over the years, they had time to experiment and develop a new organization that would not alienate their tribal followers but which would have a centralized bureaucracy. This transformation of the Mu-jung from tribal group to a mixed state was the work of the long-lived Mu-jung Hui (r. 283–333). His half-century rule provided the stability and continuity for major changes to be implemented.

Mu-jung Hui began his reign at the age of fifteen as a tribal leader in the mold of his father. As long as China was united there was no viable alternative. China was still too strong for a single Hsien-pi tribe to overcome. This did not mean that Hui was any more subservient than this father, for he continued to alternate peace and war, but with his Chinese education he saw other opportunities than raiding or being part of the tributary system. Chinese education stressed the importance of agricultural production and a bureaucratic state. In Manchuria it was possible to control small agricultural areas without confronting the whole might of China.

In 285, Hui directed his campaign against such areas in neighboring Liao-hsi as well as agricultural areas like the Fu-yü kingdom to the north. Fu-yü, sandwiched between Korea and the Hsien-pi nomads near the upper Sungari River, was a small but prosperous state with a well-armed population of around 80,000 living in towns protected by walled forts. The economy was based on growing crops and craft production. Fu-yü also raised horses, and traded sable skins, red jade, and pearls with China to the south, with which it had had sporadic relations during Ch'in and Han times. Hui destroyed all the forts and cities of Fu-yü and took 10,000 captives home, but was not able to incorporate the territory. The economic importance of the Korean borderland for the mixed states in lower Manchuria has probably been underestimated because we know so little about them and because so much of the data on frontier relations is derived from Chinese records, which depend on official reports.[25]

Hui's attacks on Liao-tung, also an agricultural urban area, were repulsed the next year. Hui then made peace with China and impressed its officials with his knowledge of Chinese etiquette when he came on an official visit. Raids against Fu-yü continued and Hui grew rich selling his captives to China. This must have been a big business for the Chin emperor tried to ban the trade and prohibited the ownership of such slaves around the capital and in the northeast.

Hui's state became more solidly grounded when, in 294, he founded a new walled capital and encouraged farming, an enterprise begun by his father. He tried to produce his own silk by requesting worms and mulberry bushes from the Chin court. These programs must have been highly successful, for Hui sent grain to China when floods wrecked much of Yu province in 301. The Mu-jung were not the only sophisticated Hsien-pi group in this region. They had rivals in the Tuan Hsien-pi, with whom they established a marriage alliance, and the Yü-wen, to whom they paid tribute.

Chinese records give few details of these or other changes, nor do they emphasize that they were watershed events. Nevertheless, it is possible to recognize three major innovations. First was the adoption and encouragement of agriculture and craft production. The outer and inner frontier strategies both had treated grain and cloth as items to be gained by trade, as gifts or plunder. Hui and his Hsien-pi neighbors were beginning to take administrative responsibility for the organization of this production, albeit on a small scale. Hui's ability to export grain to China points to a self-sufficient state. Second, Hui was employing Chinese administrators to run this new part of the economy. It is unlikely that Hui convinced the Mu-jung to become farmers, but there were plenty of Fu-yü captives and frontier Chinese who could be used for this purpose. A Chinese-style bureaucracy was needed to administer them. Undoubtedly this began as a purely pragmatic step, for Hsien-pi nomads were hardly suitable for this role, but within a few years there was a full fledged administration along Chinese lines. Third, Hui used Chinese advisors to reorganize his army. The high command remained in Hsien-pi hands and units still retained a tribal organization, but the ability for local tribal leaders to act on their own was reduced. In battle and in planning they were taking orders from a central command.

The new army included infantry led by Chinese officers and it had the technical ability to engage in siege or defend fixed positions. The superiority of the Mu-jung army was demonstrated in 302, when it was twice attacked by the

Yü-wen. In both cases, the Yü-wen were routed with heavy losses in spite of their numerical superiority. Impressed by this feat, a number of Hsien-pi tribes defected to Mu-jung Hui.

The victory of the Mu-jung could not have been better timed. The Chin court was engaged in fratricidal civil war and soon lost most of north China to the Hsiung-nu. The northeastern Hsien-pi, therefore, had complete autonomy. Heavy fighting made central China a continual battlefield. The Mu-jung refused to be drawn into the fight. Apart from some local battles with his neighbors, Mu-jung Hui had almost twenty years of peace after his victory in 302 in which to develop his kingdom. The impetus for this development was the influx of Chinese refugees from the south. Though denigrated as barbarian, the various Hsien-pi kingdoms offered food and safety. While the majority of refugees were farmers, their numbers also included artisans and former officials. All the Hsien-pi states received such refugees, but Mu-jung Hui appears to have gone out of his way to attract them, in order to increase the productivity of his state. Chinese officials became an important part of the Mu-jung court advising Hui on strategy and government. Hui, who had declared himself "Great *Shan-yü*" in 308, soon began to play Chinese-style politics and lay the foundation for a dynasty.

This change was the result of advice from Hui's Chinese councillors. They urged him to contact the Chin court to receive an imperial appointment that would confirm his rule. As an autonomous Hsien-pi leader, Hui had no need of such recognition from a rump dynasty dismembered by the Hsiung-nu. However, he realized that such an appointment had great meaning to the Chinese officials he was trying to attract to his service. They were uncomfortable serving a "barbarian" court. Their service could be more easily justified if Mu-jung Hui was acting in the capacity of "vassal" to the legitimate Chin dynasty in the south. If Mu-jung Hui wished to expand his state into China, such a cover would prove useful. A tribal leader without a classical Chinese education might simply have dismissed such suggestions, but Hui was familiar enough with China to realize that symbols of legitimacy were important political tools. He sent an envoy to the Chin court and was duly recognized.[26]

Of more immediate importance, his Chinese advisors brought visions of wider possibilities for expansion. It was they who broached the possibility of ruling China itself. They argued that Hui's disorganized tribal neighbors could be united and then used as an invasion force to conquer China. Around 322 the Mu-jung began attacking the neighboring Hsien-pi states. Each conquered tribe was incorporated into the state as a separate unit, increasing the size of the army. Border Chinese were also conquered and put to work under civil administration. The power of Mu-jung Hui greatly increased to make him far more than just a tribal leader. Chinese statecraft was being used to harness the military power of the northeastern tribes. By the time of Hui's death in 333 he was the head of an emerging dynasty.

Mu-jung Hui's military strategy was conservative. He concentrated on defense rather than aggressive expansion. Such a strategy was characteristic of the Hsien-pi border states in Manchuria, as well as in China's northwest frontier province of Liang. Against the powerful armies in central China they stood little chance in an open battle, but, well supplied and protected by walled cities, they could usually induce the retreat of an enemy. Rulers of these states concentrated their attention on internal organization and the economy. When they did expand, it was opportunistically, to take advantage of a rival's defeat. The effectiveness of this strategy was proved in 338, when Shih Hu moved a huge army against the Mu-jung but could not maintain his siege at their capital. In his retreat from Manchuria, Shih Hu lost tens of thousands of troops and the Mu-jung actually increased their territory.

The transformation of the Mu-jung from a nomadic tribe to a Chinese state moved rapidly under Mu-jung Hui's successor, Mu-jung Huang. Initially, there had been some trouble connected with this. The Hsien-pi had a long tradition of lateral succession, a tradition which was in conflict with the Chinese ideal of primogeniture. A compromise developed in which the ruler succeeded in Chinese fashion, but appointed his brothers and uncles to key posts. The best generals and advisors were members of the imperial lineage who looked upon the state as their common property. The chances of civil wars of succession occurring were thereby lessened, but not eliminated because the ruler often displayed personal animosity or jealousy toward his relatives. Huang, for example, was jealous of his talented brothers and initially drove them to exile or rebellion.

In terms of symbols, Huang's greatest innovation was to proclaim himself King of Yen in 337. Yen was the name of the old northeastern kingdom in the Warring States period. By claiming such a title Huang was moving away from identification with a particular tribe toward a claim of universal rule. By an example established at the time of Wang Mang's usurpation of the Han, there was an appropriate political procedure to seize the mandate of heaven from an expiring dynasty. A pretender first made himself a king, and from there might be in a suitable position to proclaim himself emperor. From Huang's reign onward, the Mu-jung state referred to itself as "Yen" and officially downplayed its tribal origins.

The use of Chinese titles and rituals was politically important but the real change was the economic transformation of the Manchurian frontier which gave these titles meaning. Here Chinese advisors played a critical role in guiding the Hsien-pi rulers toward pragmatic policies that increased the state's power. It was they who overcame traditional tribal objections about the importance of farming. Refugees in particular could become a burden rather than an asset if they were not properly employed. By the time of Mu-jung Hui's death, the population had increased tenfold from the start of his reign, and a Chinese advisor, Feng Yü, pointed out that 30 to 40 percent of them were idle for lack of land, which it was the duty of the state to provide. He went on to explain to Mu-jung Huang:

Your land has been extended 3,000 *li* and the population increased by 100,000 families. Now you must divide the pasture and transform it into farmland to give the newcomers work. The farmer who has no draft animal should acquire one from the government.

Since the farmer is your subject, the cattle remain your property. In this manner you will win the people and in the event of war, Shih Hu's subjects will prefer you to their own sovereign.[27]

In spite of his Chinese education, it is clear that Huang had to be persuaded that less intensive pastoralism needed to make way for more intensive farming if Yen as a whole were to advance. The memorialist went out of his way to reassure Huang that by letting his oxen be used by farmers he was not giving them away, showing he was still imbrued with traditional Hsien-pi values. Indirectly the Chinese advisors were forcing Huang to realize that he was ruler of both nomads and farmers – and with no old land available, some pastoral lands would have to be sacrificed. By small steps, the state of Yen was adapting itself to new responsibilities.

Feng Yü pressed for a greater reorganization of the Yen state along traditional Chinese lines and proposed a six-point program:

1   Waterworks should be repaired and maintained.
2   More refugees put to work farming.
3   Excess officials be dismissed.
4   Excess merchants and craftsman should be forced to take up farming.
5   The number of students should be cut and the excess forced to farm.
6   The ruler should listen to criticism.

These six points reflected the Chinese attitude that farming, farmers, and irrigation were vital state concerns, with a Confucian bias against artisans and merchants. It was an attempt to graft Chinese agricultural, political, and social policy onto the Mu-jung's tribal military power. In making their points the Chinese advisors never strayed into tribal affairs – there was not even a hint that excess Hsien-pi become farmers, only that refugees under Chinese-style administration be better employed.

Mu-jung Huang's response was favorable except for the suggestion that the number of officials be reduced. After all, Huang noted, he was fighting a war and expanding his state. This called for giving money and positions freely. This view reflected the old steppe tradition of leadership in which a ruler was expected to give with an open hand and not count his money. One of the problems Manchurian border states faced was that in order to buy allies, support large numbers of troops, and maintain a large bureaucracy, they tended to become financially overextended. As long as the state was expanding, new resources could always fill the gap. Once they had moved into China and stopped expanding, the large number of endowed positions which no longer served a critical political purpose created a potential crisis. One sign of sinicization was the need at this time for a cost accounting emperor who was not of the steppe tradition to proclaim that the empire was no longer common patrimony of the tribal elite, but rather the exclusive property of his dynasty.

In 348 Mu-jung Chün succeeded his father on the throne. The Yen state he inherited included most of Manchuria and the Chin court formally recognized his claim as king. When the Chao state collapsed in civil war, Yen followed its old strategy of picking up the pieces. Chün began moving south in 350, after letting various Chao leaders destroy one another. Yen forces never faced their opponents' full strength, only its remnants. Chün now saw himself as an emperor of China. In 352, Yen forces captured the Chao emperor Jan Min. Riding a crest of victory, Chün berated Jan Min for calling himself emperor. Jan Min's cutting reply reflected much of China's attitude toward the new foreign dynasties: "If while the empire is in turmoil barbarians like you, who belong to the brutes rather than the human race, presume to call yourself emperors why should I, a hero of the Chinese people, not call myself an emperor?"[28] The insult must have cut – Jan Min received 300 lashes for his views – because Chün was making preparations to officially declare himself emperor.

Mu-jung Chün was determined to become emperor, but for the official history he portrayed himself (or more likely was portrayed by his court historians) as unworthy, to prove perhaps that he was no greedy barbarian and could take power in a fully Chinese manner. When his officials petitioned him to take the imperial title he responded in an unctuous manner designed to appeal to Confucian sensibilities:

Our home was originally the desert and steppe, and we were barbarians. With such a background how could I dare place myself in the distinguished line of Chinese emperors? Just because you are longing for promotions and dignities to which you have no right cannot be a reason to comply with your wishes.[29]

Of course in China's eyes, the Mu-jung would always be barbarians, but for seventy years they had been developing a state capable of ruling China. Unlike the Hsiung-nu, the Mu-jung did not just overrun Chinese territory, they incorporated it into a functioning government. For three generations their leaders had been given Chinese educations. Mu-jung Chün's hypocritical refusals followed the Chinese model of statecraft. Good manners and humility would help legitimate the new dynasty, and win over those influential Chinese who were torn between the attractive positions in Yen and their almost mystical attachment to the old Chin dynasty. This had been one of the great weaknesses of the Hsiung-nu Chao states which had made little attempt to win support among the Chinese. Whether Chün actually made such customary polite refusals is less significant than his awareness of the political importance of working within a Chinese cultural context. Chün declared himself emperor in early 353.

The Yen state spent the next few years crushing small rebellions and bringing eastern China under its rule. Western China fell under the control of Fu Chien, a ruler of Tibetan stock who had served the Chao court. The Yangtze region to the south remained in the hands of the old Chin dynasty. In 357, Yen turned its attention to the danger of the steppe tribes. The Ch'ih-le nomads had grown powerful and because they sat on Yen's flank they were a threat. Yen sent an army of 80,000 which inflicted a severe defeat on the Ch'ih-le, who reportedly lost 100,000 people as casualties or captives, together with 130,000 horses and a million sheep. This victory so impressed the Hsiung-nu *Shan-yü* that he took his 35,000 subjects and allied himself with the Yen state.[30]

This steppe campaign displayed a strikingly different strategy from similar attacks on the nomads by Chinese dynasties. Dynasties of frontier origin had a very different approach to the problem of steppe confederacies that was far more effective than those developed by the Han. Foreign dynasties, in spite of their Chinese-style courts, continued to employ steppe tactics and strategies in their frontier wars. They understood how steppe confederacies were organized and where their strengths and weaknesses lay. The Chinese approach had relied on defensive walls, gifts and trade, and periodic massive attacks on the nomads. The Manchurian strategy was more sophisticated. Tribal leaders could be won over by a complex series of marriage alliances which linked them to the dynasty. Tribal politics revolved around such marriage exchanges and it was natural to extend this network to include new peoples. Manchurian rulers also knew from experience how difficult it was to produce tribal confederations on the steppe and took every opportunity to disrupt such formations by supporting rival leaders or knocking out a growing power directly. When an attack was made on the nomads it involved fast moving troops who knew steppe conditions. The aim of Manchurian commanders was not just the defeat of an army in the field but the capture of whole peoples. The Ch'ih-le captives and animals were removed to Yen territory for resettlement. As a state with dual organization, Yen could effectively utilize such people whereas traditional Chinese dynasties saw them only as a threat. Foreign dynasties combined tribal and Chinese traditions in a way that produced a powerfully effective frontier policy. The foreign emperor could call upon China's wealth and manpower to try to disrupt the steppe. Unhindered by traditional Confucian disapproval of steppe campaigns, he had a knowledge of his enemies that traditional Chinese emperors never possessed.

Throughout the time of foreign rule in China, in this and later periods, the nomads found it difficult to form powerful confederations. The nomads were most successful, almost invincible, against traditional Chinese dynasties and least successful when dealing with their cousins who became rulers of China. Little is heard from the steppe until the fall of the foreign dynasties and rise of both the Sui/T'ang dynasties in China and of the Turks on the steppe, which recreated the old bipolar world.

In spite of Yen's long period of organization its hold on China was short-lived. The conservative military strategy which had insured its survival when other states collapsed began to prove a liability. Yen's efforts to conquer all of north China fell victim to court politics and a desire to exploit what they already had.

The problem with this approach was that it exposed the financial weakness of the Yen state. Large numbers of grants and official positions had been distributed to the political elite by the Mu-jung rulers. Their liberality had attracted both Chinese officials and tribal leaders to the Mu-jung cause. As the leader of a dual organization, the Yen emperor was forced to be generous to his largely tribal military leaders, while at the same time seeing that their demands did not become too great a burden. The system prospered under strong rulers who could maintain a balance between the needs of the state as whole and the stipends to the political elite. Under weak rulers, the system was unstable because the political elite tried to divert as much of the state's revenue as possible into their own estates with dire consequences for Yen as a whole.

This structural tension was exacerbated by the uneasy compromise between Chinese and Hsien-pi succession systems. The Hsien-pi preference for the selection of the most able of an emperor's sons, and their willingness to pass the throne to a brother if there were no suitable son, produced strong rulers. However, the Chinese court officials' preference for royal primogeniture forced the Yen state to pick an heir regardless of talent. This tendency was mitigated to some extent by the use of talented brothers and uncles as important generals and advisors. When Emperor Chün died in 360 the throne went to his young son Wei. This disturbed many at court who questioned his fitness to rule because even his father had complained that Wei lacked talent. They tried to persuade Mu-jung K'o, Chün's brother, to take the throne, arguing that by the old Hsien-pi custom of lateral succession it was his right. K'o refused to take the throne directly, but he did become regent and from that position effectively ruled the state. During his regency Yen reached its height of power as he led it to new conquests.[31]

A child emperor meant that whoever was regent would effectively set policy. On his deathbed in 367, K'o recommended his brother Mu-jung Ch'ui as his successor. Ch'ui was, along with K'o, one of Yen's best commanders and a very talented man. He had long been out of favor at court because Mu-jung Huang had once proposed Ch'ui as a possible heir apparent to replace his eldest son Chün. From that time, Chün and later his heirs had been jealous of Ch'ui and refused to grant him key posts. K'o now argued that Ch'ui was the only man of vision worthy of acting as regent. He labelled the other candidates as short-sighted and avaricious. One of his major targets was Mu-jung P'ing who, by uniting Ch'ui's enemies, seized power and reduced Ch'ui to a minor position.

The Yen state declined quickly under P'ing's control. Confucian historians characteristically attributed this to moral weakness, but there was a more important structural problem. In building the Yen state, K'o and the previous emperors had kept a tight rein on the political elite. They were generous with rewards but were careful to make the elite serve the empire for the benefit of the dynasty. P'ing represented an older tribal tradition that saw the state as property to be shared out among the elite in proportion to each individual's power. The temptation to sit back and divide the spoils was strong because Yen had expanded so quickly into eastern China and thus had the possibility of obtaining heretofore undreamed of wealth. It took a strong central authority to prevent the elite from dominating the state to serve its own interests. K'o maintained such control and was willing to make sacrifices for the benefit of the dynasty. At his death the emphasis shifted. The young emperor himself was an exemplar of conspicuous consumption. His harem housed 4,000 women and 40,000 servants, at a cost of 10,000 ounces of silver daily. The political elite, which had been granted estates with an assigned number of tenants, began to expand their domains and deprived the treasury of revenue.

This was a grave situation because Yen faced strong military rivals, Ch'in in the west and Chin to the south. One official, Yüeh Wan, brought the problem to the court's attention:

At present, three states stand opposed to one another. Each has the intention of annexing the other two. In this dangerous situation the fundamental laws of our country are not being upheld. Powerful nobles behave in such a lawless manner that they (by enlarging the number of their tenants) severely reduce the number of taxpayers, so, as a result, taxes are not coming in. Consequently the officials cannot receive their regular salaries, and also, the stipends for soldiers have been stopped. The officials borrow grain and silk to support themselves. Such conditions ought not to become known among our enemy neighbors; moreover they do not contribute to the peace of our country. We ought to do away with tenants and return them to the jurisdiction of the districts and prefectures.[32]

A brief period of reform revealed that this was no exaggeration, over 200,000 families (out of a total population of 2.5 million families) had been removed from the tax rolls in the months after P'ing took power. The reforms ended with the assassination of Yüeh Wan in 368. The next year a similar memorial complained that the most basic tasks of government were being neglected. Unjust taxation, abuse of conscription and corvée labor demands had ruined the efficiency of the army, inducing widespread desertion. Mu-jung Ch'ui, who had defeated an invasion force that year, was forced to flee for his life to Fu Chien, Yen's most bitter rival in the west. In 370, only three years after K'o's death, the Yen state collapsed under the weight of an invasion by Fu Chien, in which the whole country was conquered and the court taken captive.

THE OTHER NORTHERN STATES: CH'IN AND LIANG

The Ch'in dynasty was established in 352 during the turmoil that followed the collapse of Chao. Its leaders were of the Ti people, relatives of the Ch'iang, who had long been settled in Kuan-chung. The choice of the dynastic name Ch'in recalled the glory of the Warring States kingdom of the region which had also had Ch'ang-an as its capital. Both the choice of dynastic name and capital were auspicious since it was the earlier Ch'in dynasty that had first unified China under the rule of a universal emperor, the goal toward which Fu Chien was striving.

The Ch'in state was founded by Fu Chien's uncle, and was organized along different lines than those employed by the Mu-jung in Yen. The Mu-jung Yen state was the product of seventy years of gradual development and until the time of its last king it had proved remarkably stable. The Ch'in state was, on the contrary, an immediate byproduct of the instability which led to the destruction of the Hsiung-nu dynasties on whose ruins it was founded. Its leaders were opportunists who took power in their own localities and then destroyed rival warlords. Succession to leadership was usually violent – Chien rose to power upon the murder of his uncle and brother – and its dynasties were short-lived. Their greatest problem was trying to create a central government which could control the fractious tribal peoples while at the same time providing an administration acceptable to the Chinese. The first Hsiung-nu Chao dynasty had fallen because the nomads thought the court was too Chinese and had deserted it. The second Chao dynasty of Shih Le and Hu had fallen because it was unable to provide a competent government for its Chinese subjects, who revolted and engaged in an anti-foreign pogrom when its military might weakened.

The Yen state had used the principle of dual organization as a way to create a state that maintained a civil bureaucratic structure along Chinese lines, while keeping its tribal elements and military under a separate administration. This idea was the logical outcome of their experience in Manchuria where the Hsien-pi had had to deal with a variety of peoples and economies before they entered the north Chinese plain. Those dynasties established within China proper had a much more narrow outlook and could think only in terms of a single administration for civil and military affairs in which different groups, Chinese and foreign, struggled for dominance. The Ch'in state was, like the Hsiung-nu states before it, a military bureaucracy in which civil officials also acted as army commanders.

Most warlords, Chinese or foreign, were attracted to a Chinese-style administration because it vested power in a supreme leader to whom everyone was subject. The foreign peoples who came out of a tribal position tended to look upon the state as a structure based on consensus in which power was often shared. When it was not shared, then a leader like the Hsiung-nu *Shan-yü* was at least expected to give precedence to his own people when giving out territories to rule or distributing the state's economic resources. It took a great deal of time and finesse to handle such a problem. Fu Chien's difficulty was how to maintain the support of his own ethnic group while running a Chinese-style government. The Ti did not have a strong tribal organization like the Hsiung-nu, so Fu Chien initially was able to reduce them to a subordinate status in his autocratic state. This laid the seeds for the revolts which led to his own murder and the demise of his dynasty.

The operation of the Ch'in government was in the hands of a trusted but ruthless Chinese chief minister, Wang Meng, who took on the task of reducing Ti power. He controlled the entire administration and did his best to destroy tribal influence at court. For example in 359, Fan Shih, an influential Ti leader of the Fu clan complained:

"Though my group participated with their Majesties of yore in launching the undertaking, we are not now entrusted with momentous powers. You had not even the hardship of making your horse sweat, how dare you arrogate yourself the control of a great trust? Isn't this a case of our plowing and sowing and your eating the product?" Meng said, "Then we should make you chef. Why should you just plow and sow?" Shih was greatly enraged; he said, "I will surely hang your head on Ch'ang-an's city gate; if I do not, I'll not abide in this world!"[33]

Fu Chien supported Meng in his approach because he wanted to reduce the power of his own family and relatives in order to convince them they had no special claim on the state. He executed Fan Shih, provoking a riot by Ti tribesmen who objected to Meng's tyranny. They were beaten out of the palace with whips. A year later Chinese officials led a vicious purge in which twenty members of the imperial and consort families, together with other powerful individuals, were executed. The court adopted many of the trappings of Confucian administration such as setting up literary academies and persecuting merchants. However, in these troubled times many Chinese officials at court also acted in non-traditional roles as army commanders. Wang Meng in particular proved to be a formidable general.

The alienation of the Ti and the royal clan in particular almost proved fatal to the Ch'in. The better organized Yen state was on the move and in 365 their great general Mu-jung K'o captured Lo-yang and moved toward Kuan-chung. To the north, the Hsiung-nu took the opportunity to revolt. As soon as these and other attacks were dealt with, the governors of the western provinces, members of the royal clan, revolted in 367. In order to put down the rebellion, Fu Chien had to strip his eastern defenses. Yen was unable to take advantage of these difficulties because of its own internal problems. One of its best generals, Mu-jung Ch'ui, defected to Ch'in and with his aid Fu Chien was able to march on Yen and conquer it in 370. Within a few years, all the other northern states fell to him, making Ch'in master of north China.

The lack of a well-developed state structure became apparent after the conquests of the other northern states. The Ch'in administration was characterized by the wholesale incorporation of conquered officials into the government. Wang Meng died in 375 just after these conquests and the dynasty had no one of similar ability and loyalty available to replace him. Former opponents like Mu-jung Ch'ui thereafter became a major political figures at the Ch'in court. In fact, the whole Yen political edifice lay just below the surface in eastern China and a similar state of affairs existed in the western province of Liang. As long as officials submitted to the Ch'in hegemony they stayed in place. Thus, although he conquered all of north China, Fu Chien was no real unifier. His government was stable only as long as his subordinates feared his power. In 383, he mounted a large campaign against the south which failed at the Battle of the Fei River, inducing many regions to revolt. The old states of Yen and Liang reappeared as did the T'o-pa Tai state now known as Wei. In 385, Fu Chien was strangled by the leader of the Yao, a rival Ti clan, who seized control of Kuan-chung and established his own successor state. The large number of regional states and powerful clans that emerged following Fu Chien's death showed that local elites had not been displaced, only temporarily suppressed.

The northwestern state of Liang occupied the Kansu corridor, a string of oases running from the Ordos desert toward Hami and Turkestan. To the north, it was bordered by the edge of the Mongolian steppe and was subject to incursions by nomads from there. To the south, it bordered on mountainous terrain occupied by the sedentary Ch'iang and Ti peoples as well as the T'u-yü-hun nomads who used the pastures around Lake Koko-nor. To the west were the oases of Turkestan, which had close cultural and economic ties with Liang. The Kansu oases themselves had a large Chinese population and since the time of Han Wu-ti the region had been an integral part of the Han dynasties' frontier defense.

The Liang region, like the northeastern frontier, was the home of a number of new dynasties, following the collapse of the Chin dynasty in the early fourth century. These dynasties incorporated a wide variety of nomads, sedentary villages, and cities to form mixed states. Yet unlike the northeast, it played only a marginal role in the political history of China during this period. The reasons for this are related to the region's strategic position and its economic structure.

Liang's economy was built around a series of self-sufficient oases. Because of the long distances between settlements and because of difficulties in transporting grain, each oasis was forced to provide for itself. The external trade which brought wealth to the province was not based on the export of subsistence crops, but on the caravan trade in luxury goods, pastoral products, and minerals like salt in which Liang played a key role. The oases also were part of a regional economy in which agriculture and pastoralism were inextricably linked. Therefore, rulers based in Liang were largely insulated against outside economic pressures. Even when they were on hostile terms with states to the south they could extract considerable revenue from the caravan trade because exotic goods were always in demand at the courts of whoever happened to be ruling China proper.

Strategically, Liang made an excellent base for revolt, but a poor base for expansion. It was far too distant from the population and power centers in China to have much influence there. Any army marching from Liang would find itself dangerously separated from its source of supplies and reinforcements, so that a defeat would be disastrous. No dynasty based in Liang ever conquered north China, even temporarily. On the other hand, Liang's defensive position was excellent. Opponents had to expend their own resources even to reach the region and then move from oasis to oasis.

The contrast with the northeast is striking. Whereas Liang was isolated from central China by distance and arid terrain, the Liao area was geographically isolated from the north Chinese plain only by a few mountains and a narrow pass. An army moving on China from there was close to its base of supply and reinforcement, and should it be defeated it had a nearby place of retreat. Therefore, when China collapsed into anarchy both its northwestern and northeastern frontiers became autonomous, but it was only the northeast that was able to develop local autonomy into a politically and militarily effective stage for the domination of the rest of north China. The culmination of developments in Liang would at best produce a powerful regional state like the Tangut state of Hsi Hsia (990–1227); normally it simply fell victim to whichever state unified the rest of north China.

Governors sent out from the capital to govern Liang were the most important figures in establishing new dynasties because they were in command of the local governments and military garrisons. Chang Kuei, the former Chin governor, founded the Former Liang state (313–76) which, although independent, maintained close formal relations with that dynasty's successor state in the south. The dynasty was organized along traditional Chinese lines and stayed free from interference until Fu Chien dispatched his general Lü Kuang there with an army which destroyed the old dynasty and extended Ch'in control over a number of states in Turkestan. Following the collapse of Fu Chien's government Lü Kuang used his troops to establish a Later Liang state (386–403). Within his lifetime, Liang began to unravel and at the time of his death collapsed completely to form three states: Northern Liang (397–439), Southern Liang (397–414) and Western Liang (400–21). These dynasties were formed by the various tribal leaders of the region and lasted until the T'o-pa Wei dynasty incorporated them into a unified north China.

THE T'O-PA: THIRD WAVE CONQUEST

Out of the anarchy following Fu Chien's collapse came a new power – the T'o-pa or Tabgatch. As unifiers and rulers of north China for the next century and a half they stood out. Yet in origin and structure they cannot be understood without reference to Yen and the Mu-jung Hsien-pi. For the T'o-pa would not have been able to succeed without the adoption of the Mu-jung innovation of dual organization.

The T'o-pa were the most westward of the Manchurian Hsien-pi tribes (with the exception of the T'u-yü-hun who had moved entirely out of the region). Of all the Hsien-pi in the northeast they were the least sophisticated and most nomadic, remaining closer to the old steppe tradition than their cousins, who had taken responsibility for ruling cities and governing farmers. The early T'o-pa kingdom was called Tai, after the Chinese district of that name to the south. This kingdom was never recognized as one of the Sixteen Kingdoms in Chinese history, in part because it was an ill-organized confederation of nomads that maintained a precarious existence. For most of this period the T'o-pa paid allegiance to their more powerful neighbors or fled into the mountains when attacked. When Fu Chien invaded Tai in 376 their leader, Shih-yi-chien, died while hiding in the mountains. Unlike other regional states, the T'o-pa had no capital of their own beyond the temporary stockade of their leader. T'o-pa Kuei, the founder of the dynasty (r. 386–409) had no permanent court for half his reign. The question that must be asked, then, is how such a group came to triumph and create a stable state where others had failed.[34]

Earlier, we noted that the first peoples to benefit from the collapse of China were those that could field a powerful military force: they failed because of their inability to administer their conquests. Border states like Yen survived such periods by stressing defense and internal organization. Their innovation was the dual organization for tribesmen and Chinese, both in the service of the Yen state. It was Yen that was best prepared to pick up the pieces when the Hsiung-nu Chao state fell apart. Then its conservative policies became a liability, however, for Yen did not go all out to capture north China. Even after Fu Chien's temporary conquest, Mu-jung officials used Yen's stable organization to again take control of eastern China.

In a situation like this, the T'o-pa held an advantage. Their steppe tradition gave them a military base and their leaders proved aggressively expansionist. They could have ended up like the Hsiung-nu Chao or Fu Chien's Ch'in dynasties, but in their conquests they made a significant advance over the strategies of the military states. When they moved into eastern China the T'o-pa first considered distributing agricultural land piecemeal and acting as local overlords to the Chinese, an attractive idea to a tribal people. It was obvious to their leaders that this would make the small numbers of T'o-pa very vulnerable to revolt by the large Chinese population. It would also reinforce the power of local tribal elites in their battle to avoid losing power to a central administration. The solution was to adopt the Yen pattern of dual organization which they found already in place. It had been developed by their cousins the Mu-jung to overcome the very problems the T'o-pa now faced. Chinese areas would be ruled by Chinese administrators in charge of civil affairs. Tribal peoples and military affairs would fall under a separate administration. Thus the T'o-pa attached an aggressive leadership to a political structure that was best suited to their needs.

The T'o-pa did not develop the system of dual organization, they inherited it and the officials who knew how to make it work. Many Yen officials were Hsien-pi themselves, sharing a common language and tribal heritage with their more backward cousins. They provided the means for the T'o-pa to establish a state organization in which the Mu-jung and other Hsien-pi would retain their old benefits. The dual organization also attracted many Chinese advisors, who understood that they could gain more influence by collaborating with a dynasty that needed and rewarded the elite that ran the civil bureaucracy. The advantage to the T'o-pa rulers was that such a system concentrated great power in the hands of the emperor at the expense of the older egalitarian Hsien-pi traditions.

The course of events following the collapse of Ch'in is evidence of this process. T'o-pa Kuei declared himself emperor of a new Wei dynasty in 396. His first target for conquest was Yeh, the capital of the former Yen dynasty which fell in 396, and by 410 he controlled the entire northeastern region of China and southern Manchuria. In spite of these victories, the new dynasty remained largely confined to this area for the next twenty years. It was during this period that the state developed the capacity to rule northern China by incorporating Mu-jung soldiers and Chinese officials into its administration. The Wei state structure was almost entirely adopted from the Yen model of government already in place in the northeast. Following Yen's lead, Kuei abolished his people's steppe confederacy organization. Most tribesman, T'o-pa and others, became registered subjects of the state organized as military units in state service. They were allocated land and forced to settle on it, acting as garrison communities. Nomadism was prohibited. The T'o-pa capital was established at P'ing-ch'eng, a steppe area at the center of the dynasty's military power. In spite of large population movements to provide the city with farmers and craftsmen, a palace complex, and tree plantings, the place was described as an overgrown frontier town by visitors from the more sophisticated south. Yet when the Chin dynasty fell into civil war in 420 with the founding of the (Liu) Sung dynasty (420–78), the Eastern Chin royal house fled to Wei, for Wei was far more attractive to the southerners than its rival: the Hsiung-nu Hsia state.[35]

The Hsia dynasty (407–31) was founded by Ho-lien P'o-p'o, another in that seemingly indestructible line of descendants of Mao-tun. Unlike his immediate predecessors who had adopted Chinese ways and the royal Han surname of Liu, P'o-p'o stressed steppe traditions and returned to the old Hsiung-nu imperial clan name of Ho-lien. The government there was self-consciously tribal and rejected Chinese forms of administration. Hsia became powerful when it seized Kuan-chung from Chin troops who had invaded the area from the south in 415, but little effort was made to expand out from this base. This allowed the T'o-pa Wei to outflank Hsia by gaining control of the Chinese plain (with the capture of Lo-yang in 423) and the northern steppes (during major campaigns in 425 and 429). In 430, the T'o-pa made their move and captured Ch'ang-an and the Hsia dynasty was destroyed within a year. The last remaining border state of the Northern Liang fell in 439 bringing all of north China under Wei control.

THE JOU-JAN: FOREIGN DYNASTIES AND THE STEPPE

The Jou-jan empire was founded around the turn of the fourth century by Mu-i-lu (r. 308–16). He put together a confederation of tribes during the turmoil of the Chin civil wars. The Jou-jan were not very powerful, and only the names of their next five leaders have survived. Toward the end of the century, they were divided into eastern and western branches under the rule of two brothers, P'i-hou-pa and Yün-he-t'i respectively (table 3.1). They fell victim to an attack by the Wei emperor T'o-pa Kuei in 391, in which half of the Jou-jan were reportedly captured by the Wei, while the rest were forced to flee. In 394, She-lun, leader of the west, attacked and killed his uncle P'i-hou-pa to become the paramount Jou-jan chieftain. P'i-hou-pa's sons fled to the Wei were they were granted titles, linked by marriages with the T'o-pa, and then incorporated into the dynasty. The power of the Wei dynasty was such that She-lun did not confront it. Instead he moved north where he united the tribes and declared himself khaghan. In 399 the Wei army returned north and defeated the other major tribe on the steppe, the Kao-ch'e, taking a reported 90,000 of them captive. A few years later She-lun was able to take advantage of their weakness and conquer the Kao-ch'e along with some other northern Mongolian tribes, aided in large part by the defeats these tribes had already suffered at the hands of the T'o-pa.[36]

The rise of the Jou-jan empire followed the usual pattern by which unity in north China was reflected on the steppe, and the Jou-jan were indirect beneficiaries of the T'o-pa conquests in China. Before the Chinese frontier solidified under the T'o-pa Wei dynasty, the nomadic tribes on the steppe could easily act as free agents, moving south to join in alliances or fleeing north to avoid trouble. Some of the Hsiung-nu tribes had formed their own kingdoms like the Hsia or the Northern Liang, while the K'ao-ch'e (Ch'ih-le) nomads simply had moved south from the Lake Baikal region to better pastures. In this fluid environment even a great military leader had difficulty holding subject peoples with so many alternatives at hand. The T'o-pa conquests changed this. The frontier was now under firm control and all tribes in the area fell under direct control of the T'o-pa. Thus when the Jou-jan defeated the K'ao-ch'e in 402 to became paramount on the steppe, their subject tribes had few choices. If they failed to accept Jou-jan hegemony they would have to take the risky course of revolt, or defect south to China where they would fall under the more rigorous rule of the T'o-pa Wei state. The T'o-pa conquests, therefore, acted

Table 3.1   Succession and dates of reigns of Jou-jan khaghans

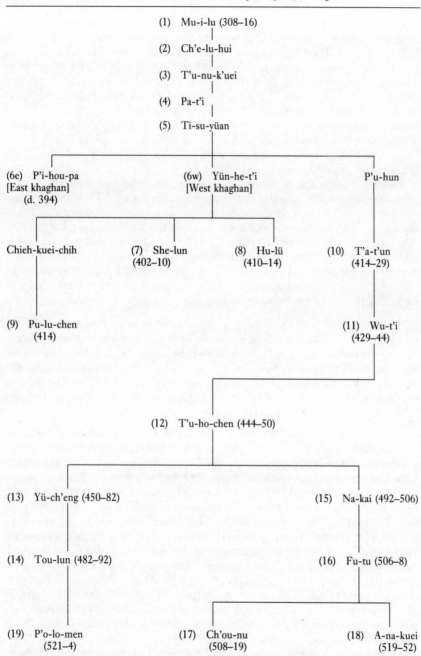

as the anvil against which the previously autonomous tribes were hammered into a steppe confederation by the Jou-jan.

From the beginning, the Jou-jan were weak compared with the great Hsiung-nu steppe empires. The outer frontier strategy, which had worked so well throughout Han times, failed against the Wei. Until the end of the Wei period, the Jou-jan proved unable to extort China's wealth by raiding or by gaining tributary benefits. As a result, their empire was structurally weak and prone to internal revolt. Then, at the beginning of the sixth century, the situation appeared to radically change. The Jou-jan empire took on new life and became much more successful in raiding, forcing political concessions from the Wei dynasty and its successor states. To understand the initial failure of the Jou-jan and their later success we must look to the frontier policies of the T'o-pa Wei dynasty.

Foreign dynasties took a very different approach toward dealing with the nomads in the north than did their Chinese counterparts. The T'o-pa rulers did not view the Jou-jan as aliens, but as a tribal people less sophisticated than themselves with weaknesses that could be exploited. Dual organization gave the T'o-pa a powerful military arm, free of control by Chinese civilian bureaucrats. Military policy and strategy were in the hands of men who knew the nomads well. When a Chinese advisor gave T'o-pa Tao the traditional lecture about the danger of steppe warfare, his objections were dismissed by a military man who explained that, far from being invincible, the nomads had their own problems.

In the summer their men and animals are scattered while in the autumn they all come together, their animals well fed. In the winter they change course and move south to plunder our frontiers. If we but come upon them by surprise [in the spring] with a great army and attack them, unprepared as they are, they will scatter in panic and flee. The stallions will be guarding their herds, and the mares will be chasing their foals, all flee in disorder. In a few days they will be unable to find grass or water, the men and animals will weaken, and we can bring about the enemy's sudden collapse.[37]

The Chinese had fought nomads for centuries, and many of their frontier commanders knew the enemy well, but the court had never attempted to understand the nomads. The tribal peoples of the steppe were external enemies to be dealt with only when wars within China were complete. Therefore during the wars that established both the Former and Later Han dynasties fighting the nomads had the lowest priority. The founders of both Han dynasties, Kao-tsu and Kuang-wu, only confronted the Hsiung-nu after they were secure in China. This allowed the nomads on the steppe to organize themselves without interference. Once Chinese dynasties were established there were always practical and ideological constraints that limited frontier policy. In ideological terms, the civilian court officials argued that a good ruler always put the ideal of civil action (*wen*) ahead of military force (*wu*). Rulers that ignored this advice, like Han Wu-ti, were condemned for their actions. The civilian bureaucracy also strongly opposed active frontier policies because they enabled the military to gain an important role in government.

As conquerors with a nomadic past, the Wei rulers took a very different approach. The T'o-pa leadership had the advantage of Chinese education combined with intimate knowledge of steppe warfare, and were less bound by the advice of Chinese advisors when it came to military affairs. Wei policy did not depend on destroying their nomadic enemies, instead the T'o-pa sought to disrupt them to such an extent that they no longer posed a threat. To this end the Wei maintained a well-supplied cavalry force that could strike deep into the steppe when necessary. The dynasty also understood the workings of a tribal system and how to manipulate it. Most important, they saw the steppe border-land as a key part of their empire. They campaigned there at the same time they were deeply engaged in wars within China, so that the nomads did not have a chance to develop their own strength.

The T'o-pa Wei frontier policy was aggressive. The dynasty's emperors conducted a series of campaigns over the course of many decades which kept the Jou-jan off balance. T'o-pa Kuei mounted his first campaign against the Jou-jan in 391, and the Kao-ch'e in 399, before the Wei had even consolidated its power in China. His successor, T'o-pa Ssu (r. 409–23), mounted an attack on She-lun in 410, but the Jou-jan retreated out of range. She-lun died during this campaign and his successors, Hu-lü and Ta-t'an, stayed away from the frontier until T'o-pa Ssu's death when the Jou-jan invaded China. T'o-pa Tao (r. 423–52) repulsed the invasion and in 425 he ordered a counterattack deep into northern Mongolia. When his troops reached the southernmost part of the desert, they abandoned their heavy weapons and proceeded north into Mongolia with a team of crack troops and provisions for fifteen days. The nomads were taken completely by surprise and defeated. In 429, T'o-pa Tao organized a hugely successful campaign on the steppe in which a reported 300,000 Jou-jan and Kao-ch'e were taken prisoner and deported to the frontier, along with millions of animals. While the figures may be exaggerated, their magnitude reveals that Wei policy was aimed at depopulating the steppe to undercut Jou-jan power. These campaigns occurred while Wei was still deeply involved in wars to conquer north China.[38]

The khaghan Ta-t'an died during the Wei invasion and was succeeded by his son Wu-t'i, who sent envoys to present gifts to the Wei court. A marriage alliance was arranged in which the khaghan married one of the emperor's daughters, while the emperor married one of the khaghan's sisters. Such marriage alliances had been employed in the Han, but had been one-sided, with the Chinese sending out royal women to steppe leaders. Foreign dynasties on the other hand tried to employ reciprocal marriage alliances in order to make the bonds more secure. However, as soon as Wu-t'i felt strong enough he began attacking the Wei frontier. Wei responded with a series of campaigns in 438, 439, 443, and 444 which were only marginally successful because the Jou-jan always retreated out of danger. It was not until 449, when T'o-pa Tao personally mounted a major invasion, that the Jou-jan were severely defeated and retreated from the frontier. Wei continued its dominance under T'o-pa Chün (r. 452–65), who organized an attack on the Jou-jan in 458 which employed 100,000 troops and 150,000 supply carts. This invasion forced the Jou-jan west and they lost control of many of their subject tribes. In response, the Jou-jan turned more of their attention to Turkestan, seizing Turfan (460). That they focused on an area beyond the range of the T'o-pa military is evidence of how pressed they were in the east.[39]

The pattern of the T'o-pa military campaigns was to make at least one major invasion a generation. Such invasions were designed to destroy the economic and political base of the nomadic state by robbing it of people and animals to such an extent that it would take at least ten to twenty years for the Jou-jan to recover. The Wei was able to make good use of the tribesmen it captured by distributing them over the frontier as military units based in six major garrisons. These garrisons were designed both as jumping off points for campaigns into Mongolia and as a buffer to prevent the Jou-jan from coming too close to the frontier. Essentially, Wei was attempting to control the steppe by removing most of the nomadic population to within its frontier where it would become part of the T'o-pa military machine. Such a strategy would have been rejected by a Chinese dynasty, for it meant settling masses of enemy tribal peoples within the frontier where they could potentially pose an even greater danger. Because the T'o-pa were from a tribal background themselves, they did not have this fear. Their dual organization allowed them to incorporate frontier peoples under a separate administration, designed to be compatible with their customs and one that could make good use of their military potential. The Wei policy of massive deportation of nomads from the steppe left the Jou-jan with a hollow empire. Each time they were about to recover, the Wei mounted new offensives.

Beginning in 485 the Jou-jan began attacking the Wei frontier on an annual basis. The khaghan Tou-lan (r. 482–92) was particularly aggressive, and this provoked a Wei campaign against him in 492. Compared with previous campaigns, this one did not result in the wholesale capture of people and animals, but it did manage to split the Jou-jan. Tou-lan became unpopular because he was constantly losing battles and many nomads wanted him replaced by his uncle Na-kai, who had been militarily successful. After the Wei attack a rebel faction formed around him, killed Tou-lan, and made Na-kai khaghan.

The Wei campaign against Tou-lan was the last major attempt by that dynasty to follow its traditional policy of disrupting the nomads. After this time there was no military response from the Wei, for it was undergoing a radical shift in foreign and domestic policy. As the dynasty sinified, its frontier policy began to resemble that of native Chinese dynasties, relying on fixed defenses and payoffs to the nomads. Under these favorable conditions the nomads began to grow in power.

THE SINIFICATION OF THE T'O-PA WEI

In a dual organization it was the emperor who was responsible for maintaining the balance between the Chinese and tribal elites that were the pillars of the dynasty. Any change in the balance of influence between these two groups had a critical impact on the Wei dynasty. The location of the Wei capital at P'ing-ch'eng in the tribal borderlands exemplified the compromise, in spite of the fact that it was hard to supply and not central for administration. Chinese, Hsien-pi, and imported Buddhist customs could all be found co-existing there. The balance changed with the death of T'o-pa Chün. His wife, the dowager empress Feng, began an attempt to sinify the Wei state. By Hsien-pi custom, the mother of the heir was supposed to be executed to prevent her from having influence at court, but Feng, of Chinese origin, managed to avoid that fate by ruling through a stepson, T'o-pa Hung (r. 465–71), who later abdicated in favor of his infant son and then died in 476. The dowager empress Feng continued ruling through her stepgrandson, T'o-pa Hung II (r. 471–99) until her death in 480. Hung II, better known by his Chinese titles of Kao-tsu or Hsiao-wen, was fully in favor of this policy, which he greatly expanded when power finally came into his hands.[40]

Kao-tsu promoted a series of changes aimed at removing Hsien-pi influence in the Wei state, beginning with staffing of the government almost exclusively with Chinese. Attempts were made to ban Hsien-pi rituals and to encourage the intermarriage of the T'o-pa and Chinese elites. The key event, however, was the choice of a new capital at Lo-yang in 494. This separated the government from its tribal elements, made them marginal to the state, and impoverished many tribal clans, which had derived their wealth by provisioning the capital. To make even more clear its anti-tribal bias, the court banned the wearing of Hsien-pi clothes (494), banned the use of Hsien-pi language at court for young officials (495), integrated the tribal and Han elites into a single ranking system (495), and abandoned the surname T'o-pa, replacing it with a Chinese one – Yüan (496). In 496 a brief revolt among the frontier tribes slowed the pace of the reforms, but the dynasty had already been redesigned on a Chinese model.

The sinification at court had a profound effect on the northern frontier, particularly since the death of Kao-tsu in 499 left the Wei government in weak hands. The move to Lo-yang drastically changed the relation of the frontier troops to the dynasty. Previously they had been well supplied, their leaders had received favor at court, and the northern border got constant imperial attention. After the move, the traditional Chinese view of the northern frontier as a marginal region gained strength. Tribal troops were no longer viewed as pillars of the state, but as politically unreliable. Garrisons were cheated of their rations by corrupt officials, who were assigned to frontier posts as a form of exile along with convicts sentenced to frontier service. The Wei policy of aggressive disruption of the Jou-jan was replaced by a conservative approach of walled defenses and tributary benefits. Thus, when the court tried to implement a model Chinese government it reverted to the traditional approach to frontier affairs developed by the Han. The major difficulty was that it still depended on troops of tribal origin for staffing the imperial guard, for putting down peasant revolts, and for frontier defense. In 519, for example, the imperial guard in Lo-yang rioted when a Chinese official proposed that soldiers be excluded from the higher government posts. This proposal was in line with Confucian values, but the government was forced to give into the soldiers' demands that it not be implemented.

The changes produced by the sinification scheme were most apparent in the way the Jou-jan khaghan A-nu-kuei manipulated the Wei court. He had been made khaghan in 519 following the death of his brother, but within a few months had lost the throne to a rival, P'o-luo-men. The next year he appeared at the Wei court seeking aid to regain his throne. In an audience before the emperor he asked for troops and weapons. The Wei had received rival Jou-jan factions in the past, but its response on those occasions had been to incorporate them into the Wei elite by granting them titles and wives. A-nu-keui was seeking to employ the inner frontier strategy, used by Hsiung-nu factions in similar situations. The Wei court supported him in the hopes of dividing the Jou-jan into permanent rival factions, but they failed. A-na-kuei no sooner had regained his throne than he mounted a massive Jou-jan attack in 523 resulting in the capture of a huge number of animals.

The Wei called up its frontier garrisons and sent them in a futile pursuit of the Jou-jan. Under stress from neglect and maladministration, this campaign set the stage for a revolt by frontier troops the next year. The immediate spark was a corrupt official's refusal to issue grain to starving troops. The revolt quickly spread to most of the frontier. The Wei court's only allies, ironically, proved to be the Jou-jan. A-nu-kuei devastated the frontier region and temporarily put down the rebellion. To forestall further trouble, the Wei moved many of its rebellious troops south where it was thought they could be more easily controlled. This proved to be a grave error, for they revolted again in 525 and 526, putting the capital itself in danger. The emperor sent letters of praise to A-nu-kuei, and formally recognized him as an equal.

A Chieh tribal leader, Erhchu Jung, marched on Lo-yang in 528 to put a new heir on the throne. When he arrived there, he murdered the entire Wei court, between 1,300 and 3,000 people. At one stroke he wiped out Wei's experiment in Chinese-style government. Lo-yang was soon deserted and the Wei state split into a Western Wei (Chou), representing Hsien-pi values, and an Eastern Wei (Ch'i) with a more Chinese style. Both sides greatly feared the nomads and made attempts to placate A-na-kuei with gifts and marriage alliances.

The collapse of the Wei marked the end of Manchurian rule in China. With the split began the process of transferring power back to the Chinese with the country's unification under Sui/T'ang. The end of the Wei showed that as a foreign dynasty became more imbrued with Chinese values it left itself vulnerable both to disaffected tribal elements and to a xenophobic north Chinese elite. The tribal military felt betrayed when the dynasty reduced its importance by promoting Chinese to the most powerful positions at court and reduced the economic and political benefits that had previously been taken for granted. The north Chinese elite, however, never fully accepted foreign rule even after a dynasty had adopted Chinese institutions and met the political criteria for legitimacy. Although foreign dynasties could claim to have succeeded to power by orthodox rules of dynastic succession, and were included in the standard dynastic histories of China, they never lost the taint of their "barbarian" origin.

The fall of the Wei also brought to a close a great cycle. We noted earlier that steppe empires and Chinese dynasties like the Han and Hsiung-nu were contemporaneous in origin and demise because of their interdependence. In the anarchy that followed, we argued that it was tribes of the northeast with their dual organizations that could first survive and then exploit the anarchy to establish strong states in north China. As time went on, such dynasties, given a choice between frontier and Chinese problems, abandoned the frontier in order to keep a grip on China. Without a tribal military such a grip could not be maintained and, ultimately, Chinese forces unseated them. Yet the time they had devoted to China, neglecting the steppe, had given the steppe tribes an opportunity to organize unopposed. By the time the Chinese had thrown the Manchurians out they faced a united steppe ready to implement the outer frontier strategy with a power unseen since the time of the Hsiung-nu.

NOTES

1 The history of the Wu-huan and the neighboring Hsien-pi during the later Han from which this account is drawn is found in the *Hou han-shu* (HHS), chapter 90 (120 in some editions). Other details are supplied by the *Wei-shu*, chapter 30, in the *San Kuo Chih* (SKC) [*Chronicle of the Three Kingdoms*], which covers much the same material. Schreiber, "Das Volk der Hsien-pi zur Han-Zeit" provides the most complete account of the Hsien-pi during this period.

2 HHS 90:1b–3a; Parker, "History of the Wu-wan or Wu-hwan Tunguses of the first century; followed by that of their kinsmen the Sien-pi," 20:73, 75.

3 HHS 90:9b; Parker, ibid., 20:93.

4 HHS 89:18b; Parker, "Turko-Scythian Tribes," 21:266.

5 HHS 90:10b; Parker, "History of the Wu-wan," 20:94.

6 HHS 90:14b–15a; Parker, ibid., 20:97.

7 HHS 90:20a; Parker, ibid., 20:88, quoted from SKC Wei 30:2a–2b.

8 The account below is drawn largely from Ssu-ma Kuang, *Tzu Chih T'ung Chien* (TCTC); cf. Crespigny, *The Last of the Han* and Fang, *The Chronicle of the Three Kingdoms*.

9 Michaud; "The Yellow Turbans."

10 Yang, "Notes on the economic history of the Chin dynasty."

11 HHS 48:15–15b, HHS 90:17a; Yü, *Trade and Expansion in Han China*, pp. 109, 132; Parker, "History of the Wu-wan," 20:98.

12 TCTC 1915–16; Crespigny, *Last of the Han*, pp. 70–1.

13 TCTC 1885–6, 1889; Crespigny, ibid., pp. 34, 38. Cf. Haloun, "The Liang-chou rebellion."

14 TCTC 2057–8; Crespigny, ibid., pp. 231–2.

15 Ibid.

16 TCTC 2072–3; Crespigny, ibid., pp. 247–8.

17 TCTC 2146–7; Crespigny, ibid., p. 327; Boodberg, "Two notes on the history of the Chinese frontier," p. 292.

18 K'o-pi-ning's biography can be found in SKC *Wei* 30:7b–9b.

19 This is one of the most ignored periods in Chinese history. Comparatively little research has been devoted to it, particularly on the short-lived foreign dynasties established in the north. The basic history of the period is recorded in the *Chin shu* (CS), but because of the complexity of peoples and events most historians rely on Ssu-ma Kuang's *Tzu Chih T'ung Chien* as a guide.

20 SKC *Wei* 28:19ab; Fang, *Chronicle*, vol. 2, pp. 85–6; CS 56; cf. Boodberg, "Two notes," pp. 292–7.
21 Yang, "Notes on economic history."
22 Wright, "Fu-t'u-teng," notes an alternative hypothesis that Chieh could also refer to mercenaries from the west and thus indicate occupation rather than ethnic identity.
23 Gardiner, "The Kung-sun warlords of Liao-tung 189–238."
24 Schreiber, "The history of the former Yen dynasty," provides an exceptionally detailed study of the Mu-jung drawing on a variety of sources.
25 Ikeuchi, "A study of Fu-yü."
26 Schreiber, "Former Yen," 14:125–30.
27 TCTC 97:3064; Schreiber, ibid., 14:475.
28 TCTC 99:3126; Schreiber, ibid., 15:28.
29 TCTC 99:3150; Schreiber, ibid., 15:32.
30 TCTC 100:3162; Schreiber, ibid., 15:47.
31 Schreiber, ibid., 15:59ff, 120–2.
32 TCTC 101:3211; Schreiber, ibid., 15:81–2.
33 CS 113:2b; Rogers, *The Chronicle of Fu Chien*, p. 116.
34 The basic history of the T'o-pa is found in the *Wei-shu* (WS), see also Eberhard, *Das Toba-Reich Nord Chinas*.
35 Jenner, *Memories of Loyang*, pp. 20–5.
36 *Jou-jan tzu-liao chi-lu* [Collection of historical source material on the Jou-jan], pp. 3–6.
37 Kollautz and Hisayuki, *Geschichte und Kultur eines völkerwanderungszeitlichen Nomadenvolks*, vol. 1, p. 110; WS 35.
38 *Jou-jan*, pp. 6–10.
39 *Jou-jan*, pp. 10–18.
40 Jenner, *Memories*, pp. 38–62 for the details of the move to Lo-yang, and Holmgren, "The Empress Dowager Ling of the Northern Wei and the T'o-pa sinicization question", for politics that brought down the dynasty.

GLOSSARY OF KEY NAMES

MAIN TRIBES ON THE STEPPE FRONTIER

HSIEN-PI
successors to the Hsiung-nu in northern Mongolia (130–80)
founded dynasties in Manchuria and north China (4th–6th centuries)
HSIUNG-NU
divided into smaller groups on both sides of China's frontier
Mao-tun lineage of *Shan-yü*s remained active until fifth century
JOU-JAN
dominant tribe in Mongolia (380–555)
known mostly for defeats at hands of the T'o-pa Wei
K'AO-CH'E (CH'IH-LE)
subordinate tribal group of the Jou-jan

T'U-YÜ-HUN
  nomads of Hsien-pi origin who lived around Lake Koko-nor
TI
  Ch'iang subgroup settled in the Ch'ang-an area (3rd–5th centuries)
WU-HUAN
  nomads along the northeastern border of China
  culturally similar to the Hsien-pi
  disappeared as political group after 300

KEY TRIBAL FIGURES (ALL FAIRLY OBSCURE)

T'AN-SHIH-HUAI
  only Hsien-pi ruler to unite the steppe tribes (r. 156–80)
K'O-PI-NENG
  Hsien-pi leader during collapse of Han dynasty
SU-P'U-YEN
  Wu-huan leader following collapse of Han dynasty

DYNASTIES IN NORTH CHINA FOLLOWING THE COLLAPSE OF THE HAN

CHINESE WARLORD DYNASTIES
  NORTHERN (TS'AO) WEI (220–66) (N)
  WESTERN CHIN (265–316) (N)
  Liang (313–76) (NW)

DYNASTIES OF HSIUNG-NU ORIGIN
  Han/Chao (304–29) (N)
  Later Chao (319–52) (N)
  Northern Liang (397–439) (NW)
  Hsia (407–31) (N)

DYNASTIES OF HSIEN-PI ORIGIN
  Former Yen (348–70) (NE)
  Later Yen (383–409) (NE)
  Southern Yen (398–410) (NE)
  Northern Yen (409–36) (NE)
  Southern Liang (397–414) (NW)
  NORTHERN (T'O-PA) WEI (386–534) (N)
  WESTERN WEI (534–57) (N)

DYNASTIES OF TI ORIGIN
  CH'IN (352–410) (N)
  Later Ch'in (384–417) (NW)
  Later Liang (386–403) (NW)
  Western Liang (400–21) (NW)

(N) = central north China

(NE) = northeastern China
(NW) = northwestern China
UPPERCASE = ruled all of north China
lowercase = ruled part of north China

KEY CHINESE FIGURES

KUNG-SUN FAMILY
warlord dynasty of Liao-tung governors (189–237)
TS'AO TS'AO
Chinese warlord (155–200)
founder of Wei dynasty succeeded Later Han dynasty
suppressed border tribes
YÜAN SHAO
Chinese warlord allied with the nomads
lost to Ts'ao Ts'ao

KEY FOREIGN FIGURES

FU CHIEN
warlord of Ti origin
briefly united north China under Ch'in rule
LIU YÜAN
Hsiung-nu founder of Han/Chao dynasty (r. 304–10)
first *Shan-yü* to establish state in China
MU-JUNG
Hsien-pi clan that founded Yen dynasties (circa 300–400)
created dual organization for government administration
family name of Yen ruling house
HUI: established Mu-jung as frontier state (r. 283–333)
CHÜN: first declared Yen emperor (r. 348–60)
SHIH LE AND SHIH HU
Chieh Hsiung-nu warlord rulers of Later Chao dynasty
wreaked destruction across north China
T'O-PA
Hsien-pi clan that founded Wei dynasty (circa 400)
united all of north China
family name of Wei ruling house
KUEI: founder of the dynasty (r. 386–409)
HUNG (II) (*aka* Kao-tsu or Hsiao-wen) Wei emperor (r. 471–99)
carried out sinification policy, induced revolt

4

The Turkish Empires and T'ang China

The unification of China under the Ch'in/Han dynasties and the steppe under the Hsiung-nu after centuries of anarchy occurred within a single generation. Three hundred years later, dissolution of central power in both China and the steppe also took place within a generation. It was no accident that the steppe and China tended to be mirror images of one another. Ultimately the state organization of the steppe needed a stable China to exploit. The Turkish empires and the T'ang dynasty provide an unusual opportunity to test this hypothesis. The policies used by both closely resembled those employed by the Han and the Hsiung-nu centuries earlier under similar circumstances. However, there were a number of important differences because China had been profoundly affected by the period of foreign rule. This influence was so strong that for a short period a native Chinese emperor, Li Shih-min (T'ang T'ai-tsung), was able to create a polity within which he was accepted as ruler over both the steppe and China. His successors, however, failed to carry on his policies and reverted to the defensive strategies toward the steppe characteristic of the Han dynasty. This change showed that once a native dynasty established itself in China strong forces came into play to implement defensive foreign policies that preserved the power of the literate bureaucrats in their struggle with the merchant and military classes. In the end, this led to a situation in which a weak T'ang dynasty was actually preserved by the nomads and protected from internal revolts and invasions because of the benefits it provided. A relationship that began as predatory became symbiotic. When the Uighurs fell in 840, the T'ang dynasty lost its protector and collapsed in internal revolt within a generation.

THE FIRST TURKISH EMPIRE

The T'u-chüeh, the most famous of the nomadic Turkish tribes, enter the Chinese historical record in the middle of the sixth century.[1] Their home was in the Altai Mountain region, although some sources suggest they may have originally come from the P'ing-liang area in eastern Kansu. They were subjects of the Jou-jan and renowned for their skill in ironworking. The Jou-jan had only periodically been in firm control of the steppe. The attacks of the T'o-pa Wei had beaten them back from the frontier immediately after they had established their empire. Later, when the Wei moved to Lo-yang and abandoned its aggressive frontier policy, the Jou-jan were too divided by their own disputes to take advantage of the change. Indicative of their weakness was the existence of another independent nomadic group, the T'u-yü-hun in Koko-nor who controlled the trade routes to Turkestan. China was able to use Tu-yü-hun territory to bypass the Jou-jan.[2] The Jou-jan also never fully subjugated the Kao-ch'e (T'ieh-le), who periodically revolted against their overlords. In 546, the Turks came to prominence when they defeated the Kao-ch'e for the Jou-jan, capturing 50,000 tents. The Turkish leader T'u-men sought a marriage alliance with the Jou-jan khaghan A-na-kuei as a reward for this service. Instead he received a stinging rebuke that called the Turks impudent slaves. T'u-men killed the envoys who delivered the message and began a revolt.

T'u-men strengthened his political position by making an alliance with the western Wei state of Chou in 551. The next year, he engaged the Jou-jan in battle and defeated them. Their khaghan A-na-kuei committed suicide. T'u-men also died that year and was succeeded briefly by his son K'o-lo who mounted another attack on the Jou-jan. He also died and was succeeded by his brother Mu-kan, who chased the remnants of the Jou-jan leadership into eastern China where he killed them. He went on to conquer the T'u-yü-hun and greatly extended the Turkish empire, with the aid of his uncle Istämi, until it reached from Manchuria to the Caspian Sea.

The empire was organized as an imperial confederacy. Like that of the Hsiung-nu, it had three basic levels: an imperial government and court bureaucracy, imperial appointees governing tribes throughout the empire, and indigenous tribal leaders running the local affairs of their own people.

The highest imperial rank was that of khaghan, but unlike the Hsiung-nu rank of *Shan-yü*, it was not always exclusive. The senior khaghan sometimes appointed lesser khaghans to rule over parts of the empire. The heir apparent to the khaghan held the title of *yabghu*. Before the establishment of the Turkish empire this title appears to have been the highest, for the T'u-chüeh first became powerful under the leadership of the "Great Yabghu" when still part of the Jou-jan empire. The imperial governors of the empire held the title of *shad*. They and the *yabghu* ruled over the component tribes of the empire. Those holding these titles were the sons, brothers, and uncles of the khaghan, called *tigin* (princes). All were members of the ruling A-shih-na clan.

The tribes making up the empire all had their own native rulers, *bäg*. Leaders of powerful tribes held the title of *iltäbär*, those from less powerful tribes were called *irkin*. They were all under the authority of one of the imperial governors. Collectively these local tribal groups were divided into eastern and western wings: the *Tölis* and *Tardush*. Tribes not directly ruled by the Turks were watched over by *tudun*, agents appointed by the khaghan to extract tribute and maintain the loyalty of more distant tribes. According to Chinese records there were 28 ranks, all hereditary, in the whole system.[3]

From what information is available it appears that the Turkish empire was not as centralized as that of the Hsiung-nu. The khaghan's willingness to appoint lesser khaghans who were often autonomous created fractures in the state structure and reduced the senior khaghan's ability to command. The Turks lacked the decimal system of military organization (commanders of 10,000, 1,000, etc.) and the khaghan had less power over his subordinates than had the Hsiung-nu *Shan-yü*.

The rise of the Turks, like that of the Hsiung-nu, was due to their military might. As soon as they had established themselves, the Turks began to extort subsidies from the two rival courts in north China, Chou and Ch'i. The Turks did not need to invade China to impress them. Both courts had been terrified by the earlier destruction of the Jou-jan and the conquests on the steppe. The Turks received lavish gifts from each court. On occasion they acted as mercenaries, aiding Chou in attacks on Ch'i. Trade flourished, with the Turks exchanging horses for silk. In 553 the Turks brought 50,000 horses to the frontier. During Mu-kan's reign (553–72) the Chou court made an annual gift of 100,000 rolls of silk to the khaghan and was forced to lavishly maintain a host of Turkish visitors in the capital as a goodwill gesture. Ch'i was not far behind in making its bribes. Both courts feared that the Turks would side with their rival. The khaghan enjoyed being the focus of such a competition, which made the Turks enormously wealthy. The khaghan is reputed to have said, "My two children in the south are always filial and obedient, so why should I fear poverty?"[4]

The silk trade was a major agent binding the Turkish empire together. The eastern Turks extracted the silk from China and the western Turks traded it to Iran and Byzantium. Each ruler had his own power base which permitted great autonomy. As long as the kinship bonds between the two rulers were close there was peaceful cooperation. After the death of the empire's founders these links gradually weakened, and their successors began a civil war which left the empire permanently divided. The Turkish empire was at the height of its power when war began. The problem was similar in origin to that faced by the Hsiung-nu: the difficulty of running a political system in which lateral succession was the norm. Lateral succession became the bane of the Turks because they could not agree on how to exclude potential heirs. Unlike the Hsiung-nu, the Turks did not have a clear hierarchy of ranks that determined who was in line for the throne once a set of brothers was exhausted. Ultimately, succession could be guaranteed only through the use of force. The association of violence with succession disputes on the steppe was a legacy of the Turks.[5]

The Turkish empire split into hostile eastern and western khaghanates around 581 during the period the eastern Turks were engaged in a civil war. Both the split and the civil war can be explained by the difficulty the Turks encountered when power had to be passed to a new generation.

The informal division of the empire was a legacy of T'u-men. He had granted his brother Istämi the right to rule over the west as Hsi-mien khaghan

(khaghan facing west). When T'u-men died in 553, Istämi appears to have made no attempt to become the supreme ruler of the empire. The title of senior khaghan passed to his nephews, T'u-men's sons. Istämi outlived most of his brother's sons and died during the reign of T'o-po in 576. Istämi's son Tardu became ruler of the west. If Tardu was not satisfied with his position of nominal subordination to his cousins, he did not immediately revolt. T'o-po (or Tapar) was slightly senior in genealogical terms and, more importantly, he was well-established in power and had been accepted as senior khaghan by Istämi.

Tardu only caused serious trouble after T'o-po died when he refused to recognize the rights of the next generation. In kinship terms Tardu was now the senior male of his generation and thereby outranked the sons of his cousins. He could argue that since all the sons of T'u-men were now dead, the highest honors should go next to any of the surviving sons of Istämi. It was an excellent opportunity for the powerful western khaghanate to renegotiate the terms on which the empire had been founded. Tardu was aided in this task by the eastern Turks' difficulties in transferring power to a new generation. They could not agree on how to do it peacefully.

The eastern Turks had gained a long period of stability by passing the throne from elder brother to younger brother until the sons of T'u-men had all died. This system of succession was most vulnerable when the throne had to be passed to a new generation. Cousins had little to bind them together and each set could make some claim as sons of former khaghans. Once power did pass to a new generation all but one of these lines would find themselves permanently removed from the possibility of future successions. In theory there should not have been a problem. By seniority the eldest son of the eldest brother was entitled to the throne after all the younger brothers had died. Only after he and his own brothers died would the throne then move to any surviving cousins representing junior lines of the same generation. (This was the essence of Tardu's right to succeed.) However, this model of succession by strict seniority ignored some major political difficulties. The most senior male of the junior generation was often the son of a khaghan dead for many decades, while the sons of more recent khaghans were closer to real power and could employ their fathers' political allies in their own struggles. Regardless of the technical rights and privileges, the end of a line of brothers created an opportunity for sets of cousins to vie for the throne on the basis of their political and military strength. The sudden decline of the first Turkish empire, which was at its height of military and economic power, was the consequence of division at the top.

The dynamics of such a succession struggle are best illustrated by looking at the details of the first civil war. The khaghans and their relationship to one another are outlined in table 4.1. In the first succession, power passed from T'u-men to his son K'o-lo. Istämi had already received the western part of the empire and a khaghan title before his brother died. Although Istämi was potentially more powerful than his nephews, and by the rights of lateral succession could have attempted to become the senior khaghan, he did not contest his nephew's elevation. K'o-lo died almost immediately after becoming khaghan and was succeeded by his younger brother Mu-kan, who ruled for the next eighteen years. Mu-kan was the most powerful ruler of his generation. It

Table 4.1   Reigns of khaghans of the first Turkish empire

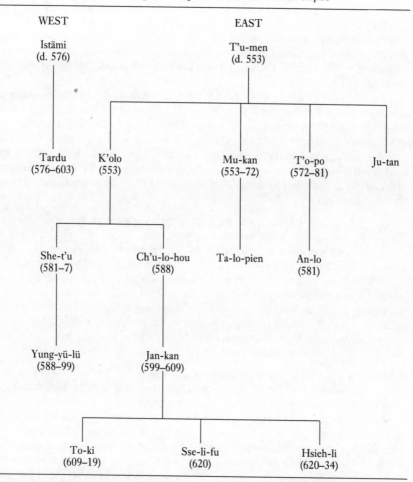

was during his reign that the Jou-jan were finally destroyed and the Ephthalites driven from Afghanistan by his uncle Istämi. However, even he appointed his younger brothers to lesser khaghan positions. T'o-po resided in eastern Mongolia as the Tung-mien khaghan (khaghan facing east), in charge of overseeing tribes along the Manchurian border and attacking the Khitans. Ju-tan was named Pu-li khaghan in charge of western Mongolia.

When Mu-kan died in 572, his brother T'o-po became khaghan. This succession was peaceful but there was evidence of tension growing within the ruling house. Sons of khaghans had been passed over in favor of their uncles; and the new generation was pushing to take power as soon as T'o-po, the last living son of T'u-men, died. In the meantime, many of them were appointed junior khaghans. T'o-po appointed a son of his younger brother Ju-tan Pu-li khaghan, while K'o-lo's son She-t'u became Tung-mien khaghan. Istämi died soon thereafter and his son Tardu became Hsi-mien khaghan. Of the four khaghans, Tardu was the most powerful, although T'o-po outranked him. She-t'u was also militarily strong. T'o-po was already losing his grip on the empire as the lesser khaghans gained in power. This devolution of power meant that when he died in 581 the struggle for the throne became intense. A civil war erupted.

The Turkish khaghan was chosen from the potential heirs by an elective council seeking a consensus, but unlike similar Hsiung-nu elections there were more open disputes during the process. The candidates in 581 included the descendants of the four sons of T'u-men who had held a khaghan title. The major contest was among An-lo, the son of T'o-po; Ta-lo-pien, son of the long-lived Mu-kan; and She-t'u, son of the eldest brother Kolo and representative of the genealogically senior line of descent. The election was fraught with threats of violence.

When [T'o-po] died, his people at the head of the administration were about to set up Ta-lo-pien; but in view of his mother's humble status the masses were dissatisfied. An-lo was truly well-born and possessed the Turks' esteem. She-t'u was the last to arrive, and he addressed the assembly saying, "In the event of An-lo being set up, I and my brothers will of course serve him; but if Ta-lo-pien is set up, I shall certainly hold my own territory and deal with him at the point of a sword and lance." She-t'u being the senior, and formidable to boot, the assembly did not oppose him, and so An-lo was set up as successor. Ta-lo-pien, not having secured the succession, was at heart unsubmissive to An-lo, and on several occasions sent persons to revile him. An-lo was powerless to control him, and therefore abdicated in favor of She-t'u.[6]

She-t'u became Sha-po-lüeh khaghan. He appointed An-lo Second khaghan as a consolation prize. When Ta-lo-pien objected that only he was without a khaghan title, She-t'u named him A-po khaghan.

She-t'u's hold on the empire was tenuous. Not only did he have strong rivals on the steppe but, just as he took power, China cut off its subsidy payments. In 581, the Sui dynasty had unified north China and was moving to recover the south to form a single empire. When its founder Sui Wen-ti (r. 581–604), destroyed the Chou state two of his first acts were to send all the Turks living at court back to the steppe and to stop making the huge silk payments. This was a great threat to the Turkish empire because it had grown wealthy and powerful on the trade and gifts that it had extracted from the weak successors of the T'o-pa Wei. She-t'u's response of both of these problems was to organize an enormous raid on China in 582. This invasion was intended both to reward the Turkish tribes with loot and to induce the Sui court to adopt a more accommodating policy towards the steppe.

The raid was a great success. The Turks carried off practically all the livestock along the frontier. It did not resolve the internal power struggle, however. She-t'u remained concerned about the loyalty of Ta-lo-pien, although he had come to aid She-t'u in repelling Sui counterattacks that followed the Turkish invasion of China. So while Ta-lo-pien was away fighting the

Chinese, She-t'u attacked his rival's people in an attempt to destroy his power base. This attack opened a period of violent civil war that lasted for two decades.

She-t'u's attempt to wipe out his rival failed. Ta-lo-pien fled west to seek Tardu's aid. Tardu used the breakup of the eastern Turks as an opportunity to declare himself an independent khaghan and was looking to become the paramount Turkish leader. He was more than eager to help Ta-lo-pien. He equipped an army which soon defeated She-t'u, who was forced to flee for safety to the border of China in 584.

In seeking China's aid after a defeat on the steppe She-t'u was following the inner frontier policy which had been employed by the southern *Shan-yüs*: exchanging submission to China for protection and aid against rival tribal leaders. This is not to say that She-t'u was aware of the parallel, although the Chinese were. Rather it was one of the few options open to a defeated leader. The Jou-jan leaders had unsuccessfully sought such protection when they fled to Ch'i following their defeat by the Turks. Ch'i, fearful of Turkish retaliation, had delivered them back to be murdered. Sui was in a much stronger position and welcomed the defection as a way to perpetuate division on the steppe. It protected She-t'u from attacks by both his Turkish rivals and the Khitan tribes from Manchuria.

China had strong ideological reasons for welcoming the submission of a Turkish khaghan. After centuries of foreign rule, China was now united under a native dynasty. In the minds of Confucian historians, the formal submission of a Turkish khaghan, stripped of power though he was, was another indication that the "Mandate of Heaven" was truly held by the Sui dynasty. It recalled the more glorious days of Han. For this reason the Chinese underplayed the political nature of She-t'u's actions. He was by no means pleased to find himself dependent on China and acted in a surly manner towards Chinese envoys, although he was portrayed as polite in his written communications with the court. She-t'u had allied himself with China because he needed a base from which to rebuild, not because he was an admirer of the Sui.

She-t'u died in 587 and was succeeded by his brother Ch'u-lo-hou, who led an offensive against Ta-lo-pien. Many of the Turkish tribes, assuming that Ch'u-lo-hou was supported by Sui military aid, defected to him from Ta-lo-pien. In the ensuing battle Ta-lo-pien was captured and died soon thereafter. Ch'u-lo-hou extended his attacks further to the west but was killed in battle. He was succeeded by She-t'u's son, Yung-yü-lü (Tu-lan khaghan).

Ta-lo-pien's defeat did not mean the end of the civil war. Tardu still controlled most of the steppe and had ambitions to become the sole ruling khaghan. Even within the eastern Turkish ranks order could not be restored easily because of new conflicts when a new generation began its own wars over the throne. As during the earlier conflict, this new battle involved rival sets of cousins.

Yung-yü-lü had succeeded his uncle because he was the eldest of the senior line. Ch'u-lo-hou's son Jan-kan had declared himself T'u-li khaghan, ruling over the T'ieh-le (Kao-ch'e) tribes in the north. Yung-yü-lü's succession displaced Ch'u-lo-hou's sons, yet it had been Ch'u-lo-hou who restored the fortunes of the eastern Turks while She-t'u had been responsible for their loss. The Sui courts was well aware of this rivalry and encouraged its growth. They granted Jan-kan a Sui princess in marriage and sent many gifts in 597. The flood of gifts to Jan-kan – 370 missions were sent to him in a little over a year – infuriated Yung-yü-lü, who attacked the Sui frontier and allied himself with Tardu. Jan-kan suffered major defeats at their hands and had to retreat behind Chinese walls.

It was during this period that Tardu's fortune reached its height. After Yung-yü-lü was murdered by his retainers in 599, Tardu declared himself the sole legitimate khaghan of the Turks. He then made wide-ranging attacks in an attempt to wipe out the eastern Turkish line. His attacks threatened the Sui capital of Lo-yang in 601 and the next year Jan-kan came under attack in the Ordos. In attempting to sow discord on the steppe the Sui had reaped a fiery whirlwind of frontier warfare that threatened to unite the Turks under a leadership of the aggressive Tardu.

Fortunately for the Sui and Jan-kan, Tardu's campaigns so far east of his own territory left him vulnerable to revolt at home. The Tölis tribe took advantage of his absence to throw off Turkish domination. Tardu abandoned Mongolia to the eastern Turks and returned west, where he died. With Sui help Jan-kan took control of the tribes in southern Mongolia, but his grip on the tribes north of the Gobi was weak. When Jan-kan died in 609, the khaghan title was passed on to his son To-ki (Shih-pi khaghan), and, until their destruction by T'ang, the eastern Turks were ruled successively by him and his two brothers.

In comparison with the Hsiung-nu, the Turks were much more prone to civil war. This was due to both the large number of potential heirs and to their inability to eliminate collateral claims except by force. In analyzing the theoretical problems of such systems the anthropologist Jack Goody has noted:

With each succeeding generation the problem of determining seniority becomes more complex, and the number of possible candidates becomes too great even for elective or appointive succession. The system cannot continue indefinitely. By the third or fourth generations, you get strong pressures towards a reduction in the number of potential successors.

One possibility would be to concentrate at [the third generation of potential heirs] on the offspring of a single brother. This results in modified unigeniture. But it would be a most explosive system since it means that a man may be king and his children not. Indeed I know of no actual example of this possibility.[7]

The first Turkish empire would seem to be such a case, and, as predicted, such a system was highly explosive when power moved from one generation to the next. Ultimately, potential heirs could be excluded only by death. Civil wars therefore became extremely common because the number of potential heirs in a society that permitted polygyny was bound to be large. In Ottoman times, the Turks solved this problem of lateral heirs by killing all the new sultan's brothers, a brutal but effective method.

A CHINESE KHAGHAN

Jan-kan owed his position to the Sui and the dynasty began to look upon the eastern Turks as important allies. In 605, the Sui dispatched 20,000 Turks against the Khitans, who were soundly defeated. However, Sui Yang-ti (r. 605–16, d. 618) found that he could not always count on their help. During a visit to the khaghan's court in 607 he discovered that Jan-kan was negotiating with envoys from Korea, and the next year, after agreeing to help the Sui with the capture of Hami in Turkestan, the Turks did not show up. But the Turks, in spite of their unreliability, had become an important part of Yang-ti's plans for expansion. For example, he threatened the Koreans with an attack by the Turks if they did not submit to his rule. In order to maintain China's alliance with the Turks, Yang-ti organized border markets for the nomads, gave their leaders gifts, and held hostages at court. However, he also constructed defenses along the Yellow River to protect China in case the nomads turned hostile.[8]

Yang-ti's reliance on the Turks was based on the Sui's long support of Jan-kan. As khaghan, he had built a career on accommodation with China. The situation changed quickly after he died in 609 during a state visit to Lo-yang. His son To-ki (Shih-pi khaghan) came to power and he was far cooler towards China than his father. When Sui Yang-ti attacked Korea with a huge army, expecting Turkish support, he found himself isolated whey they failed to arrive. This and two other Korean campaigns ended so disastrously that revolts broke out all over China. Initially, the Turks remained allied to the dynasty – at least to the extent of collecting their tributary benefits – until 615. That year, they became overtly hostile and attacked Yang-ti who was vacationing near the frontier. The Sui empire fell further into civil war. Yang-ti was murdered in 618.

The Turks sat by while China collapsed. They happily received envoys from all the contenders who were sending gifts. They also received many refugees, including part of the Sui court, with whom the khaghan was related by marriage. In spite of their overwhelming power, the Turks did not play the role of king-makers nor did they attempt to conquer China. They supported about a half-dozen rebel groups, to whose leaders they granted titles, with horses and small numbers of troops, but the khaghan himself did not take an active military role. Like the nomadic empires before them, the Turks worked through intermediaries. They were content largely to sit by and wait to see what would emerge from China. They preferred to exploit China from a distance or raid. They shifted support periodically to make whoever was in power uneasy. Even as the new T'ang dynasty unified China, it was forced into a policy of appeasement toward the Turks. The outer frontier strategy was once again effective in making the Turks rich and powerful throughout the reign of the first T'ang emperor.

North China had been under foreign rule for three hundred years. In that time China's foreign rulers had become largely sinified, the policies of the T'o-pa Wei dynasty at Lo-yang being an example. The steps in this process have been subject to considerable scrutiny, but the reverse process of the "barbarization" of north China has received far less attention. The emergence of the T'ang dynasty is usually seen as a restoration of traditional Chinese values and policies. Yet a look at the Li family which founded the new dynasty shows that the Chinese elite in the north had been profoundly affected by the centuries of alien rule. Their values, habits, behavior, and policy all display a strong steppe influence. This influence was so pervasive that by the end of his reign Li Shih-min, the second T'ang emperor, was able to rule over both China and the steppe as the accepted ruler of both societies. His successors were unable to fill both roles and this unique combination reverted to its former bipolar form.

The impact of alien rule in north China was illustrated by the many debates between southerners from the Yangtze region, which had remained under Chinese rule, and the northern Chinese who had lived in China's ancient heartland under foreign rule. The southerners thought of themselves as the inheritors of the old Han culture. They considered the northerners to be lacking in literary ability and manners, but skilled in military affairs, more casual in their personal relationships, and unconcerned with form. In the north women had much greater freedom. They handled legal affairs, business, and lobbied for themselves at court. A sorry state of affairs that could be attributed to the steppe traditions of the T'o-pa Wei, according to southern writers – who secluded women. Yoghurt thinned with water, not tea, was the drink of the northern courts. Northerners laughed at the effete southern habit of drinking tea. A longer list of traits could be enumerated, but it was clear that a large number of steppe customs had been integrated into ordinary life in the north, particularly among the Chinese elite that served at court.[9]

Politics and military affairs were profoundly altered by steppe influence. The unification of China had been led by families of northwestern origin. After the breakup of the northern Wei dynasty, the unification of China was begun by the northern Chou dynasty, the heir to those rebels who had objected to the sinification policies of the last Wei emperors. It had come very close to succeeding in this task, but fell victim to a succession struggle which enabled the founders of the Sui to take advantage of their position as imperial in-laws to start a new dynasty which reunited all of China. The Li family, which founded the T'ang dynasty, was also part of this same elite. The northwestern aristocracy placed strong emphasis on martial virtues, and personal participation in warfare or hunting was highly valued, activities more in keeping with nomadic Turkish cultural traits than traditional Chinese ones. They did, however, have traditional Chinese educations, even if horse riding was preferred to calligraphy. In ethnic origin these families were a mix of old frontier Chinese, Hsien-pi, Hsiung-nu, and Turkish background, but over the centuries they had lost specific tribal ties and become a social class with a strong aristocratic tradition.[10]

When Sui fell the Li family was only one of many pretenders to the imperial throne. Li Yüan, the future T'ang Kao-tsu, was an important frontier commander in T'ai-yüan who had stayed loyal to the dynasty. As the anarchy in China increased, he took advantage of his military position to revolt in 617. In order to be successful it was necessary to strike a deal with the Turkish khaghan, who had more power than any single rebel army in China. While not seeking a formal alliance with the Turks, as some of his rivals had done, Li Yüan promised to give the Turks all the loot taken during the campaign. He also argued that by restoring order to China it would be possible to reestablish the old tributary system which had so much benefited the nomads. The khaghan provided Li Yüan with thousands of horses and a few hundred men. With the aid of armies raised by his sons (and one by a daughter), Li Yüan quickly took the capital at Ch'ang-an and declared himself emperor of a new T'ang dynasty in 618. Battles to unify China lasted until 623. Many of the most outstanding military exploits were carried out by Li Shih-min, Li Yüan's second son.[11]

Li Shih-min's tactics in many of his battles displayed the influence of the frontier. He was master of the strategic retreat, letting larger armies exhaust themselves before he attacked. He personally led troops in battle and had four mounts shot from under him. He enshrined these horses in stone, with an accurate rendering of each horse's physical traits, including the number of arrow wounds. Such concern with detail about horses and battles was characteristic of steppe leaders, but not of founders of Chinese dynasties. Many were great generals but few were capable warriors and they generally avoided personal combat. Yet at the same time, Shih-min's education included standard training in the classics and calligraphy. His skill in the latter was admired long after his death. Together with these scholarly virtues, he also met the steppe's standard of achievement as an excellent horseman, great archer, and warrior.

Steppe politics, particularly the use of violence, marked the beginning of T'ang. Li Shih-min came into conflict with his elder brother Li Chien-ch'eng, who, by Chinese tradition, had precedence in succession. The heir and a younger brother, who were at court, plotted against Shih-min. They were fearful of his military power, for in 621 Kao-tsu had made him military and civil commander of the eastern plain based in Lo-yang. Beyond that, Shih-min's prestige in the empire as a whole was much greater than that of the heir. Chien-ch'eng feared that Shih-min would use his reputation to replace him. A bitter political struggle ensued between the two brothers. For some time it appeared that the heir had the advantage and that Shih-min would fall victim to plots to murder him. He avoided this fate by taking direct action against his elder brother in 626. He led a group of followers to the palace gate where he laid an ambush for the heir and his younger brother, who were both shot dead in a hail of arrows. Kao-tsu was informed that his services were no longer required and he was forced to abdicate a few days later in favor of Li Shih-min who became T'ang T'ai-tsung.

This was shocking to the sensibilities of Confucians, for whom fratricide and lack of filial piety were crimes against nature. Such actions were more in keeping with traditional Turkish power struggles or with Mao-tun's creation of the Hsiung-nu empire. Other nomadic features of early T'ang included the importance of a hereditary aristocracy. Under the northern Wei, the idea of a hereditary aristocracy had taken deep root. The northwestern aristocracy remained closer to Turkish ideology in this matter than to the old Chinese ideal of a meritocratic bureaucracy, and ranks and offices could be legally inherited (known as the *yin* privilege). Government administration also initially featured the dual military/civilian organization that was characteristic of the Hsien-pi dynasties. While the establishment of the T'ang marked the restoration of native Chinese rule to a unified empire, it was not a sharp break from the recent past.

Turkish influence within the royal line was even more pronounced in Li Shih-min's son and heir Li Ch'eng-ch'ien. He was fond of Turkish music and customs and surrounded himself with Turkish retainers. He ignored the traditional standards of Chinese behavior and used violence against anyone who offended him. He was rebuked for conduct unbecoming to an heir and stripped of his Turkish retainers. Outwardly, he then comported himself correctly. However in his palace he chose Chinese attendants that looked like Turks and spoke Turkish. He constructed a yurt in the courtyard complete with wolf's head banners. For amusement he once held a khaghan's funeral and played the corpse himself surrounded by wailing mounted nomads. He often expressed the desire to move to the steppe where he could lead a less restricted life. Ch'eng-ch'ien never ruled. He plotted against his father in 643, was exiled, and died a year later.

The details of Ch'eng-ch'ien's Turkish habits were recorded in lurid detail by court historians intent on proving he was unfit to rule. But his behavior, even at its most bizarre, was not unusual in his times. Except for the explicit Turkish overlay, his actions followed Li family tradition. One of Li Shih-min's younger brothers, when given rule of a province, had delighted in terrorizing the capital's inhabitants by shooting arrows at people from the palace walls. At night in the company of congenial thugs he broke into private houses for amusement. Li Shih-min himself had murdered two of his brothers and they had tried to poison him. He forced his own father from the throne. Moreover, Yang-ti, the last Sui emperor, was notorious for his ruthlessness. The palace culture for which T'ang was justly famous in later times should not hide the fact that the early T'ang elite in the northwest was close enough to the frontier Turks in so many ways that Li Shih-min could become their khaghan without stepping out of character.

With the fall of the Sui, the Turks regained their position as the dominant power in northeast Asia. All the steppe tribes and the new rulers in China recognized the Turkish khaghan's superiority. The new T'ang dynasty went out of its way to appease the Turks who had sent men and horses to aid in the seizure of Ch'ang-an.

When Kao-tsu had mounted the throne, the presents he [Shih-pi khaghan, To-ki] received from first to last were quite innumerable. Shih-pi, presuming on his services, grew more and more insolent and was always sending envoys to Ch'ang-an, most of whom were very overbearing. Kao-tsu always behaved with utmost tolerance, as China was scarcely settled down.[12]

To-ki died in 619 and was succeeded by his brother Sse-li-fu, the Ch'u-lo khaghan. T'ang declared an official period of mourning and delivered 30,000 pieces of silk as a funeral gift. Sse-li-fu died the next year and was replaced by his brother, the Hsieh-li khaghan. Under Hsieh-li the Turks became more aggressive, and he mounted frequent raids on the frontier that far surpassed any previous ones. About two dozen invasions were recorded for the 75 years preceding his reign, but triple that number were carried out in the first decade of his rule.[13] Yet in 630, the whole Turkish people came under T'ang control and their khaghan was taken prisoner. This rapid shift in power was the result of recurring succession problems among the Turks and the unusually creative foreign policy conducted by Li Shih-min.

The constant raids by the Turks under Hsieh-li's leadership forced the T'ang to maintain a large imperial army even after it had unified China. For his part, Hsieh-li was employing a classic version of the outer frontier strategy. He organized innumerable raids for loot, destroyed Chinese armies that ventured too close to the steppe, and retreated from armies that seemed well organized and powerful. His ultimate aim was undoubtedly similar to previous khaghans and *Shan-yüs*, that is, to get a peace agreement from the T'ang which would support his state with trade and subsidies, as the Chou and Ch'i states had subsidized his grandfather and great-uncles. He had the military power to achieve such an end but, as before, even when the Turks were at the peak of their power their leadership was fatally divided over the rights of succession. This proved to be even more dangerous than usual because the new Chinese emperor, Li Shih-min, had a subtle grasp of steppe politics and was finally able to manipulate the Turks to China's advantage. In particular, he understood the importance of personal leadership among the nomads, a concept that was alien to most Chinese emperors, who were secluded behind palace walls and were rarely seen.

The Turkish state was weaker than it appeared because of a dispute after To-ki's death. Following the lateral tradition his two younger brothers were fully entitled to the throne, but To-ki's son Shi-po-pi could claim some support for his right to succeed as the representative of the genealogically senior line who was now of age. The Turks could never come to an agreement over where to draw the line separating the rights of brothers from the rights of sons. Shi-po-pi was named T'u-li khaghan in recognition of the strength of his claim and put in charge of the tribes in southeastern Mongolia. This was the traditional way of resolving such problems, but Hsieh-li managed to keep all the other pretenders at the rank of *shad* and centralized power to a much greater degree than his predecessors.

Hsieh-li's extraordinary number of raids on China may well have been induced by his need to consolidate power on the steppe. Successful raids brought wealth to the tribal leaders within the empire and kept them busy fighting an external enemy. T'ang attempts to beat off the Turkish attacks initially proved unsuccessful in spite of their experienced generals and battle-tested troops. After receiving reports of famine on the steppe in 622, T'ang forces mounted an invasion. The army was destroyed by the Turks who then raided deeper into China.

T'ang encounters with the Turks were more successful under the leadership of Li Shih-min, who understood where the Turks were vulnerable. His tactical aim was to force the retreat of the Turks. He argued that, given enough time, the Turks would destroy themselves through internal disputes. In the tradition of the foreign dynasties that had preceded him, Shih-min became a master at the game of steppe politics. In this he displayed a profound knowledge of steppe culture and tradition. His use of personal charisma, bluff, nomad ceremonies, and battle tactics marked him as a leader at home in the very different worlds of the Chinese empire and nomadic horsemen.

In 624, the Turks invaded the Ch'ang-an region and panicked the T'ang troops. Li Shih-min left the army, and with a hundred men rode out to challenge Hsieh-li to personal combat. When he refused the T'ang prince sent a message to Shi-po-pi and challenged him to a duel. He also refused. Li Shih-min then advanced alone toward the Turkish lines. This convinced the suspicious Hsieh-li that his rival Shi-po-pi must have struck a bargain with the Chinese, and he offered to negotiate. Li Shih-min then, "sent mischief makers to work with T'u-li who was delighted and took his part, expressing unwillingness to fight. Uncle and nephew being thus at loggerheads, Hsieh-li was unable to fight even if he wished it . . ."[14]

The Turks' inability to fight should not be exaggerated, however, for after opening negotiations the T'ang was forced to pay a huge sum in order to get the nomads to go home.

In 626, the Turks again invaded the Ch'ang-an region just after Li Shih-min had deposed his father and become emperor. He was urged to stay behind the walls of the city because his advisors felt they had too few troops to defeat the Turks in open battle. Li Shih-min ignored their advice and with only six men

he galloped out of the Hsüan-wu gate and proceeded to the River Wei, speaking with the khaghan across the water, and moreover reproaching him with forsaking his agreement. The group of chiefs, seeing the emperor, were startled and all got off their horses to salute. Suddenly the bulk of the army came up with a brave show of flags and cuirasses, and with quiet but imposing ranks. The bandits were in consternation. The emperor and Hsieh-li dropped their bridles motioning to the troops to draw further back. Hsiao Yü, kneeling before his horse, remonstrated with him at this despising of an enemy. The emperor said: "I have thought this well out; it is not the sort of thing for you to understand. Now the Turks, in sweeping their territory of men for a raid on us, think that because we have newly had internal troubles we cannot muster an army. If I were to close the city, they would loot our territory wholesale. Hence I go out alone to show that there is nothing to fear, and I make a show of force to make them know I mean fighting. To their surprise, I have been able to thwart their original plan, and they, having now advanced a good way into our territory, are afraid they won't be able to get back. Hence if we fight with them, we win; if it is peace, things are strengthened. It is by this move that we get the whip hand of the enemy."[15]

The ploy worked. Hsieh-li made a peace proposal which was accepted and confirmed by a horse sacrifice the next day.

In both these incidents Li Shih-min displayed qualities admired by the Turks. With brotherhood ceremonies and horse sacrifices he had established personal links with most of the important Turkish leaders. In defense of China he did not attempt great campaigns on the steppe until the nomads were divided. Chinese troops were most effective within China where fortifications and supplies were near at hand. His prediction that the Turkish empire would collapse if left to itself proved correct.

After agreeing to peace with China, the Turks returned home, where in 627 they were faced with a rebellion by subject tribes. Hsieh-li sent Shi-po-pi to deal with them, but he failed. Hsieh-li was angry at this and had Shi-po-pi imprisoned for a while. That year was also one of great hardship on the steppe because heavy snows had killed many sheep and horses. Shi-po-pi rebelled the next year, beginning a new civil war. He had a strong base of support because Hsieh-li had turned over much of the administration of the empire to foreigners, probably Sogdians from the west, who tried to run it like a sedentary state. This meant that many of Hsieh-li's relatives were denied positions in the government, which they resented. It also appears these advisors tried to introduce the concept of regular taxation. When the pastoral disaster struck the steppe, these officials continued to collect at the regular rate. Thus, there was discontent at all levels with Hsieh-li and the revolt spread. The T'ang intervened in 629 by sending large numbers of troops to the steppe. Important Turkish leaders, including Shi-po-pi, surrendered en masse and Hsieh-li fled. He was attacked the next year and finally captured by T'ang troops. Within a few years all the remaining Turkish tribes either went over to the T'ang or fled west.

China's problem was now what to do with the large number of Turks now under T'ang control. One minister proposed that they be moved south and forced to become farmers. The emperor rejected that idea. Instead he settled them in the Ordos, divided into small tribes, choosing 500 leaders from the Turkish elite to rule over them. Another hundred served at court while several thousand prominent families were moved to Ch'ang-an. In doing this, the emperor incorporated the Turkish tribal structure into the T'ang government; Turkish leaders became T'ang officials. The Turks accepted this new position, in part because LiShih-min had all the personal qualities of a steppe khaghan, and because he treated them well. Turkish troops under the T'ang banner expanded China's borders deep into central Asia. For the next fifty years, the Turks proved faithful allies, bound to the "heavenly khaghan."

THE RISE AND FALL OF THE SECOND TURKISH EMPIRE

The combination of T'ang administration backed by a Turkish military expanded China's power to new heights. The T'ang conquests far surpassed those of the great martial emperors of the past – Ch'in Shih-huang-ti and Han Wu-ti. Drawing on the lessons learned during three centuries of foreign rule, Li Shih-min appeared to have solved the northern frontier problem to China's advantage. By employing the Turks as the T'ang's military arm in remote places, he created a huge buffer between China proper and T'ang frontiers in Mongolia, Turkestan, and Manchuria. The Turks became a well-ordered part of the T'ang administration, receiving benefits in return for loyalty to the dynasty. Yet, after Li Shih-min's death, the system began to decay; and before the end of his son's reign, the eastern Turks reunited and again resumed attacks on China. China responded by reverting to the defensive policies employed by the Han.

Why were the lessons of Li Shih-min and the foreign dynasties forgotten, and an effective frontier policy abandoned in favor of static defenses and a defeatist attitude toward the nomads? The answer has more to do with administrative development in China than with a change by the steppe tribes. By taking advantage of leadership divisions among the Turks, the T'ang emperor had altered the balance of power. In the tradition of a steppe leader he maintained their loyalty by rewarding them and employing them on extensive military campaigns. Li Shih-min had all the traditional steppe criteria for personal leadership and was an active ruler, capable of seeing through his policies. Employing the Turks as part of the T'ang administration meant violating a number of classical Chinese norms. The Turks were allowed to retain their own tribal structure and customs. Their talented generals became powerful members of the T'ang elite on the basis of their military ability. In other words, Li Shih-min was perpetuating a modified tradition of dual organization, in which the frontier tribes were military specialists; however, the Chinese were the senior partners. This was a logical progression from the period of foreign dynasties, which came naturally to the T'ang elite because it was northwestern origin itself and heir to Northern Wei.

To continue such a system required that Li Shih-min's successor be personally adept in dealing with the steppe tribes, or that the system be institutionalized in a way that would bind the Turks to T'ang administration. Had Li Ch'eng-ch'ien, the Turcophile heir apparent, taken the throne, it is possible that his familiarity with and love of steppe life would have given China a second "Chinese khaghan" who would have led the Turks to greater glory. Instead he was succeeded by Emperor Kao-tsung (649–83) who proved sickly and was soon enmeshed almost entirely in court intrigues. Without a strong-willed emperor, administration fell either to court favorites or to the growing class of professional bureaucrats recruited by the examination system. It was in their interest to prevent the recruitment and advancement of Turks in the administration. The bureaucrats in particular tried to reduce the importance of military men at court. As long as the empire was expanding, this conflict was muted. Indeed the Turks under T'ang defeated the western Turks in 657 and China was able to impose new leaders on them. When expansion stopped and T'ang was put on the defensive, the problem became acute. The Tarim Basin fell to Tibetan attack in 670 and the western Turks also became hostile. Ministers at court recommended the abandonment of aggressive wars in distant regions. This put the eastern Turks in difficulty, caught between Tibetan and western Turk advances while getting less and less support from T'ang. There was also a generational problem – the generals loyal to Li Shih-min were gone and their sons did not have the same strong ties to Kao-tsung. The Turks felt mistreated, and revolted in 679.

In the Orkhon inscriptions the Turks recorded their complaints – the first voice directly from the steppe:

Those chieftains who were in China adopted Chinese titles and obeyed the Chinese emperor. They gave their services and their strength to him for fifty years.... They surrendered to the Chinese emperor their empire and their own law. Then the Turks and all the common people said as follows: "I used to be of a people who had an empire. Where is my empire now? For whose benefit am I conquering realms?" They said "I used to be of a polity that had an emperor. Where is my emperor now? To which emperor do I give my services and strength?" they said. By saying so they became foes of the Chinese emperor.[16]

The first attempt at establishing autonomy near the Chinese frontier failed because the T'ang was able to attack the Turks before they were fully reorganized. A number of tribal leaders then abandoned the frontier for the old Turkish homeland of Ötükän in Mongolia. Among these was Khutlugh, a *shad* from the royal clan, who was named Iltirish khaghan in 680. He led only around 200 men at the time, but by successful attacks on other tribes he gained strength and the Turks gathered around him. Within ten years, he had mounted forty-seven campaigns and engaged in twenty battles, according to the Turkish inscriptions, gaining control of most of the steppe and raiding China. When he died in 692, he was succeeded by his brother Mo-ch'o (Khapaghan khaghan) who incorporated more tribes until this second Turkish empire approached the size of the first.

Under Mo-ch'o, the Turks turned to the outer frontier strategy with a vengeance. Having served the T'ang for fifty years, the Turks were familiar with the internal structure of the empire. Their major field commander, Tonyukhukh, had been born in China. The Turks also benefited because at the same time as they were establishing their control over the steppe, China had been preoccupied by a political coup in which the T'ang throne had been seized by Empress Wu. She had been a major influence in the latter half of Kaotsung's reign and after his death she dispossessed the legitimate heirs and ruled herself. Mo-ch'o was therefore able to raid China and pressure the court in the name of the restoration of the T'ang heirs. Some have concluded from this that Mo-ch'o had ambitions to conquer China. This would not have been in keeping with the usual strategies of steppe empires, nor did the pattern of raids and negotiations demonstrate any such intent.

Mo-ch'o organized a frontier alliance against the T'ang and raided deep into western China in 693. However, his hostility to China was strategic. When the Khitan broke away from Turkish control and raided China on their own, Mo-ch'o immediately opened negotiations with the T'ang court for a war against them. In return for huge gifts from China, he attacked the Khitan and defeated them in 696. Yet that same year he also mounted three raids on the Chinese frontier himself. Similarly, two years later, after negotiating a marriage for his daughter to a nephew of Empress Wu, Mo-ch'o refused to complete the deal when the young man arrived on the steppe, on the grounds he was not a legitimate heir to the Chinese throne.[17] The khaghan then conducted a dozen raids on China that year. A flurry of raids was also carried out in 702 and 706.

These raids brought large numbers of captives and huge wealth to the Turks. However, for the rest of Mo-ch'o's reign there were few raids on China because of his attention to conquests in the west. The abandonment of heavy pressure on China occurred exactly at the moment when China was most vulnerable. Empress Wu had been dethroned in 705, and China's government was rife with feuding factions. Had the Turks truly been interested in conquering China, this would have been the time to intervene. Like the steppe empires before them, however, they were interested not in conquest, but in exploitation.

In 706 after displaying their power in a series of raids the Turks received a new marriage proposal and gifts of silk from the Chinese court. These negotiations were renewed in 710 and a princess was named as a bride for the khaghan, although because of coups at the T'ang court the marriage never took place. The successors to Empress Wu were anxious to avoid Turkish attacks. Since marriage proposals were always accompanied by substantial gifts, it is reasonable to conclude that Mo-ch'o, having established a satisfactory subsidy treaty with China, had gotten what he wanted and shifted his attacks to his western frontier. From the Turkish point of view, campaigns in the west were more important than continued hostilities with China. The raids on China had not been a prelude to conquest: they had been designed to fund the empire and induce China to make concessions. The weaker the dynasty's position in China the more likely it was to be accommodating. Therefore Turkish raids tended to coincide with times of strength in China, when the court was predisposed to reject Turkish demands. Raids slacked off when the dynasty was in turmoil because the contenders for power were all willing to pacify the Turkish khaghan by meeting his demands.

The Turks themselves understood the nature of their relation with China and Mo-ch'o's successor, the Bilgä khaghan, recorded the essence of the outer frontier strategy in stone for the edification of his descendants. It stressed the importance of exploiting China at a distance and the danger of coming too close to the Chinese frontier:

A land better than the Ötükän does not exist at all. The place from which the tribes can be [best] controlled is the Ötükän mountains. Having stayed in this place I came to an amiable agreement with the Chinese people.

They [the Chinese] give (us) gold, silver, and silk in abundance. The words of the Chinese people have always been sweet and the materials of the Chinese people have always been soft. Deceiving by means of their sweet words and soft materials the Chinese are said to cause remote peoples to come close in this manner. After such a people have settled close to them, (the Chinese) are said to plan ill will there. The Chinese do not let real wise and brave men make progress. If a man commits an error, they do not give shelter to anybody (from his immediate family) to the families of his clan or tribe. Having been taken in by their sweet words and soft materials, you Turkish people were killed in great numbers. O Turkish people, you will die! if you intend to settle at the Choghay mountains and on the Togultun plain in the south, O Turkish people you will die. There ill willed persons made harmful suggestions as follows "if people live afar (from them), they (the Chinese) give cheap materials (to them), but, if a people live close to them then (the Chinese) give them valuable materials." Apparently such harmful suggestions made the ill willed persons. Having heard these words you unwise people went close to the Chinese and were killed in great numbers. If you go to those places O Turkish people you will die. If you stay in the land of the Ötükän and send caravans from there you will have no trouble. If you stay in the Ötükän mountains you will live forever dominating the tribes.[18]

Table 4.2   Reigns of khaghans of the second Turkish empire

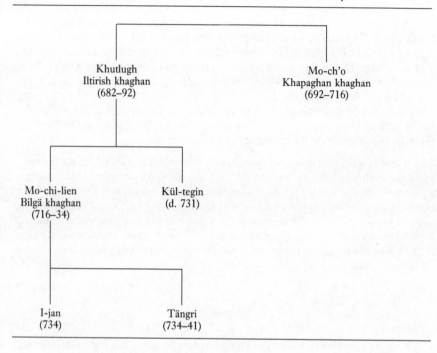

The Turks did not live forever dominating the tribes. Mo-ch'o lost his head in an ambush laid by his enemies among the western Turks in 716 and a civil war erupted. As before, this was a war of the cousins. Mo-ch'o had named a number of his sons junior khaghans, positioning them to succeed. The senior line, sons of Khutlugh, were given lower ranks. The main actor in the war was Khutlugh's son Kül-tegin. He defeated Mo-ch'o's sons, killing all members of that line and all of Mo-ch'o's advisors except for his father-in-law, old Tonyukhukh. Kül-tegin did not become khaghan himself but placed his elder brother Mo-chi-lien on the throne as the Bilgä khaghan. They spent much of their time reconquering tribes that had broken away in the civil war struggle.

After a brief war with China in 720, they gained a peace settlement the next year which was quite lucrative. In 727 the T'ang reported that Emperor Hsüan-tsung (r. 713–56) presented the khaghan with a yearly gift of 100,000 balls of silk. The Turks grew so wealthy that Mo-chi-lien planned to build a city on the steppe. Tonyukhukh dissuaded him by pointing out that the Turks depended on flexibility to survive. If they had a city one defeat would mean their end, while as nomads they could advance or retreat depending on the strength of the enemy.

Mo-chi-lien was assassinated in 734. Power passed to his son I-jan who died the same year. Tängri, a young boy, became khaghan under the regency of his mother, the daughter of Tonyukhukh. The empire was soon effectively divided up among Tängri's "uncles," men of a senior generation of the royal house but probably from a different line of descent. The situation proved unstable. The left *shad* murdered Tängri in 741, and the component tribes of the empire broke away. An alliance of subject tribes, the Basmil, Kharlukh, and Uighurs, defeated the old dynasty in 744. The Uighurs then defeated their allies to found a new empire. This imperial confederacy consisted of thirty tribes, twelve Turk and eighteen Oguz. The Uighur tribes made up half the Oguz under the leadership of the Yao-lo-ko clan.[19]

The Turks brought about their own end by the constant feuding within the ruling tribes. They were aware of this defect and the Bilgä khaghan had chided them in his inscription for their earlier civil wars:

You, Turkish and Oguz lords and peoples, hear this! If the sky above did not collapse, and if the earth below did not give way, O Turkish people, who would be able to destroy your state and institutions? O Turkish people, regret and repent. Because of your unruliness, you yourselves betrayed your wise khaghan who had (always) nourished you, and you yourselves betrayed your good realm which was free and independent, and you (yourselves) caused discord. From where did the armed (men) come and put you to flight? From where did the lancer come and drive you away? You people of the sacred Ötükän mountains, it was you who went away.[20]

THE UIGHUR EMPIRE

Traditional histories have always cast the steppe nomads as dangerous enemies whose ultimate intent was to rule China. My argument has been that while the nomads were a danger to China, they were intent on exploiting it indirectly. The Uighur policy toward the T'ang dynasty was perhaps the best example of this phenomenon. From the very beginning, the Uighurs provided support for a weakening T'ang dynasty, preserving it from internal rebellions and foreign invasions. In exchange they received huge quantities of silk that made them the richest nomads yet to have appeared in Mongolia. They established a capital city of impressive proportions and developed a high degree of culture.

This favorable relationship occurred because when a native Chinese dynasty weakened it was in desperate need of allies. The steppe nomads were an obvious source of military strength that could be bought. A dynasty in such a position came to depend on outside help and yet at the same time was fearful because only a constant flow of wealth to the steppe could maintain that support. From the nomads' point of view, this was the best of all situations. A weak dynasty ruling China had access to an immense amount of revenue which out of fear and need it was willing to spend. Part of this wealth could be channeled through the leader of a steppe empire to finance an impressive state structure. Any threat to the Chinese dynasty was indirectly a threat to the nomad state. Thus, a nomad ruler preferred to maintain the lucrative status quo against any attempts at change. A rebellion in China or a foreign invasion that might topple the dynasty would bring new groups to power, who might prove far less willing to appease the nomads. For this reason the Uighurs had a vested interest in preserving the T'ang dynasty. When the Uighur empire was destroyed in 840, the T'ang lost this protection and fell in all but name to the next revolt in China.

In many ways the Uighurs were similar to the Turks in customs, titles, and political organization. Yet in other respects the Uighurs were quite different. They remained at peace with China and acted as T'ang allies, their political structure was much more stable, and they developed a greater degree of civilization, which became an important legacy for Inner Asia long after their empire was gone. Each of these aspects helps explain the reasons for the Uighurs' success and the complex system of trade, government, and military that made their empire work.

The strength of the Uighur state was based on the military domination of the steppe and foreign aid from China. In the first years of the empire, the Uighur khaghan Ku-li sent embassies to China to open relations. In 745, he forwarded the head of the last Turkish khaghan to the T'ang as proof of Uighur control of the steppe. Like the Turks before them, the Uighurs wished to control the lucrative silk market and, although they mounted no attacks on China, they followed the outer frontier strategy of exploiting China at a distance. China responded favorably to these requests because it feared provoking the nomads. The T'ang court under Emperor Hsüan-tsung was already having problems controlling its frontier commanders and was in no position to refuse Uighur embassies.

In 755, a major revolt broke out in China led by An Lu-shan, a former court favorite of mixed Turkish and Sogdian parentage. He had been removed from court and given command of the frontier armies in the northeast. In league with other frontier commanders, he declared himself independent and the founder of a new Yen dynasty the next year. His armies were powerful, consisting of a mix of frontier Chinese and foreign tribes. They overran Lo-yang and Ch'ang-an, forcing the T'ang court to flee to the southwest. An Lu-shan was assassinated soon after this, but the rebellion continued under the leadership of his son. The T'ang court appeared doomed to extinction.[21]

In desperation, the T'ang court reached out for allies. A T'ang prince was sent to open negotiations with Mo-yen-ch'o in 756. Mo-yen-ch'o had completed the work of his father by conquering the steppe and had established the Uighur capital city of Karabalghasun. The khaghan agreed to aid the T'ang. To conclude the alliance, he married his adopted daughter to the T'ang prince. Mo-yen-ch'o then led a Uighur force to the frontier, where they defeated a T'ieh-le tribe that had joined the rebels. The khaghan appointed his heir apparent, the *yabghu*, to lead an expeditionary force into China.[22]

The Uighurs arrived in China during the middle of 757 with 4,000 horsemen. This was a tiny force in comparison to the huge land armies employed by each side, yet their aid proved decisive. Late that year in a battle outside Ch'ang-an the Uighurs attacked the rebels from the rear and put them to flight. The nomads urged the T'ang generals to pursue the enemy immediately, but they refused. This pointed up a major difference in strategy between the steppe and China. In battle, the nomads looked for weak spots where a quick attack would be decisive, while the Chinese relied on masses of heavy infantry to overwhelm the enemy. Nomadic tradition demanded that a defeated enemy always be run to ground, while traditional Chinese strategy cautioned against pushing a defeated army too far, lest in desperation it inflict a defeat on its pursuers. A few weeks later the armies met again near Lo-yang. Again the Uighurs surprised and disrupted the rebel rear, allowing a T'ang victory. The two old capitals of China were now back in T'ang control.

There was a high price for this help. The Uighurs had demanded the right to loot the captured cities. They were dissuaded from sacking Ch'ang-an on the grounds that the war was not over, but when Lo-yang fell

The Uighurs pillaged the Eastern capital savagely for three days. Evil men led them around and the treasure houses were stripped bare. The Prince of Kuang-p'ing [the T'ang heir apparent] wanted to stop them but could not. However the elders [of the city] bribed the Uighurs with enormous quantities of silken fabric and embroidery and got them to discontinue the pillage.[23]

In addition to this loot, the Uighurs were given an annual present of 20,000 rolls of silk and their leaders got honorary titles and gifts. Having proved his power to T'ang, the Uighur khaghan demanded a marriage alliance. He was given a daughter of the emperor. While previous dynasties had made such marriage alliances, T'ang was one of the few to send true daughters of the emperor – an indication of the important position of the Uighurs. Such a marriage was accompanied by huge gifts. It was also during this period that the Uighurs established the lucrative horse exchange with T'ang. The Uighurs got forty pieces of silk for every horse brought to China. This was an extortionate rate of exchange, for on the steppe a horse was worth only one piece of silk, and the Turks had managed to collect only four or five pieces per horse. The Uighurs took tens of thousands of horses to China annually. To add injury to insult, the horses were of the poorest quality the Uighurs could find. China could not refuse the offer of horses, but the court often withheld payment for years.[24]

The Uighurs were also busy campaigning on the steppe. They reported winning a great victory over the Kirghiz, their nomadic neighbors to the north, in 758. The next year the Uighurs returned to aid China, but with little success, and went home. A few months later Mo-yen-ch'o died. He was succeeded by Iti-chien, under the title Mou-yü khaghan. His older brother, heir apparent and *yabghu*, had been killed earlier.

The Uighur victories in China had restored T'ang power but had not put an end to the disorder. The long simmering rebellion in China soon heated up as the rebels retook Lo-yang. In 762, the T'ang emperor Hsüan-tsung died. The rebels took this opportunity to seek Uighur assistance. They reported that the emperor was dead and stated that the T'ang dynasty was no more. The Uighurs moved south with the hope of profitable raiding and the chance to impose a new client dynasty in China. An army of 100,000 was reported on the banks of the Yellow River. In fact, the Uighurs had sent only their usual 4,000 soldiers. A T'ang envoy, a brother-in-law to the khaghan, was able to convince them that the T'ang was still in power under Emperor Tai-tsung, who had fought alongside the Uighurs in earlier campaigns when he was heir apparent. The khaghan abandoned the rebel cause and offered his assistance to the T'ang. Tai-tsung sent his heir apparent, Li Kua, to negotiate with the Uighurs. Unlike his father, who had been quite skillful in dealing with the nomads, Li Kua proved obstinate in matters of form and provoked trouble. He refused to salute the khaghan and then became embroiled in a controversy over performing a ceremonial dance. The Uighurs took their revenge by beating his advisors to death before returning the heir to his camp. The Uighurs were no mere vassals come to aid their masters, but a major power of equal strength to the T'ang. In spite of this incident, the Uighurs were in the field with T'ang forces in late 762 near Lo-yang. The battle and its outcome was similar to that fought five years earlier, and the rebels abandoned Lo-yang. The Uighurs looted the city with terrible intensity. People fled for protection to the towers of two Buddhist temples. The Uighurs set them afire, killing over 10,000. The Uighurs then plundered other parts of the country. The T'ang was forced to overlook these actions and provided the Uighurs with rewards for their aid in putting down the rebels before they went home.

The Uighurs returned to China three years later but this time it was to aid a new rebel against the T'ang. The Chinese general Huai-yen, who had earlier helped save the dynasty, had been pushed into revolt. His daughter was married to the khaghan and so a contingent of Uighurs (but not the khaghan himself) came to his aid, as did a large number of Tibetans. Huai-yen died soon after their arrival, however, and the Uighurs offered their support to the T'ang. They defeated their erstwhile allies the Tibetans with great slaughter. The T'ang was forced to pay them 100,000 pieces of silk to get them to go home, bankrupting the treasury.

This was the last Uighur campaign within China, but the Uighurs and their Sogdian allies had become important agents of trade and money-lending in Ch'ang-an. Marriage alliances continued to bind China and the steppe together. This alliance had made the Uighurs rich, but an attempt was made to abandon it by those Uighurs who preferred a more aggressive policy. Ever since the second sacking of Lo-yang, the Mou-yü khaghan Iti-chien had developed a dependence on Sogdian advisors to whose religion, Manichaeanism, he had converted. When Emperor Tai-tsung died in 779, these advisors urged him to attack China. Iti-chien was predisposed to follow their advice, having permitted a serious raid in China the year before. Iti-chien's cousin Tun was opposed to this change and to the Sogdians. He killed Iti-chien and declared himself khaghan, purging the Sogdians from government. China's huge annual payments to the Uighur elite would have been put at risk by a war policy and it would have deprived the Uighur elite of an important source of revenue. Down to the end of the Uighur period, their policy remained one of extortion.

The Uighurs no longer campaigned in China, but the fear of their power forced China to increase payments to the steppe. The T'ang court continually anticipated that small Uighur attacks might be precursors to a full-scale invasion. Uighurs and their Sogdian allies in China exploited this fear to commit crimes with impunity because China feared offending the khaghan. However, in 780, the Chinese, thinking that the Uighurs could not respond because of Iti-chien's death, murdered a large number of Uighurs and Sogdians who had organized a caravan to leave Ch'ang-an. A hundred thousand pieces of silk were also seized. Tun was very angry when informed of this and demanded compensation to the extent of 1,800,000 strings of cash, which was still owed for horses the Uighurs had previously delivered. The T'ang agreed to pay the Uighurs this amount in gold and silk, reinforcing Tun's position that extortion was more lucrative than raiding. Some idea of the burden this put on the dynasty is revealed by the annual revenue of a fertile southeastern sub-prefecture, which was about 200,000 strings of cash. In 787, the Uighurs requested and received a new marriage alliance. Such an alliance cost heavily in gifts, by one calculation made some years later the treasury estimated the total at 5,000,000 strings of cash, although other officials argued that the cost was only a small fraction of that amount. Nevertheless, expensive gifts were in addition to the regular frontier defense expenses that ate up one-third of the annual government budget.[25]

In spite of these payments, the Uighurs had grown weaker on the steppe as a result of Tibetan attacks. In 790–1, they attempted to aid the T'ang in protecting the Turkestan oasis town of Pei-t'ing. The campaign proved a failure; the town fell and an army attempting to retake it was destroyed. This marked a low point for the Uighurs, but following the defeat there was a dynastic change. Their new khaghan, Ku-tu-lu, took power in 795 and revived Uighur fortunes. Relations with China were dropped for about ten years as Ku-tu-lu campaigned on the steppe, recapturing Pei-t'ing. Order was restored and embassies again began arriving in 805. A proposal for a new marriage alliance was at first refused but the Uighurs continued to press. The T'ang finally agreed to this expensive proposal in 820, just before the death of Emperor Mu-tsung. Fear of the Tibetan attacks and a desire to reduce frontier defenses forced the T'ang to keep up good relations with the Uighurs. In 822, the Uighurs sent troops to help the T'ang fight new rebels. Remembering the sacking of Lo-yang, the T'ang declined the aid, but it had to pay the Uighurs 70,000 pieces of silk to get them to go home.

The final decades of the Uighur empire were marked by large increases in the silk subsidy. Payments for horses reached record levels, fifty pieces of silk per horse. The T'ang entries reported payments of silks in batches by the hundreds of thousands, whereas before they had usually been in tens of thousands. The Arab traveller Tamim ibn Bahr was witness to this flow of wealth, for he visited Karabalghasun and reported that the khaghan annually received 500,000 pieces of silk from the T'ang.[26]

From this account a number of patterns emerge. The Uighurs understood the importance of the Chinese connection and immediately replaced the Turks upon their defeat. By aiding the T'ang against rebels, they preserved the dynasty while at the same time terrifying it. The small number of Uighur cavalry employed made this an extremely cheap venture for the khaghan, and the loot from the two sacks of Lo-yang was immense. From that period of direct aid, almost 75 years followed in which the Uighurs did little, yet the amount of silk recorded going to them increased inexorably, reflecting the T'ang's desperate need of a protector. The Uighur protection was double-edged. It had saved the dynasty on a number of occasions, but the T'ang always feared the

Uighurs might revert to attacks. The Uighurs it seems had taken the Orkhon inscriptions to heart. From deep in the steppe they successfully exploited China without allowing the Chinese a chance to interfere in nomadic affairs.

The Uighurs were vastly more successful than the Turks in running a steppe empire, although their conquests were not as extensive. This was due in large measure to the stability of their imperial government. The Turks often reached great heights of power but always fell into civil wars because of lateral succession disputes. The Uighurs avoided this problem by employing a lineal succession pattern. This is not to say things were always peaceful, but disputes among the elite did not lead to civil wars. Like the Hsiung-nu, the Uighur elite remained united and forestalled attempts by component tribes to break away.

The political organization of the Uighur empire was largely a copy of the Turkish one it replaced. The titles and offices appear to have been the same. It was an imperial confederacy, with the state structure monopolizing foreign affairs and imposing order upon the steppe. Within the state structure, sedentary Sogdians formed an important corp of literate ministers, probably made necessary by Uighur involvement in long distance trade and the administrative responsibility of running a true city on the steppe.

The stability of the empire was evident in its imperial politics. Assassination replaced civil war as a means to power, and the number of potential heirs to the throne was greatly restricted. Table 4.3 lists the khaghans of the two Uighur dynasties. In the Chinese records the relationships of succeeding khaghans were always noted for the first dynasty but only occasionally mentioned for the second.[27]

The pattern of Uighur successions shows that they employed a lineal succession rule. Power passed without violence from Ku-li to his son Mo-yen-ch'o to his son Iti-chien. In 779, Iti-chien proposed changing Uighur policy and going to war with China. His cousin and first minister Tun opposed this plan, assassinated his cousin and took power himself. When Tun died, the khaghan title went to his eldest son To-lo-ssu who was soon murdered by an unnamed younger brother. The Uighurs refused to accept this usurpation and executed him, placing To-lo-ssu's young son on the throne. He died without heirs and the throne passed into the hands of a new dynasty.

In the case of the first and second Turkish empires, struggles for power broke out upon the death of a khaghan and resulted in civil war. Among the Uighurs, political opposition most often resulted in the murder of a ruling khaghan by a rival, who replaced him. For example, Tun killed his cousin Iti-chien, who had been on the throne for twenty years, and in order to secure his power Tun then killed all members of Iti-chien's line. In spite of this violence, the elite did not divide into warring factions and the empire remained stable. Similarly, the empire did not split when Tun's sons challenged one another for the throne. Although succession to leadership among the Uighurs was often violent, they never had a civil war, even during the change of dynasties in 795. Until that time, all the khaghans had come from the Yao-lo-ko clan, but during the reign of A-ch'o real power was in the hands of a Uighur general. He was of the Hsieh-tieh clan and had been orphaned and adopted by a powerful chieftain. When A-ch'o died without heirs this general was declared

Table 4.3   Reigns of Uighur khaghans

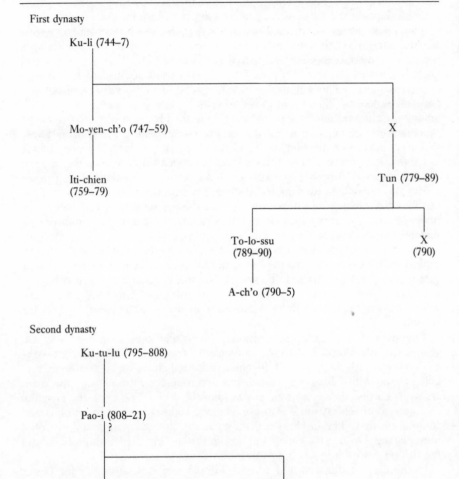

First dynasty

Ku-li (744–7)

Mo-yen-ch'o (747–59)   X

Iti-chien   Tun (779–89)
(759–79)

To-lo-ssu   X
(789–90)   (790)

A-ch'o (790–5)

Second dynasty

Ku-tu-lu (795–808)

Pao-i (808–21)
?

Ch'ung-te (821–4)   Ho-sa (824–32)
?   ?

Hu (832–9)   Ho-sa II (840)

khaghan. As a precaution, he exiled all of A-ch'o's relatives to China.

The relations of the succeeding khaghans are less clear because of the lack of genealogical information. After a great restoration under the khaghans Ku-tu-lu (r. 795–808) and Pao-i (r. 808–21), the reigns of succeeding khaghans were shorter and more fraught with violence. The Ch'ung-te khaghan died in

824 after only three years on the throne. He was succeeded by his younger brother Prince Ho-sa who was murdered by his ministers in 832 and replaced as khaghan by his nephew Prince Hu (Ch'ung-te's son?). In 839, Hu uncovered a conspiracy against the throne and executed the plotters. One of his ministers then allied himself with the Sha-t'o Turks who lived to the east on the T'ang frontier and attacked the khaghan in retaliation. Hu committed suicide and the minister, Prince Ho-sa II, a member of the royal line, became khaghan. He ruled for only a short time before the Kirghiz, taking advantage of the political turmoil among the Uighurs, attacked and looted the capital in 840 bringing about the collapse of the empire. Like the previous two Turkish empires, the Uighur state fell when disputes between rival lines of descent weakened its unity and made it vulnerable to rival tribes.

A STEPPE CIVILIZATION

The Uighurs are most remembered for the degree of civilization they bought to the steppe. They ruled their empire from a permanent city, kept written records, maintained agricultural communities on the steppe, and became increasingly tied to the Iranian world in religion and government. Whereas most nomadic empires left only a legacy of great conquests, the Uighurs maintained their unique cross of steppe traditions and civilization even after they lost their dominance. The Uighur tradition became a bridge between the world of the nomad and surrounding civilizations. The Mongols, 400 years later, relied heavily on Uighur advisors to organize their government.

The idea of a city on the steppe did not originate with the Uighurs. The Hsiung-nu had on occasion built and abandoned cities. The Turkish khaghan Mo-chi-lien had proposed building a city, but had been dissuaded. The Uighurs established their capital Karabalghasun soon after the empire was founded. The Arab traveller Tamim ibn Bahr who saw it in the 830s described it as a large town with twelve iron gates enclosing a castle. It was "populous and thickly crowded with markets and various trades." The countryside was surrounded by intensive cultivation.[28] This city was deep in the heart of nomad country on the Orkhon River, near where the Mongols would later establish Karakorum.

Because the association of cities with an agricultural base is so strong, it has often been assumed that the Uighurs were sedentary. This is unlikely to have been the case. A nomadic empire was capable of bringing farmers deep into their country where they could establish cultivation, but a city built for nomads was not a natural development out of a growing agricultural base. Rather, a city established by nomads was willed into existence by fiat and continued because of its position as the center of tributary wealth. The Uighurs extracted huge amounts of silk and other gifts from China. They needed a place to store these goods, receive traders, and hold court in a way that would centralize their role as middlemen in the lucrative export of silk. The intensive farming that grew up around the city was a secondary phenomenon, serving the needs of a place founded and maintained by international trade. Such a city located deep in

Mongolia did not need to be economically viable using solely local resources. Like the imperial confederacy itself, it grew as the result of the extortion of the Chinese economy. It was the flower of a plant that had its roots in Ch'ang-an. Had the Chinese connection been destroyed, the city on the steppe would not have long survived. Even the local agriculture depended on the stability of the Uighur government. Agriculture was possible in Mongolia when the nomads could be prevented from raiding and destroying farming communities. Once these communities were destroyed they disappeared, for there was no reserve agricultural population available to move in and rebuild. The whole complex of urban life, agricultural production, and centralized trade was tied to the continuance of Uighur control of the steppe.

The model for the city of Karabalghasun was not Chinese, but Sogdian. The success of the Uighur civilization was due in large measure to the much greater applicability of Iranian models of organization to the steppe. Iranian influence first became apparent in Mongolia near the end of the first Turkish empire, when one of the complaints against Hsieh-li was his extensive use of Sogdian officials. Before this period, the eastern steppe's only model for civilization was China. Based so strongly on an agricultural economy and with many values antithetical to the nomad way of life, Chinese models of organization had never taken root on the steppe. The Iranian world did not draw such a sharp distinction between the nomadic and sedentary peoples. Governments there had long dealt with nomadic pastoralists. They had close ties to stockraisers who were scattered throughout the area and who tended to have close relations with the villages and cities of the region. Indeed, large parts of the Iranian world had at times been ruled by dynasties founded by powerful tribes. The Yüeh-chih had ruled the Oxus region in this manner. The ecology of the region allowed them to remain nomadic pastoralists engaging in seasonal migration, while remaining in close contact with the sedentary population. In a similar manner the Western Turks had been part of a much more complex system than their cousins in the east, who were sharply divided from agricultural China.

The Sogdians controlled the oases of Turkestan. They were famous as merchants and had established trading communities in China. The traditional Chinese government attitude toward foreign trade was negative, therefore from the beginning Sogdian and other foreign merchants had sought to ally themselves with powerful nomadic empires. The nomads valued trade, forced China to open markets, and extorted silk. Foreign merchants then rode on the coat tails of steppe embassies to engage in private trade. In addition, these merchants were also in a position to act as buyers of extorted silk and other goods for trade in the west. Moreover, the nomads controlled most of the territory linking the Iranian world with China. Therefore in order to conduct the caravan trade it was necessary to establish cordial relations with the steppe tribes. Finally, the Sogdians considered the steppe tribes allies, not enemies, and could offer themselves as officials who knew how to combine a wide range of interests. Both groups held the view that trade was a vital resource.

The Sogdian connection with the Uighurs became quite close after the second sack of Lo-yang. There the khaghan had been introduced to the Manichaean religion espoused by the Sogdians, and he subsequently adopted it, bringing priests and a large number of Sogdian advisors onto the steppe. They introduced the Sogdian alphabet to the Uighurs. The Manichaean religion, with its emphasis on vegetarian diet and pacific pursuits, might have seemed unsuitable for nomads, but the true rigors of the faith were only expected to be followed by an elect. Like the adoption of Buddhism before and after this time, the steppe tribes' interest in these world religions was always tempered with a pragmatic acceptance of war and animal-raising as a normal part of life.

There was a reaction against Sogdian influence among the Uighurs that culminated in the murder of Iti-chien in 759, but within a generation their influence was as strong as ever. The Sogdians benefited tremendously from this relationship. Their trading communities in China came under Uighur protection, giving them diplomatic immunity. They became influential moneylenders and major silk buyers. Iranian culture permeated the Uighur elite, who had found a model that was much more flexible than the older steppe borrowings from Chinese culture.

The Uighur conversion to Manichaeanism and the establishment of their city on the steppe is often presumed to have made them "soft" and prey to other nomads. While the fall of the Uighurs is intimately related to their city, their defeat by the Kirghiz was not because they were any worse soldiers than before. More subtle factors were at work that made the Uighurs vulnerable to the type of attack that destroyed them. When Mo-chi-lien proposed founding a Turkish city, Tonyukhukh argued that it would create a danger for the Turkish state, which relied on mobility. While nomadic, the Turks could always retreat, but if they had to defend a fixed point, then it would take but one loss to destroy them. The Uighurs must have been aware of this liability; the Hsiung-nu had abandoned a city for those reasons. To any nomadic group a fixed defense spelled danger. But creating a city had many positive aspects. A walled town served as a protective warehouse for trade goods. The more such goods a nomadic society acquired, the less mobility it had, hence, at some point, one was more vulnerable trying to protect a rich treasure house by moving it than by fortifying it. In addition, a walled city rarely fell prey to nomadic raids because nomads were incapable of besieging a city or storming its walls. The great Mongol conquests with their rapid destruction of walled defenses have tended to obscure this fact. In the beginning, the Mongols could not take walled towns and developed the ability only after they acquired skilled Muslim and Chinese engineers, who employed their specialties under Mongol supervision. On the negative side, a rich city remained a natural and permanent target for other nomads. Nomadic empires often suffered a series of defeats, only to regroup and later restore their power, but if too much of an empire's strength and wealth were tied up in a capital city its fall would prove fatal.

The Uighurs had too much wealth not to have a permanent fortified capital. This meant it would have to be defended in all circumstances. There were plenty of opponents willing to try to take it. They could suffer a dozen reverses in the hope of a single victory. The Kirghiz, who lived to the north, were one such group. They had been at war with the Uighurs since about 830. In 840, when there was civil unrest at Karabalghasun, the Kirghiz took advantage of the situation, capturing and looting the city. Uighur power on the steppe suffered a fatal blow. The elite retreated to the oases of Turkestan, where they preserved themselves as the leaders of the Kan-chou (840–1028) and Khocho (840–1209) kingdoms.[29] Though small in scope, the Uighurs' model of organization later acted as a bridge between nomads and sedentary societies. The name Uighur still carries enough prestige to have been chosen as the common ethnic label of the oasis peoples of Xinjiang in the People's Republic of China today, more than 1,100 years after they ceased to dominate the steppe.

NOTES

1 The history of the first two Turkish empires is recorded in the succeeding Chinese dynastic histories for this period, each of which contains a chapter on the nomads. The Turks' relationship with the successors to the Wei dynasty and the end of the Jou-jan is found in the *Chou-shu, Peh-shi* (99) and the *Sui-shu* (84). The relationship of the Turks with the T'ang dynasty is described in the *Chiu T'ang-shu* [CTS] (144) and the *Hsin T'ang-shu* [HTS] (215). Although these two sources cover the same period, each has slightly different material. Liu Mau-tsai [*Die chinesischen Nachrichten zur Geschichte der Ost-Türken (T'u-küe)*] brings all of this material together in a German translation.

2 Molè, *The T'u-yü-hun from the Northern Wei to the Time of the Five Dynasties*.

3 Mori, *Historical Studies of the Ancient Turkic Peoples* (in Japanese with an English summary, pp. 3–25).

4 *Sui-shu* 84:5a; Ecsedy, "Trade and war relations between the Turks and China in the second half of the 6th century," and "Tribe and tribal society in the 6th century Turk empire."

5 Fletcher, "The Mongols: ecological and social perspective," p. 17.

6 *Pei-shi* 99:6b–7a; Parker, "The early Turks," 25:2.

7 Goody, *Succession to High Office*, pp. 35–6.

8 Wright, *The Sui Dynasty*, pp. 187–94.

9 Ibid., pp. 21–53.

10 Twitchett, "The composition of the T'ang ruling class," pp. 47–87.

11 Bingham, *The Founding of the T'ang Dynasty*.

12 CTS 144A:1aff; Parker, "Early Turks," 25:164.

13 Liu Mau-tsai, *Geschichte der Ost-Türken*, pp. 433–9.

14 CTS 144A:3aff; Parker, "Early Turks," 25:166.

15 HTS 215A:5bff; Parker, "Early Turks," 24:238–9.

16 Pritsak, *The Origin of Rus'*, vol. 1, pp. 75–6, translated from the memorial inscription of Kül-tegin. I have substituted the "empire" for "pax" which is his term to denote nomadic empires as opposed to sedentary ones.

17 The story of this prince, Wu Yen-hsiu, is quite interesting. After remaining with the Turks for a few years, he returned to China where he cut a striking figure with his Turkish clothes and manners. He married a princess in 708 but died in a palace coup in 710, cf. *Cambridge History of China*, vol. 5, *Sui and T'ang*, pp. 317, 324, 335.

18 Tekin, *Grammar*, pp. 261–2.

19 The tribal composition of the Uighur state is still the subject of considerable debate, see Pulleyblank, "Some remarks on the Toquz-oghuz problem."

20 Tekin, *Grammar*, p. 267.
21 Pulleyblank provides the background of court politics and frontier commands that led to this revolt (*The Background of the Rebellion of An Lu-shan*). The war itself is chronicled by Levy, *Biography of An Lu-shan*, and des Rotours, *Histoire de Ngan Lou-chan*.
22 The Uighurs relationship with China is described in the CTS 195 and the HTS 217. Mackerras, *The Uighur Empire*, provides side by side translations of these two histories as well as an extensive analysis of the material contained there.
23 HTS 217A:3b; Mackerras, *Uighur Empire*, p. 59.
24 Mackerras, "Sino-Uighur diplomatic and trade contacts."
25 HTS 219A:7b–8a, 217A:11a, 217B:1a; Mackerras, *Uighur Empire*, pp. 89–93, 113–15.
26 Minorski, *Hudud al-'Alam "The Regions of the World": A Persian Geography 372 A.H. – 982 A.D.*; Mackerras, "Sino-Uighur diplomatic and trade contacts."
27 Mackerras, *Uighur Empire*, pp. 191–3.
28 Minorski, "Tamim ibn Bahr's journey to the Uighurs," p. 283.
29 Pinks, *Die Uiguren von Kan-chou in der frühen Sung-Zeit (960–1028)*.

GLOSSARY OF KEY NAMES

MAIN TRIBES ON THE STEPPE FRONTIER

JOU-JAN
  destroyed by their erstwhile vassals the Turks in 555
KHITAN
  nomadic tribe of Manchuria
  crushed between Turkish and Chinese attacks
KIRGHIZ
  tribe from the Lake Baikal region
  loot Uighur capital in 840 and destroy empire
  fail to form their own empire
TURKS (T'u-chüeh)
  first empire (552–630)
    controlled entire steppe from Manchuria to Caspian Sea
  second empire (683–734)
    controlled Mongolia
UIGHURS
  replace Turks with new empire (745–840)
  major military ally of T'ang dynasty

KEY TRIBAL FIGURES

A-NA-KUEI
  last khaghan of the Jou-jan (519–52)
HSIEH-LI
  last khaghan of first Turkish empire (r. 620–34)
  captured by T'ang forces

ISTÄMI
co-founder of first Turkish empire with brother T'u-men
Turkish khaghan in charge of the west (d. 576)
KHUTLUGH (Iltirish khaghan)
founder of second Turkish empire (r. 680–92)
KÜL-TEGIN
victor in second Turkish empire civil war over Mo-ch'o's heirs
appointed his brother Bilgä khaghan (r. 716–34)
MO-CH'O (Khapaghan khaghan)
khaghan of second Turkish empire (r. 692–716)
brother of Khutlugh, reconquers western Turks
MO-YEN-CH'O
Uighur khaghan (747–59)
aids T'ang in suppressing An Lu-shan rebellion
MU-KAN
Turkish khaghan in the east (r. 554–72)
son of T'u-men, military commander at height of Turkish power
T'U-MEN (Bumin)
co-founder of first Turkish empire with brother Istämi
Turkish khaghan in charge of the east (d. 553)
TARDU
Turkish khaghan in the west (r. 576–603)
son of Istämi, main contender for power in first civil war
TONYUKHUKH
military commander for Khutlugh, Mo-ch'o and Kül-tegin
most influential political leader in second Turkish empire

FOREIGN DYNASTIES IN NORTH CHINA

Northern Chou (557–81)
Northern Ch'i (550–77)

NATIVE DYNASTIES RULING ALL CHINA

Sui (581–618)
T'ang (618–907)

KEY CHINESE FIGURES

AN LU-SHAN
court favorite of Sogdian origin
almost brings down T'ang dynasty in 755 rebellion
EMPRESS WU
only woman to rule in her own name as a Chinese emperor (660–705)
paid off second Turkish empire khaghans
LI SHIH-MIN (T'ang T'ai-tsung)
second T'ang emperor (626–49)
"Chinese khaghan" after conquest of first Turkish empire

YANG-TI
 second and last Sui emperor (r. 605–16)
 military campaigns bring down empire
HSÜAN-TSUNG
 T'ang emperor (r. 713–56)
 makes military/marriage alliance with Uighurs
 cost of silk payments to nomads jumps

5

The Manchurian Candidates

The Kirghiz victory did not lead to a Kirghiz empire, but to anarchy. All the Turkish empires had relied on China to finance their state formation. The Kirghiz, wild nomads from the edge of Siberia, had no conception of how this relationship worked and made no attempt to deal with China. Neither did they move to dominate the other steppe tribes the Uighurs had conquered. They appeared content with the loot from Karabalghasun and went home. The internal order which the Uighurs had maintained on the steppe was ended. Tribes were free to do as they pleased, but none had the power to restore central rule. When the Chinese got word of this defeat, they smugly recorded the end of their enemies, noting that their empire did not rise again. The rejoicing was premature. The destruction of the Uighurs, troublesome as they were, now left China vulnerable to both internal revolt (which the Uighurs had proved so helpful in quelling) and to the Khitans of the Manchurian steppe, who had been kept in line throughout the T'ang period by the Turk and Uighur domination of their nomadic rivals.

The Kirghiz failure to implement a policy of imperial expansion is striking. For 300 years, successive Turkish and Uighur dynasties had pursued this goal. The Turks had made the establishment of a relationship with China their first priority after attacking the Jou-jan. The Uighurs sent envoys immediately to China upon the defeat of the Turks to announce their victories and demand that the old tributary benefits now be delivered to them. Both the Turks and Uighurs understood that the stability of their imperial confederacies depended on Chinese subsidies or loot from raids. Over the years they had raised the extortion of the T'ang court to a high art, preserving the dynasty against internal opposition in order to maintain the huge flow of tributary silk. Yet the Kirghiz sat content in the Orkhon, allowing the steppe to fragment and ignoring China. Mongolia fell into anarchy from which it was not to emerge for another 350 years, when the Mongols took power.

An imperial confederacy was not a simple or natural form of steppe political organization. It required sophisticated leadership to build and maintain. This the Kirghiz lacked. The Kirghiz came from southern Siberia on the upper Yenisei River. This was the very northern margin of the steppe, bordering the great forests inhabited by hunters and reindeer herders. Historically it was a poor but generally self-sufficient region, on the fringes of international trade routes. The Kirghiz may have been involved in the fur trade, for which the northern forests were famous, but they lacked the sophistication of the Turks and Uighurs who had long standing ties to great centers of world civilization – China, Sogdia, Persia, and Byzantium. The Kirghiz were, in short, a militarily powerful but ignorant tribe of nomads. To them Karabalghasun was a source of great wealth in itself. Their only desire was to take it. Unsophisticated nomads had appeared at China's doorstep before with similar aims – but there was a fundamental difference between looting a Chinese city and the Uighur capital. A Chinese city was the product of a sedentary agrarian civilization which had the power to renew itself from its own resources. The Uighur capital was a trade city based on the projection of nomad power. It could not renew itself unless the Kirghiz recreated the old network. They did not. Karabalghasun returned to sheep pasture.

The situation might have taken a different turn had the Kirghiz incorporated the old Uighur elite into a new state. Uighur advisors could have instructed the Kirghiz on the means necessary to maintain the tributary connection. Instead the Uighur elite fled south and regrouped as rulers of two sedentary oasis city states in Turkestan. These states of Kan-chou and Khocho gave the Uighurs a new base to continue their role as middlemen. It was they, not the Kirghiz, who continued to send envoys to China trading horses and jade for silk. Although they had lost their military power to extort huge subsidies, they maintained their importance in international trade. Khocho survived as an independent state until the time of the Mongols, on whom the Uighurs were to have a great influence. Nor did the Uighurs forget the importance of their ties with T'ang. In the last years of the dynasty their oasis kingdoms still sent envoys to court and even offered military aid to China.[1]

The Kirghiz, though initially victorious, turned the Orkhon into a backwater. They were driven from it fifty years later by Khitan armies, for the Manchurian Khitans were the ultimate beneficiaries of the anarchy on the steppe.

T'ang welcomed the collapse of the Uighurs. In 843 they attacked and destroyed those Uighur tribes which had fled toward the safety of the Chinese frontier. By remarkable coincidence the threat of Tibetan invasion disappeared at the same time, as the last king of Tibet was deposed and the country fell into turmoil. The Kirghiz showed no signs of attacking China. In one short period it would appear that T'ang frontier problems were at an end. Such was not the case. The end of central control in Mongolia and Tibet increased the importance and autonomy of smaller tribal leaders. Though no major threat to China, they caused enough trouble to force T'ang to maintain the old border defenses.

The main problem the dynasty faced was one it refused to recognize: the T'ang owed its continued existence to nomad military support. In spite of their arrogance and expensive demands, the Uighurs had proved faithful allies, most notably intervening to put down the An Lu-shan rebellion. Unwilling to admit its obligation to the nomads, the T'ang could not see that their fall stripped the dynasty of a major military prop that could be used in emergencies. The end of the Uighurs foreshadowed the T'ang's own doom.

Trouble within China was no new problem for the T'ang. Even before the time of the An Lu-shan rebellion the northern part of the empire had been split among a large number of autonomous military governors who respected the legitimacy but not the power of the court in Ch'ang-an. Over time the court had become increasingly dependent on revenue from the south, in the growing Yangtze River valley and beyond. As taxes increased so did disturbances in this area, but at the time the Uighurs fell the dynasty was able to put down bandit attacks with its own resources. However, within twenty years the situation got beyond the control of Ch'ang-an. In 859–60 a bandit leader, Ch'iu Fu, managed to organize a large number of robber bands into an army and began to create a government in the coastal territory south of the Yangtze. The T'ang put down the rebellion after fierce fighting, but the imperial commander felt it necessary to import several hundred Uighur and Tibetan mercenary cavalrymen in order to stiffen his force.[2]

This rebellion opened a whole series of troubles in the south, including a number of garrison insurrections. The most notable of these was led by P'ang Hsun. He was a frontier commander in the south when his troops revolted at the order to serve another tour of duty. Marching north they overran much of the Yangtze and cut the canal that supplied Ch'ang-an in 868–9. Government forces were only able to put down the rebellion with the assistance of the Sha-t'o Turks. Their leader, Chu-yeh Ch'ih-hsin, commanded 3,000 troops, a similar number to the force the Uighurs provided the T'ang with to attack An Lu-shan. As with the Uighurs, this small number of cavalrymen proved decisive in a number of battles. The Sha-t'o leader was granted the use of the imperial surname as an honor and became known as Li Kuo-ch'ang.

In both these campaigns T'ang commanders depended on foreign troops. Unlike the Uighurs, however, the Sha-t'o Turks lived near the frontier and used their new power to extract territorial concessions in the north. Nevertheless, the Sha-t'o were to prove more loyal to the T'ang than most of the Chinese military governors. Like most steppe nomads they had no desire to take on the responsibility of ruling all China. They would support T'ang to the bitter end. It was the barbarians who proved to be the strongest T'ang loyalists.

The collapse of the T'ang empire began in 875 when an enormous popular rebellion led by Huang Ch'ao broke out in the south. In 880, the rebels occupied both Lo-yang and Ch'ang-an, and the T'ang court fled to Szechwan. T'ang counterattacks stopped Huang Ch'ao's expansion a year later, but military governors feared losing their troops and maintained a defensive strategy. In desperation, the T'ang turned to its only sure supporters, the Sha-t'o Turks, even though they had been attacking other tribes supported by China. Under the leadership of Li K'o-yung, the son of their previous chief, the Sha-t'o formed an army of 35,000 and rode against Huang Ch'ao in 883. Joined by provincial Chinese troops, Li attacked and destroyed a much larger rebel force. Huang Ch'ao abandoned Ch'ang-an and retreated south. In spite of a number of further reverses he held out against new T'ang attacks. The court again called on Li K'o-yung, who moved east with an army of 50,000 in 884. After a series of military defeats and natural disasters, Huang Ch'ao fled with a small force pursued by the Turks. Finally trapped, he committed suicide rather than allow Li K'o-yung to get the credit for his capture.

Li K'o-yung was granted the military governorship of much of the north. This grant merely legitimized his power, for China was now divided into a large number of militarized provinces under autonomous governors. Indeed, the Turks could have abolished the dynasty, whose writ no longer ran outside the capital. Instead, the Turks were able to preserve the fiction of central rule until 907, when a Chinese warlord put an official end to the T'ang.[3]

THE KHITAN LIAO DYNASTY

The political situation on the frontier and within China following the collapse of T'ang was structurally similar to the succession of foreign dynasties after the Han dynasty. In analyzing that period it was suggested that a type of political ecology was at work and that certain foreign dynasties had advantages in certain situations, which led to a predictable order of replacement. This model identified three basic types of foreign dynasties, their origin, and organization:

1 *Steppe nomads*　Situated on China's northern frontier, they used their tribal military organization to become rulers of large parts of north China. These dynasties bore the brunt of fighting with native Chinese warlords, and formed the first foreign dynasties in China. However, constant fighting, an inability to provide stable administration, and difficulty in resolving the conflicts of being both tribal and Chinese-style rulers, led to their swift collapse.

2 *Conservative Manchurian frontier states*　Coming from the northeast, they began their history as small kingdoms combining steppe nomads, forest tribes, and Chinese rural and urban dwellers. These dynasties were organized with dual administrations, one branch, staffed by tribesmen, in charge of tribal affairs and war; while the other branch, staffed by Chinese bureaucrats, handled civil affairs. Both were under the control of the emperor, who manipulated each group of officials, using Chinese rules to weaken tribal autonomy, and tribal military organizations to prevent rebellion by the civil population. This style of dual organization was the product of decades of development and could only occur in areas of relative stability, beyond the major battle zones in China. Such states were conservative, moving into China only after the collapse of the steppe dynasties. They were scavengers rather than conquerors and at best controlled only a portion of north China. While such border states developed in both the northeast and northwest, those of the northeast had the strategic advantage, being much closer to the north China plain.

3 *Aggressive Manchurian frontier states*　These were founded by the leaders of "wild" tribes, who came either from the forest or the steppe. Originally they were frontier clients of the conservative Manchurian states. The failure of these states to incorporate all of north China under their rule meant that they

ultimately suffered severe fiscal problems, which created discontent among the mass of bureaucrats and army officers. The unsophisticated and aggressive tribes of the frontier took advantage of these military and economic weaknesses to displace the dynastic elite, revitalizing the state and beginning an aggressive policy of wholesale expansion to bring all of north China under their rule. They employed both the dual organization of government already in place and incorporated most of the old ruling class into the new political order.

The Liao dynasty established by the Khitans is a prime example of a Manchurian conquest, longer lived but similar in form to the Yen dynasty of the Mu-jung Hsien-pi of the fourth century. Its policy toward the steppe tribes and China provides data on how such dynasties arose and maintained their power.

The Khitans were pastoral nomads and the major tribal power in the northeast at the end of the T'o-pa Wei period. However, every one of their numerous attempts to create an autonomous state was put down by China or a steppe empire, because neither was willing to see a new frontier power come into existence. Evidence for this can be seen from the large number of failed rebellions the Khitans mounted against their overlords during the Sui–T'ang period. In 605, they attacked China, and the Sui dynasty responded by using Turkish troops to crush them. The Khitans later accepted the rule of the T'ang dynasty in 648 and were controlled by a governor-general until 695. At that time they revolted because famine relief failed to arrive, and because their chiefs felt mistreated by the Chinese administration. The Khitans advanced south, fortifying the region around modern Peking. Although China was at war with the eastern Turks, the T'ang temporarily combined with them to crush the Khitans in 697; China attacking the Khitan army in the south, while the Turks invaded the Khitan homeland. The rebellion collapsed and the Khitan gave their allegiance to the Turks. When Turkish power weakened in 714, the Khitans returned to China's rule. Local Khitan rulers increased their power until in 730 they proclaimed their independence. For the next ten years, the Khitans beat off both T'ang and Turkish attacks, but by 740 they had once again fallen under Chinese control, but only after the T'ang military forces along the frontier had been substantially increased. This frontier militarization, along with the troubles in organizing a campaign against the Khitans in 745, led to the rise of An Lu-shan, who commanded the T'ang northeastern defenses. The Khitans did not become active again until the Uighurs were destroyed by the Kirghiz.[4]

This tale of unsuccessful rebellions displays a consistent pattern. As long as the steppe and China were united, they maintained a bipolar world in which frontier peoples fell under the sway of one of the two powers. Maintaining a bipolar frontier was so important that when rebellions against Chinese control got out of hand, they were put down by the nomads from the central steppe. The rise of a Manchurian state following the collapse of central authority in both China and Mongolia was to be expected. Manchurian leaders had for 300 years tried to establish such a state but could only expect to claim power in such a strategically important area when they faced no outside opposition. In less sensitive areas located to the north along the Korean frontier, the Po-hai people had already established a kingdom that was organized along Chinese lines at the beginning of the eighth century. The Po-hai state maintained its independence because it was located in a region marginal to both China and Mongolia, whose troops suppressed their potential rivals to the south. With the Sha-t'o Turks preoccupied with their struggle to defeat Chinese warlords and the Kirghiz quiet on the steppe, the Khitan rulers began the process of state building that would lay the groundwork for a new and powerful dynasty.

At the end of the ninth century, the Khitans were divided into eight tribes under the rule of a supreme chieftain from the Yao-lien lineage. This leader had only a limited amount of power because the component tribes were largely autonomous. Confederation leadership itself occasionally moved from one tribe to another following military defeats. At the tribal level central authority was even more restricted, with leaders being elected to three-year terms. Over a period of four generations the I-la tribe, for example, had twelve chieftains chosen from the large Yeh-lü lineage. Succession was generally lateral, with brothers and cousins expecting to hold office in turn. Most of these men served only a single term, but one, T'ieh-la, held the office for twenty-seven years, indicating that strong personalities could come to dominate their tribes. However, his long rule failed to change the basic structure of Khitan tribal organization because leadership continued to rotate after his reign. If, as Chinese records state, the Khitans were descendants of the Hsien-pi, it would seem that the tradition of elective leadership and local autonomy remained strong in the northeast.[5]

The destruction of the tribal Khitan political order began during the turmoil surrounding the collapse of Uighur and T'ang power. Yeh-lü Sa-la-ti, a leader of the I-la tribe, gradually increased his power by broadening his tribe's economic base. He arranged a marriage alliance with a neighboring Uighur Hsiao tribe that possessed a developed tradition of ironworking. Sa-la-ti established the first iron smelters for toolmaking among the Khitans, while his brother was instrumental in encouraging the production of cloth and the construction of towns. Farming had been previously pioneered by their father and had made the I-la rich.

When Sa-la-ti's son, A-pao-chi, became ruler of the I-la tribe in 901, he used this base to expand his own power. In 902, he mounted a major attack on the Chinese frontier, reportedly capturing 95,000 people and 100,000 animals. In the following years he attacked and defeated neighboring Turkish tribes to the east, the Jurchens in the north, and a warlord in northeast China, Liu Shou-kuang. In early 907 he declared himself "emperor" of the Khitans.[6] This was a sharp break away from the traditional egalitarian tribal structure. It was made possible only by A-pao-chi's destruction of the old political organization with the help of Chinese advisors and the resources from conquered areas.

Sung records, hostile to the Khitans, recorded the bloody story of how he transformed the Khitan from a confederation of tribes into a state:

At this time Liu Shou-kuang was despotic, so that the people of Yu and Cho fled to the Khitans. A-pao-chi, taking advantage of this opportunity, crossed the frontier, attacked and seized the cities, and captured their people. Following the prefectures and counties of T'ang, he built cities to settle them.

The Chinese told A-pao-chi that there was no case of a Chinese ruler being replaced on the throne. Thereupon A-pao-chi made increasing use of his power to control the tribes and refused to be replaced. After nine years the tribes reproached him for not being replaced after such a long time. A-pao-chi had no choice but to pass on his banner and drum [symbols of authority]. But he said to the tribes, "The Chinese whom I have obtained during the nine years of my rule are numerous. I should like to organize an independent tribe to govern the Chinese City. Is this permissible?"

The tribe consented to it.

The Chinese city which was situated southeast of Mount T'an and on the Luan River, enjoyed the advantages of salt and iron. . . . Its land was suitable for the cultivation of the five grains. A-pao-chi led the Chinese in cultivating the land and constructed a city, houses, and markets after the system of Yu prefecture. The Chinese were satisfied with this and had no thought of returning.

A-pao-chi, realizing that people could be used, followed the plan of his wife Sho-lü and sent emissaries to inform the tribal chieftains: "I own the salt-lake from which you eat [salt]. But though the tribes know the advantages of eating salt, you do not realize it has an owner. Is that fair? You should compensate me."

The tribes considering this to be right, all assembled at the salt-lake with oxen and wine. A-pao-chi placed soldiers in ambush nearby. When the wine had begun to take effect, the hidden soldiers came forth and killed the tribal chieftains. Then he set himself up and was not replaced.[7]

A-pao-chi's strength was derived from his combination of tribal cavalry and a Chinese agricultural base. The massacre of tribal leaders placed A-pao-chi in an unchallenged position. It was his acquisition of Chinese subjects that made the difference, bringing new craft skills, agriculture, and sedentary administrative officials to the Khitans. Because of the civil wars within China frontier states could count on an influx of refugees or captives to help increase production. The I-la tribe's concern with fostering economic growth enabled them to grow more powerful than the other tribes and eventually to dominate them.

A-pao-chi's military campaigns, and those of his successors, reflected the conservative strategy common to new Manchurian border states. They never expanded deeply into China, and usually won territory by alliance or upon the collapse of their rivals. On the steppe, the Khitans practiced a policy of containment, controlling nearby tribes and disrupting more distant ones. The growth of the Khitan Liao state was relatively slow, with each conquest undertaken after prolonged planning.

The Khitans' initial campaigns were directed against their tribal neighbors rather than China. In 916, A-pao-chi defeated a number of Turkic tribes on the steppe, including the Sha-t'o, and in 924 his troops reached the abandoned Uighur city on the Orkhon River. There A-pao-chi ordered that an old stone engraving commissioned by Bilgä khaghan be reinscribed with a narrative of his own deeds.[8] These campaigns made the Khitan effective masters of the steppe, but not of a steppe empire. As a border state with interests in China, they considered Mongolia a marginal region. They planned steppe campaigns in order to clear their flank of dangerous rivals. Tribal wars in Manchuria were another matter. Forest tribes such as the Jurchens and steppe tribes such as the Turkish Hsi were forcibly integrated into the Khitan state.

The transformation of the Khitans from a confederation of tribes into a bureaucratic state under the control of an emperor was no simple task. A-pao-chi's murder of his tribal rivals eliminated the opposition from other Khitan clans and tribes, but the old ideal of collective rule continued to live on within the imperial family. Although he retained a strong sense of loyalty to his own family, A-pao-chi refused to share supreme power with them, restricting his relatives to subordinate, but important, positions within the state structure. His brothers and other collateral relatives, however, still favored the traditional Khitan tribal customs of limited terms for chiefs and lateral succession, and this issue became the focus of tribal discontent with the new imperial system.

Active revolts began only in 911, after A-pao-chi's traditional three-year term would have expired, had he not abolished the tribal system of circulating leadership. In response, A-pao-chi's brothers, uncles, and cousins organized a series of plots and outright rebellions in an attempt to seize power. The first two attempts failed, but the emperor pardoned his brothers and even gave them important offices. In 913, they led a large-scale insurrection which also ended in defeat. A-pao-chi executed most of the rebel leaders, although he could not bring himself to kill his brothers, and in the end they were set free. A final rebellion took place in 918, with the same results. These rebellions demonstrate that the concept of autocratic rule was not easily accepted. A-pao-chi's unwillingness to execute his rebellious brothers may have been due in part to his own uneasiness about breaking Khitan tribal law, under which his collateral relatives had rights that he was violating. At any rate, they and all their descendants were permanently excluded from the line of succession, although throughout the dynasty's history, the leadership for coups and rebellions tended to be drawn from alienated brothers, cousins, and uncles of the ruling emperor.

The struggle to implement a lineal succession rule was also supported by Chinese advisors who encouraged A-pao-chi to adopt more of Chinese culture. In 916, he announced a Chinese-style reign title and designated his eldest son as heir. These actions, and his public praise for Confucian philosophy, were all attempts by the new emperor to identify himself with an ideology that justified his centralized rule, for such a concept had no basis in the egalitarian Khitan tribal tradition. When, for example, A-pao-chi's uncle Hsia-ti was interrogated about his role in leading a revolt in 913, he sardonically expressed the tribal Khitan view of the new situation (perhaps too sardonically since he was executed shortly thereafter): "At first I did not realize how exalted a Son of Heaven is. Then Your Majesty ascended the throne. With your guards of attendants you were extremely dignified and in a different class from the common run of people."[9]

A-pao-chi laid the foundation for the Liao state by first establishing control over a number of Chinese cities in Liao-tung, gaining hegemony over the

Khitans, and then defeating other rival tribes on the steppe. Towards the end of his career he turned his attention to sedentary areas, such as the Korean kingdom of Po-hai, which he conquered just before his death in 926. He was succeeded by his second son Yao-ku (also known as Te-kuang or T'ai-tsung) who, with the aid of his powerful mother, displaced the heir designate, his elder brother, to become emperor. Yao-ku continued his father's policy of expansion and, taking advantage of the breakup of warlord states in the south, began making attacks on northeastern China.

Under the reigns of A-pao-chi and Yao-ku, the Liao state grew and developed in relative security for a period of forty years before it expanded into north China. It was during this time that the dynasty refined its system of dual organization, which became the key to its stability in China. From the beginning, A-pao-chi realized that he could not rule Chinese cities in Liao-tung the same way he ruled the Khitan tribes. He needed Chinese officials, with their knowledge of administration and taxation, to make these conquests productive. Therefore, Chinese officials were kept at their posts where they continued to use the T'ang system of organization. However, A-pao-chi was astute enough to realize that the adoption of completely Chinese-style government would alienate his tribal military. A dual organization allowed him to administer his new state in a way that centralized power in his hands and yet allowed each group to be ruled by its own customary law.

Such a system of government had been developed by the Mu-jung Hsien-pi in the Yen dynasty and inherited by the T'o-pa Wei. Its re-emergence centuries later was not the result of conscious imitation, but was rather a natural solution to the problem most founders of Manchurian states faced: how to organize a single state that contained both tribal peoples, who often lived a nomadic existence, and a sedentary Chinese population. The nomads from the central steppe, with their own ideas of hierarchy, had not been able to solve this problem effectively because they vacillated between adopting a purely Chinese administration, which alienated their tribal supporters, or imposing tribal leaders on the Chinese, which led to maladministration and economic collapse. In Manchuria leaders like A-pao-chi could experiment in a limited area and moreover, because the northeastern tribes did not have a hereditary aristocracy, they needed Chinese advisors and political philosophies to justify their usurpation of power. This process began simply enough when A-pao-chi asked permission to rule the Chinese he had conquered as an "independent tribe" and then employed the officials already in place there. After the Liao state expanded, the system became more complex, and under Yao-ku a formal dual administrative structure was created:

In the old Khitan way of life their affairs were simple, their official duties specific, and their governmental system plain and unsophisticated and not confused by terminology. Their rise was rapid indeed. In 921 an edict was issued concerning the regularization of grades and ranks. When T'ai-tsung [= Yao-ku] came to rule over China, he divided the government into North and South. The Khitans were governed according to their own national system, while the Chinese were governed according to their own system. The national system was plain and simple. In the Chinese system the usage of traditional terminology was preserved.

The government of the Liao state was divided into a Northern and a Southern division. The Northern Region administered the affairs of the camps, tents, tribes, lineages, and tributary states, while the Southern Region administered the taxes and the military affairs of the Chinese prefectures and counties. To govern according to custom is indeed to achieve what is proper.[10]

Perhaps the strangest aspect of this dual administration, at least to the Chinese, was that throughout the history of the dynasty the emperors made a habit of leaving the capital to move seasonally from one temporary camp to another. Chinese officials were therefore often left in charge of everyday management of the southern government by a court that was out fishing, hunting tigers and bears, visiting its tribal subjects, or just enjoying the fresh air. These officials were expected to periodically travel to these temporary camps for court conferences:

During the first ten days of the first month of every year, when the emperor started out, the officials from the prime ministers on down returned to the Central Capital where they remained on duty dispatching all matters concerning the Chinese and appointing officials simply by orders for temporary commissions. They awaited receipt of orders after discussions in the emperor's temporary residence and then issued the imperial certificates of appointment. Civil officials from county magistrates and recorders on down were permitted to be selected by the Secretarial Council without informing the throne by memorials. Military officials had to be reported to the emperor. During the fifth month, when the emperor enjoyed the coolness of his temporary residence, conferences were held with the northern and southern officials. During the tenth month, when the emperor spent the winter in his temporary residence, conferences were similarly held.[11]

For forty years the Liao state confined itself largely to campaigns in Manchuria and on the steppe. A-pao-chi never attempted a serious attack against north China. From the early part of his reign he had allied himself with the Sha-t'o Turks, the most powerful warlords in north China, who bore the brunt of fighting there. When their Later T'ang dynasty (923–36) fell apart, the Khitans did not attempt to conquer north China, but instead supported the rulers of a successor dynasty, the Later Chin (936–47), which then became their client state. The Liao court protected it from rivals in return for which the Khitans received a small amount of territory in China. A more aggressive state would have taken all the territory for itself. However, the Khitans were content with indirect control, because, like other Manchurian dynasties that were designed primarily to survive periods of anarchy, they moved to conquer north China only after the more militaristic warlord states had destroyed themselves.

It was not until the Chin court attempted to break its links with the Liao in 945 that the Khitans invaded China. Initially they were quite unsuccessful, being soundly defeated at Pai-t'uan-wei where the Liao emperor was forced to flee the battlefield on the back of a camel. Despite this setback, the Khitans overwhelmed the Chin armies in 946–7 and captured their capital of K'ai-feng. However, within months, the Khitans lost most of this territory when internal political disputes resulting from the death of Yao-ku, Emperor T'ai-tsung, and local rebellions forced them to withdraw north. It remained in the hands of local warlords until the establishment of the Sung dynasty in 960.[12]

The Liao dynasty's conservative approach to conquests in China was even more evident in its relationship with the new (Northern) Sung empire which had conquered all the small kingdoms in China, with the exception of the Khitan territories, to unite the country under a national dynasty. The Sung was able to seize a number of important kingdoms allied with the Khitans without substantial opposition. In 979 and then in 986, the Sung attacked the Khitans themselves. They were repulsed on both occasions, the second time disastrously. In addition to a tenacious military defense, the Khitans also responded in 990 by recognizing the new Tangut kingdom of Hsi Hsia, located in northwestern China, whose existence threatened the Sung frontiers. The balance of power began to shift in favor of the Liao, and in 994 the Sung court sent two embassies to negotiate a peace, but both were rejected. By 1004, the Khitans were in a strong enough position to carry out a counterattack against the Sung, forcing that dynasty to sue for peace on the Liao's terms. A treaty was signed in 1005 which called for the Sung to deliver 200,000 bolts of silk and 100,000 ounces of silver annually to the Khitans, who promised to recognize the old frontier. This effectively ended fighting between the Sung and the Khitans for a hundred years.[13]

The Khitans' ability to survive the Sung attacks and then go to war against them depended on a strong military. Under their dual system of administration, military affairs were under the control of the Northern Chancellor, that is, within the tribal sphere of influence. While a few Chinese did become military leaders, members of the Chinese administrative structure were excluded from discussions involving military affairs. All military appointments had to be approved by the emperor himself. However, while tribal troops were the backbone of the Liao army, they also posed a threat to the dynasty because they remained under the leadership of the old tribal elite. It was this tribal elite that was most dissatisfied by the imposition of imperial rule. A-pao-chi and his successors therefore attempted to reduce their influence by recruiting a permanent class of soldiers of mixed tribal, and even Chinese, background to act as their personal shock troops and imperial guards. These troops, known as *ordo*, were distributed in strategic parts of the empire, and were the first to be mobilized in the event of war.

T'ai-tsu [A-pao-chi], after ascending the throne through the I-la tribe, split his own tribe into the Five Divisions and the Six Divisions, which were governed by the imperial clan. But a personal guard was lacking. Therefore the ordo system was established, the prefectures and counties were divided, and the households and individuals were parted so as to strengthen the trunk and weaken the branches. This device was transmitted to posterity; an ordo guard was set up for each reign. When the emperor entered [his residence] it settled down to protect him, and when he went out it escorted him. After his burial it then guarded his mausoleum. In case of military activities the Control Bases of the five capitals and two prefectures quickly sent out notices and assembled [the troops] so that it was unnecessary to wait for the mobilization of the prefectures, counties, and tribes for an army of a hundred thousand mounted soldiers was already in existence.[14]

Actually the ordo armies probably never numbered a hundred thousand troops, but they were always the core for the much larger number of troops, as many as million, that could be drawn from the population as a whole. As the Liao state expanded so did the number of ordo troops and associated households, although some new ordos were created by taking manpower away from older ones.[15]

Time period	Households	Adult males	Mounted soldiers
926	15,000	30,000	6,000
951	51,000	102,000	24,000
969–83	73,000	146,000	36,000
pre-1031	110,000	220,000	61,000
1101–25	140,000	280,000	76,000

The Khitans established a more stable state than had the Mu-jung Hsien-pi of the fourth century. The Liao dynasty effectively reduced the power of its tribal elite through the development of ordo troops and by its tighter control over members of the imperial clan. Initially, it avoided the financial problems that plagued the former Yen dynasty. The Yen had found that maintaining the large number of officials required for a dual organization put too great a burden on its limited territory. The Liao might have faced a similar problem except for the large tribute benefits it received from the Sung as a consequence of the peace treaty of 1005. Finally the Liao state was blessed with a series of very long-lived emperors, so that the political turmoil brought on by succession disputes was greatly reduced.

The Liao and Yen strategy for expansion, however, was quite similar. Both were Manchurian dynasties that survived and expanded in periods of anarchy by employing a conservative military policy: defending themselves with great skill when attacked, but conquering relatively little of north China. The Liao dynasty proved unable to hold captured Chin territory in the face of local rebellions and it accepted Sung control of much of north China, even when its armies proved superior to those of its southern neighbor. It was willing to recognize the Tangut Hsi Hsia kingdom which, while a useful third power to use against the Sung, effectively ceded Khitan authority in the northwest. The peace treaty with the Sung which accepted the old borders in return for money and silk showed that the Liao court was primarily defensive in dealing with the south. "Surrounded on four sides by militant peoples, [Liao] crouched in their midst like a tiger whom no one dared to challenge."[16]

In dealing with the steppe and Manchuria the Khitans were more aggressive. Khitan control over the frontier tribes had both political and military components. They appointed tribal leaders loyal to the dynasty who were expected to provide tribute to the Liao court. The burden of meeting the Liao demands for goods and services was often heavy, and the dynasty was unpopular with its subject tribal leaders. They periodically rebelled, often murdering their Liao-appointed chiefs. Having put down a Jurchen rebellion in 986, the Liao court was aware of the danger from its tribal subjects. The Sung peace treaty, with its large annual tribute, allowed the Khitans to transfer troops north and pay for expensive military expeditions against frontier tribes and kingdoms. Campaigns were launched against Korea beginning in 1010 and lasting for about ten years, but they gained no real success. Armies also marched on the Uighurs in the west, against the Turks on the steppe, put down a major Po-hai rebellion in 1029, and launched a number of punitive attacks on the Jurchens. These military campaigns, like previous frontier expeditions, kept tribal groups either under direct Khitan control or, in more remote areas, forced them to acknowledge Khitan dominance. The main tool employed by the Khitans for this purpose was a series of frontier posts. Even as the dynasty entered a long period of prosperity following the conclusion of the Sung wars, the northeastern frontier became more and more difficult to control.

The garrisons along the northeastern border centered around two cities and seventy fortified places manned by 22,000 regular troops. The largest garrison numbered 10,000 while the smaller forts were staffed by several hundred troops. Soldiers were often conscripted for such service and expected to provide most of their own provisions. Similar frontier posts were also found on the northwestern frontier. From an early date, the dynasty faced problems in maintaining these defenses because conditions at these posts were very bad. One minister, seeking to reform the system, described conditions sometime between 983 and 1012, when the dynasty was still at the peak of its power.

In the northwestern regions, during the agricultural seasons for each person engaged in patrol service, another cares for public land and two render service to the *chiu* officers. Generally none of the four adult males lives at home. The work of grazing and herding devolves on their wives and children. Once robbed or plundered they immediately become impoverished. During the summer and spring they are relieved by compassionate actions [of the government]. The officials, however, frequently mix [the government grain] with chaff, thus adding to their exploitation so that after a few months they again face distress. . . . Further, because of desertions and deaths, the soldiers on guard at the frontier are continually being replaced by persons who are not accustomed to the natural conditions of the region. Thus the deterioration goes on day after day, and the inroads continue month after month, so that they are gradually reaching complete exhaustion.[17]

The situation did not improve. A report two generations later (circa 1034–44) on the northeastern frontier ran as follows:

Recently we have been selecting for the protection of the frontiers wealthy individuals who can supply their own provisions of grain. The way is long and difficult so that the trip takes a long time. By the time the garrison stations are reached, the supplies are already more than half consumed. Consequently hardly an ox or cart returns.

The families without adults [capable of military service] offer double prices for hired [substitutes], but these men fear the hardship and run off in the middle of the journey, so that provisions for the frontier troops frequently cannot be supplied. If they seek a loan from a person, tenfold interest has to be paid. Things go so far that repayment is impossible even if both children and fields are sold. Whenever there are permanent desertions from the service or deaths in the army, replacements are made with young and able-bodied men. Such in general is the frontier garrison service east of the Yalu River.

Furthermore the Po-hai, Nü-chih [Jurchens], and Koreans form alliances. Punitive expeditions are always taking place. The rich join the army, the poor become the patrols. Besides, the occurrence of floods and droughts and the fact that beans and millet are not flourishing increase the distress of the people daily. This is because the circumstances make it so.[18]

THE JURCHEN CHIN DYNASTY CONQUERS NORTH CHINA

The 1005 treaty with the Sung ushered in a stable period in Liao history. The Liao court had abandoned hope of any major expansion and worked to preserve the status quo. For a dynasty established by conquest this invited trouble because the Liao state's dual organization was expensive to maintain even with the aid of Sung tribute. Increasingly frequent wars along its northern flank drained the dynasty, for victories brought no new revenue. Since the army and bureaucracy were maintained by state revenue, this problem was of critical importance. A fiscal crisis developed in the latter half of the eleventh century, in spite of a new treaty with the Sung signed in 1042 that greatly increased the amount of tribute from the south. Substantial amounts of tax revenue were lost to the state as powerful Khitans became landlords. Elite Khitans who had been previously involved almost exclusively with military affairs, acquired property during the long period of peace with the Sung and used their influence to avoid taxes. This weakened the Liao state's financial base while diverting the Khitan elite's attention more toward financial affairs. The expansion of Khitan land-holdings also fomented rebellion among Chinese farmers who were pushed off their land or forced to become tenants. Banditry and widespread migrations by displaced persons became so commonplace that by 1087 the government declared the situation in many rural areas to be out of control.[19]

On the frontier, frequent revolts by the Jurchens and Po-hai were a consequence of harsh Khitan rule. Unrest among the frontier tribesmen and the declining state of the frontier garrisons in the northeast presented the greatest danger to the dynasty. The Jurchens, in particular, complained of abusive officials and the disproportionate work they expended in providing exotic furs and animals as tribute to the Liao court. Such tribes had always formed the nucleus of opposition to the dynasty, but as long as the Khitans remained well-organized there was little they could do. When internal weakness of the Liao state reduced its ability to coerce its neighbors, frontier leaders began to break free. The Jurchen opposition manifested itself openly in 1112, when their chief, A-ku-ta, pointedly refused an order to dance given by the Liao emperor who was making his annual fishing trip among the forest tribes. Such a refusal was an act of defiance equivalent to a declaration of rebellion. In the next few years, A-ku-ta gathered the Jurchens together under his banner and attacked the Liao positions.

The Jurchens lived in the territory to the north of the Liao homeland of the Khitans. They had a mixed economy that combined farming with stockraising, hunting, and fishing. The climate and land provided the Jurchens a low standard of living, but in spite of their poverty they had a fine cavalry. The

Khitans had incorporated some Jurchens into the Liao state, who were called "tame" Jurchen, while their more remote kinsmen not under Khitan control were known as "wild" Jurchen. Early accounts of the Jurchens reveal a fragmented political structure with no overall leadership. Individuals gained local influence by mediating disputes between villages that often led to blood feuds. Within a lineage leaders were elected to the position of *po-chin* (*bogile*) and they commanded their people in times of war. After the establishment of the Khitan Liao dynasty, the Jurchen tribes became more centralized. The Wan-yen clan from the Korean borderland expanded its dominance over the other "wild" tribes during the eleventh century, governing through a council of tribal leaders who held the title *po-chi-lieh*. The founder of the Jurchen Chin dynasty, A-ku-ta, was a member of the ruling Wan-yen lineage who inherited leadership from his brother, following the Jurchen tradition of lateral succession.[20]

A-ku-ta inherited an aggressive but poorly organized confederation of tribes. The Jurchens had no writing when they began their conquest of China and no administrative system for organizing a government. The transformation of a tribal rebellion into a conquest of north China was no mean feat. The writers of the official history of the Chin dynasty, written in Yüan times, attributed the rise of the Jurchens to their martial character and tough conditioning.

The causes for such swift success were that their customs were fierce, giving them great strength, and that their people were tenacious and vigorous. All the brothers, sons, and nephews were talented generals. All the tribes and basic units were good soldiers. In addition, their land was small and poor, and products few. In peacetime they worked hard in the fields to earn a living; in case of war they devoted themselves to fighting in order to capture booty. They constantly practiced physical exercise to that they could endure cold as well as warm weather. The way they drafted and sent soldiers to the battleground was like a family affair. The commanders were brave and had one spirit; the soldiers were skilled and possessed great strength. Once they rose and transformed themselves from a weak tribe to a formidable one, they were able to conquer a vast population with a few people.[21]

Yet many frontier tribes could boast of strong kinship ties and good fighters. The rapid success of the Jurchens after their initial attack on the Khitans in 1114 was aided by the collapse of the Liao defenses. Had the Liao military stood strongly behind the dynasty the Jurchens would have been unable to expand into China. However, the Liao had been plagued by a series of peasant rebellions which weakened them and sowed disaffection against the court even among the Khitans themselves. When the frontier came under attack, neither the tribal Khitans nor the imperial armies put up a sustained defense. In 1115, only a year after A-ku-ta mounted his first campaign, an imperial army of enormous proportions (reportedly 700,000 strong) disintegrated after losing the first battle to a much smaller number of Jurchens, allowing most of Manchuria to fall under their control. The eastern capital of Liao fell to the Jurchens the next year and imperial clansmen serving in nearby districts surrendered. The Liao northeastern army dispersed without fighting in 1117.[22]

The dissatisfaction of the Liao's non-Khitan subjects is easily understood, but the defection of the Khitans in their home territory, the collapse of impressive armies, and the surrender of imperial clansmen, demonstrated that the dynasty had lost touch with its own people. The decline in agricultural revenue, lack of expansion, and the promotion of policies that benefited only the Khitans at court, meant that tribal Khitans could no longer be rewarded for their support of the dynasty. This was particularly true for the front line troops defending the northeast, who bore the brunt of the court's neglect of the frontier garrisons. The Jurchens promised these groups loot from battles and new conquests. This was typical of tribal conquests because a tribal leader was initially an alliance builder seeking support for greater battles to come.

Jurchen tribal organization served as its military framework. Conquered tribes were easily absorbed as new military units under the command of their own leaders. Originally the Jurchen army was composed of units of one hundred (*mou-k'e*) and one thousand (*meng-an*), but A-ku-ta increased the size of these units so that each *meng-an* consisted of ten *mou-k'e* of 300 households. Even Chinese who surrendered could expect to receive tribal titles and be incorporated into this structure whose leaders provided the elite core within the Jurchen state. Thus, for many Khitan tribal leaders and Chinese officials the invading Jurchens offered a far better prospect than remaining with the declining Liao dynasty, which could no longer reward them. For these reasons the Jurchens had far greater success than the Sung in taking advantage of the divisions within the Liao government. The Sung could not offer the Khitan elite such a bargain, for it aimed at their destruction and courted the Jurchens as a means to that end.

By 1126, the Jurchens had not only conquered the Khitan Liao state, but all of north China. Their invasion of Liao territories was so swift that it is almost better described as a coup than a conquest. The structure of the Liao state remained intact – the Jurchens had no other administrative model – and they replaced an unpopular and defensive court with more aggressive leadership. Sinified Po-hai and Khitan officials modified the Liao administrative structure to fit the needs of the Jurchens. Many Khitan officials benefited, for the new dynasty invigorated the top levels of the former Khitan state and greatly expanded it, producing more revenue and new government positions.

The conquest of north China was a severe blow to the Sung dynasty, which was driven out of this territory. Ironically, they had encouraged the Jurchen to attack the Khitans in hopes of regaining the Chinese territory held by the Liao. The alliance was of little military value to the Jurchens, for Sung military failures only exposed the southern dynasty's weakness. Following their conquest of the Khitans, the Jurchens refused to allow the Sung to reclaim its old districts and in 1125 they opened hostilities. Within two years all of north China, including the Sung capital of K'ai-feng, was in their hands. These campaigns were spearheaded by Jurchen cavalry, although they were also quick to adopt the sophisticated Chinese weapons and infantry needed to take cities. Like previous foreign conquerors, the Jurchens proved unable to drive the Sung out of southern China, even after many attempts, because their cavalry was ineffective in the swampy ricelands of the south. The Jurchen Chin dynasty never developed an adequate navy to challenge Sung control of the waterways which, as for other dynasties in the south, were the bulwark of its defenses. The failure to overcome the south initiated a period of co-existence similar to that which had prevailed between Sung and Liao.

Jurchen military skill was far more sophisticated than their political or administrative understanding. The governing of all of north China put a great burden on the rulers of the new Chin dynasty. The Jurchens were quick to employ old Liao officials – Chinese, Po-hai, and Khitans – in their administration. Having had no experience in government, the Jurchens readily adopted the Khitan model of dual administration. It was particularly attractive to the Jurchens since it allowed tribal groups to be ruled differently from the Chinese population. In fact, dual administration was even more viable for the tribal Jurchens than for the Khitans at the end of the Liao period, when the distinction between Chinese and Khitans had become blurred. The Khitans had established a system that was adapted to the needs of a conquering tribal people, and the Jurchens expanded it throughout north China.

The Chin dynasty was noted for the high degree of sinification it achieved during its 120 year history. Much more so than their Khitan predecessors or Mongol successors, the Jurchens adopted Chinese philosophy and administrative practices. By the time of the Mongols they had produced a dynasty more Chinese in style than the Liao had ever been. A mark of this cultural assimilation were the discussions held by the Chin emperor on a metaphysical problem about which elements, according to Chinese tradition, were the most appropriate for the dynasty as the armies of Chinggis Khan overran north China.[23]

The reasons for the more intense sinification of the Jurchen are complex, but the growth of Chinese influence was intimately connected to their political development. The Chin ruled over all of north China, not just a part of it as the Liao had done. The Jurchens were forced to employ Chinese advisors and institutions on a much larger scale because Chinese territory represented the bulk of their empire. Whereas the ratio of Chinese to Khitans had been around 3:1 in the Liao state, the Chinese outnumbered the Jurchens 10:1. In this larger empire the Manchurian borderland played a less central role, particularly after the Jurchens resettled most of their people in China proper. The resettlement of the Jurchen meant that there was no tribal reservoir which might have counteracted Chinese influence. Even at the end of Liao many Khitans still lived in the border region where, ironically, they replaced the Jurchens as frontier troublemakers, Khitan revolts becoming a major problem for the Chin in its later history.[24]

Another important factor was the low level of cultural development among the Jurchens when they conquered north China. Before the Khitans expanded out of Manchuria they had developed a writing script and their own ideas about government. During the course of a few generations their leaders built a border society that combined both tribal and Chinese culture to some degree. Thus, when the Khitans began their advance into northeastern China, it was the culmination of almost a century of local development. Under A-ku-ta the Jurchens were catapulted directly into north China without any such development. Their traditional values, customs, and even language were lost at a rapid rate in the new environment, particularly among the elite at court, in spite of periodic government programs and edicts designed to protect Jurchen culture. However, it was not a case of the Jurchens having greater affinity for Chinese culture than the Khitans, rather it was that their own cultural traditions were inadequate for dealing with the complexities of their new way of life. Because Chinese culture was the only model of civilization readily available to them, the Jurchen were absorbed by it.

The process by which the Chin dynasty adopted Chinese culture was part of a political struggle over who should control the state. After the conquest a large number of districts were in the hands of Jurchen warlords. From 1123 to 1150, cliques whose influence depended on the emperor struggled for power against these warlords whose right to rule was based on conquest. Since their justification was rooted in Jurchen customary law, which emphasized the shared nature of power within the tribal system, the Chin court saw an advantage in strengthening the Chinese-style administration as a way to destroy tribal autonomy. Such struggles had characterized the formation of the Mu-jung Yen and the Khitan Liao kingdoms, but they had been resolved before entering China. The Jurchens made this transition while ruling China. The court rapidly adopted Chinese political institutions, with their focus on the emperor, as a means of strengthening the dynasty at the expense of tribal leaders. While the Chin needed its tribal reserves as a dependable military force, it administered them directly by the court and not through the mediation of tribal leaders.[25]

Centralization was accompanied an increased emphasis on Chinese culture. Under Emperor Tan (r. 1135–49) the *po-chi-lieh* tribal council was eliminated. A government reorganization was implemented using T'ang and Sung models of administration along with Confucian rites and rituals at court. Centralization reached its height under Emperor Liang (r. 1149–61), the fourth Chin emperor, who was an unabashed supporter of Chinese culture. He ended the system of dual administration in 1150 and executed many Jurchen military leaders, including those imperial clansmen who opposed him. In 1153 he transferred the capital south to better control Chinese territory, adopted a whole series of Chinese court rituals, and abolished earlier laws that had been part of a "Jurchenizing" campaign to maintain traditional customs begun in 1126. In 1158, Emperor Liang began a massive construction project at the Northern Sung capital of Pien (K'ai-feng), which he viewed as the center of a great empire which would emerge after he conquered the south. The project came to naught when the emperor was assassinated in 1161 after an unsuccessful campaign against the Sung. The Jurchen elite had his name expunged from the official list of emperors.

The fifth Chin emperor, Yung or Wu-lu (1161–1189), attempted to reverse his predecessor's policies which had alienated the dynasty's tribal supporters. He promoted hunting, encouraged the use of the Jurchen language, increased the number of Jurchen appointments to the government, and redistributed land to Jurchen commoners.[26] These policies failed because the process had gone too far. Structurally, the government remained based on a Chinese model because that was to the emperor's advantage. "Tribalizing" the government in any real sense would have necessitated a devolution of power to local tribal leaders, a course the central government was not prepared to take. Most of the encouragement was aimed at reviving Jurchen culture, but traditional tribal customs had little relevance to the Jurchens in China proper. Nor could a superficial return to tribal customs bring about fundamental change. The Chin dynasty appeared to outsiders, if not to the Chinese themselves, to be a typical Chinese dynasty in government and style. However, in terms of foreign policy, the Jurchen Chin dynasty was far from sinified. It played tribal politics along its northern frontier to keep the nomads divided. When it was suddenly faced with the most serious invasion ever mounted from the steppe by the Mongols of Chinggis Khan, it responded with all its military might. The Chin refused to agree to a peace in which it would have been forced to pay subsidies to the nomads, as did the Han and T'ang, or as the Sung had long done. Though the Mongols might view the Chin as a Chinese state, it was not. When under attack the Jurchens threw up strong, if eventually futile defense, that kept northern China embroiled in war for more than a quarter of a century before the dynasty was destroyed in 1234.

THE STEPPE DIVIDED

The conquest of northern China by dynasties of foreign origin put the nomads of Mongolia at a disadvantage. They were familiar with tribal politics and customs, maintained large numbers of cavalry troops, and were more creative than native Chinese dynasties in their dealings with nomadic tribes. One special advantage was their adoption of dual organization which allowed separate laws and administrative practices to be employed in frontier regions. Dual organization also freed the army from the control of Chinese bureaucrats so that military leaders were able to pursue more active campaigns. Perhaps the greatest difference in the policies was psychological. Chinese dynasties found the nomads to be alien, more like birds and beasts than men, whose actions and social organization were inexplicable. Foreign dynasties took a broader view because from the start their states included frontier peoples of steppe and forest origin as well as Chinese peasants and cities. Tribal organization and pastoral nomadism were parts of their own background. In dealing with the steppe, foreign dynasties knew where to find weaknesses.

This difference was most apparent in their strategy of attacking the steppe. Foreign dynasties were not intent on fighting crucial battles, but in capturing as many people and animals as possible. Because the steppe economy and peoples were mobile, it was possible to undermine the power of nomadic leaders by the wholesale removal of resources. The Chinese only rarely carried out such a policy because it meant carrying the enemy home to live within the empire, possibly to disrupt it. For foreign dynasties there was little danger because they were already equipped to control tribal peoples with their dual administrative structure. A similar flexibility was shown in trade. Chinese dynasties often refused to allow the nomads to trade or put severe restrictions on them. Negotiations for regular markets were a source of perennial disputes. With foreign dynasties this issue was moot, the frontier was not absolute and steppe tribes appear to have been able to trade without difficulty. This removed a major cause of raids and took away an excuse that steppe leaders had traditionally used to justify their authority.

The specific policies employed by foreign dynasties differed depending on the threat. The T'o-pa Wei relied on strong garrisons along the frontier which were used to attack the Jou-jan and keep them away from the border. They also attempted to sow discord among the Jou-jan to keep them fragmented politically. The Khitan Liao and the early Jurchen Chin had fewer difficulties because the steppe was in anarchy with no semblance of central authority. These dynasties employed a zone defense, incorporating tribes close to the frontier as buffers against attack from more distant tribes. Those tribes which fell under the direct control of the Liao or Chin authorities were closely watched and tightly controlled, a policy which led to discontent and frequent rebellions by trans-border populations. For tribes further away the policy was more flexible. While forts were sometimes established in steppe territory to threaten the tribes, the Liao and the Chin made far greater use of internal rivalries among the nomads. They threw their weight behind lesser tribes in order to destroy greater ones, who in their turn would be betrayed. Their basic policy was to keep the steppe in anarchy by preventing the rise of any powerful figure.

The Mongols first enter the historical record as victims of this Jurchen divide and rule strategy. They were only one of the many small tribes north of the Gobi that could have caused trouble. All had ambitious leaders who wished to bring the steppe under their control. Tribes such as the Tatar, Kereyid, Naiman, Merkid, and Önggüd were all potential rivals to the Mongols. Nor were the Jurchen alone in watching the frontier. From the Pamirs to the Pacific all the steppe frontier was in the hands of powerful foreign dynasties with tribal backgrounds and cavalry-based military. In the west, Turkestan was ruled by the Qara Khitai, a state founded by a Khitan prince who had mobilized local Turkish nomads to control the strategic oases of the region. The Kansu corridor and the Ordos were controlled by the Tangut kingdom of Hsi Hsia. Rich from trade, it could boast many walled cities and a strong defense. In the east, from the Ordos through southern Mongolia and Manchuria, Jurchen garrisons and fortresses protected the dynasty from incursions and provided aid to allied tribes. Potential nomadic leaders faced not one, but three, powerful states on their southern border.

The Jurchen often dealt with the tribes in the north by giving them gifts and inviting their leaders to visit. When such positive policies failed, they applied force. When Khabul Khan first became a powerful leader of the Mongols, he was invited to the Chin court where he was royally entertained. Later, deciding he was too great a danger to leave unmolested, the Jurchen organized a campaign against the Mongols in 1137. The Jurchen advanced into Mongol country but could not find the nomads. When the expedition ran short of supplies and had to return to China, the Mongols attacked and defeated them. Khabul Khan died soon thereafter and was succeeded by his nephew Ambaghai. The Tatars betrayed Ambaghai to the Jurchen who executed him in China. The Mongols regrouped under the leadership of Khutula, a son of

Khabul Khan, and retaliated by raiding the frontier. The Jurchen counter-attacked in 1143, but with no success. The Mongols were too far from China to be easily pursued, and the Chin's best troops and efforts were devoted to its wars in the south with Sung China. In 1147 a Chin general recommended seeking a peace treaty as the best way to deal with the Mongols. As part of this agreement the Chin agreed to withdraw a score of forts that threatened the Mongols and pay them a subsidy. On the surface this looked like a great defeat for the Chin and a reversion to policies common to native Chinese dynasties, but this was not so. The Chin had only devised a more subtle indirect policy against the Mongols.

As soon as the peace treaty was arranged the Mongols attacked the Tatars to avenge the death of Ambaghai, opening a long period of active hostilities. However, the Mongols suffered from internal divisions which produced a civil war in which Khutula and most of his brothers were killed. The Chin court was aware that the Mongols had many jealous neighbors who would work for their downfall, and took the opportunity to ally themselves with the Tatars for a joint expedition in 1161 to crush the Mongols. This victory raised the power of the Tatars to new heights, which caused the Jurchen to seek new allies, the Kereyid, to counter them. In 1198, Kereyid, Mongol, and Jurchen troops allied to destroy the Tatars.[27]

These events well illustrate the Jurchen policy of divide and rule. It was a long-term strategy which put growing tribal confederations under intense pressure. The Jurchen cultivated the leaders of weaker tribes to curb the power of stronger tribes. When the time was right, the Jurchen would change alliances and destroy the most dangerous confederation, often recruiting the very tribes they had defeated a generation earlier. In the case of the Mongols this was a period of twenty-five years, in the case of the Tatars, thirty-seven years. Implementing such a policy required that the Chin court keep close watch on the nomads throughout the reigns of successive emperors. Of course this policy did have a potential drawback: in supporting minor powers against major ones, the Jurchen might help to create a situation in which a new leader proved unstoppable by employing traditional tribal rivalries.

NOTES

1 Hamilton, *Les Ouïghours à l'époque des Cinq Dynasties d'après les documents chinois.*
2 *Cambridge History of China: Sui and T'ang* pp. 688–92.
3 Wang, *Structure of Power in the Five Dynasties.*
4 Pulleyblank, *The Background of the Rebellion of An Lu-shan.*
5 Wittfogel and Feng, *The History of Chinese Society: Liao.* Wittfogel and Feng have organized a partial translation of the *Liao Shih* (LS), a history of the Khitan (Ch'itan) Liao dynasty, into topical sections which provides the basic source material for this account.
6 LS 1:1-2b; Wittfogel and Feng, *Liao*, pp. 573–4.
7 *Wu-tai Shih-chi* by Ou-yang Hsiu (WTS) 72:2b-2a; Wittfogel and Feng, *Liao*, p. 142.

8 LS 1:9a, 2:4b-5a; Wittfogel and Feng, *Liao*, p. 576.
9 LS 112:12a; Wittfogel and Feng, *Liao*, p. 412, cf. 398–402.
10 LS 45:la-b; Wittfogel and Feng, *Liao*, p. 473.
11 LS 32:3b-4a; Wittfogel and Feng, *Liao*, p. 484.
12 LS 4:9b-16a.
13 LS 9:3a, 11:4a, 13:5a–b, 14:5b–6a; cf. Tao, "Barbarians or Northerners: Northern Sung images of the Khitans."
14 LS 35:lb; Wittfogel and Feng, *Liao*, p. 540.
15 Wittfogel and Feng, *Liao*, p. 516.
16 LS 46:14b; Wittfogel and Feng, *Liao*, p. 554.
17 LS 104:2a-b; Wittfogel and Feng, *Liao*, p. 556.
18 LS 103:2a-3b; Wittfogel and Feng, *Liao*, p. 557.
19 Wittfogel and Feng, *Liao*, pp. 286, 377, 406.
20 H. Franke, "Chinese texts on the Jurchens." The dynastic history of the Jurchens is found in the *Chin-shu* (CS).
21 CS 40:1a; Tao, *The Jurchen in Twelfth Century China*, pp. 21–2.
22 Wittfogel and Feng, *Liao*, p. 596.
23 Chan, *Legitimation in Imperial China: Discussions under the Jurchen-Chin Dynasty (1115–1234)*, p. 116.
24 Tao, *Jurchen*, p. 51.
25 Chan provides a concise yet detailed account of the Jurchen political struggles, *Legitimation*, pp. 57–72.
26 Tao, *Jurchen*, pp. 68–83.
27 Martin, *The Rise of Chinggis Khan*, pp. 55–9.

GLOSSARY OF KEY NAMES

MAIN TRIBES ON THE STEPPE FRONTIER

HSI (10th–11th centuries)
Turkish nomadic neighbors of Khitan
targets of Liao steppe campaigns
JURCHEN (10th–11th centuries)
tribes which inhabited northern forests of Manchuria
conquered by Khitan
JURCHEN (12th century)
tribes which inhabited northern forests of Manchuria
move south and conquer Khitan Liao dynasty
establish Chin dynasty
KHITANS (10th–11th centuries)
nomadic tribe of Manchuria
established Liao dynasty in northeast China in early tenth century
KHITANS (12th century)
nomadic tribe of Manchuria
state destroyed by Jurchen neighbors in early twelfth century
nomadic tribes remain on Manchurian steppe
settled Khitans become important Chin officials

KIRGHIZ (10th century)
 displaced from old Uighur area by Khitan attack
MONGOLS (12th century)
 small tribe in Mongolia
 suffered at hands of Jurchen Chin dynasty
PO-HAI (10th century)
 kingdom on Korean frontier
 fell to Khitan attack
SHA-T'O (10th century)
 Turks allied with the Uighurs, then T'ang court
 establish Later T'ang dynasty (923–36)
 displaced by Khitans

IMPORTANT TRIBAL KINGDOMS AND CHINESE DYNASTIES

CHIN (1115–1234)
 Jurchen dynasty that ruled over most of north China
HSI HSIA (990–1227)
 Tangut kingdom in northwestern China
LIAO (907–1124)
 Khitan dynasty in northeastern China
QARA KHITAI (1143–1211)
 state ruling over Turkestan
 established by refugee Khitan royal house
SUNG (Northern 960–1127; Southern 1127–1279)
 native Chinese dynasty that succeeded T'ang
 ruled most of China in northern phase
 confined to southern China by Jurchen Chin

KEY FIGURES

A-KU-TA
 founder of Jurchen Chin dynasty
A-PAO-CHI
 founder of Khitan Liao dynasty
LI K'O-YUNG
 Sha-t'o Turk leader
 provided military aid to T'ang
LIANG (Ti-ku-nai)
 fourth Chin emperor (1150–61)
 instituted sinification policy

6

The Mongol Empire

Temüjin, the future Chinggis Khan, was probably born in 1167, at a time when the Mongols had little independent power. Their confederation had been destroyed by Chin and Tatar attacks, and the component tribes of the Mongols were either allied with the Kereyid or under Tatar control. Temüjin's father was Yesügei Ba'atur, a son of Khutula Khan's only surviving brother. He was leader of the Kiyad lineage of the Borjigin clan, which had united the Mongols under Khabul Khan. Even in defeat there remained a rivalry between the Borjigin and the Tayichi'ud, the clan of Ambaghai and his descendants, over which should rule the Mongols. They were fairly equal in power and the khan title had moved from one clan to the other, but after their civil war the Mongols became so fragmented that they no longer had a khan. Temüjin, therefore, came from lineage that had provided Mongols with leaders, but such ancestry brought him few immediate advantages, for clans gathered around a capable leader in times of success and deserted him if he failed or when he died.[1]

Because Chinggis Khan's life was recorded in detail, it has often been assumed that he was typical of founders of steppe empires. Lattimore has argued that only a member of minor nobility would have both the social position to gain followers and the desire to disrupt the status quo in order to build a new state.[2] In fact, men in such positions were not typically founders of nomadic states.

Founders of pre-Mongol steppe empires can be divided into three major types. The majority were the hereditary leaders of established united tribes already powerful in one part of the steppe. Rulers of these tribes could count on their own tribe's consistent support. From this base they expanded their power by conquering neighboring tribes and incorporating them into an imperial confederacy, which eventually encompassed the whole steppe. The elite of the founding tribe became the imperial elite of the empire, but local tribal groups, while subservient to imperial authority, usually retained their traditional leaders and internal organization. Mao-tun of the Hsiung-nu, Bumin of the Turks, and

Kuli of the Uighurs all founded classic empires in this manner.

A second type of leader established an empire by reorganizing a nomadic state that was falling apart or which had been recently destroyed. These dynasties were founded by members of the existing political elite by means of coups, civil wars, or wars of reincorporation. The southern *Shan-yüs* of the Hsiung-nu were of this type, coming from the ruling elite of the old empire. A more powerful example was the foundation of the second Turkish Empire by Khutlugh Elterish. With only a small number of supporters initially, he re-created the old Turkish state, helped greatly by the living memory of the first empire's prestige and authority. Among the Uighurs the coup by Ku-tu-lu led to an increase in power under his dynasty. In all these cases the secondary founder had the advantage of working within an established tradition of centralized rule.

A third category consisted of rulers by election. Tan-shih-huai of the Hsien-pi, a man of lowly birth but great talent, was elected head of a confeder-ation which dominated the steppe under his leadership. Such confederations were weakly structured and could not be passed on to descendants. They were typical of the Manchurian steppe areas, where the concept of a hereditary right to rule never developed to the same extent as among the nomads of the central steppe. The Khitan Liao founder A-pao-chi was elected to leadership in this tradition, but he destroyed the tribal system to create a border state on radically different principles.

Chinggis Khan's own rise to power fits none of these patterns. While he was born into a ruling clan, the Mongols had no supratribal leadership of their own and they never provided Chinggis Khan with a secure base. The Mongols constantly deserted him during the many wars he fought before unifying the steppe. Chinggis could not be considered a secondary founder. The last steppe empire, that of the Uighurs, had been gone for more than 300 years. There was no tradition, or even memory, of a steppe empire that could be used as a model. Nor did Chinggis Khan owe his power to election. While he was asked to be khan of the Mongols early in his career, about half the clans refused to accept his leadership and even those that swore to follow him forever deserted at the first sign of trouble. Unlike Tan-shih-huai, who was elected at an early age and used his position to increase Hsien-pi rule, Chinggis Khan was elected to be khan when the Mongols were junior partners of the Kereyid confederation without full autonomy.

Chinggis Khan rose to the leadership of a great nomadic empire from an extremely marginal position. He lacked a secure base of tribal support and encountered a series of obstacles in his attempts to gain power and unite the nomads. His bitter experiences with steppe politics and the fickleness of tribal military units shaped his ideas about military strategy and political organization, which gave the Mongol empire a unique structure. Chinggis Khan took more risks in battle than other steppe leaders because he needed victories to establish himself, for without a firm base of tribal support, he could not rely on the strategic retreat to avoid powerful enemies. The army and the empire were commanded by men who owed their personal loyalty to Chinggis Khan, while members of his own lineage were generally excluded from major positions.

Because Chinggis Khan trusted neither his close relatives nor the Mongol clans, he saw autocracy as the only way to preserve his power.

At the time of Temüjin's birth the steppe was in anarchy. Segmentary opposition was the basic form of political organization: opposing tribes or clans would unite against a common foe, only to separate and continue fighting one another when the common enemy was defeated. There was some safety to be had in joining tribal confederations, but none of them proved capable of permanently dominating the others. Any leader who gained power also gained enemies and provoked new alliances against himself. It took very little effort by the Chin court to exploit these rivalries and intervene against any confederation that got too powerful.

At the level of the individual, life and property were insecure. Tribal wars, small-scale raids, ambushes, stocktheft, kidnapping, and murder were common. Temüjin's early life was full of such dangers, and his conquest of the steppe and imposition of order on it consumed most of his adult life. Temüjin was barely more than a child when his father was murdered and the Mongols rejected his family. Yesügei had arranged a marriage for his nine-year-old son with a girl from the Unggirad and, following custom, had left Temüjin with his future father-in-law. On the way back Yesügei was met by some Tatars who poisoned him. His widow, Hö'elün Üjin, attempted to keep her husband's people together, but the Tayichi'ud incited them to leave. Deserted by everyone, the family moved into the mountains where they survived by hunting marmots and birds, fishing, and gathering wild foods. Harmony within the family was disrupted by sibling rivalry between Temüjin and his half-brother Begter. Temüjin murdered him. Hö'elün Üjin was furious:

At the moment when you have no companion other than your shadow;
At the moment when you have no whip other than your tail,
At the moment when you are not able to suffer the bitterness of the Tayichi'ud brethren and at the moment when you are saying, "By whom shall we take vengeance?" you do this to each other. Saying "How shall we live?" . . . she was exceedingly displeased with her son.[3]

Soon problems got worse. The Tayichi'ud feared that having survived exile, Temüjin would take revenge as he matured. They raided his camp and took him prisoner, but Temüjin engineered an escape.

Around the age of sixteen Temüjin entered the world of tribal politics when he returned to the Unggirad to marry his betrothed, Börte, as arranged by his father. Part of her dowry included a sable coat which Temüjin presented as a gift to To'oril Khan, the leader of the Kereyid confederation. To'oril had been a sworn brother (*anda*) to Yesügei and, pleased by the valuable gift, promised to help Temüjin recover his father's people. However, Temüjin soon needed more practical aid after some Merkid attacked his camp and carried off Börte. To'oril Khan raised an army against the Merkid and rescued Börte. This expedition was the first time Temüjin had the opportunity to lead a large number of troops, and the victory over the Merkid enhanced his reputation, allowing him to recover leadership of his father's people.

Temüjin was just one of many ambitious young men in the Kereyid confederation. He had a rival among the Mongols, Jamukha, who had sworn brother-hood with Temüjin when they were boys. After the Merkid war they camped together but, because they were ultimately in competition for leadership of the same tribe, they split up and relations deteriorated as many of Jamukha's followers deserted to Temüjin. At this point (1190?) the leaders of his tribe, the senior descendants of Khabul Khan, elected Temüjin khan of the Mongols. The politics behind this move are obscure, but Temüjin's clansmen may have renounced their own rights in order to support a proven rival of Jamukha, whose leadership threatened to take power away from the descendants of Khabul Khan. In any event, Temüjin was khan only to a fraction of the Mongols, for he and Jamukha could both put about 30,000 men each into the field. To'oril Khan was pleased with the election. Noting the Mongols needed a khan, he warned them not to later break their promises. His warning was evidence that the title may have been more glorious than the reality. Initially, Jamukha did not protest the election, but when a raid by some of Temüjin's followers resulted in the death of his cousin he raised his tribes and attacked. Temüjin was defeated and forced to retreat. Jamukha boiled some of the prisoners alive, offending a number of clans who then deserted to Temüjin.

In terms of steppe-wide politics, Temüjin's role did not become important until 1196 when he aided To'oril Khan in regaining control of the Kereyid. To'oril Khan had long been unpopular because he had murdered two of his younger brothers when he took power, and forced a third to flee to the Naiman. In 1194 this brother overthrew To'oril Khan who sought aid from the Gur Khan, the ruler of the Qara Khitai. This was refused and a year later he arrived at Temüjin's camp as a poor refugee. Temüjin raised an army and restored his patron to power. He then defeated an attack by the Merkid who had hoped to exploit the weakness of the Kereyid. Temüjin sent the captured booty to To'oril Khan. In 1198, the Chin decided to enlist the help of the Mongols and Kereyid in an attack against the Tatars, who had grown powerful. The Mongols were eager to avenge themselves on their old enemies, and the combined force defeated the Tatars. To'oril Khan received the title Ong (Wang) Khan from the Chin in recognition of his service; Temüjin got a minor title.

The destruction of the Tatars changed the balance of power on the steppe, leaving the Naiman and Kereyid confederations as the most dominant in northern Mongolia. The Chin attack also proved that the Jurchen were far from losing control of their frontier, remaining active and powerful players in steppe politics. After the defeat of the Tatars, Temüjin did not attempt to create an independent role for himself. He still controlled only part of the Mongol people and remained a junior member of the Kereyid confederation. It appears he tried to link himself more closely with Ong Khan in hopes of becoming leader of the confederation at his patron's death. However, Temüjin's rising influence and Ong Khan's reliance on his support had the effect of inciting the Kereyid leader's fear and jealousy. Ong Khan tried to keep the Mongols as subordinate partners in the confederation by constantly switching his support from Temüjin to Jamukha.

When the Naiman confederation split after the death of its khan, Ong Khan organized an attack against it. Both Jamukha and Temüjin participated. The night before the battle, Jamukha convinced Ong Khan to withdraw and leave Temüjin alone against the Naiman with the expectation that his force would be destroyed. The ploy failed because the Naiman ignored the Mongols and pursued the Kereyid instead. Ong Khan was forced to call on Temüjin's aid to drive the Naiman off. Temüjin also fended off an attack by the Merkid who had hoped to take advantage of the situation.

Fear of Kereyid power led the other tribes to organize a new coalition under the leadership of Jamukha, who was named Gur Khan. After a fierce battle Jamukha was defeated. Temüjin used the opportunity to follow and destroy the Tayichi'ud, a tactic which he also then employed against the remaining Tatars. For his aid in saving the confederation, Ong Khan adopted Temüjin as his son. Ong Khan's own son bitterly opposed his father's action, and when Temüjin requested a marriage alliance to reinforce this bond, Ong Khan's son and Jamukha (who was now back in Ong Khan's good graces) convinced him to reject the proposal as insulting. They also accused Temüjin of plotting with the Naiman. Sensing that Temüjin was losing Ong Khan's favor, many Mongol clans deserted him. An unsuccessful attempt was made to poison Temüjin, and a Kereyid attack followed. Temüjin was forced to retreat, a failed leader. Now at his low point, only 4,600 troops were still with him when he camped at Lake Baljuna. Temüjin attempted to open negotiations with the Kereyid, but was rebuffed. He was saved by exploiting a stroke of good fortune, for his envoy reported that the Kereyid were now busy feasting – meaning they were mostly drunk. Temüjin immediately attacked them. After three days of fighting Ong Khan was forced to flee and he lost his head soon thereafter. Temüjin was now ruler of the Kereyid confederation, which weeks before had been on the verge of destroying him.

This sudden change in fortune provoked an alliance of his enemies led by the Naiman. A year later (1204), after reorganizing his army, Temüjin met his enemies in battle. If he had lost, his career would have been at an end, but he won a major victory, defeating the Naiman and scattering their allies. While many campaigns would follow, from this point he was master of Mongolia. In 1206 he held a great meeting, *khuriltai*, where he was proclaimed Chinggis Khan.

MONGOL POLITICAL ORGANIZATION

Chinggis Khan created a steppe empire by organizing a personal following rather than by depending on tribal loyalties. Most of the Mongol clans had proved fickle, electing him khan one year and deserting him the next. Even his uncles and brothers had at various times allied themselves with rivals. This experience had a strong impact on Chinggis and he was never willing to delegate power to his own relatives or to other Mongol leaders without in some way limiting their autonomy. The Mongols never had the close relationship with Chinggis Khan that developed among the Hsiung-nu with their *Shan-yü* or among the Turks with their khaghan.

Traditionally Mongol political organization centered on lineage and clan leaders who were lords (*tus*) of their respective kinship groups. In times of anarchy, however, loyalty to such leaders was conditional and not reliable. Chinggis Khan himself had been deserted by his father's people when he was a boy. Leaders were forced to rely on building a personal following in addition to their kin. Rising leaders attracted companions, *nökör*, who swore their personal allegiance as free men to their patron. They acted as bodyguards, personal units in war, and agents of their leader. The most heinous act that could be committed in the eyes of Chinggis Khan was betrayal by a *nökör*. He executed the *nökör*s of his enemies who had betrayed their trust and rewarded those who had proved faithful even in battle against the Mongols. A man who had betrayed his oath once was not to be trusted again. A second type of follower was a household retainer ("slave of the threshold") who was pledged in service to a particular family. While not a relationship of free choice, such men often became integral parts of the family and rose to prominent positions. When Chinggis Khan was first elected khan of the Mongols, his choices for army commanders were his two closest aides, Bo'orchu, a *nökör*, and Jelme, a household retainer.

Both these types of positions stressed personal loyalty between followers and leaders. Between leaders the concept of sworn brotherhood (*anda*) created a similar bond but with a stress on equality. This allowed the creation of alliances beyond the bounds of kinship. An *anda* gave not only his personal promise to aid his sworn brother, but was expected to bring the support of his group with him. Temüjin used the *anda* relationship his father had established with To'oril Khan to gain his aid in recovering Börte from the Merkid. Perhaps the most famous sworn brotherhood was that between Jamukha and Temüjin, which soured over time. Unlike the forsworn *nökör* for whom there was no mercy, Chinggis Khan looked upon his *anda*'s opposition with more regret than anger. After Chinggis Khan's unification of the steppe, the *anda* relationship all but disappeared, for nomadic leaders became part of the new imperium and were no longer autonomous actors.

When Chinggis was proclaimed master of Mongolia in 1206, he had moved far from his low point at Lake Baljuna three years earlier, but his reorganization of the army reflected his own recent insecurity. The highest positions did not go to family members or traditional tribal leaders, but to Chinggis's most loyal commanders. In addition, the personal bodyguard (*keshig*) was transformed into an imperial guard. Throughout the remainder of his life Chinggis Khan remained suspicious of anyone, particularly family members, who might be tempted to usurp his position. It was not until after his death that family members began to play a dominant role in running the affairs of the empire.

The army itself numbered 95,000 in 1206. Chinggis Khan divided it among eight-six "captains of a thousand." Most of these units were of mixed tribal background. Exceptions to this rule were made for those tribes or clans whose leaders had continually supported Temüjin since his first election to khan around 1190, or who accepted his rule voluntarily after he had united the Mongols and entered into marriage alliances to become "brothers-in-law" (*güregen*). They often led more than a thousand men in their units. Others were allowed to gather together scattered clansmen as a specific award for their service. The commanders of a thousand could be divided into three categories. The first were long-term supporters of Chinggis (20 percent) who received special favors or higher ranks for their services. It was from this group that came the famous commanders of the Mongol conquests. A second group consisted of commanders connected by marriage or adoption to Chinggis Khan (10 percent), who played prominent roles in administration or warfare. The vast majority (70 percent) had no past connection recorded in the *Secret History*, nor were they prominent as individuals later. They were probably the traditional clan leaders (*tus*).[4]

The largest tactical unit in the Mongol army was the *tümen*, which consisted of 10,000 men, although not all such units contained their full complement of troops. The *tümen* were under the control of Chinggis's most trusted friends and *tümen* leaders had direct command of about half the troops in the army. Bo'orchu, Chinggis's first *nökör*, commanded a *tümen* based in the Altai Mountains. Mukhali, a household retainer, was given command of a *tümen* on the Manchurian border and granted the hereditary title of Gui Ong. Khorchi, an early supporter and prophet of Chinggis's success, was given a *tümen* to control the forest tribes of the north. Naya'a who had brought Chinggis his Tayichi'ud enemies without compromising his honor, commanded a *tümen* in the center. Ghunan was made commander of a *tümen* delegated to Chinggis's son Jochi. A few others commanded four or five thousand of their own tribal people. The command of the whole army was in the hands of Khubilai, the younger brother of Chinggis's best friend Jelme, who were both household retainers.[5]

What was remarkable about this division was the exclusion of patrilineal relatives from command positions. None of Chinggis's uncles, cousins, brothers, sons, or nephews (with the nominal exception of Jochi) initially received any direct control over military units. When, some time later, he finally did distribute troops to his family he was parsimonious (see table 6.1 below) although the number of troops under Mongol control had increased with time. Those troops who were distributed to the family came with commanders of a thousand with proven loyalty to Chinggis. Chinggis's fear was partially justified, for no sooner had the troops been divided than plots to control them arose.

Chinggis Khan's distrust of his own patrilineal relatives was marked throughout his life. Whenever possible he entrusted major affairs to his personal supporters. These men, whom he had recruited himself, proved both loyal and remarkably talented. In his dealings with them he was generous and outgoing, confident that his judgment of their character was sound. With relatives he showed a very different disposition of suspicion, ill-will and jealousy. He resented almost anyone who had a kinship claim upon him, as if, being unearned, it was an affront. The mere rumor that a close kinsman was encroaching on his rights or power sent him into a rage, and the number of his relatives he put to death, or threatened to put to death, was about a dozen – practically everyone in the patriline who had a claim to power. Chinggis's attitude was determined by three key experiences: the desertion of his family at the death of his father, the desertion of those kinsmen who had elected him khan, and disputes with his relatives after he became supreme ruler.

Probably the most traumatic event in Chinggis's life occurred when the Tayichi'ud convinced the Mongols to desert Yesügei's family after his death. The family was left destitute and received no aid or support from Yesügei's younger brother. From this point the *Secret History* stresses the importance of Chinggis's personal followers. As if to underscore his dependence on non-kin, it was during this exile that a resentful Temüjin killed his half-brother because he did not like him. When the Mongols made Temüjin their khan around 1190 there were more senior candidates for the position, like Temüjin, all descendants of Khabul Khan, who gave their support to him. Within a few years these men deserted and then attacked him. Chinggis made a point of killing them all. Sacha Beki and Taichu (who were of the most senior line) he captured and executed. Büri-bökö, who had caused trouble for Chinggis, had his back broken on the khan's order. Altan, the son of Khatula Khan, was too powerful to destroy until after the defeat of the Naiman, when he too was killed. Even Dagharitai, Chinggis's uncle, was to be executed until the khan's companions convinced him it would be too unseemly. By these killings Chinggis wiped out all the other competitive lines of succession.

Chinggis's suspicion of relatives was also evident in a lethal dispute with his step-brother Teb Tenggeri, the son of Münglig, that evolved after the *khuriltai* of 1206. Teb Tenggeri was no ordinary man. He was feared by the Mongols for his powers as a shaman, a seer who could communicate with the spirits of heaven to cure illness, curse an enemy, or predict the future. His earlier pronouncements that Chinggis Khan had been chosen by heaven as the supreme ruler had done much to legitimate the new empire. Although Münglig had married Chinggis's mother, been named the first "captain of a thousand," and is referred to in the Secret History as "Father Münglig," neither he nor his seven sons had received a *tümen* command or personal allocation of troops. When Chinggis's mother Hö'elün Üjin died, Teb Tenggeri moved to seize control of the 10,000 troops she and Chinggis's youngest brother Temüge Odchigin had been given. When Temüge Odchigin demanded their return the sons of Münglig refused and then insulted him. Chinggis was usually ruthless in dealing with such threats to his authority but, because the Mongols were in awe of Teb Tenggeri's shamanistic powers, he hesitated to act until Börte pointed out that any man who could humiliate Chinggis's brother was a threat to the family as a whole. Teb Tenggeri was surprised by guards on his next visit and Temüge Odchigin broke his back. Münglig was then warned not to count on past favors to protect him or his sons in the future. They were not to be granted a special inheritance.[6]

While this dispute has often been interpreted as a struggle between secular and spiritual power among the Mongols (in part because it is one of the very few times when a shaman even appears in the history of steppe politics), it is more explicable as an attempt by Münglig's sons to claim a share of power they felt was theirs by right of inheritance. Teb Tenggeri saw himself as a step-brother entitled to rule at least some of the tribes, while Chinggis was determined to retain exclusive power at all costs. Even after he had decided on a successor, Chinggis still remained sensitive to any sign of insubordination by his sons. For example, he was furious with them when they divided the loot of Urgench

Table 6.1   Distribution of troops to Chinggis's family

First distribution (1206–10)	
To collateral relatives:	
Mother and Temüge	= 10,000
Khasar	= 4,000 (secretly reduced to 1,400)
Alchidai	= 2,000
Belgutai	= 1,500
To lineal descendants:	
Jochi	= 9,000
Chaghadai	= 8,000
Ögödei	= 5,000
Tolui	= 5,000
Total	= 44,500
Distribution of troops at Chinggis's death (1227)	
To collateral relatives:	
Mother (deceased)	= 3,000
Temüge	= 5,000
Alchidai	= 3,000
Khasar's sons	= 1,000
To lineal descendants:	
Jochi	= 4,000
Chaghadai	= 4,000
Ögödei	= 4,000
Kolgen	= 4,000
Total	= 28,000

Source: Secret History 242; Cleaves, p. 175; Hsiao, Military Establishment, p. 11

without reserving a share for him and threatened dire punishments before being calmed down by his advisors. At the end of his life Chinggis almost went to war with Jochi because of unfounded rumors that he was plotting rebellion.

It is possible that because of these incidents Chinggis reduced even further the number of personal troops attached to his family, for the number of troops assigned to them at the time of his death differs significantly from the first allocation (table 6.1). In the first distribution 44,500 troops out of 95,000 had been allocated to immediate family members (47 percent). In 1227, this number had been reduced to 28,000 out of an army of 129,000 (22 percent), both an absolute and relative decline. The sons got an equal number of people, but less than before. For the first time Kolgen, a son by a favorite secondary wife, was included along with the others. Tolui got no personal people because, as the youngest son, he inherited the paternal hearth consisting of the command of the 110,000 man imperial Mongol army. Collateral relatives who inherited people also show a change. Khasar's descendants still suffered from Chinggis's quarrel with his brother and got the least. The descendants of Belgutai, a half-brother, were dropped from the rolls. Only Alchidai and his sons, the descendants of Khachi'un, Chinggis's brother who died before he came to power, got an increase. All in all, companions fared better than relatives in their dealings with Chinggis.

The greatest innovation of Chinggis Khan was the establishment of the *keshig*. It has its origins in his personal bodyguard of 70 day guards and 80 night guards. Later this number was raised to 800 night guards (and presumably 700 day guards), together with special quiver bearers, messengers, and household stewards. From this base the *keshig* was expanded in 1206 to 10,000 men drawn from all the units in the army. Ten units of one thousand were established. The most important was the night guard which was restricted to personal service to the khan. Then came an elite unit of quiver bearers, a *ba'atud* (picked warriors) and seven units of day guards. Those who had served in the old *keshig* were considered senior to newcomers.[7]

Chinggis recruited members of the *keshig* from all ranks. The leaders of the *keshig* were all sons, or sometimes younger brothers, of the captains of a thousand. Its members were therefore from junior lines or generations:

When one shall enroll the guards of us, when the sons of captains of ten thousands, of thousands, and of hundreds, and the sons of ordinary people shall enter [our service], let one enroll those who have ability and [are] good of appearance. When one shall enroll the sons of captains of thousands, let them come [each] with ten companions and bringing with them a younger brother. When one shall enroll sons of captains of hundreds, let them come [each] with five companions and bringing with them a younger brother. When one shall enroll the captains of tens or when one shall enroll the sons of ordinary persons, let them come [each] with three companions and also bringing with them a younger brother . . .[8]

The *keshig* was more than just a picked body of troops in the service of Chinggis Khan. By recruiting sons and younger brothers into an imperial force they were both hostages for their families' loyalty and the first large group that owed its advancement to the imperial government rather than to their own tribes. The older generation was likely to remember the old freebooting days of shifting alliances and might in the future think of breaking away to regain their autonomy. Sons and younger brothers who saw their future tied to the empire would be a strong cohesive force. To emphasize the *keshig*'s importance Chinggis Khan decreed that they were to outrank their tribal counterparts who made up the bulk of the regular army commands:

My guards are higher than the outward captains of thousands. The companions of my guards are higher than the outward captains of hundreds and of tens. If outward captains of thousands, making themselves equal unto my guards and equaling themselves unto [them], quarrel with [one of] my guards, we shall punish the persons which are captains of a thousand.[9]

The guard allowed the services of talented men to be put to use for the empire and the guard became a training ground for future Mongol leaders. So effective was this strategy that as the empire expanded the old tribal divisions became irrelevant. No man, under pain of death, was allowed to move to another unit without permission. This rule and the imperial guard gave the Mongol army much more stability than seen previously on the steppe. The army was strictly disciplined, subject to central authority, and trained to fight as a group rather than as individuals. Those who broke ranks to loot or who engaged in personal combat without regard to orders were severely punished.

Many of Chinggis Khan's military ideas were not new. The decimal system of organization was used by the Hsiung-nu. The Khitans appear to have been the first to create a truly disciplined cavalry force: both the Hsiung-nu and Turks were known for their disorganized, though dangerous, armies. The expansion of the *keshig* and an attempt to reduce the importance of tribal organization for the empire were new, and appear to have resulted from Chinggis Khan's position as a steppe leader without a secure tribal base. All previous steppe rulers had a personal following, but only Chinggis Khan elevated his multi-tribal elite above his own family. Mongolian political organization was not, therefore, the culmination of a long evolving steppe tradition, but a deviation from it. Like Manchurian rulers, Chinggis was trying to create an institutionalized state that was not based on the principles of confederation. For this reason it was more effective than any previous steppe empire, and also unique. After the fall of the Mongol empire nomads returned to the older and less effective imperial confederacy model of organization.

THE MONGOL CONQUESTS

Of all the foreign dynasties to rule north China, only the Mongols came from the northern steppe. Earlier nomad empires from this area, confronting native Chinese dynasties, were concerned solely with exploiting China from a distance. It was dynasties of Manchurian origin, arising from the chaos that followed the collapse of central authority both in China and the steppe, which were interested in conquest of agricultural land and its administration. It was also Manchurian dynasties that traditionally prevented the rise of steppe empires or their expansion. The Mongols, therefore, were anomalous in two respects. They rose to power and expanded against the opposition of a firmly entrenched foreign dynasty, and they eventually conquered north China to found their own dynasty. This made the Mongols different from other steppe nomads, but not by choice. The Mongols appear to have initially employed the outer frontier strategy to exploit China. The strategy failed because the Jurchen Chin dynasty refused to respond in the traditional Chinese fashion of appeasement. Instead the Jurchen responded militarily and fought the Mongols until the Chin dynasty was itself destroyed. The Mongols' immense scale of killing in north China, their initial refusal to accept responsibility for government, and their frequent withdrawals from conquered cities and regions all point to an older pattern of nomadic warfare. The conquest of China was not a primary goal of the Mongols, but, ironically, simply a consequence of their having completely destroyed the Jurchen Chin regime which they had planned to extort.

The outer frontier strategy had been developed to correct a fundamental weakness in a nomadic state: its inability to survive and maintain a state organization just on the resources of an extensive and relatively undifferentiated pastoral economy. China was a traditional source for such agricultural and manufactured goods. The outer frontier strategy as practiced classically by the

Hsiung-nu, Turks, and Uighurs in their dealings with the native Han and T'ang dynasties was designed to wrest trade and subsidies from Chinese dynasties loath to aid the nomadic empires but at the same time fearful of disruption of the border areas with its accompanying military expense which posed a danger to internal stability. The nomads had no interest in conquering China and breaches of the various peace treaties were aimed at increasing subsidies, not destroying the relationship.

Foreign dynasties in China employed a different policy. First they attempted to prevent unity on the steppe. The Jurchen campaigns against the Mongols and later the Tatars were attempts to prevent any tribe from becoming dominant. Later the Jurchen Chin threw its support behind the Naiman attempt to destroy Chinggis Khan, although, because it was preoccupied with a southern border war with Sung, it did not intervene directly. Should a tribe overcome this obstacle, in making raids on China it faced the prospect of a stiff battle with border garrisons equipped with a cavalry arm equal to the nomads' own. The Jou-jan, for example, proved unable to practice a policy of extortion against the T'o-pa Wei until the very end of that dynasty when its border garrisons revolted.

The Mongols faced a similar problem. They were vastly outnumbered by the Jurchen who maintained an interlocking series of frontier fortifications. Although the China court was significantly sinified, its military was still effective, aggressive, and capable of considerable resistance. Unlike Sung China, which had a long-standing policy of paying heavy tribute to the Khitans and Jurchens, the Chin dynasty used payments only to buy enough time to raise new armies. Thus when the Mongols employed the outer frontier strategy, they did not gain a lucrative peace but an escalating war which devastated north China. The ultimate victory of the Mongols over the Chin dynasty was the result of a fierce fight. No steppe power had ever fought so tenaciously against a dynasty so firmly entrenched and capable of self-defense.

The Mongol conquest of China, most of southwest Asia, and eastern Europe created a new empire of unparalleled power and extent. It united the eastern and western parts of Eurasia into a single political order, facilitating the flow of people, trade, and ideas. On the other hand, the creation of this empire resulted from conquests which were conducted with unprecedented loss of life and destruction of property. Conquered areas were often abandoned, and those incorporated into the empire were ruled with far less sophistication than previously. Mongol military strategy, governmental policies, and values puzzled both contemporary and modern historians.

Some of these questions can be resolved by looking more closely at Chinggis Khan's policies as an attempt to employ traditional steppe strategies of extortion by terror in parts of the world where this was counterproductive, or against dynasties in China that refused to respond in the usual fashion. Although Chinggis's successors proclaimed their right to universal rule, he himself had a more limited view that centered on the control of the steppe. The conquests of large sedentary civilizations appears to have occurred almost by default rather than by plan until the time of Chinggis's grandsons.

At the time of the unification of the Mongols, Chinggis Khan would brook no rivals on the steppe, but he was inclined to extort rather than conquer his sedentary neighbors, and he welcomed alliances with them. When Barchukh, the Uighur ruler (*Iduq qut*), broke from the Qara Khitai to join the Mongols, he was welcomed as a "fifth son" by Chinggis and promised a daughter in marriage. The Uighur oases remained autonomous throughout Chinggis's reign and later took precedence as the premier client state in the empire. This began a long-standing policy of seeking out local rulers who would become clients in return for local autonomy.[10]

The invasions of the Tangut state in 1207 and 1209 had similar goals. Chinggis mounted his campaign against them just after the *khuriltai* which made him ruler of Mongolia, for it was now necessary to raise revenue to keep the new steppe polity intact. The initial attack was aimed at gaining loot on a fairly small scale. The second expedition was much larger and put the Tangut capital under siege. Even though the Mongols had problems in dealing with walled fortifications, the Tangut king came under great pressure. He accepted a peace agreement in which the Tanguts pledged to send troops to aid Chinggis in future wars and to provide the Mongols with camels, woolen cloth, and hunting falcons for which the Tanguts were famous. The Tangut king also married his daughter to Chinggis Khan. It is clear from this peace treaty that the Mongols had no intention of actually conquering the Tanguts, but were satisfied with an agreement that provided for subsidies and troops. Neither the Uighur nor Tangut leader was forced to renounce his sovereignty.

Campaigns against the Jurchen were begun in 1211. Ostensibly the war was in revenge for the Jurchen attacks on the Mongols a half-century earlier. As the richest state bordering the Mongols Jurchen China made an inviting target, but it was by no means an easy prize. The Chin had constructed a complex of fortified cities designed to obstruct any invasion from the north. Maintaining a strong cavalry force and a large infantry, the dynasty had recently defeated both the Sung and the Tanguts. In September, the Mongols attacked a huge Chin force at Huan-erh-tsui and routed them to gain control of key passes into China. Separate columns raced across Manchuria and from the Ordos to prevent the Jurchen from bringing up reinforcements. In spite of capturing a number of fortress cities, the Mongols withdrew from all the territory they overran (except for key passes) and returned to southern Mongolia in February 1212. Chin reoccupied the abandoned areas.[11]

In the fall of 1212 the Mongols returned, this time aided by a Khitan revolt in Manchuria whose leader had formed an alliance with the Mongols. These Khitan were nomads who, before the Mongol invasion, had been the major threat to the Chin frontier because of their frequent revolts. As with the Uighurs, the Khitan gained autonomy within the empire by joining with the Mongols. During this campaign the Mongols again overran much territory, but when Chinggis Khan was wounded, the army abandoned all its gains to the Chin and retired to the north.

The third Mongol invasion in the fall of 1213 was the most devastating. The Chin capital was surrounded, but proved too strongly fortified to be taken. Instead the Mongols turned south, riding over the north China plain eastward through Shan-tung, south to the Yellow River, and west through Shansi. By the winter of 1214 they had overrun most of the Chin territory before returning to besiege the capital, Chung-tu. After considerable political unrest within the Jurchen court, the Chin negotiated a peace settlement with the Mongols. The emperor gave the daughter of his predecessor in marriage to Chinggis together with horses, gold, and silk. The Mongol army, loaded with this and the loot seized in the south, again withdrew from China: "Our soldiers lading [their beasts with] satin and goods as many as they could carry, tied their burdens with silk and went away."[12]

In sharp contrast to the policies of the Khitan and Jurchen, who had both declared Chinese dynastic names as soon as possible after occupying Chinese land and directly administered Chinese territory under their control, the Mongols followed the steppe strategy of maintaining only indirect control of sedentary areas. At the time of their agreement with the Chin they had established such relationships with the Uighurs, Khitan, and Tanguts. Negotiations were in progress along similar lines with the Khwarazm Shah in the west. A peace based on payments to the Mongols was made with Korea in 1218. Those areas which accepted the new situation (Manchuria, Korea, Uighur oases) avoided destructive campaigns by the Mongols and retained their own leaders. Those areas which rejected the Mongol peace terms or reneged on previous agreements (Chin China, western Turkestan, and the Tangut kingdom) became the scenes of numerous campaigns that wiped out much of their population and productivity. In Chinggis' lifetime wars of destruction were aimed at leaders who violated previously agreed peace terms. These campaigns were so devastating that they led to the overthrow of the ruling dynasties and, by default, their direct incorporation into the Mongol empire.

In spite of their wide-ranging attacks, the three Mongol campaigns against Chin had not resulted in any significant territorial gain, nor had the Mongols attempted to replace the Jurchen as rulers of China. They had simply gone home with their loot. The Chin emperor, however, felt extremely vulnerable to Mongol pressure in Chung-tu and resolved to move to a more defensible position. Some officials argued that, as a Manchurian dynasty, the court should retreat to Liao-tung which was more easily defended and from where it could draw on tribal reserves. It was a mark of how sinified this dynasty had become (and all other Manchurian dynasties in similar situations) that this course was rejected. Instead, the emperor moved south of the Yellow River to K'ai-feng, the former Sung capital, in the heart of their Chinese territory.

The Mongols were immediately suspicious of the move because the capital at Chung-tu had held the dynasty hostage in the north: the Mongols had less leverage when it was transferred to the south. Chinggis Khan saw it as a step toward new resistance, saying, "The Chin Emperor made a peace agreement with me, but now he has moved his capital to the south; evidently he mistrusts my word and has used the peace to deceive me!"[13] In light of the later conquests of the Mongols, Chinggis's complaint could be passed off as an excuse for a war long planned. However, the history of other steppe leaders, Hsiung-nu or Turk, has shown that wars of conquest were not normally undertaken, and the *Secret History* alleges that it was the refusal of the Chin emperor to allow Mongol envoys to deal directly with the Sung court that provoked the renewed Mongol attack.[14] During this period a policy of accommodation might still have preserved Chin from further Mongol incursions.

The Mongols surrounded Chung-tu in the autumn of 1214, but the city was so heavily fortified that they could only blockade it with the hope of eventually starving the defenders into surrender. The army consisted of Chinese and Khitan, as well as Mongol troops, because Chinggis Khan had actively recruited men from the ranks of defeated Chin armies, not only to increase his numbers, but to gain commanders skilled in siegecraft and infantry tactics. Not until early summer of 1215 was the city deserted by its commanders and allowed to fall to the Mongols. Chinggis Khan was not present, having gone north earlier. In spite of its surrender, the city was sacked with great loss of life and whole sections of the town were reduced to ash. An embassy from the Khwarazm Shah reported that the soil was greasy from human fat and covered with rotting bodies.[15]

The fall of Chung-tu marked the first real incorporation of Chinese territory under Mongol rule. Large numbers of Chinese, Khitan, and Jurchen troops fell into Mongol hands. Many quickly rose to prominence as military leaders and administrators. Under their influence the Mongols took the first halting steps toward assuming responsibility for governmental policy in China. Nevertheless, Chinggis Khan himself gave further conquests in China a low priority. He and the bulk of the Mongol army returned to the steppe to campaign against remnants of the Naiman and Merkid. Chinggis Khan's personal retainer Mukhali was left in China with a force of 20,000 Mongols which acted as a nucleus of a larger composite army of Chinese, Jurchen, and Khitan. Chinggis Khan himself took no further part in the Chin war, which was finally ended in the reign of his son Ögödei with the fall of K'ai-feng in 1234. Even then the Mongols withdrew so many troops after their victory that Sung attempted to seize much of the area. The Mongols sent troops to throw them out.

Chinggis Khan's other campaigns into sedentary areas showed a similar pattern. When envoys of the Khwarazm Shah arrived following the fall of Chung-tu, Chinggis assured them that he considered the Shah to be ruler of the west (Transoxiana and Iran), as he was ruler of the east, and asked only that merchants be allowed free transit between their empires. A Mongol embassy arrived in Khwarazm during the spring of 1218 to confirm a treaty of peace. Although the Shah bridled at Chinggis's reference to him as a "son," he agreed to the treaty. However, within a few months a Mongol treaty caravan was massacred by the governor of Utrar. A Mongol envoy sent to protest this act was killed. By Mongol custom, the murder of diplomats and breaking treaty provisions were heinous crimes that demanded revenge. Chinggis Khan mobilized almost the entire army for an invasion of the west. In 1219, Utrar was destroyed. In 1220, the great cities of Transoxiana – Bukhara, Samarkand, Tirmidh, and Urgeneh – fell with great loss of life. The following year the Mongols overran Khorasan, destroying Merv, Balkh, Herat, and Nishapur. By 1222 the Mongols had reached the banks of the Indus. A separate Mongol force rounded the Caspian Sea in 1223, defeating the nomads of the Kipchak steppe in southern Russia.[16]

This was the first time that a major nomadic power direct from the Chinese frontier had invaded the sedentary states of the west. The outer frontier strategy of devastation and terror wreaked havoc with the more fragile ecology of the region. China might replace large population losses within a relatively short period, but here the damage was more long lasting. Cities whose populations numbered in the hundreds of thousands were completely destroyed. Irrigation systems were ruined, severely hampering economic recovery. Writing about conditions in the region one hundred years later, one observer still spoke of the,

ruin (in the present day) as a result of the eruption of the Mongols and the general massacre of people which took place in their days. . . . Further there can be no doubt that if for a thousand years to come no evil befalls the country, yet it will not be possible to repair the damage, and bring the land back into the state it was formerly.[17]

As in China, Chinggis Khan withdrew his troops from most of the area he overran. Only Khwarazmia was put under Mongol control with government in the hands of non-Mongol administrators. As puzzling as the severe harm done to the area was its quick abandonment. Nomads who had previously entered southwestern Asia from the steppe had always attempted, usually successfully, to found new dynasties and become rulers. The Mongols with their heritage from the Chinese frontier refused to take administrative responsibilities.

Chinggis's final invasion of a sedentary area was his war against the Tanguts. The Tangut king had refused to provide troops for the western campaign saying, "Since his might is not able to overcome others, why go so far as to become khan?"[18] When the war with the Khwarazm Shah was over, Chinggis Khan threw the Mongol army at him, utterly destroying the Tanguts and their cities. As with the other campaigns, this invasion was not mounted because of a lust for conquest, but as a punishment for breaking treaty obligations. During the last of these battles, in 1227, Chinggis died.

MONGOL STRATEGY AND POLICY

The outer frontier strategy of extortion had failed because of Chinggis Khan's enormous military success. A policy designed to disrupt China and extort it for revenue ended in the area's destruction. The Mongols appear to have been unwilling to recognize the extent of the political failure of their policy and continued to act as if China were simply a place to loot rather than to govern.

Other nomads had raided deeply into China: the Hsiung-nu once looted the suburbs of Ch'ang-an and the Turks had attacked both Ch'ang-an and Lo-yang on several occasions. The Mongol invasion, however, was mounted with better organization, discipline, tactics and – most important – siegecraft, than was possessed by other steppe armies. The Mongols quickly recruited engineers in China who had the skills necessary to besiege cities, whereas other nomads could only raid around walled fortifications. The combination of speed, striking power, and technical abilities put the Mongol army ahead of all its contemporaries, in spite of its numerical inferiority. The Mongols developed a blitzkrieg approach to warfare still studied by modern military strategists.[19]

In one important respect Chinggis Khan differed from all other nomadic leaders: he had a penchant for fighting decisive battles. The traditional nomadic approach, when confronted with a large well-organized force, was to withdraw and delay giving battle until the enemy was exhausted and had begun retreating. The campaigns of the Persians against the Scythians or Han Wu-ti against the Hsiung-nu demonstrated the effectiveness of this approach. Nomads traditionally advanced before weakness and retreated before strength. Chinggis Khan, on the contrary, was willing to risk all on the effectiveness of his force and tactics in an open battle. His attack on Ong Khan and then the Naiman were early indicators of his approach. Of course he was experienced at using the tactical retreat to lead an enemy into ambush – the most common Mongol trap – but he never employed the strategic retreat of withdrawing long distances to avoid the enemy. Instead he sought the best tactical position and attacked.

This was best displayed in the first Mongol invasion of Chin territory. At the critical battle of Huan-erh-tsui in 1211 his 65,000 horsemen faced at least 150,000 Chin troops, including a cavalry equal in size to the whole Mongol force.[20] Most nomadic leaders would have withdrawn rather than risk battle with such a formidable army. Chinggis Khan attacked and routed the Chin force. Chinggis Khan's willingness to risk such danger was based on two factors. On the positive side was the discipline of the Mongols in battle. They could be counted upon to carry out their instructions as units, and the Mongol *tümen* commanders were talented generals themselves. On the negative side was Chinggis's fear of the consequences of retreat. Lacking a firm tribal base, it would have been politically difficult to withdraw back into Mongolia without having the newly united tribes desert him. Chinggis had become ruler of the steppe by taking great risks and winning a string of victories: the loss of any early battle – against the Kereyid, Naiman, or Jurchen – could have ended his career. Even after he had solidified his position, he maintained his old style of aggressive response to all dangers.

Chinggis Khan's vision of his world was centered on the steppe. At his death the Mongol empire consisted of the old steppe land formerly ruled by the Turks and the sedentary territory marginal to it. Control of the steppe tribes, not the conquest of China or Iran, was his initial goal. Sedentary border areas were seen as useful adjuncts to a steppe polity – the opposite view from that of the sedentary advisors to the Mongols, for whom the steppe was an adjunct to neighboring civilizations. The great transformation of the Mongols into rulers of settled empires occurred with Chinggis's grandsons, who finally lost the nomadic perspective.

Nowhere was the impact of the ideology of a steppe-centered world more pronounced than in the Mongol destruction of cities and farms. Violent raiding was an old steppe tactic, but the Mongols carried it to excess. They were extremely conscious of their small numbers and employed terror as a tool to discourage resistance against them. Cities, like Herat, that surrendered and then revolted were put to the sword. The Mongols could not maintain strong garrisons and so preferred to wipe out whole areas that appeared troublesome. Such behavior was inexplicable to sedentary historians for whom the conquest of productive populations was the goal of warfare. Of greater importance was the traditional lack of established ties between the Mongols and sedentary communities. In their relation with China the steppe tribes of the north had only indirect ties with agricultural producers. They traded at border markets and got gifts directly from the Chinese court. To the nomads China became known as a fabulous storehouse of wealth. But how this wealth came to be produced, or how the Chinese organized its administration and the taxation of millions of peasants and artisans, was of no interest to the Mongols. Chinese peasant production, the basis of the Chinese economy, was belittled by the nomads who considered peasants to be no more a part of a political universe than were the domestic animals of the steppe. Peasants fell into the category of useless people who, as individuals, could provide no special service to the Mongols. They were used as human shields in wave attacks on cities, displaced from their homes, and prevented from returning to productive farming. A Chin census of 1195 showed a population of about 50 million people in north China. The first Mongol census of 1235–6 counted only 8.5 million.[21] Even accepting a large undercount of 100 or 200 percent because of the disorder in the north or exclusion of the population under the control of individual Mongol fief holders, clearly the population and productivity of north China had collapsed. As noted earlier, the situation was, if anything, proportionately worse in the west where a policy of destruction as political terrorism expanded beyond any practical purpose.

Widespread destruction was just one result of the Mongol attitude that China was to be looted or its government extorted. For a long period of time they also refused to accept their responsibility for administration. The Mongols extracted grain, silk, and silver, as well as weapons of war produced by captured artisans, but, unlike previous foreign dynasties, the Mongols did not rely on a Chinese civil bureaucracy that had played such an important role in maintaining traditional governmental values. When pressed, the Mongols tended to respond in an *ad hoc* fashion, delegating the task of ruling to an expatriate staff which carried out its work under Mongol supervision. For the first time knowledge of written Chinese was unnecessary to rise in government. Traditional forms of Chinese administration, maintained by the foreign Liao and Chin dynasties, were neglected. This was particularly true in taxation policy. The Mongols initially depended on tax farming, allowing Central Asian Muslims who were members of trading corporations (*ortakh*) to extract revenue from China. Equally destructive to the revival of China's economic life, land and people were often given out as apanages to Mongol leaders and members of the royal family. The Mongol census of 1235–6 showed that of the 1,730,000 registered households in north China, 900,000 (over 50 percent) fell into this category.[22]

Not until the fall of the Chin dynasty was Ögödei's prime minister, Yeh-lü Ch'u-ts'ai, able to set up proper administration in China. He proposed an end to tax farming, together with more reasonable and progressive tax rates, although in fact the malpractices, particularly the use of tax farming, were little reduced until much later. In spite of ruling a huge empire, however, Ögödei's values were still firmly based on steppe culture. Ögödei listed his four proudest accomplishments as the defeat of the Jakhud tribe, the creation of the Mongol post system, the digging of wells to open new pastures, and the stationing of occupation troops in sedentary regions.[23] As previously recommended by the

Orkhon inscription, Chinggis Khan wished to keep the nomads free of foreign entanglements. For thirty years after the great conqueror's death, his descendants clung to the belief that the empire could be centered around their steppe city/encampment at Karakorum, which for that short time was the political power center of Eurasia.

Mismanagement was most apparent in the Mongol policies toward agricultural production and its peasant producers. The sheer number of Chinese peasants had always given the Mongols pause. Considered unfit as soldiers and possessing no special skills such as did artisans, merchants, or scholars, it was proposed to Ögödei that these useless people be exterminated and their land allowed to revert to pasture. Yeh-lü Ch'u-ts'ai argued strongly against the proposal, explaining that if he were allowed to set up a system of taxation and let the peasants work in peace, he could produce annual revenues of a half million ounces of silver, 400,000 bags of grain, and 80,000 pieces of silk. Only the tribes of the northern steppe, with no personal experience of the realities of sedentary civilization, would have failed to understand that the surpluses they wanted were based on peasant production. As the goods flowed into Karakorum the talk of eliminating peasants ceased.[24]

Not until the reign of Khubilai (r. 1260–94) was the half-century of Mongol misrule in China brought to an end. In a civil war with his younger brother, Khubilai's troops in China cut off Karakorum's food supply and exposed the weakness of the capital. Mongol power in east Asia shifted to China and Khubilai transferred the Mongol capital from the steppe to Peking. In 1271 he proclaimed the Yüan dynasty. All previous foreign dynasties had proclaimed dynastic names long before they conquered Chinese territory, trying to make themselves at least minimally acceptable to the Chinese. It never occurred to Chinggis Khan to think of himself as a Chinese emperor and no attempt was made to link Mongol government into China's historical tradition. Khubilai's policies were more sophisticated, for he saw himself as a Chinese emperor as well as a khaghan of the steppe.[25]

From Khubilai's reign, the Yüan dynasty followed more traditional Chinese patterns of administration with an eye to preserving and enlarging the productivity of the state. Those nobles with apanages continued to get revenue, but it was channeled through the central government. Nowhere was this new attitude more clear than in the conquest of Sung China. Khubilai's attacks there were aimed at bringing down the government, not in providing loot for the troops (who were now in the main Chinese infantry and more suitable for fighting in the south). Comparatively little damage was done to the economy and the landowning classes were allowed to remain in place. The Sung conquest was conducted while preserving the south's economic base, and it was not marked by the reckless pillage that had ruined the north. However, in other parts of the empire the old outer frontier strategy was alive and well. Khubilai's brother Hülegü conquered Iran and the Near East to establish the line of Il-Khans. There it took another thirty years before Ghazan, his great-grandson, imposed a proper administrative order on the conquered territory.

Some positive aspects also emanated from the Mongols' steppe traditions, particularly in trade and communication. China had long devalued trade as a government policy, in spite (or because) of its growing importance to the economy. Native dynasties held to the ideal of a self-sufficient state and officially placed the farmer on a superior plane to that of the merchant. Merchants were usually forbidden from taking imperial examinations to enter the government. In this way a potentially powerful class was excluded from political power and lived under the threat of confiscations of their assets by the state. The Mongols and other nomads of the steppe held the opposite view from the Chinese, encouraging merchants to visit their territories and providing protection for their caravans. Unable to be self-sufficient to the same degree as China, the nomads profited by the exchange of products. Whereas the Chinese government tended to view international trade as a potential drain on resources, the nomads saw it as a way to create wealth. Chinggis Khan's main concern in sending envoys to the Khwarazm Shah had been to ensure the safe transit of caravans across his frontier. In the wake of the Mongol conquests merchants found it easier to move goods throughout Eurasia. The Mongol government facilitated this by issuing paper money and even financing merchant ventures. The safe transit of goods throughout Mongol territory was also a major impetus to new trade. However, this does not mean that north China or Iran were more prosperous – so greatly had they suffered in the Mongol conquest – only that the Mongols viewed trade in a fundamentally different way than native Chinese dynasties and gave it more recognition and support.

Communications was another Mongol wonder. News and important people could travel rapidly across the vast empire using a system of post stations with fresh horses and relays of riders. Concern with rapid communication had always been a priority for nomads. Such post stations had linked the Uighur empire. The Mongols considered a network of post stations to be one of the most vital elements in holding their empire together. Ögödei thought it one of the major accomplishments of his reign. These stations appear to have been a major expense to the state however and were subject to abuse – the unauthorized use of horses being a consistent complaint at court. But without such a system the Mongol world order would have collapsed far sooner than it did.

POLITICAL SUCCESSION IN THE MONGOL EMPIRE

The vast Mongol empire was faced with even greater problems than the old Turkish empires in remaining united. The problems grew more acute with the succession of each new khan. Increasingly, Mongol leaders put their own local interests ahead of those of the whole Mongol state. This was inevitable in so large an empire, but the process was accelerated by the persistent difficulties in choosing a supreme ruler. Like the Turks, the Mongols did not have one clear rule of succession, but rather a number of guiding principles (some in contradiction to others) that could justify various outcomes. In the end the right to rule had to be ratified by the control of sufficient military power to overawe or actually defeat any rivals. Military success had always justified irregular successions on the steppe.[26]

Both the Mongols and the Turks faced similar problems in passing on a united empire to the grandsons of the founder. The Turkish pattern of lateral succession had insured stability while the sons of the founder ruled, but resulted in bitter disputes and civil war when power had to be passed on to the next generation. Each set of cousins could make some claim to the throne, and eventually all but one would have to be excluded. The Mongols were to face similar struggles, but lacking a firm lateral rule of succession their politics were more complex. To examine the problem, let us outline the principles used by the Mongols in choosing a supreme leader.

Among the Mongols, succession was both a legal and political struggle. Each clique would present a case for itself and point up the defects in their rivals. It is from the speeches, insults, and rationalizations that accompanied each succession, and which were recorded in various contemporary accounts, that an outline of the basic principles of Mongol succession can be discerned. That these histories were as much political documents as descriptions of events is useful for this analysis because they try to justify what took place.

The only firm rule of succession in the Mongol empire was that the new Great Khan must be a male member of the house of Chinggis Khan, usually interpreted to mean Chinggis Khan's four sons by his principal wife and their descendants, although initially it could have included Chinggis Khan's brothers. This limited the number of legitimate pretenders, but implied no automatic choice or exclusion. Descendants were judged on purity of lineage in two ways. First, there should be no doubt about their parentage. In a patrilineal society tracing a pure genealogy was of great importance. Doubt about the paternity of Chinggis Khan's first son, Jochi, was always held against him and his line. Second, each line of descent could be ranked hierarchically by generation, status of mother, and order of birth. In such a system the sons of the principal wife were always ranked higher than sons by secondary wives or adopted sons. Just as elder brothers outranked younger brothers, senior generations were assumed to have superior rights over junior generations, but there were two different ways to judge seniority – lateral and lineal – and the Mongols used both. In practice rules of seniority only set the parameters of succession struggles. They determined who could compete, not who would emerge victorious.

Lateral succession placed emphasis on generation. In a lateral succession scheme political power passes within a generation from elder brother to younger brother before dropping to the next generation. In the next generation the eldest son of the senior lineage should inherit, and again the succession moves through a set of brothers. This pattern stresses generational seniority because the throne always reverts to the most senior member of the most senior lineage in the line of the founder. Succession should never skip a generation in this system.

Another way to look at seniority is to follow a lineal succession in which emphasis is placed on passing the throne from father to son – usually, but by no means always – to the eldest son. In this pattern, an office moves to a new generation each time, always going from father to son. Its fundamental stress is on the links between generations (father to son) at the expense of links within a generation (elder brother to younger brother). By this logic, a younger brother could only inherit if his elder brother had no sons. At its most extreme, the throne would go to a grandson (son of a deceased heir apparent) before it went to a son (brother of the heir apparent).

A third way of looking at succession turned the seniority principle on its head. By Turco-Mongolian custom the youngest son inherited the paternal hearth and household, and was viewed as the trustee of his father's estate – the practice of ultimogeniture. This concerned a man's private property, for inheritance of property and inheritance of office were quite distinct (unlike English common law in which they were inseparable). While an office might go elsewhere, the paternal estate went to the youngest son. However, as trustee of his father's estate, an argument could be made on behalf of the youngest son that the political office should go to him as well, ignoring more senior relations.

Far from being a simple choice, the Mongols could argue from two different principles of seniority and one of ultimogeniture, each contradicting the others. A rather large number of people could consider themselves not only candidates for the throne, but cheated if they failed to obtain it. Each system had major problems. If succession was lateral, a civil war inevitably arose among cousins because the principle of seniority which demanded that the throne revert to the senior line of the new generation conflicted with the political fact that the sons of the deceased khan were unlikely to permit power to be transferred without a fight. The lineal system often alienated brothers, particularly when at the death of a khan the younger brother was in his prime and the khan's sons were still young. In practice there was an alternating pattern here. The lateral system was often defeated by sons demanding lineal rights to the throne in an attempt to exclude their uncles or cousins; and the lineal system was often endangered by strong brothers who usurped the throne at the expense of their nephews by asserting lateral rights. No wonder the steppe polity seemed forever breaking out in civil war, but there was always a logic behind these wars.

In order to avoid some of these difficulties, the Great Khan usually attempted to name an heir. Theoretically he could override any rule and his wish was expected to be followed. For practical purposes, however, naming an heir was not always effective. The Great Khan's choice could never be ignored, but with the passage of time it had less and less impact unless supported by powerful leaders within the empire. "Khan's choice" became just another ingredient in the stew of steppe politics.

The principles enumerated above could all be used to demonstrate a right to compete for the throne. There were, in addition, five practical considerations which often had a decisive impact on the selections of the Great Khan.

1 *The regency* In most cases the death of a Great Khan was followed by a regency, usually in the hands of the old Great Khan's principal wife, more rarely in the hands of a youngest son or brother. The regent was supposed to rule until a new Great Khan could be elected in a tribal assembly, the *khuriltai*. The Mongol empire was so vast that it often took years for such an assembly to be gathered. By controlling appointments and the imperial treasury during the interregnum, the regent was in a position to push her or his candidate (in the case of a wife, usually her son), at the expense of other pretenders. The regent's wishes as de facto ruler carried great weight.

2 *Control of imperial military forces* Command of an army at the time of succession brought great political power, which could be used indirectly so that the commander became a power broker, or directly if the commander was a pretender to the throne. Right to succession was ultimately upheld by the ability to fend off rivals, by force if necessary. Holding a standing army was a distinct advantage over rivals who had to build a coalition army from scratch.

3 *Distance* (a) Distance of apanage: The Mongol empire was so large that those leaders who held distant territories took far less interest in imperial successions than those closer to the center of power. Their role was usually a passive one, supporting more central candidates who would respect their interests.
(b) Personal distance: The death of a Great Khan threw the empire into disorder. The contender to the throne who was first to arrive in the capital had an advantage over his rivals. At the very least he could protect his rights from usurpation, at the most he could seize power while his rivals were still distant and ill-organized.

4 *Reputation* The popularity of a contender, his general character (war-like, honest, generous, drunken, stingy, etc.), type of friends and advisors, state of health, youth or age, were all factors in tipping the scales of election. No factor, positive or negative, was in itself decisive. Instead they gave some idea of how much popular support a contender was likely to have. Personal factors were often cited to explain irregular exclusions of an heir. The most popular exclusions were youth and ill-health. If a war broke out the loser would usually be condemned in Mongol histories for personal defects rather than strategic difficulties, and conversely the victor would be ascribed all manner of good attributes to explain his victory at the expense of such factors as a better army or source of supply.

5 *The* khuriltai The final element of Mongol succession was the election of a Great Khan by a *khuriltai*, a tribal assembly of all the great men of the empire. The *khuriltai* was not an election in the sense that rival candidates were voted for and the winner elected, rather the *khuriltai* was the legal confirmation of a single candidate. The choice of Great Khan was the end point of a period in which rivals traded threats, consolidated support, and displayed their power. At some point one candidate would be seen as preeminent, and the *khuriltai* confirmed this political reality by its unanimous decision. Strong objections to a candidate were expressed by not coming to a *khuriltai*. Absence of enough key leaders could be used as evidence that the *khuriltai* lacked legitimacy.

The rules of succession, tribal politics, and military force, all played major roles in determining who would become Great Khan. The importance of each of these variables changed over time. The Mongol political scene was not static, but in a state of flux, and any analysis that treats Mongol succession in synchronic terms is deceptive. Although the principles remained the same, there was a movement away from rules in which rights of succession and legal reasoning were the most important factors, to a situation in which might made right.

The election of Ögödei following the death of Chinggis Khan was highly deterministic. The founder's selection of an heir was the paramount factor. The succession of Güyük was highly political. Legal rights served only as a gloss to exclude other candidates, and there was the threat of military action against dissenters. Only his sudden death prevented the outbreak of civil war. Möngke used a similar means to gain office and military power formed the basis of his succession. Open warfare was avoided because Möngke executed his rivals and their supporters on the charge of treason. Khubilai, the last universal Great Khan, took power after a civil war and a traditional *khuriltai* was never convened to confirm him. We will now turn to the specific cases to see how the principles of succession and political restraints came to life as part of a complex and changing matrix.

Struggles for power: the four Great Khans

The prospect of passing power to a successor was an eventuality no one, friend or family, had been willing to broach before Chinggis Khan. His jealous reaction to any thought of sharing power was well known and feared. Not until the beginning of the campaign against the Khwarazm Shah in 1218 did one of his favorite concubines dare to remind him that even great conquerors die, and urged him to name a successor. Following custom, he was set to name his eldest son, Jochi, when Chaghadai angrily objected that Jochi was probably fathered by a Merkid and therefore not entitled to the throne. This charge referred to the kidnapping of Börte before Jochi's birth. Chinggis had always accepted him as his son and this charge of bastardy was the culmination of a long-standing feud between the two brothers. As a compromise, Chinggis picked his third son Ögödei as his successor. He was well liked by all his brothers, though known to be somewhat lazy and a heavy drinker. Elder brothers Jochi and Chaghadai along with younger brother Tolui all swore to accept the decision. Reminding them of the punishment of Altan and Khuchar, who had sworn to support Chinggis and then deserted, he warned them to be faithful. At the same time, Chinggis also appointed successors from brothers' sons to lead their own descent groups.[27]

This appointment does not appear to have established an exclusive right to Ögödei's line. Chinggis declared:

So thinking, making one of my seed to govern, not violating my decree, if you destroy [it] not, you will not err and you will not miss. If the seed of Ögödei be born [so void of valor that]

> If one wrap it in green grass,
> It will not be eaten by an ox;
> If one wrap it in fat,
> It will not be eaten by a dog,

will there not be born among my seed [even] one [which may be] good?[28]

Table 6.2   The Great Khans

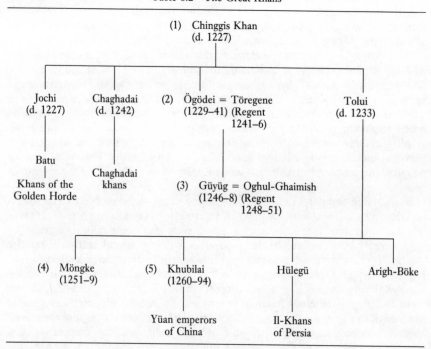

Chinggis Khan's choice of Ögödei produced an acceptable compromise for his quarreling sons, who liked Ögödei, even if they disliked each other. When Chinggis died in 1227 a two-year interregnum ensued. Although as regent Tolui had control of the army, he did not dare to take power himself in opposition to his father's will, his sworn word, and Chaghadai's opposition. (Jochi had predeceased Chinggis.) Ögödei's customary first refusal speech expressed many of the legal principles that had been overridden by Chinggis's choice, as recorded by later (pro-Toluid) Persian sources:

Although Chinggis Khan's command was to this effect, yet there are my elder brother and uncles, and in particular my younger brother Tolui Khan is more worthy to undertake and accomplish this task, for in accordance with Mongol custom and usage the youngest son from the eldest house succeeds his father and administers his house and *yurt* and Ulugh Noyan [Tolui] is the son of the eldest *ordu* and was ever in attendance on Chinggis Khan . . . Seeing that he is alive and they are here present how may I succeed to the Khanate? The princes all said in one voice "Chinggis Khan has confided this task to thee of all his sons and brothers, and entrusted the tying and the untying thereof to thee. How can we admit any change or alteration in his firm decree and inflexible command?"[29]

This speech neatly addresses the four legal principles outlined previously. By objecting that Chinggis Khan still had living brothers, Ögödei recognized the tradition of lateral succession – elder brother to younger brother. By objecting that he still had an elder brother, he affirmed the right of lineal succession – from father to eldest living son. By objecting that he had a younger brother, he affirmed the Mongol custom of ultimogeniture. (The long-winded praise of Tolui's rights is an attempt to demonstrate the legitimacy of his descendants who founded the Yüan and Il-Khanid dynasties, but of all those mentioned he had the weakest formal claim.) In accepting the office, Ögödei recognized the right of the Great Khan to name his own successor and set aside other rules in doing so. The fact that these four principles were all in the conflict explains much about the potential for division among the Mongols. Competing ideas about succession were an open invitation to conflict as time passed and the personal bonds among Mongol leaders weakened. Among Turco-Mongolian peoples, the unity of brothers was almost universally followed by the enmity of cousins.

In choosing Ögödei, Chinggis Khan hoped to avoid the problems that would be created by a Great Khan who was interested in consolidating power. Even at his death he saw the empire as a creation of the steppe and as basically indivisible. Each son had been given an *ulus*, or personal territory, on the steppe. Jochi's descendants received the northwestern territories and the Kipchak steppe. Ögödei appears to have inherited the Altai region and upper Yenisei River, while Chaghadai occupied the Ili Valley region. Tolui, as the youngest son, got the old Mongol heartland. These *ulus* are nowhere exactly described, so there is some dispute about their actual boundaries, but they were initially relatively close together and did not constitute the empire's entire territory. In distributing these lands, Chinggis was not dividing the empire, for he had allotted his sons only 4,000 families each as personal retainers. Unlike the Turkish empires, the Mongols never accepted the division of the khan title. There was only one legitimate Great Khan in the Mongol empire who was expected to rule the patrimony as the agent of the entire imperial family. Chinggis thought only in terms of providing each son with pastoral lands of their own; the rich sedentary conquests remained under the control of the Great Khan and were administered by imperial appointees. While the grants of people and land later formed the basis for the Mongol khanates, these came into being only during the reign of Ögödei and his successors. For example, when Chaghadai attempted to control Transoxiana himself, he was rebuked by Ögödei for overstepping his authority. Nevertheless, Ögödei thereafter gave Transoxiana to Chaghadai as a personal apanage which later became the basis of the Chaghadai khanate. However, during the lifetime of the sons of Chinggis Khan, imperial authority was generally respected.[30]

Ögödei's election raised him and his line to a position of superiority, but Tolui also inherited his father's personal forces which made him extremely powerful. Chinggis Khan had declared,

The business of government is a difficult business: let Ögödei administer it. But such things as my yurt and house and the property, treasures, and troops I have gathered together, let these be administered by Tolui.[31]

A balance of power existed between the sons. Tolui retained a considerable amount of personal influence as army commander. Chaghadai, while a loser at the imperial level, inherited some of the best territory in the empire, combining the wealth of the cities of Transoxiana together with the excellent pasture for his nomadic followers. Jochi, who had been at odds with Chinggis Khan, left his descendants with the least, but, after the defeat of the Chin in 1234, Ögödei dispatched the Mongol army west to assist Batu, Jochi's heir, in extending his territory. With this imperial support Batu conquered a huge area of the Russian steppe extending on into the central European plain and established a khanate equal to any in the empire.

Ögödei's death in 1241 marked the end of the generation of sons of Chinggis Khan. Tolui had died early in Ögödei's reign (perhaps poisoned[32]) and Chaghadai survived Ögödei only by a few months, opening the succession of the Great Khan to dispute. The contestants were no longer a set of brothers, but fractious cousins. There were two major questions: would the succession remain in Ögödei's line, and if it did would Ögödei's choice of heir apparent be respected?

It was by no means certain that the succession would have to stay in Ögödei's line, for Chinggis Khan had declared Ögödei his successor without endowing his line with any dynastic rights. Following a lateral succession pattern, the throne could go to Jochi's sons, who were the most senior heirs of the next generation, or, if Jochi's line was considered tainted by suspicions of illegitimate birth, then Chaghadai's sons would be proper candidates. With an ultimogeniture twist, an argument could be raised for the succession of the eldest son of Tolui's line representing the founder's trustees. More remotely, but still in a lateral pattern, Chinggis Khan's brother Temüge Odchigin could claim a right as senior member of the house of Chinggis Khan (and senior by two generations), although he was obviously not a descendant of Chinggis Khan.

Ögödei's sons pressed for the recognition of lineal rights to office by which one them would inherit. Acceptance of this lineal right had broad implications because it could potentially exclude other lines from future succession by creating the presumption of a dynastic tradition limited to Ögödei's descendants. The situation was further complicated by Ögödei's choice of a grandson for Great Khan. Initially, he had chosen his third son Köchü as heir, but when Köchu died Ögödei replaced him with Köchü's son, Shiremün. This effectively disinherited Güyüg, Ögödei's eldest son, and Köden, his second son whom Chinggis had once praised as a future Great Khan.

At Ögödei's death his principal wife Töregene became regent. By custom she was expected to rule until a *khuriltai* could be assembled to elect a new Great Khan. Many important Mongols were in Europe at the time campaigning with Batu. They were victorious everywhere but suffered from internal disputes that would later be reflected in conflicts about the succession to the throne. In particular Güyüg, Ögödei's eldest son, and Büri, one of Chaghadai's grandsons, were at odds with Batu. This resulted in complaints to the throne and the recall of Güyüg to Mongolia in disgrace. News of Ögödei's death ended the campaign in Europe and Batu also started back towards Mongolia. Because of his recall, Güyüg had a head start, and he hurried to be the first to arrive at the Mongol capital of Karakorum. Proximity to the center of power was a great advantage over more distant rivals, and by his presence Güyüg could better insure that his rights and those of his family would be respected. The need for haste became obvious when word reached the capital that Chinggis Khan's brother Temüge was on the march with a large army. He intended to seize the throne himself, but hesitated in the face of opposition, and finally retreated when he heard that Güyüg had arrived in the capital.

Töregene, the regent, had no intention of following her husband's instructions to place Shiremün on the throne. Instead she plotted to set him aside in favor of her son Güyüg. The powers of the regency aided her in this task. With her access to the treasury, she distributed gifts to influential people to buy support for Güyüg. She also issued decrees that deprived her opponents of office, thereby enabling her to run the empire directly. By the time the *khuriltai* was convened in 1245, Güyüg was preeminent. Bowing to political reality, Shiremün and Köden were set aside, and Güyüg placed on the throne. The political decision to ignore Ögödei's choice was rationalized legally by pointing out the defects in Güyüg's rivals:

Since Köden, whom Chinggis Khan had appointed to be successor to *Kha'an* [Ögödei], is somewhat sickly, and Töregene Khatun favors Güyüg, and Shiremün, *Kha'an's* heir, has not yet reached maturity, it is advisable that we set up Güyüg Khan, who is the eldest son of *Kha'an*.[33]

Güyüg accepted the office with assurances that the succession would in the future be reserved to Ögödei's descendants.

This was a major victory for Ögödei's line. Only his descendants had been considered for the office, although many others could have made a valid claim by lateral principles. Töregene had effectively engineered her son's election and kept power in Ögödei's line even if she had ignored his expressed wishes. Güyüg's election was not unanimous. Batu, heir to Jochi's line, refused to attend the *khuriltai* of his enemy, though he did send his brothers. As has been said, in Mongol politics one did not attend a *khuriltai* to elect a Great Khan, but to confirm a previously developed consensus. Strong disagreement was expressed by refusing to come to a *khuriltai* and ratify its choice. Since Batu was the senior descendant of Chinggis Khan and was on poor terms with Güyüg his absence had political importance.

Güyüg had a much sterner reputation than his hard-drinking and easy-going father Ögödei. He immediately moved to increase his personal power and tighten his grip on the empire, for being elected ruler of the Mongol empire was only the first step in becoming master of it. By limiting succession to the Ögödei line, Güyüg was creating a royal dynasty that would eventually exclude the other lines of descent from imperial power and reduce their autonomy. He first demonstrated his power by executing Chinggis Khan's younger brother, Temüge Odchigin, for treason because of his attempt to seize the throne. Güyüg also curbed the corruption that had developed during Töregene's regency, when there was a wholesale abuse of power to draw upon the Mongol treasury. Güyüg publicly confronted the Mongol notables with their misdeeds and severely punished the worst offenders. The major victims of this purge were the unpopular advisors of his own recently deceased mother, who were put to death by Güyüg.

Güyüg's conception of imperial order demanded that the autonomy of the other Chinggisid lines which held apanages be broken. He implemented this policy first by interfering with succession in the Chaghadai line. Chaghadai had designated his eldest legitimate son, Mütügen, to be his successor, but when Mütügen predeceased his father, Chaghadai had ignored his surviving sons and chose his grandson Kara Hülegü, Mütügen's eldest son, as his heir. Güyüg annulled this appointment, stating, "How can a grandson be heir when there is a son?", and appointed Yesü-Möngke, a son of Chaghadai, to the position.[34] Yesü-Möngke was a political ally of Güyüg, and by this move Güyüg hoped to ensure the loyalty of the Chaghadai territory. The Chaghadai line became divided over the issue because Kara Hülegü was both popular and the choice of his grandfather. The succession from eldest son to eldest son had justification by lineal logic, particularly since Chaghadai had considered Yesü-Möngke unfit, and Güyüg's objection was self-serving – he had ignored his father Ögödei's own selection of a grandson as heir to the throne.

Güyüg attempted to curb the power of Tolui's line by reducing the number of imperial troops under their command. Under the leadership of his widow Sorkhaghtani Beki, the family had avoided charges of corruption and outwardly gave complete support to Güyüg, making no public protest over losing their military units. Behind the scenes, however, she quietly befriended many of Güyüg's opponents, building widespread political support for her sons. Güyüg's most difficult problem was dealing with the heirs of Jochi, who posed the greatest threat to his power. Batu's dislike of Güyüg was well known and, because of the campaigns in Europe, he commanded a powerful army. Güyüg organized the armies of the east and marched on Batu. Sorkhaghtani Beki warned Batu of his advance and it looked like the beginning of the first civil war among the Mongols, but Güyüg died on the march in 1248, after ruling only two years. The succession struggle for the throne began anew.[35]

Oghul-Ghaimish, Güyüg's widow, became regent, but she was unable to maintain authority in the empire as whole because everyone was sending out his own orders. Ögödei's line was also faced with serious problems. Güyüg's sons were both young and in competition with their cousin Shiremün. The other lines were in a better position than they had been when Güyüg was elected, since his consolidation of power had only begun and his widow did not have the strength of her mother-in-law Töregene. Batu, as eldest descendant of Chinggis Khan, called for a *khuriltai* to be held in the west because he suffered from gout and was unable to travel. The divisions over succession soon became public. The sons of Ögödei, Güyüg, and Chaghadai refused to participate, later arguing that a legal *khuriltai* could only be held in the Mongol heartland. Sorkhaghtani Beki saw her opportunity to gain the throne for Tolui's line. She instructed her sons to travel to Batu's camp where he declared Möngke his choice for Great Khan. He attacked Güyüg's succession as an usurpation because Ögödei's choice of Shiremün had been ignored, but he did nothing to right this wrong. Instead, using the logic of ultimogeniture, he explained:

Today it is Möngke *Kha'an* who is best fitted and most suitable to be ruler. He is of the family of Chinggis Khan, and what other prince is there who by his penetrating thought and straight-hitting counsel can administer the Empire and the army, except Möngke *Kha'an*, who is the son of my good uncle, Tolui Khan, who was the youngest son of Chinggis Khan and held his chief *yurt?* (It is well known that according to the *yasa* and custom the position of the father passes to his youngest son.) Therefore Möngke *Kha'an* has all the qualifications of kingship.[36]

Batu's support of Möngke was critical. As the senior descendant of Chinggis Khan, Batu actually had more of a right to the throne than Möngke. By nominating Möngke, Batu renounced those rights, but at a high price. In exchange, he got full autonomy in the west. European sources even declared that Batu was Möngke's co-ruler in the empire.[37] The reason for this bargain is not hard to see: Batu's land in the west was most distant from the imperial homeland and was itself immense. Batu would have undoubtedly faced overwhelming difficulties trying to run the empire from Karakorum and yet still manage to control his own territory. He compromised by accepting a de facto split in the empire, similar to the Turkish division of east and west in their oversized first empire. With Batu began the real history of the independent Golden Horde, as his khanate was later called.

The alliance of Batu and Möngke put the Ögödeyid descendants in a poor position. They had some allies among the Chaghadayid princes, but other Chaghadayids supported Möngke, including Kara Hülegü who had been deprived of office by Güyüg. The first line of Ögödeyid defense was to make complaints that the *khuriltai* was illegal because it had not been held in Mongolia. To meet this objection, Batu ordered his army to march with Tolui's forces into Mongolia so that a *khuriltai* could be held in the traditional manner and reconfirm his decision. The Ögödeyid and many Chaghadayid princes then refused to come to the *khuriltai*, in the belief that without their presence a *khuriltai* could not be held. Instead they sent protests to Batu expressing their objection to the transfer of power from their line: "We dissent from this agreement. The kingship belongs to us. How can thou give it to another?"[38]

Batu answered that he had made his choice and that the job was too demanding to be left to the Ögödeyid candidates because they were too young. After receiving a series of threats, the recalcitrant princes decided to attend the *khuriltai*, but they travelled very slowly. Batu's brother Berke, who was his agent at the *khuriltai*, sent word to him that the delay was getting out of control, "For two years we have been waiting to set Möngke *Kha'an* on the throne, and the sons of Ögödei and Güyüg Khan and Yesü-Möngke, son of Chaghadai have not come." Batu's curt response marked an end to the sacrosanct nature of the Mongol *khuriltai*, "Set him on the throne. Whoever turns against the *yasa* let him lose his head." Möngke was declared Great Khan in 1251 by this rump *khuriltai*.[39]

The Ögödeyid princes were still en route to the *khuriltai* when the election took place. When word reached Möngke that Shiremün, Ögödei's heir, and Nakhu, who was Güyüg's son, were travelling with an armed force, he had them intercepted and arrested. It is not absolutely clear if they actually plotted revolt, or if this charge was concocted by Möngke to remove his rivals. In any event, a purge ensued in which the regent, the plotters, supporters of the Ögödeyid line, and many military commanders were put to death. Mongol succession had moved a further step away from politics towards violence as the key tool of statecraft. The purge also enabled Möngke to reward his allies. Kara Hülegü was restored as head of the Chaghadayid line. Batu, in addition to full autonomy, received his old enemy Büri, a Chaghadayid grandson, whom he put to death. This ended the succession struggle and the office now passed permanently to the house of Tolui, but at the cost of the empire's first de facto division.

Möngke was the last Great Khan who had his power base on the steppe in Karakorum. With civil strife at an end, Möngke resumed the reforms Güyüg had initiated. Internally he strengthened imperial control, in part because he had purged many powerful leaders and replaced them with men more beholden to him. The wars of expansion, which had only halted during the succession struggles, began anew. Significantly, Möngke did not renew the European campaign, for after gaining autonomy Batu's realm was no longer entitled to aid by imperial troops. Instead Möngke divided the imperial forces in half and sent one group to Iran under his brother Hülegü, while the remainder attacked Sung China. Iran should have been part of the Jochid inheritance, but Möngke used his position as Great Khan to create a new khanate for his family. These new campaigns into populous civilized regions had a profound impact on Mongol political structure because they set the stage for a transfer of power from those Mongols on the steppe to those Mongols who held the more productive centers of agriculture and industrial production. It would be Möngke's line which established the Yüan dynasty in China and the Il-Khanid state in Iran, shifting the balance of power in the empire.

After a poor start in the war with Sung, Möngke took direct control of the army in China. He was accompanied by his younger brother Khubilai and left Arigh Böke, the youngest brother, in charge at Karakorum. While campaigning in 1259 Möngke died. Both Arigh Böke and Khubilai declared themselves Great Khan without benefit of proper *khuriltai*s. Arigh Böke had the support of the tribal leadership on the steppe and Khubilai was supported by the army in China; Hülegü in far off Iran took no direct part in the dispute.

This struggle and its consequences were profoundly different from previous contests of power on the steppe because the issues involved concerned the basic direction the government should take. Arigh Böke, following the policy set down by Chinggis Khan and the succeeding Great Khans, viewed the steppe with its capital at Karakorum as the power center of the empire. Occupation of agricultural areas and cities had proved useful, indeed necessary, to supply the steppe, but real power came from control of the Inner Asian heartland. Khubilai, who held command of the troops in China, recognized the center of power was no longer on the steppe, but in the conquered agricultural regions. At the death of Chinggis Khan these regions comprised a small part of the empire, but with Ögödei's conquest of the Chin dynasty, Hülegü's invasion of Iran, and Möngke's attacks on Sung China, the balance had tipped. Control of the conquered non-steppe territory was now the key to power. The struggle was not between nomad and sedentary powers – both Arigh Böke and Khubilai had a steppe background – the struggle was between those nomads who controlled agricultural regions and those on the steppe. As Khubilai demonstrated, China was the future center of Mongol power in east Asia and the Mongol heartland would become peripheral, thereby reducing the influence of the nomadic elite who held territories on the steppe.

Khubilai's war with Arigh Böke proved that the balance of power in east Asia had already shifted. He defeated Arigh Böke in battle and cut off Karakorum: "It had been the custom to bring food and drink for Karakorum on wagons from Khitai. Khubilai *Kha'an* banned this traffic and there occurred a great dearth and famine in the region."[40] The Mongol capital was dependent on outside supplies to maintain itself. Although the center of a command economy, it was not in a productive region itself. Khubilai demonstrated that he who controlled the source of supply, controlled Karakorum. Arigh Böke was forced to turn elsewhere for a source of supply. Initially he moved northwest to the Yenisei region which was more productive than the Mongolian steppe, but still inadequate.

Arigh Böke was at his wit's end and said: "The best thing is for Alghu, son of Baidar, the son of Chaghadai . . . to go administer his grandfather's residence and *ulus* and send us assistance and provisions, and arms and guard the frontier along Oxus so that the army of Hülegü and the army of Berke cannot come and aid Khubilai *Kha'an* from that direction."[41]

Even defenders of the virtues of the steppe needed sedentary areas of agriculture and industry to supply them. Arigh Böke's plan failed when, after seizing the Chaghadai territory, Alghu refused Arigh Böke the right to raise supplies there. Instead he murdered Arigh Böke's representatives and allied himself with Khubilai – at a price. Khubilai recognized his ally's aid by splitting the empire, giving up the west to maintain primacy in the east, saying in a message,

The lands are in revolt. From the banks of the Oxus to the gates of Egypt the Tazik lands must be administered and well guarded by thee, Hülegü; from the Altai on the far side to the Oxus *el* and *ulus* must be administered and maintained by Alghu; and from the Altai on this side to the shores of the Ocean Sea [all lands] will be maintained by me.[42]

The land from the Kipchak steppe to Europe had previously been divided by Möngke and given to Batu, hence Khubilai was in no position to make decisions about it. Berke, Batu's brother, stayed out of the dispute and attempted to mediate between the warring factions.

Arigh Böke was soon surrounded and defeated. He surrendered to Khubilai and was spared, but his supporters were executed. Thus ended the united world empire established by Chinggis Khan, now divided into four great khanates: the Golden Horde on the Russian steppe, the Il-Khanate in Iran, the Chaghadai khanate from the Oxus to the Altai, and the Yüan dynasty in China and Mongolia.

THE YÜAN DYNASTY

Khubilai faced opposition from the steppe, notably from Khaidu of Ögödei's line, but these conflicts were no longer civil wars but conflicts between a foreign dynasty in China and its neighbors on the steppe. The policies of Khubilai Khan and his Yüan dynasty successors toward Mongolia were similar to those of other foreign conquerors of China. Like them, the Mongols were adept at using the resources of China and their own knowledge of the steppe to control the tribes along China's frontier. They could campaign effectively on the steppe, but their aim was to protect their holdings in China. Khubilai turned most of his attention to China and the conquest of the Sung.

The reign of Khubilai Khan marked a major change for Mongol government in China with important consequences for the nomads on the steppe. Moving the capital from Karakorum to Peking and the selection of a dynastic name was symbolic of the shift away from the steppe towards China. The formerly "marginal" agricultural areas had become the central power base for each Mongol khanate. While Chinggis Khan had envisioned an empire based solidly on the steppe, his grandsons found it necessary to combine their nomadic pastoral economy with a sedentary base. The Chaghadai khanate depended on the resources of Transoxiana, the Il-Khanate on the economy of Iran, and the Golden Horde on the towns and taxes of the Slavs in Russia. Ögödei's descendants, whose *ulus* had no such base, disappeared as an independent khanate.

Yüan dynasty government in China was quite unlike its Manchurian predecessors. They had all relied on a form of dual organization with separate administrative structures for the Chinese and tribal populations. In such dual organizations the civil bureaucracy was in the hands of Chinese officials who played a strong role in government. They also acted as a counterbalance to the tribal elite which dominated the military structure and the frontier regions. From the very beginning Manchurian dynasties had been quick to employ, and had become dependent on, Chinese officials with their administrative skills. The Mongols, on the contrary, initially ignored them as a group and employed aliens from western and central Asia to serve as officials. Using their own methods, foreign languages and alphabets, they by-passed the need for literate Chinese officials and their cultural baggage. They were not bound by the Chinese administrative precedents that even earlier foreign dynasties had felt compelled to recognize.

In place of dual organization the Mongols employed a single system of government with a hierarchy of ranked ethnic preference groups to maintain their control in China. This ethnic hierarchy consisted of four categories: Mongols, *se-mu* (western and central Asians), *han-jen* (north Chinese, Manchurians, and Koreans), and *nan-jen* (south Chinese). The populations of these groups were far from equal. The 1290 Yüan census data showed the following approximate breakdown:[43]

Mongols	1,000,000
se-mu	1,000,000
han-jen	10,000,000
nan-jen	60,000,000

The Mongols and their *se-mu* allies held about 30 percent of all official positions, including most of the top military and civilian offices. They also held a virtual monopoly on positions in the Imperial Guard, the successor to the older *keshig*, from which many high officials were recruited. Even when the Yüan implemented such classic Chinese recruitment devices as the examination system, the number of degrees awarded remained the same for each group. This gave the Mongols and *se-mu* who took the tests a far better chance of succeeding than their Chinese counterparts. They also got easier tests. In order to overcome these barriers some Chinese studied foreign languages and adopted foreign names to pass as members of more favored categories – a tactic the Yüan government periodically tried to stamp out. Nevertheless, unlike systems of dual administration, the Chinese were represented in all branches of government.[44]

Khubilai's reorganization of the Mongol government in China displayed a number of steppe characteristics. With its court and hierarchical ministries subject to an all-powerful emperor, the Yüan government appeared highly centralized and autocratic. Yet an examination of the provincial administration and the limits of direct imperial rule showed much regional autonomy and a surprising lack of integration with the central administration.[45]

Stripped of its Chinese veneer, the Yüan government had much in common with a steppe imperial confederacy. The Yüan court maintained a monopoly on foreign relations and economic policy, yet the imperial government ruled directly over only the large Metropolitan Province and the steppe region. Provinces within the empire, such as Yunnan and Kansu, were treated as separate kingdoms. Even provinces more closely tied to the central government were not handled directly, but through the use of *darughachis*, Mongol or *se-mu* officials whose job it was to oversee provincial or district administration and ensure that the proper amount of revenue was obtained.[46]

This use of agents to oversee local administration had a long steppe tradition, in which local tribal leaders conducted their people's affairs under the supervision of an imperial governor. China was not tribally organized, but the Mongols adapted their customary practices to a sedentary bureaucracy. Therefore, like the imperial confederacy, the Yüan government presented two strikingly opposed impressions. The top levels of government presented a picture of authoritarian central control, while those familiar with local administration were impressed by provincial autonomy. Whether on the steppe or in China, the weak link lay in the relatively brittle relationship between the central government and local leaders. This relationship was exacerbated in China by the need to regularly extract large amounts of tax revenue, whereas in a traditional steppe empire exactions were both irregular and less of an economic burden. In both systems a breakup was prevented by the central government's use of imperial armies to put down rebellion and its ability to reward those who participated in running the empire.

The Mongols constituted the elite group of the empire, but the condition of ordinary Mongols in China or on the steppe declined markedly under the Yüan government's increasing demands. The Yüan government considered its Mongol troops to be a hereditary and self-sustaining military force. Although the Mongols were only a minority of the troops involved in the conquest of China, they were seen as the dynasty's most loyal bulwark. Following the last major campaigns that led to the conquest of Sung in 1279, large Mongol garrisons were established along the area of the lower and middle course of the Yellow River, north of the Huai River. The Huai marked the ecological and old political boundary between north and south China. Mongol encampments north of that line retained their effective steppe cavalry, while occupying a strategic position that protected the capital region to the north. These troops could also be called upon to move against any rebellions in the south, but the wet rice regions there were not suitable for calvary and the dynasty employed Chinese troops under Mongol and *se-mu* supervision for the bulk of its garrison forces.

The ideal of a self-sustaining hereditary army was an old steppe tradition that was difficult to transplant. Nomadic pastoralists made little distinction between civilian and military life. Every man was subject to military call-up on short notice. In addition, nomad troops were expected to provide most of their own equipment, weapons, horses, and supplies for campaigning. This was possible in a nomadic pastoral economy where skills in riding and archery were a natural part of the culture. Labor demands could be shifted to those left behind, allowing each household to provide one or two soldiers, a ratio not possible in sedentary agricultural societies. War also generally supplied loot that allowed wars to be carried out at a profit.

Once garrisoned in China, however, it was far more difficult to maintain such a tradition. The Yüan government initially granted land, of which there was a surplus in north China, and slaves to work it, so that ordinary Mongols would have the resources to devote themselves to their military obligations. The land allotments proved inadequate to both support the Mongols and pay for the expense of military duty. Many Mongols were forced to sell their land to equip and supply themselves for action in distant frontier wars, and these wars did not provide loot which might have compensated their losses. The rate of conscription common on the steppe was also economically harmful to Mongol families trying to oversee their agricultural holdings. As time passed, the number of Mongols attached to the hereditary garrisons declined both in numbers and effectiveness when a series of rebellions broke out toward the middle of the fourteenth century, the Mongol garrisons proved incapable of suppressing them alone.[47]

One reason for the decline in the effectiveness of the garrison troops in China was the long series of expensive wars fought by the Yüan government in Mongolia and Turkestan against rival Mongol leaders. Beginning with the struggle between Khubilai and Arigh Böke, Mongolia became a battleground. Arigh Böke's defeat had shown that Mongol princes depending on steppe resources alone stood little chance against other Mongols equipped and supplied from China. Nevertheless, Mongolia and Turkestan were far enough away from China so that nomads in the region could be defeated only at great expense. Unlike earlier foreign dynasties, which simply attempted to promote anarchy on the steppe, the Yüan ruled northern Mongolia directly and defended its frontiers. As the empire's original heartland, the homeland of Chinggis Khan held great symbolic value for the Mongols and the dynasty never considered abandoning it.

The flanks of Mongolia, particularly in the Altai Mountain region and the Turkestan oases to the south, were scenes of conflict because they acted as buffer zones between Yüan China and rival khanates. After Khubilai defeated Arigh Böke in 1264, fighting broke out four years later when Khaidu, an Ögödei descendant, allied himself with the Chaghadai khanate and mounted a series of attacks that lasted throughout Khubilai's reign. His example induced the descendants of Temüge Odchigin in Manchuria to revolt in 1287, but they were quickly suppressed. Only in 1303, a few years after both men's death, was peace restored.

To meet these military threats the Yüan government posted 300,000 troops in Mongolia and Turkestan. In order to supply them it was necessary to ship huge quantities of grain, initially 200,000 *shih* annually, rising to 300,000 *shih* by the beginning of the fourteenth century. Even after peace was arranged with Khaidu's descendants, the threat of attack from the Chaghadai khanate remained sufficiently strong that the Yüan government still maintained large garrisons in the north. By 1311 the Yüan court reported that one-third of all government revenue (6–7 million *ting*) was consumed by the defense of Mongolia.[48] This enormous expense would not have been sustainable without the steady stream of revenue gained from the conquest of Sung China. Ironically, Mongol control of their old homeland was only possible because the Yüan dynasty had access to control of Chinese revenue from the south, a resource unavailable to all previous foreign dynasties.

To maintain its control over the frontier, the Yüan court absorbed Mongolia into the provincial system in 1307, posting Chinese garrison troops in Karakorum. The plight of the average nomad was bleak because the continual demands for troops, supplies and horses put a tremendous burden on the steppe economy. Even with aid from China, the nomads became progressively more impoverished. A whole series of relief measures granting emergency food were recorded involving hundreds of thousands of families. Grain was provided directly by the central government while other relief was channeled through local Mongol princes. Potentially the center of opposition, these princes were co-opted by the dynasty with generous stipends derived from fiefs in China. Probably at no time until the Manchu period was the control of Mongolia by China so tight or the nomads so badly off.[49]

THE DISSOLUTION OF YÜAN CHINA

Following the reign of Khubilai Khan the Yüan dynasty was plagued by severe factionalism at court. The Mongols had retained their customary rules of

Table 6.3 The Yüan emperors of China

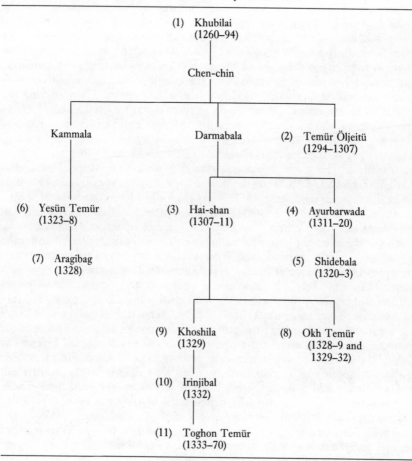

succession that allowed both lineal and collateral branches of the imperial line to become pretenders to the throne. They also retained the institutionalized violence of steppe politics in which the murder of an emperor was a common tactic. This resulted in a dynastic history punctuated by coups, murders, poisonings, and purges. Indeed the dynastic table of the Yüan rulers (table 6.3) bears a stronger resemblance to those of the Turkish khaghans than it does to any other dynastic table of Chinese emperors. By Chinese standards there were an unprecedented number of assassinations and improper successions to the throne of younger brothers and nephews. Although the Mongols may have adopted many Confucian values and institutions in running their court, when it came to power struggles they reverted to their own traditions with very different standards.

One result of these conflicts for the throne was the emergence of strongmen at court who ruled in the emperor's name but who set policy themselves. By the 1320s imperial politics revolved around a series of these strongmen who seized power and controlled the government until they were suddenly replaced by rivals. Such short-term conflicts in the capital diverted the central government's attention from the growing problems in the provinces where famine, misrule, and peasant discontent threatened to explode into serious rebellion. Such rebellions erupted in various regions in south and central China during the 1330s. While the central government put them down they remained an economic threat, for the Yüan government depended on grain and money from the Yangtze region to finance and feed itself. Any disruptions in the canal system, sea routes, or in the agricultural regions of the south had a direct impact on Yüan control. The grain shipments from the south to the capital peaked at 3,340,306 *shih* in 1329. During the next decade they declined by 25 percent.[50]

Conditions worsened after this. In 1344 the Yellow River flooded and altered its course to the north, bringing immediate ruin to 6,000 square miles of agricultural land and putting the Grand Canal out of action. The sea route, which was the alternate means for supplying the north with grain, fell under the control of a pirate warlord, and local garrison troops failed to cope with widespread banditry. Nevertheless, under strong leadership the Yüan establishment was far from helpless, for a former court minister, Toghto, retook power in 1349 and reversed the decline. He immediately organized a massive diversion scheme to rechannel the Yellow River and reopen the Grand Canal. After only six months work in 1351 the project was completed, removing some of the leverage of the sea pirates on the dynasty. This spectacular capital investment allowed the continued bulk transport of grain to the north even after the Yüan had fallen. Another of Toghto's schemes was a huge agricultural resettlement program that would make the north less dependent on imported food. These were not the actions of a man who believed the dynasty was beyond help.[51]

After the completion of the river project, a major rebellion broke out in the Huai region led by a group known as the Red Turbans. In spite of their initial victories and the spread of the rebellion to the Yangtze region, by 1354 Toghto had suppressed it with the aid of Chinese troops. In the same year he also besieged the stronghold of a warlord who was blocking the Grand Canal at Kuo-yü. While he was gone from the capital he fell victim to court politics and was stripped of office. Power devolved onto Chinese and Mongol warlords with regional bases who fought with each other and the Yüan court. Out of this morass arose Chu Yüan-chang, founder of the Ming dynasty. Based in the south Ming forces moved against rival warlords and in 1368 seized Peking after the Yüan court had decamped for Mongolia.

To retreat from north China in the face of attack was not the usual pattern of response by a ruling dynasty. Every other major foreign dynasty in Chinese history had fought tenaciously to hold onto its Chinese territory. But these dynasties had been of Manchurian origin, each with an ideology of conquest and a well-developed administrative structure. The Mongols were of steppe origin and heirs to the outer frontier strategy. Under Chinggis Khan the Mongols had refused to administer or defend their Chinese conquests. Only after the collapse of the Chin dynasty in 1234 did the Mongols began to take administrative responsibility for agricultural production, and not until the reign of Khubilai Khan did the Mongols transfer the capital into China and establish a formal dynasty.

The Mongol retreat from China is understandable only in the light of one of the oldest steppe traditions – that of strategic retreat. When confronted with a determined Ming advance from the south, the Mongols chose retreat in favor of last ditch resistance, which could well have succeeded in maintaining a Yüan foothold in China, as the Khitans had done when attacked by the northern Sung. Nomads always preferred a mobile defense, in which they chose the time and place to fight, to the risks of holding fixed positions. This made sense on the steppe where there were no cities or farmlands to be occupied by an enemy. But in withdrawing from China this was not the case. The Yüan was leaving Mongol troops behind and sacrificing its key bridgehead in China. The Yüan leaders may have hoped to rely on their troops in Mongolia, who had been defending the frontier there, to aid them in a counterattack, but once the dynasty had retreated, it stood little chance of returning to China. In nomad fashion, though long removed from steppe life, the Yüan leaders abandoned China in the same casual way their ancestors acquired it – without thinking too much about the consequences.

NOTES

1 The basic source for political and social conditions in Mongolia during Chinggis Khan's lifetime is the *Secret History of the Mongols* (SH) written sometime soon after his death, although the exact date of its composition is still in dispute. It concentrates largely on tribal history and provides only sketchy details on Mongol campaigns in sedentary areas. Cleaves provides a complete English translation of this work. I have consistently substituted "you" for "thee" for readability. See also Vladimirtsov, *Life of Chinggis Khan*. The *Yüan-shih* (YS) provides the dynastic records of the Mongols in China.

2 Lattimore, *Inner Asian Frontiers of China*, pp. 543–9.

3 SH 78; Cleaves, *Secret History*, p. 24.

4 SH 202; Cleaves, *Secret History*, pp. 141–2.

5 SH 205, 206, 207; Cleaves, *Secret History*, pp. 145–50.

6 SH 243–6; Cleaves, *Secret History*, pp. 176–82.

7 Hsiao, *Military Establishment*, pp. 34–8; cf. Allsen, "Guard and government in the reign of the Grand Qan Möngke."

8 SH 224; Cleaves, *Secret History*, p. 162.

9 SH 228; Cleaves, *Secret History*, p. 166.

10 Allsen, "The Yüan dynasty and the Uighurs of Turfan in the 13th century," pp. 243–80.

11 Martin, *The Rise of Chinggis Khan and his Conquest of North China*, has attempted to reconstruct the probable course of the Mongol campaigns against the Chin using Chinese sources.

12 SH 248; Cleaves, *Secret History*, p. 185.

13 Martin, *Conquest of North China*, pp. 173–4.
14 SC 251; Cleaves, *Secret History*, p. 186.
15 *Cambridge History of Iran*, vol. 5, pp. 303–4.
16 Barthold, *Turkestan down to the Mongol Invasion*, pp. 381–462; Boyle, *The History of the World Conqueror*.
17 Le Strange, *The Lands of the Eastern Caliphate*, p. 34.
18 SC 256; Cleaves, *Secret History*, p. 198.
19 Liddell-Hart, *Great Captains Unveiled*.
20 Martin, *Conquest of North China*, pp. 336–7.
21 Bielenstein, "Chinese Historical Demography, AD 2–1982," pp. 85–8; cf. Ho, "An estimate of the total population of Sung-Chin China."
22 Schurmann, *The Economic Structure of the Yüan Dynasty*, pp. 66–7.
23 SC 281; Cleaves, *Secret History*, pp. 227–8.
24 de Rachewiltz, "Yeh-lü Ch'u-ts-ai."
25 Dardess, "From Mongol empire to Yüan dynasty: Changing forms of imperial rule in Mongolia and central Asia."
26 Fletcher, "The Mongols: ecological and social perspectives."
27 SH 254; Cleaves, *Secret History*, pp. 184–94.
28 SH 255; Cleaves, *Secret History*, p. 197.
29 Boyle (trans. from Rashid al-Din), *The Successors of Genghis Khan*, pp. 30–1.
30 Barthold, *Turkestan*, pp. 392–3, 464–5.
31 Boyle, *Successors*, pp. 17–18.
32 Fletcher, "Mongols," pp. 33–9.
33 Boyle, *Successors*, p. 181.
34 Ibid., p. 182.
35 Ibid., pp. 180–6, quote p. 182.
36 Ibid., pp. 201–2.
37 Jackson, "The dissolution of the Mongol Empire."
38 Boyle, *Successors*, p. 203.
39 Ibid., p. 204.
40 Ibid., p. 253.
41 Ibid., pp. 253–54.
42 Ibid., pp. 255–6.
43 Langlois, *China Under Mongol Rule*, p. 15, n. 34.
44 Dardess, *Conquerors and Confucians*, pp. 35–6, 60, 68.
45 Farquhar, "Structure and function in Yüan imperial government," pp. 52–3.
46 Endicott-West, "Imperial governance in Yüan times."
47 Hsiao, *The Military Establishment of the Yüan Dynasty*, pp. 17–24.
48 Ibid., pp. 59–60.
49 Serruys, *The Mongols in China During the Hung-wu Period*.
50 YS 93:21a, 97:1b–2a; Schurmann, *Economic Structure*, pp. 112–13, 125; Dardess, *Conquerors and Confucians*, p. 88.
51 Dardess, *Conquerors and Confucians*, pp. 95–146.

GLOSSARY OF KEY NAMES

IMPORTANT TRIBES ON THE STEPPE FRONTIER

KEREYID
leading tribe in Mongolia in late 12th century
ruled confederation that included Mongols
MERKID
nomad tribe in Lake Baikal area
often feuded with Mongols in 12th century
MONGOL
small tribe in Mongolia in 12th century
people of Chinggis Khan
NAIMAN
nomad tribe in Altai region
leader of powerful confederation in late 12th century
ÖNGGÜD
nomads on border of China in 12th century
frontier-guarding troops of Chin dynasty
TATAR
small tribe in Mongolia in 12th century
blood enemy of Mongols

KEY LEADERS

BATU
son of Jochi, grandson of Chinggis Khan
Mongol ruler of the Golden Horde in Russia
BÖRTE
wife of Chinggis Khan
mother of Jochi, Chaghadai, Ögödei, and Tolui
CHAGHADAI
second son of Chinggis Khan
descendants rule western central Asia
CHINGGIS KHAN (TEMÜJIN)
founder of the Mongol Empire
conqueror of much of the known world
GÜYÜG
son of Ögödei, grandson of Chinggis Khan
succeeds father as Great Khan (1246–8)
HÖ'ELÜN ÜJIN
mother of Chinggis Khan
HÜLEGÜ
son of Tolui, grandson of Chinggis Khan
founder of Il-khanid state in Iran

JAMUKHA
   anda to Chinggis Khan
   rival for leadership of Mongol tribe
JOCHI
   eldest son of Chinggis Khan
   descendants rule Golden Horde
KHUBILAI
   grandson of Chinggis Khan
   first Mongol Yüan emperor of China (r. 1260–94)
   conquers Sung dynasty
MÖNGKE
   son of Tolui, grandson of Chinggis Khan
   succeeds Güyüg as Great Khan (r. 1251–9)
MUKHALI
   Mongol commander in charge of China campaign
   personal retainer of Chinggis Khan
ÖGÖDEI
   third son of Chinggis Khan
   succeeds his father as imperial ruler (1229–41)
SORKHAGHTANI BEKI
   wife of Tolui, mother of Möngke, Khubilai Khan, and Hülegü
   establishes Toluid line as paramount
TEB TENGGERI
   famous shaman of Mongols
   step-brother of Chinggis Khan
TO'ORIL KHAN (Ong Khan)
   Kereyid confederation leader
   Chinggis's original patron
TOGHTO
   Yüan strongman of 14th century
   attempts to maintain dynasty against Chinese revolt
TOLUI
   youngest son of Chinggis Khan
   sons become rulers of China and Iran
TÖREGENE
   principal wife of Ögödei
   becomes regent of empire on his death (1241–6)
YEH-LÜ CH'U-TS'AI
   former Chin government official of Khitan ancestry
   establishes regular administration for Mongols in north China under
   Ögödei

7

Steppe Wolves and Forest Tigers

The Ming, Mongols, and Manchus

CYCLES OF POWER

The Mongol empire and its conquest of China was a unique event which disrupted the usual pattern of relations between China and its northern frontier neighbors. The traditional cycle of relations was determined by the interplay of the military power, political organization, and economic structure of three key regions: Mongolia, Manchuria, and north China. There were two basic patterns of interaction. In the first, a native dynasty ruling in China was confronted by a united nomadic imperium on the steppe. In this situation, the whole frontier fell under the control of one of the two superpowers, and such a bipolar division left no room for border states to grow. In the second pattern, a Manchurian dynasty established its rule over north China, keeping the steppe nomads divided and confining the Chinese to the south. The development of one set of relations generally excluded the other, and the breakdown of either system laid the groundwork for the rise of its complement. Thus the frontier history of Inner Asia appears to be cyclical. The dynamics of these interactions can be most clearly understood by looking at the strengths and weaknesses of each component.

The steppe imperium was most vulnerable in its formative stage when its leadership was trying to unite the nomads. Military or political interference from the outside at this time often proved fatal. Manchurian dynasties were past masters at this sort of interference and they kept the steppe in disarray. However, Manchurian dynasties were also responsible for ruling large areas of China which were key to their continued existence. When these dynasties weakened internally, they abandoned their interference on the steppe to concentrate on defending themselves against enemies within China.

During such a period steppe leaders could construct an empire with the least prospect of interference. By the time the Manchurian dynasty had fallen and been replaced by a native Chinese dynasty, the steppe was reorganized. This larger Inner Asian polity could not support itself by an undiversified pastoral economy, hence united steppe empires immediately turned to the new Chinese state as the economic base by which to finance an imperial hierarchy on the steppe. The nomads used their military power to acquire subsidies and favorable terms of trade from China. The frontier would be split between two great polities: mixed regions like Manchuria or Kansu would be dominated by China in agricultural areas, by the nomadic state in pastoral areas. Because a steppe empire could not survive without its relationship with China, it is no surprise to find the great steppe empires and the native Chinese empires not only co-existing but also simultaneously going into decline. Once the nomads had a treaty with a dynasty, they had a vested interest in its preservation and often aided declining Chinese dynasties against internal rebellion. When either empire collapsed, the other was soon to follow, the nomads because they had lost their economic base, the Chinese because they had lost their protection.

These periods of collapse on both the steppe and in China were the only times during which intrinsically weak border areas such as Manchuria could become autonomous. Taking advantage of the anarchy around them, they built small states and were able to seize north China and administer it with a dual organization of Chinese officials backed by a tribal army. Their tribal background and military also gave them the power to disrupt the political structure of the steppe and keep it disorganized. The decline of these Manchurian states set off another cycle of native rebellion leading to reunification in China and steppe reorganization.

This pattern first appeared with the simultaneous rise and decline of the Han dynasty and Hsiung-nu empire. It was followed by a period of north/south disunion in which the T'o-pa Wei dynasty conquered north China and disrupted attempts by the Jou-jan to unite the nomads. The subsequent reunification of China and the steppe in the Sui–T'ang/Turk–Uighur times ended in a second period of disunion with the Chinese Sung dynasty ruling the south while the Manchurian Khitans and Jurchens occupied north China.

The Mongols upset this pattern by creating a nomadic empire in the face of intensive Manchurian opposition. This produced an unusual situation in which a strong and united steppe empire confronted a Manchurian state in China. This confrontation was unprecedented and produced a Mongol military machine with steppe mobility and sophisticated technical skills. All of China, indeed most of Eurasia, fell before it. The experience of the Mongol conquest was not forgotten quickly and it profoundly influenced subsequent Chinese relationships with the steppe nomads. The Ming approach to the steppe was so colored by the memory of the Yüan conquest that its frontier policy was unlike that of any other native dynasty. Yet as in the past the real danger of conquest in times of Chinese weakness came not from the steppe but from Manchuria.

The Ming period was the only time in China's 2,200-year dynastic history that the nomads on the steppe failed to create a unified and stable empire in opposition to a native dynasty in China. This failure was not the result of a lack of interest or poor leadership. The steppe was unified at various times during the Ming, each supratribal leader pursuing the outer frontier strategy to extort trade and subsidies from China. With savage raids the Mongols and the Oirats pillaged China. They demanded gifts and trade as the price of peace, both sources of revenue needed to finance the nomadic state. Yet for most of its history the Ming refused to come to an accommodation with the nomads, in spite of classical precedents from Han and T'ang dynasties for such a policy. Their refusal forced the collapse of at least one nomadic imperium and led to incessant raiding on China's northern frontier, the number and intensity of the raids growing over time. This was the reverse pattern from other native dynasties, and by not accommodating the nomads the Ming suffered from more years of frontier warfare than those dynasties that acquiesced. At first glance it might be argued that the Ming succeeded where the Han and T'ang had failed, but a closer look reveals a shortsighted policy that sapped the strength of the Ming both economically and militarily. It brought no security to a dynasty that grew progressively weaker. As much as the Chinese hated the great nomadic empires, they at least brought a conservative stability to the steppe and saved weak dynasties from internal rebellions. The demise of the Ming in the face of rebel attacks and invasion from Manchuria in 1644 was at least in part the bitter fruit of a poor Ming frontier strategy.

During the Ming period steppe history was characterized by three major failures at empire building. These failures have often been cited as evidence of Mongol weakness and incompetence in the post-Yüan era, as if Mongols had somehow exhausted their energy 200 years earlier with their world conquests. Most of these critiques assume that the rise of Chinggis Khan and his organization of the empire were the culmination of an evolving steppe tradition. However, such a comparison ignores how exceptional the Mongol empire was when compared with those of the Hsiung-nu, Turks, or Uighurs. The nomads in the Ming period were not Yüan revanchists trying to recover China, they were more typical of earlier nomads employing the outer frontier strategy. They intended to exploit China from a distance and had no plans for reconquering China. The failure to produce a long-lasting nomadic empire in the Ming period by either Esen, Dayan Khan, or Altan Khan is of great significance, not because it shows the steppe in decline, but because it illuminates both the structure of steppe empires and Ming foreign policy. Comparisons with Chinggis Khan cannot reveal the structural reasons why the nomads failed when they had previously succeeded. This failure can only be understood by looking at the attempts at nomadic state building during the Ming.[1]

MONGOLIA IN THE POST-YÜAN ERA

The overturning of the Yüan dynasty was not the result of an anti-foreign uprising by nationalistic Chinese; it was a traditional rebellion against a weakening dynasty, which succeeded in toppling the Mongols while retaining many Yüan institutions and policies. The Ming founder, the Hung-wu Emperor (1368–98), encouraged the surrender of Mongol military units left in China by the Yüan retreat and incorporated them into his army. He also issued decrees that encouraged the assimilation of the large number of foreigners who had served the Mongol state in order to prevent the rise of a fifth column. Much of his state structure, particularly the initial organization of the military as a hereditary, potentially self-supporting, force was derived from Manchurian and Mongol models.[2]

For the Ming dynasty, the retreat of the Yüan court to Mongolia was both an unexpected opportunity and a danger. North China fell to the new conquerors without a protracted siege which would have strained the new dynasty's resources and capacity to supply troops. Nevertheless, the Mongols remaining on the steppe potentially threatened Ming control in the north. The survival of the Yüan rulers was also an ideological problem because it could be argued that the Ming rulers did not have an exclusive right to the throne. Foreigners or not, by uniting China the Yüan had met the Confucian requirements for legitimacy. Since the Ming had been unable to extinguish the Yüan line or force it to abdicate, Mongol claims had a certain moral force which Chinese tradition took seriously. In terms of *realpolitik*, this danger was trivial because the Mongols did not have the power to reconquer China, but to a succession of Ming rulers it remained a live issue (particularly after the dynasty's humiliating defeat at T'u-mu by the Oirats in 1449). Mongol attacks on China were often viewed as attempts to reclaim the lost empire, long after the nomads had abandoned any such pretensions.

The Hung-wu Emperor's strategic policy in the north was primarily defensive. For a dynasty with its origins and capital in the Yangtze River valley, the northern border was peripheral to its basic interests. Ming attacks against Yüan forces in Mongolia were not attempts to annex the territory there, but to destroy the military power of the old dynasty and guard the frontier from Mongol incursions. Ming troops advanced on Karakorum in three columns in 1372, but the Mongols mauled one and the other two retreated, while a second steppe campaign eight years later also ended in defeat. However, the Ming won a spectacular victory in 1388, when it caught the northern Yüan forces by surprise at Lake Bayur. In practical terms, this defeat ended the northern Yüan dynasty, and its authority on the steppe ceased to be effective.

After their defeat at Lake Bayur, Yüan dynasts continued to be proclaimed as the rulers of the steppe. During the next twelve years, five Yüan emperors quickly followed one another – each meeting a violent death. The position of khan became almost purely symbolic. As in other parts of the Mongol controlled world, formal leadership was traditionally restricted to the descendants of Chinggis Khan because only they had the right to hold the title of khan or khaghan.[3] Non-Chinggisid powerholders, therefore, found it necessary to name a Chinggisid as khan and generally adopted the title of *tayishi*, a kind of lieutenant to the great khan, for themselves. In western Turkestan, under Tamerlane, this facade was well understood: no one confused the Chinggisid khan portrayed on the dynasty's coins with the true ruler of the empire. The Chinese had more difficulty accepting the concept as a mere formality, for in the east the Chinggisids were also descendants of the Yüan imperial line. Thus, while the Mongols were naming Chinggisid khans, as required by Mongolian custom, the Chinese suspected that the appointments were made because of their Yüan lineage, i.e., that the nomads were deliberately choosing rulers with a potential claim to the Chinese throne. The Chinese, who had a penchant for following the "legitimate" line, though often confused about the role of these nominal khans in steppe politics, kept detailed records of their comings, goings, murders, and replacements. The Mongols themselves may have partially justified Ming suspicions by giving these khans Chinese-style reign titles. However, the Mongols probably did this out of custom, for the same reason that they adopted the names of Yüan bureaucratic offices as tribal titles, and not for any ulterior motives. For the Chinese, who considered tribal or "barbarian" politics incomprehensible under any circumstances, following the defunct Yüan lineage provided some sense of order to the growing anarchy in Mongolia.[4]

The fall of the northern Yüan opened up new opportunities for non-Chinggisid tribal leaders on the steppe. During the Yüan period they had been integrated into the state hierarchy and their people had been responsible for guarding Mongolia against rival khanates. This put a great burden on the nomads there, a burden which the fall of the dynasty ended. Initially, the Yüan court and its troops provided the highest political order on the steppe. Without a real economic or political base on the steppe, however, it was an alien transplant with no long-term hope of survival. Its crushing defeat in 1388 and the subsequent cycle of dynastic murders created the conditions for the rise of indigenous tribal leaders needed to build a new steppe empire.

By 1400 the nomads were divided into two rival groups competing for power. The area of the Altai Mountains was the home of the Western Mongols, or Oirats, led by Mahmud, while central and southern Mongolia was dominated by the Eastern Mongols under Arughtai. Both these leaders were of non-Chinggisid descent, marking the emergence of a new tribal elite, but the supreme title of khan was still retained by Chinggisids. The Eastern Mongols originally had the larger territory, bordering on China to the south, with the Oirats to their west and north. On the Manchurian steppe were three small, but strategically important, steppe tribes known to the Ming as the Three Commanderies or Uriyangkhai Commanderies. When Yüan domination of the steppe collapsed, a struggle for supremacy in this region erupted between the Eastern Mongols and Oirats.

After the Yüan defeat at Lake Bayur, it appeared the Ming would largely ignore the steppe and engage in a passive defense. Internal struggles within the dynasty altered the course of this policy drastically, and the northern frontier became the Ming's central foreign policy preoccupation. This change in the northern frontier's significance was initiated during the struggle for succession following the Hung-wu Emperor's death in 1398.

To control the northern frontier Hung-wu had parceled out strategic territories there as fiefs to some of his many sons. This strategy served a double purpose. Because the northern border was far away from the Ming capital of Nanking, his sons could help keep it within the dynasty's orbit. In addition, by removing his sons to distant fiefs while keeping the heir designate in the capital, Hung-wu planned to ease the problem of succession and avoid civil war. Potential rivals for the throne would be too far from the seat of imperial power to interfere. This policy, however, had the well-recognized disadvantage of undercutting imperial authority by providing each son with personal troops and a territorial base.

The Hung-wu Emperor's plans for a peaceful transfer of power were upset when his heir designate predeceased him. Instead of appointing one of his other sons as heir, he named the dead prince's son to the position. Thus a young grandson was designated to take power at the expense of his uncles. When Hung-wu died, the boy emperor's advisors moved to eliminate, by exile or execution, all the fief holders who might endanger the throne. This naturally posed a threat to Chu-ti, the oldest surviving son of the former emperor, who was a popular and experienced frontier military commander. He raised his troops in rebellion and defeated the ill-led imperial forces, which had been weakened by Hung-wu's purge of its most talented generals in an effort to reduce non-familial threats to his power. Nanking fell and its palace was reduced to ashes. Proclaiming himself the Yung-lo Emperor, Chu-ti transferred the capital north, to his former base in Peking.[5]

Choosing Peking as the dynastic capital had a profound effect on Ming frontier policy. Peking had been the site of the defunct Mongol capital of Ta-tu, and before that time had served as a dynastic capital for the Liao and Chin. For a Manchurian or Mongolian dynasty Peking was superbly situated – in the extreme north of China's traditional territory with easy access to troops and supplies from Manchuria or the steppe. For the same reason, it was a questionable choice for a native Chinese dynasty. It put the court directly on a vulnerable frontier defense line, leaving it liable to attack from the steppe or Manchuria and remote from the bulk of China's population and agricultural surplus in the south. Peking was at the end of a very long and complex distribution network which drew on the productive regions of central and southern China. The north could barely feed its own population, let alone the additional troops and government officials required by an imperial capital in Peking. Grain was shipped at great expense by barge on the Grand Canal or via ships on the sea route. These supply disadvantages had been acceptable to the Mongol Yüan dynasty because of Peking's strategic advantages, and it was they who had invested in the expensive canal system that supplied the north.[6]

For a native dynasty, a capital astride the northern frontier (a frontier which China could not successfully advance at the best of times) magnified the Mongol problem to an unwarranted degree. For a dynasty based in Nanking, nomadic incursions would have been troublesome but remote, capable of being handled with flexibility. For a court in Peking, each nomadic attack was an immediate threat to its safety. Yung-lo's choice of Peking as a capital did not take these long-term disadvantages into account. Peking was his princely fief and he was popular with the troops there. A secondary consideration was that the imperial palace in Nanking had been burnt to the ground, leaving that city far less attractive. More important though was Yung-lo's early training and frontier experience in dealing with the Mongol threat. As a northern-based leader, he took the Mongols seriously and intended to campaign against them. As a military man Yung-lo knew he could not mount effective attacks against fast-moving nomads from a southern capital. For such an aggressive emperor,

Peking offered the perfect bridgehead for a long-term policy of disrupting the nomads. Indeed, this was the very location used so successfully by Manchurian dynasties to simultaneously control China and disrupt the steppe.

Yung-lo immediately improved the canal network which the Ming had inherited from the Yüan so that he could supply large-scale military expeditions. He also restored the old frontier barriers and added new interior defense lines to protect the capital. For an activist leader like Yung-lo, who understood frontier warfare and tribal politics, a northern capital was an asset. The problem for native Chinese dynasties was that such emperors were unusual, and at their deaths their policies were abandoned by the civilian bureaucrats at court who were opposed both to activist emperors and their frontier military campaigns. Han Wu-ti's campaigns on the steppe against the Hsiung-nu lasted only while he was on the throne. Similarly, during the T'ang dynasty, the forward policies of T'ai-tsung, which had given China temporary control of the steppe, were dismantled in favor of a passive defense under the reigns of his successors. After Yung-lo's death, when the Ming dynasty reverted to the more traditional pattern of fixed defenses, the Peking bridgehead become embarrassingly vulnerable to nomad attack. The Ming court was to remain in a state of continual agitation over the nomad threat for the next 200 years.

When Yung-lo took power in 1403 the threat from Yüan forces was long past, but the threat of new nomadic confederations was growing. The collapse of Yüan political authority on the steppe provided an opportunity for new leaders to attempt to unite the steppe. Under the control of non-Chinggisid clans, two large confederations had emerged. Closest to the Chinese frontier were the Eastern Mongols who threatened to absorb the Manchurian tribes loosely allied with the Ming and then unite all of Mongolia. More distant, but still a growing menace, were their rivals, the Western Mongols or Oirats, who dominated the Altai region and had imperial ambitions to replace their cousins to the east.

In an effort to protect the Ming frontier, Yung-lo began to play tribal politics – shifting alliances between tribes and attacking those which appeared most likely to unite the steppe. To protect the vulnerable province of Liao-tung and access to Peking, the Ming had established a system of nominal alliances with the Uriyangkhai tribes – the Döen, Fu-yü, and T'ai-ning. These tribes had helped Yung-lo during the civil war when they held loyal imperial troops in defensive positions, leaving Yung-lo free to march south. As a reward the Uriyangkhai leaders were granted titles making them and their tribes military auxiliaries (*wei-so* units) in the Ming army, a form of organization copied from the Yüan. On the frontier it merely marked status. Although the Uriyangkhai were sometimes hostile to China, they maintained their "most favored barbarian" status throughout the Ming. As early as 1407 Yung-lo established horse markets for them while other nomadic groups were denied the right to trade. By means of this alliance Yung-lo protected a vulnerable Ming flank and kept this northeastern territory independent of more aggressive nomadic rulers.

To the east, in Manchurian forests, Yung-lo employed a similar policy. Manchuria had been part of Yüan-ruled China, but the Ming dynasty lacked the power to directly control this territory as had been done in Han and T'ang times. The Ming therefore granted titles to the leaders of the scattered and fragmented Jurchen tribes, recognizing about 200 small *wei-so* units. This gave the Jurchens the right to trade at border markets and visit the court to receive tributary benefits. The policy was a cheap way to expand China's influence and counter Korean ambitions in the area. The Manchurian tribes themselves were of little military consequence at this date.

Yung-lo's policy toward the steppe was aimed at preventing its unification. The rise of the Eastern Mongol leader Arughtai posed the most immediate threat. To counter his growing influence, the Ming attempted to exploit the hostility between the Eastern Mongols and the Oirats. The Ming sent envoys to the Oirats in 1409 and granted their leaders titles, encouraging them to attack Arughtai. This was the classic policy of "using barbarians to fight barbarians." The danger of this policy was that the nomads were equally skilled at exploiting Chinese aid to expand their own power. If the Chinese were not careful, their support of one tribe against another might lay the foundation for a united steppe empire.

Difficulties in implementing the policy immediately surfaced after the Oirats attacked Arughtai in 1409 and won a victory. Hoping to take advantage of his defeat, Yung-lo sent a force of 100,000 troops to attack the Eastern Mongols. It was ambushed and annihilated by Arughtai. Stung by this setback, Yung-lo raised an even larger expeditionary force and in 1410 he marched on Arughtai with 500,000 troops. This immense expedition was no mean undertaking (even if the number of troops recorded in the Ming history was inflated). Plans had begun as soon as the 1409 defeat was known. Twenty-six million pounds of grain, transported by 30,000 heavy carts, were hauled to a series of base camps, each constructed a ten-day march from the next. Additional supplies and manpower were recruited to follow the army. The expedition lasted four months and the Ming army defeated the Eastern Mongols in two battles. Impressed with Ming military power, Arughtai agreed to send tribute to court. This peace agreement did not give the Ming dynasty direct power over the Eastern Mongols, but it did reduce the threat they posed to the frontier. However, Yung-lo's victory had also left them vulnerable to China's erstwhile ally, the Oirats.

The Oirats promptly attacked Arughtai, killing his figurehead Chinggisid and appointing a successor under their control. The Oirat chieftain Mahmud sent envoys to the Ming court in 1412 to announce this victory, and demand rewards for defeating the very nomads who had just concluded a peace with China. Mahmud also requested weapons to destroy Arughtai completely. The Ming could not let the now weakened Eastern Mongols fall before an Oirat onslaught, so the next year Yung-lo broke with the Oirats and declared his support for Arughtai, granting him the title of Ho-ning Wang in 1413. Yung-lo was drawn into a power struggle on the steppe in which both antagonists sought Chinese aid. The nomad leaders had trapped the Ming into financing their own bids for power. In order to keep a balance of power, Yung-lo was forced to switch support from side to side and mount expensive campaigns in an effort to prevent either the Oirats or the Eastern Mongols from achieving domination over the steppe.

The Oirat leader Mahmud responded to the Ming support of the Eastern Mongols by gathering his tribes for an attack. Yung-lo then organized the imperial Ming army for a campaign against the Oirats in 1414. Like his earlier campaign, this expedition put a strain on Ming finances because it required a massive baggage train. Advancing into Mongolia, the Ming troops fought a battle north of the Kerulen River where they won a victory by firing cannons against the nomads, although they suffered heavy casualties themselves. Arughtai, who could have provided critical aid to the Ming, failed to participate in the battle. Instead, he sent an excuse of illness and let the Ming waste its own men and money attacking the rival Oirats. Though displeased with his ally, Yung-lo raised no formal complaint against Arughtai, and even had gifts dispatched in celebration of the victory.

The Oirat reverse at the hands of Yung-lo greatly increased Arughtai's power, which had sunk so low only a few years earlier. Without having lifted a finger, Arughtai was again in a position to renew his bid for dominance on the steppe. Leaving the Ming to cope alone with a series of Oirat raids that came in the wake of the 1414 campaign, Arughtai subjugated the Uriyangkhai in the east and attacked the Oirats in the west. In 1416, the Eastern Mongols killed Mahmud and expanded their influence far to the west. To highlight his independence, Arughtai also robbed some Chinese envoys and overran a Ming fortress in Kalgan the same year.

The Eastern Mongols now posed a direct threat to the Ming – again. Yung-lo changed sides and undertook a series of attacks on Arughtai. The Eastern Mongols were confronted with the full weight of Ming power when, in 1422, Yung-lo mounted another major campaign against the nomads. Supply figures recorded the use of 340,000 donkeys, 117,000 carts, and 235,000 cartpullers to haul 48 million pounds of grain. Arughtai simply retreated out of the range of this overwhelming force, although he was obliged to abandon a large stock of supplies to the Chinese. Unwilling, or unable, to pursue the Eastern Mongols, Yung-lo turned his military machine on the hapless Uriyangkhai tribes who had been forced into alliance with Arughtai. A small expedition was deployed the next year, but it never made contact with Arughtai. The Oirats, however, did attack and defeat Arughtai that same year. Yung-lo led his fifth steppe campaign in 1424, but Arughtai again moved out of range and it came to nothing. This was to be the last Ming offensive on the steppe. Yung-lo died en route to Peking and his successors had no taste for renewing distant steppe campaigns.[7]

While Yung-lo's death marked an end to Ming campaigns against the nomads, his activist policy left the dynasty with a situation it was unable to handle. Eastern Mongol and Oirat power had been kept in check only by frequent shifts in Chinese military aid from one side to the other. While one fell victim to Chinese attacks, the other recovered its strength. The Eastern Mongols had the misfortune to be the last victim of this policy when Yung-lo died. They had been forced to defend themselves against China, while the Oirats grew in power and conquered large areas in the west without interference. Moreover, the Oirats had become unified after Mahmud's son, Toghon, killed the two other chieftains with whom his father had shared power, to become the sole ruler of the Oirats – albeit with the usual facade of a tame Chinggisid.

This put Arughtai in a difficult position. He was forced to move east to escape Oirat power. In 1425, he conquered the Uriyangkhai and sent envoys to China seeking aid. Presumably he expected that the new Ming emperor would follow Yung-lo's policy and put troops in the field against Toghon now that the Oirats were on the rise. He was wrong. Yung-lo's successors had no intention of taking to the field. Officials at court instead had proposed that the Ming' abandon Peking for a safer place.

Arughtai's envoys' pleas for aid relieved Ming anxiety about an expected attack by the Eastern Mongols and the messengers were given gifts. The Ming now anticipated that the Eastern Mongols would act as a buffer between them and the Oirats, allowing the court to turn its attention to strengthening the walled defenses near the capital. Such passive support was of little value to Arughtai, who was soon faced with disaster. In 1431, the Oirats soundly defeated the Eastern Mongols in battle. The Uriyangkhai took the opportunity to revolt, but Arughtai suppressed it. In 1434 the Oirats struck again, killing Arughtai and scattering some of the Eastern Mongols west along the Chinese frontier. In a popular, but short-sighted, move the Ming court raised an army to destroy these remnants of Eastern Mongol power, leaving the Oirats masters of the steppe.

THE OIRATS AND THE MING

Toghon died in 1439, leaving to his son Esen the basis of the Oirat empire. It was Esen who led the Oirats to their greatest victories, but he was unable to establish a durable state, thus forestalling the creation of an empire that would have ranked alongside those of the Hsiung-nu, Turks, or Uighurs. Esen's failure, at the height of his power, demonstrates that nomadic states could not support themselves without outside aid. A nomadic leader who failed to establish a lucrative extortion relationship with China was building a political structure on sand. It would collapse at his death or even sooner.

Esen was typical of those steppe leaders who inherited steppe patrimonies and transformed them into nomadic states. Because his father had previously eliminated rival Oirat chieftains, Esen was able to devote his energies to completing the conquest of the steppe. Over the course of ten years Esen gradually increased Oirat control on the frontier until it was all secure under his command. In the east he wrested the Manchurian steppe from the Ming in 1444 by conquering two of the Uriyangkhai tribes, forcing the third to flee to China. In the west, after attacks on the Chinese protectorate of Hami in 1443, 1445 and 1448, the Oirats forced the Ming out of its bridgehead in Turkestan and also neutralized the power of tribes in Kansu who acted as Ming border guards.

Esen's wars on the frontier were only the first part of a larger plan. Like other nomads before him, Esen was preparing to implement the outer frontier strategy that utilized the political and military power of a unified steppe to extort economic concessions from China. Esen's frontier wars against minor opponents were a necessary prelude to this. As a nomadic leader he eventually had to focus his forces on a Chinese campaign; but to avoid becoming vulnerable to other nomads on his flanks and rear, all potential opposition on the steppe had to be neutralized before sustained attacks on China could begin without interruption.

The objective of these campaigns was first loot and then a peace treaty that would provide subsidies and trade. It was not an attempt to conquer China. Although steppe nomads always tried to exploit China from a distance through raids and tributary visits, at some point every sophisticated nomadic ruler realized he needed both a regular source of revenue and luxury goods to support the political elite, as well as border markets to provide trade for the ordinary nomads. Esen's campaigns against the Ming were the Oirats' attempt to transform their military domination of the steppe into permanent control, a transformation that had been successfully completed by the Hsiung-nu, Turks, and Uighurs when they had faced native dynasties in China.

Esen's control of the eastern and western flanks of the steppe permitted the Oirats to focus their energy on Ming China. The Oirats had been in touch with the Ming court since the time of Mahmud, Esen's grandfather. They sent tribute missions annually to China, in spite of the many alternations of peace and hostility between them. These embassies were small, usually under a hundred men, bringing horses and furs for which they received Chinese goods. After Esen took power and extended Oirat influence, the number of people on these missions suddenly escalated. In 1431, his first year on the throne, more than a thousand Oirats appeared as members of the tribute mission, and in 1444 an embassy of more than 2,000 arrived. The Chinese protested at this tremendous increase in visiting Oirats, whom they had to feed and reward.

The Ming attributed the rise in the number of Oirats coming on tributary missions to Esen's greed. But it was not a steppe leader's personal greed that was at the root of his economic demands on China, rather it was his need to reward the political elite of his domain. Since each envoy was feasted, presented with gifts, and allowed to engage in trade, being chosen as an envoy had practical benefits. Tributary visits provided sought after luxury goods that could be redistributed among the nomads or traded elsewhere. The Oirats were therefore anxious to enlarge these opportunities for international trade. Muslim merchants often accompanied the embassies to take advantage of this situation.

When Esen became overlord of the steppe he was burdened with new financial obligations which the increasing size of his tribute missions helped meet. The 1446 mission, for example, brought 800 horses, 130,000 squirrel pelts, 16,000 ermine pelts, and 200 sable pelts, which were exchanged for a variety of Chinese products, most of them luxury goods that the Oirats could not have acquired by raiding.[8] The Chinese later said that the nobility preferred trade to raiding because it provided luxury goods, while the common people preferred raiding in order to obtain necessities like grain, metal, and livestock. The growth of Esen's tribute missions can be interpreted as a political device to reward the elite and bind them to the new Oirat empire. Swiftly growing tribute missions, or the demand that the Ming permit such missions, were the consequence of political centralization on the steppe. While Esen was busy for ten years (1439–49) with conquests on the steppe, in his dealings with the Ming he seemed content simply to enlarge the number of people participating in the tributary visits.

In 1448–9 the tribute missions became a critical issue between the Ming and Esen. In that year an embassy of 3,500 people arrived at the border. The Chinese vigorously objected to this wholesale enlargement of the tributary system. Still they accepted it, though the Ming court tried to save money by reducing the quantity and quality of its gifts. Esen must have realized that he had now approached the outer limits of what he could expect from the Ming tribute system as it was then organized, and that it would not be enough to finance his empire. In addition, the tributary system did not benefit most of the nomads, who needed border markets. With an exception only for the Uriyang-khai, the Ming court had steadfastly refused to establish markets for the frontier nomads. The ever-increasing Oirat missions to the Ming court foreshadowed greater demands to come, for Esen had completed the last of his border campaigns a year before he sent his largest embassy. The Oirats controlled the entire frontier, had experienced troops ready, and knew that the Chinese were ill-prepared for war. It was the perfect opportunity to implement the outer frontier strategy.

Esen attacked China soon after the return of his tributary mission. He had planned a massive invasion which would allow his nomads to pillage vast areas, while forcing the Ming to renegotiate the tributary system. The Oirats split their forces into three groups: one sent to loot Liao-tung, another to harass the fortress complex of Hsüan-fu, and the last, under Esen, to invade Ta-t'ung. While these three attacks threatened all the major approaches to Peking, Esen could not have planned to attack the city itself because his cavalry was incapable of capturing a fortified city. Instead, these attacks were designed to terrorize the Ming court and dramatically illustrate the capital's vulnerability. Loot would come from the undefended towns and farming villages.

News of the Oirat invasions naturally disturbed the Ming court. The safest course of action would have been to rely on the line of walled defenses manned by imperial troops. The chief eunuch at court, however, convinced the young Cheng-t'ung Emperor (Chu Ch'i-chen), that if he took to the field himself with a half million troops Esen would flee. The Ming forces from the capital area marched toward the frontier. Esen initially avoided contact with such a formidable army, as all nomadic leaders (except Chinggis Khan) invariably did. However, the Ming army was not a proper fighting force. In the barely quarter-century since Yung-lo's death, the Ming military had become almost purely defensive in character and had declined dramatically in effectiveness. It was not prepared for a mobile campaign. The expedition against Esen was ill equipped, ill led, and poorly provisioned. To make matters worse, the weather was horrible, with constant rain. A retreat, ordered before the army even reached the frontier, became a rout when the Oirats began to harry the march. Realizing that, despite its size, this force was in no condition to fight, Esen destroyed its rear guard and then moved on the main body which was camped at T'u-mu. Here as many as half the Ming troops were killed while the rest fled. The Ming emperor fell prisoner to Esen, and only a token force stood between the Oirats and Peking.[9]

Esen was then faced with the problem of how to exploit this astounding victory. He decided to demand a huge ransom and proceeded to retreat toward the frontier. Esen's failure to march immediately on Peking, which was in turmoil because of the emperor's capture and the defeat of the region's main army, may seem surprising. However, Esen was leading only part of the Oirat force, about 20,000 men according to Chinese records, and he may have been hesitant about taking such a small force into the heart of the Ming defenses where another Chinese army could be lurking. Besides, unless the city surrendered, Esen could not hope to storm it. Esen's plan was to extort a huge ransom, perhaps arrange a marriage with the Ming imperial line, and then negotiate a favorable treaty from a thoroughly frightened ruler, much as Mao-tun had done with Kao-tsu in the Former Han. This was the traditional strategy of nomadic leaders from the steppe which had been obscured by the unusually extensive conquests of Chinggis Khan and his successors.

Esen's plan was disrupted by an unexpected turn of events. Ming court officials replaced the captured emperor with his brother and refused to negotiate with the Oirats. The nomads immediately marched on Peking, but were unable to penetrate its defenses. When Esen received word that a relief force from the south was about to arrive he returned to the steppe, looting the territory surrounding the Ming capital as he withdrew. Esen now found himself with a captured emperor who was not only worthless but a political liability. Such a prize had raised the Oirats' expectations of immense wealth from a ransom and greater treaty benefits. Esen was shocked to discover that the Ming intended to abandon their sovereign and pay nothing. In 1450, having received nothing, Esen returned the ex-emperor. This was a great blow to the nomad leader's prestige.

Esen's empire was at its height in 1450, but the failure to collect a huge ransom for the Ming emperor's return had disappointed his followers and their unhappiness was soon reflected in political opposition. Esen was forced to put down a rebellion by Eastern Mongol tribes after executing one of their leaders. He also faced a revolt by his own figurehead Chinggisid khan, Tokhto-bukha, after attempting to change the mode of succession to this office. Tokhto-bukha was killed and replaced. To centralize his administration and forestall future Chinggisid attempts to seize real power, Esen executed Tokhto-bukha's replacement and proclaimed himself khan in 1453. Before that time he had been content with the title of *tayishi*, now he was abolishing the tradition of a Chinggisid khan.

Esen's ploy might have succeeded if he had been able to gain a fat ransom and trade benefits from China that would have dampened opposition. Breaking with such a strong tradition after a period of internal trouble and unproductive relations with China was, however, very risky in view of the fact that Esen's political base, particularly among the conquered Eastern Mongols, was insecure. Nevertheless, it looked at first as if he might succeed. The Chinese finally agreed to receive an Oirat embassy which brought horses to the frontier and took home 90,000 bolts of cloth. Still, Mongol opposition to what was considered usurpation of the supreme leadership was strong. Esen was not a descendant of Chinggis Khan and his action was considered high-handed at a time when he was suffering from political trouble, expressed by revolts within the empire. Several chieftains who felt they had been insufficiently rewarded killed Esen in 1455. The Oirat empire collapsed.

Esen's political failure after a string of military victories points up the vulnerability of a steppe empire at this stage of development. The Oirat empire was still held together primarily by force and Esen's political popularity among his own people. If Esen had managed to set up a beneficial relationship with China, this fragile political control could have been stabilized by increasing and controlling the flow of goods between China and the steppe. Esen's initial invasion of China aimed at creating such a system. His capture of the emperor, however, although a great victory, was ultimately fatal to this aim. The nomads expected immediate wealth but got nothing. They blamed Esen for this and those leaders who were not happy with his rule used the opportunity to destroy him. Esen's death marked the end of the first attempt to create a nomadic state during the Ming period.

RETURN OF THE EASTERN MONGOLS

The collapse of the Oirat empire opened a period of anarchy on the steppe. The remaining Oirat leaders were unable to maintain hegemony in Mongolia and were forced to withdraw to their homeland in the west. The Chinese, however, had little time to congratulate themselves on Esen's fall because the newly autonomous Eastern Mongol tribes began a series of raids on the frontier under the leadership of their new khan, Bolai. Although he was unable to subdue the other tribes on the steppe, Bolai had great success in raiding China and sent tribute missions there. It was during his reign that the nomads began to move south, seizing marginal land along the border. Around 1457, the Ming court was informed that the Mongols had infiltrated the Ordos territories, forcing the Chinese to withdraw. The loss of the Ordos was both a strategic and an economic blow because the Ming had exploited it as a source of provisions for its frontier troops. Areas around the capital and in Kansu thereafter came under increasingly heavy attack, and by 1465, Bolai, in alliance with other nomadic leaders, was staging the largest raids since Esen. The Ming was unable to effectively deter the Mongols because its defenses were deficient. A censor, Ch'en Hsüan, presented a gloomy picture of frontier conditions to the court in 1464:

The Mongols are notorious for their propensity to make raids, but our border commanders follow their routine and grow completely lazy. The cities and fortifications have not been repaired, the ammunition and arms are in a pitiful state. Crying abuses are being practiced: the rich soldiers bribe their superiors every month, thus avoiding their services. But the poor ones must either endure cold and hunger or desert. Due to this the guarding of the frontier is in such a deplorable state.[10]

The threat to China was not critical, however, because Bolai was hamstrung by constant bickering among the divided tribes that participated in his campaigns. After overwhelming the Ming frontier, Bolai fell victim to these disputes and was murdered. Without security and unity in the steppe, no leader could devote his full attention to China.

Divisions, temporary alliances, battles, and assassinations were the hallmark of political life on the steppe after Esen's death. Several tribal leaders tried to unify the Eastern Mongols without success. Tributary missions declined and by 1500 had ceased altogether. If, as we have proposed, regular tribute missions of increasing size marked the growth of political centralization on the steppe, then their decline was evidence of political instability and devolution on the steppe. The Oirats were too far removed from China to have regular relations with the Ming. The Eastern Mongols were too busy fighting each other, and raiding China, to concern themselves with tributary exchanges.

The anarchy among the Eastern Mongols permitted the previously ignored khans of Chinggisid descent to rise in importance because they could gain easier acceptance as formal leaders, while other pretenders could obtain only short-term recognition by force. Under Bayan Möngke, or Dayan Khan, the Chinggisid line reasserted itself at the end of the fifteenth century. Dayan Khan was born in 1464 and elevated to the rulership in 1488. After the death of a rival leader, Ismael, in the west, Dayan Khan increased his domination over most of the Eastern Mongols.[11]

Dayan Khan raided China almost continually, a task simplified by the poor state of Ming defenses which had become both costly and inefficient because of corruption. Minor skirmishes with the Mongols were often portrayed as major Ming victories by the generals in command, as in 1501 when 210 officers were promoted for valor after a battle in which a mere fifteen Mongols had been killed. Ming campaigns on the steppe itself were reduced to attacks on isolated Mongol encampments inhabited by women and children.[12]

Dayan Khan encountered very different problems than Esen had in creating a nomadic state. Esen had spent the early part of his career imposing his will on the steppe. He undertook attacks on China in earnest only after he had conquered the tribes along the frontier. Dayan Khan initiated his attacks on China without first gaining control of his neighbors. He was able to engage their cooperation because he was the officially recognized khan of Chinggisid origin and the obvious leader for popular raids. However, Dayan Khan met with intense opposition whenever he imposed his will on tribal leaders in other affairs. In 1509, a revolt erupted among the tribes in Kalgan and the Ordos when Dayan Khan appointed one of sons to lead them. This revolt took about four years to suppress and Dayan Khan had to halt his invasions of China until 1514.

Before resuming his attacks, Dayan Khan reorganized the nomads and changed his tactics in order to bring even more pressure on the Ming court. He established about thirty fortified camps as permanent bases from which regular raids could be mounted on the border. Dayan Khan also trained an elite force of 15,000 for an attack on the fortress of Hsüan-fu, which was one of the Ming frontier's most strategic points. This enabled the Mongols to encircle the capital and, in 1516, a reported 70,000 Mongols attacked the area east of

Peking, overrunning a number of towns. The next year 50,000 Mongols attacked the capital district itself. In repulsing this invasion, the Ming gained one of its few successes against Dayan Khan, and forced him to withdraw. The rising tide of Mongol military pressure was only relieved when internal feuding broke out on the steppe. Dayan Khan had to abandon his attacks to put down rebels in the Ordos and Koko-nor. It was not until 1522 that he again seriously returned to the Chinese frontier, mounting a raid on the suburbs of Peking the next year while sending other nomads to invade Kansu. Dayan Khan continued these attacks on an annual basis until 1532 when he attempted to seek a negotiated peace. In spite of its growing military weakness, the Ming had considerably hardened its position for dealing with nomads since the late fifteenth century. Previously they had received and rewarded tribute missions, but now they refused even to accept envoys from the steppe. After Dayan Khan's mission was turned away, he responded with a new series of attacks which ended only with his death in 1533.

Dayan Khan left the Eastern Mongols in control of all of southern Mongolia and the eastern part of northern Mongolia. His long reign, Yüan lineage, and distinguished descendants have given him an important place in Mongolian history, but in spite of his many successes he failed to institute centralized internal authority over all the tribes on the steppe. His Yüan lineage made it easier for him to gain formal submission from local tribal leaders – Chinggisid puppet dynasties in the past had always been recognized as the nominal leaders of the steppe – but it was another thing to turn this formal recognition of sovereignty into real political power. Esen and Arughtai had both recognized this because they had used puppet Chinggisids and conducted military campaigns not only to enforce the recognition of their Chinggisid, but to enforce their own will.

Once a state was established, nomadic rulers turned to China to finance it, but Dayan Khan's troubles demonstrate that unity on the steppe was a necessary prelude to an extortion policy when dealing with a balky Chinese court. After Dayan Khan began to implement the outer frontier strategy, putting greater and greater pressure on China, it was not the Ming defenses that upset his plans, but domestic trouble in his unsecured steppe territory that forced him to break off the campaign. Large-scale wars against China required the imperial leadership's utmost attention. While imperial forces were committed to objectives along the frontier, unpacified tribal leaders at home could take advantage of their temporary absence to disobey. Hence an ambitious nomadic leader had to first impose his control on the steppe before making a serious attempt at extorting China. Once the steppe was united, a nomadic leader had to quickly turn his attention to China and alter the relationship between the ruling dynasty and the steppe. Dayan Khan had attempted to act without securing the total control of the steppe. The weakness of the Ming defenses aided him in this, as did the popularity of raiding for loot among the steppe tribes. But with each of Dayan Khan's successes in China the fears of local tribal leaders grew because they thought that he would impose himself more firmly on them. They chose to revolt before Dayan Khan could succeed in his China campaigns, thereby disrupting his efforts to build a state.

ALTAN KHAN AND THE MING CAPITULATION

Dayan Khan's descendants quickly split his territory among themselves. This division has been attributed to Mongolian custom, with scholars comparing it to the split of Chinggis Khan's empire. In fact, the Mongol empire did not formally split during the rule of the Great Khans, but remained a unified state until civil war broke it up. Likewise, there was no split of the Oirat empire from Mahmud to Toghon to Esen. The dismemberment of Dayan Khan's territory was proof of its disorganization. Dayan Khan had never achieved tribal unity, or even the beginning of a nomadic state that could be built upon by his heirs. It was a tribal patrimony in which various sons established themselves in different areas, producing a loose confederation. Dayan Khan's sons and grandsons cooperated in large ventures but none of them seriously attempted to bring the steppe under his personal control.

The most notable of these rulers was Altan Khan (1507–82), a grandson of Dayan Khan, who ruled for over forty years and became, by virtue of seniority and talent, the unofficial head of the confederation.[13] He had inherited the Tümed Mongol tribes north of Shansi, giving him control of the center of the frontier. His brother Chi-nang had received territory north of Shensi. At Chi-nang's death Altan became the most influential leader on the steppe. It was he who finally persuaded the Ming to reverse its policy and provide subsidies and border markets for the nomads. Ironically, this concession came too late to create a centralized nomadic state, for Altan Khan never attempted to monopolize the flow of tributary benefits himself, and these resources instead served to preserve a chaotic status quo on the steppe.

Altan Khan continued Dayan Khan's policy of pressuring the Ming court by means of raids. Under his leadership the Eastern Mongols invaded China on an annual basis, and for forty years there was not a single year of peace on the frontier. Altan Khan used the raids for two purposes: to directly reward the Mongol participants and to force China into resuming the tribute system and opening horse markets to provide the Mongol leadership with luxury goods. The Ming refusal to provide frontier markets was a major provocation encouraging Mongol attacks. When in 1541, for example, a Mongol proposal for border peace in exchange for frontier trade was rejected by the Ming court, the Mongols launched a devastating attack into Shansi the next year.

A pattern of rejected peace offers followed by destructive raiding continued for decades. These raids reached a climax in 1550 when Altan Khan rode to the very gates of Peking. The Chinese refused to leave the walls of the city and Altan Khan withdrew at his own pace. This attack forced the Chinese to reconsider their position. Many officials had argued that it was foolish to deny the Mongols markets and then face annual attacks. A horse fair was organized and Altan Khan was presented with a large gift of money. The markets were abolished almost immediately when the Mongols requested that grain be traded along with cloth. This, court officials argued, was a Mongol trick to get grain to feed a captive Chinese population in southern Mongolia. The Mongol response was swift. Eight major attacks fell on China in 1552, followed by raids of similar intensity during the following five years. By 1557 these raids had become so serious that the Ming court considered abandoning Peking as its capital in favor of a less vulnerable position, a proposal that had last been raised and rejected after Esen's capture of the emperor a century earlier.

This seemingly endless cycle of frontier invasions suddenly ended when the Ming court reversed its position on trade and subsidies. In 1570, Wang Ch'ung-ku, an adept Ming frontier commander, received the surrender of one of Altan Khan's favorite grandsons. In a diplomatic coup, he used the incident to secure a change in Ming policy towards the Mongols. A peace pact was negotiated with the Mongols by which the Chinese were guaranteed secure frontiers in exchange for titles, subsidies, and border markets. These had been standard Mongol demands for more than seventy years. After generations of war, this agreement brought peace to the frontier, but only after much debate within the Ming court.[14]

Yet the peace on Mongol terms did not create a nomadic state. Altan Khan was only one of a number of Mongol leaders, all related but autonomous. Thus, a deal with Altan did not automatically include the numerous tribes of the Ordos who had to be handled separately. Nor did it include the Chahar Mongols in the east who were raiding Liao-tung. They were led by the great khaghan Tümen who, as the senior Chinggisid prince, was genealogically superior to Altan. Tümen refused to take part in the system because

the Altan Khan is Tümen khaghan's subject, but now that he [Altan Khan] has received a princely title and a gold seal as big as a peck is it not as if he was made the husband, and Tümen khaghan [technically his overlord] has been reduced to the status of wife.[15]

Tümen and his descendants continued to raid Liao-tung.

The new Ming policy offered the Mongols many advantages. Subsidies and border markets were actually more profitable than raiding. Their value also grew at an incredible rate. In the three military districts of Hsüan-fu, Ta-t'ung, and Shan-hsi horse markets and subsidies amounted to about 60,000 taels in 1571, 70,000 the next year, and had risen to 270,000 taels in 1577, of which subsidies amounted to about 10 percent of the total. By 1587, subsidies alone amounted to 47,000 taels, although they may have accounted for a larger fraction of the total. The breakdown of the annual cost (in taels) of horse markets and subsidies in three frontier districts during 1612 shows just how lucrative the system was to the Tümed.[16]

District	Horse markets	Subsidies	Totals
Hsüan-fu	185,000	52,000	237,000
Ta-t'ung	100,000	22,000	122,000
Shan-hsi	40,000	14,000	54,000
Totals	325,000	88,000	413,000

In addition, the Tümed khan received a personal subsidy of 20,000 taels over and above these figures.

The treaty provided that all Mongol notables who entered the tributary system would receive titles and gifts appropriate to their rank, as well as the right to trade. The number of Mongols in the system was always expanding because those that died were never removed from the rolls and chieftains constantly requested that their subordinates be added. In essence, this policy unwittingly preserved the fragmented political structure that existed on the steppe when the treaty was signed in 1570. A centralized nomadic state financed itself with Chinese goods only by preserving its monopoly on the Chinese connection. In such a system, if a local leader wished to acquire Chinese goods, he had to work through the imperial hierarchy, for he was not permitted to negotiate directly with the Chinese court. Altan Khan never attempted to create such monopoly. Under his aegis, each nomadic leader maintained a personal relationship with China, and the right to participate in the system preserved the authority of local rulers who could gain wealth from China without giving up their autonomy.

Chinese frontier officials themselves complained about this fragmentation. Results had been far easier to obtain from a ruler like Altan Khan than from the petty tribal rulers of the Ordos, with whom they had to negotiate individually. Many of the Mongol rulers had only nominal control over the tribes in their region. Some leaders invariably found it profitable to break the peace. One frontier commander supervising the Ordos region sent a report to court explaining why his district continually encountered such trouble.

The tribes, which are nomadizing the Ho-t'ao, are not like those Mongols living east of the river. In the east, all affairs are concentrated in one hand. If we want to enter into an agreement with their chieftain, the relations will not be changed, even within a period of thirty years, once they have been established. In contrast the Ordos tribes are divided into forty-two branches, each of which claims to be the most important. . . . The whole Ordos population amounts to several tens of thousands of people; but because they are divided into forty-two branches, each of them consists of not more than 2,000–3,000, and in some instances only 1,000–2,000 people. In dealing with them, their forces must be divided and the tribute, which is brought by them, should be accepted. But those who are expressing their submission earlier, should be graciously received and rewarded, while the others must be turned away. During these procedures it is indispensable to be ready for war at any moment, in order that they all realize the strength of China.[17]

In spite of the difficulties, the peace agreements led to a period of relative peace on the frontier and immense savings on military expenditures. The army expenses of the Hsüan-fu, Ta-t'ung, and Shan-hsi military districts in 1577 were reported to be only 20 or 30 percent of what they had been before the treaty. The costs of the markets and subsidies that made the peace possible with the Tümeds were only 10 percent of the costs of maintaining troops on the frontier in the 1580s, although as the nomads increased their demands the savings became less.[18] For the Chinese the agreement even had the advantage of reducing the possibility of unity on the steppe, one of Yung-lo's concerns, by keeping many petty and jealous rulers in power who would oppose any centralization. The policy was a success, but the question remains as to why it took so long for the Ming to take the advice long proposed by its own frontier officials.

Ming policy was always divided on the issue of tribute relations with the nomads. As with previous native dynasties, tributary missions were an approved channel for providing subsidies and trade to frontier peoples. Envoys would present "tribute" (often mere tokens) and in return receive much larger gifts, lavish entertainment, and access to profitable markets. China gained the ideological satisfaction of treating envoys as if they were from subject states. This allowed the court to dispense huge subsidies, often amounting to extortion, without officially acknowledging it was doing any such thing. The appearance of a sinocentric world order, with its peerless all-sovereign emperor, was thereby maintained while the realities of power politics were handled flexibly. The rationale behind this policy was that tributary relations and markets were cheaper and less disruptive than wars. A rarely admitted benefit was that a weak dynasty could often count on military aid from the nomads to put down rebellions or repel invasions because the nomads wanted to maintain a profitable status quo. Those opposed to tribute relations objected to their expense and argued that gifts and trade for barbarians merely strengthened China's enemies. These officials pushed for either aggressive military policies or defensive isolation.

Arguments for either policy could be supported by historical precedent. Both the Han and T'ang dynasties, exemplar of Chinese policy, had made unseemly deals with the nomads at an early date in their dynastic histories. They had both relied on subsidies given through the tributary system and border markets to pacify the nomads. Military campaigns against the nomads during both dynasties were expensive and unpopular, and had proved short-lived. Treaties recognizing the value of a peaceful relationship with the northern steppe tribes became more crucial as each dynasty declined. The T'ang in particular came to rely on Uighur protection to keep it in power.

Neither dynasty had attempted the passive Ming policy of non-intercourse that had been implemented after Yung-lo's death, in which trade and subsidies were denied to the nomads while the Chinese military was confined to repelling invasions. And invasions there were: the Ming experienced more attacks over a longer period than any other Chinese dynasty. Yet the Ming refused to make accommodations with the steppe even when confronted with a deteriorating frontier situation. Even more astounding, this refusal came from a dynasty that had economic problems and military difficulties far worse than those encountered by the Han and T'ang. Ming China never directly controlled either the northeast or the northwest frontier regions and, after Yung-lo, did not campaign on the steppe. In view of these problems, military difficulties, and economic hardships, why did the Ming refuse to deal with the steppe as other Chinese dynasties had done?

The answer stems from a fundamental shift in China's perception about the type of danger the nomads posed. The Mongol conquest of China was so traumatic that it left a legacy of fear unknown to the Han and T'ang. The Ming's most basic fear was that the nomads on the steppe wanted to conquer China. The Han and T'ang had experienced nomad invasions, but they never thought of the steppe people as potential conquerors of China. This perception was correct: the other frontier strategy demanded that the nomads avoid occupying Chinese land, establishing dynasties in China only after central control there collapsed. The Ming, on the contrary, had replaced the Mongol Yüan dynasty, the single example of a direct steppe conquest of China. Following the expulsion of the Yüan from China, the Oirats and Eastern Mongols had reverted to the traditional strategy of the Hsiung-nu, Turks, and Uighurs. But the Ming was no longer willing to see the nomads as simple extortioners. To them, nomad attacks were precursors to a new conquest of China from the steppe. This suspicion was greatly magnified by the capital's location in the very heart of a troubled frontier. Even simple raids often put the capital at risk so that the Ming could not write off nomad attacks as remote border problems. The Ming defeat at T'u-mu greatly reinforced this attitude, for it was the only dynasty to have lost a reigning emperor in battle with the steppe tribes.

The Ming's other fear was that its position would prove to be more like the weak Sung dynasty than the powerful Han or T'ang. The Ming court worried that subsidies and trade would be used to increase the power of their enemies until they were powerful enough to destroy the dynasty. The Sung had paid huge sums to the Khitans, Jurchens, and finally Mongols, only to lose first northern China and then be swallowed up by the Yüan dynasty. The Ming was acutely aware that, like the Sung, it was a dynasty of southern origin that had captured most of the north in its early days and then been unable to handle frontier defense. Thus, instead of looking at payments and trade for the nomads as pragmatic tools of diplomacy, the Ming saw them as the first step on the road that had led to Sung's destruction. Some officials did argue for a more realistic policy. Frontier military men in particular urged more accommodations in meeting the nomads' demands for markets and subsidies, but they were opposed by Ming bureaucrats who worried about whether the Mongols were "sincere." In a debate over frontier policy in 1542, when Altan Khan was devastating the capital region, Yang Shou-ch'ien attacked this line of reasoning, including the Sung analogy, by pointing out that tribute relations were a sound means of preventing war which was already in use on other parts of the frontier.[19]

Tribute missions had of course been part of Ming policy in Yung-lo's time. He had opened horse markets to the Uriyangkhai and conducted the tea trade in the west as a useful way to make alliances. After Yung-lo's death and the unification of the steppe under Esen, there was a qualitative change in Ming attitudes. The Chinese lost control of the system as Esen sent more and more envoys. When the Ming objected, Esen went to war to reorganize the tributary system to increase the flow of goods to the steppe in exchange for peace. As we have seen, Esen's capture of the emperor caused unexpected problems leading to the Oirats' fall. This provided a breathing space for China because, as the steppe political organization fell apart, tribute missions from the nomads declined and then ceased. When, around 1530, the nomads demanded the system be reopened, and expanded to include trade, the Ming refused, fearing that it would fund their own destruction. These fears grew as the Ming's ability to defend itself declined.

Ming frontier officials grew exasperated at this policy. While subsidies to the nomads were expensive, they argued, it was cheaper than raising troops or building walls. They also argued that the court misunderstood the tributary system if it thought that the nomads needed to be "sincere" in their respect for China to make the policy successful. Self-interest would make it work. This advice was rejected. For seventy years Ming frontiers took a pounding unprecedented in China's history.

The change in policy in 1570 brought peace, exchanging subsidies and trade for border security. Why the change occurred at this time is not clear because the answer apparently lies in an understanding of Ming court politics rather than frontier affairs. It was true that military expenses had grown beyond the government's ability to finance, that the army was increasingly ineffective, and that the border had been terrorized for years. Annual military expenses had risen from 430,000 taels in the period 1480–1520, to 2,300,000 in 1567–72.[20] They rose even further after this time because of problems with the Manchus and internal rebellions. Without a treaty with the Mongols, the Ming government would likely have collapsed a half-century before it actually did. A deal with Altan Khan also may have been attractive because he was an old man with no great ambitions. However, the decision appears linked to a larger shift in Ming foreign relations geared to accommodate pressures in the southern coastal regions by the Japanese and Europeans. On both its northern and southern frontiers the Ming court loosened its restrictions on trade and adopted a less hostile attitude toward foreigners. Whatever its origin, the peace policy soon proved a success in establishing a more peaceful relationship with the steppe tribes. As Mongol leaders eagerly sought titles and gifts raiding slowed to minor proportions.

Nevertheless, the Ming had resolved this frontier problem too late. The real danger to Ming control had never been from the steppe, but from internal rebellions and the tribes in Manchuria, and trouble in both areas was growing. For a third time in 1,800 years, the collapse of internal order within China and anarchy on the steppe unleashed the Manchurian tiger and set the stage for the establishment of the most successful and long-lasting of all foreign dynasties.

THE RISE OF THE MANCHUS

For most of the Ming dynasty's history, frontier problems meant nomad problems. The long conflict between China and the nomads was greatly reduced with the establishment of the tributary system after the 1571 treaty was signed. Under its terms most of the numerous Mongol tribal leaders received subsidies, gained the right to trade, and were granted titles by the Ming court. The peace agreement also had the effect of freezing and perpetuating the fragmented political structure which existed in Mongolia at this time. Because every minor chieftain was independently funded, each objected to efforts at unification under the leadership of a single ruler.

Even as the Ming's frontier problems with the Mongols were easing in the late sixteenth and early seventeenth centuries, the northeastern frontier in Manchuria underwent a number of significant changes that were quite dangerous to Ming interests. Taking advantage of the Ming tributary system and the dynasty's military weakness, the fragmented Jurchen tribes began to unite and form a frontier state. Mongol power, which would have crushed such a state at an earlier time, no longer stood in the way because of the disputes among the Eastern Mongol tribes.

The Jurchens were descendants of the people who had established the Chin dynasty, which was destroyed by the Mongols. In Ming times they lived in small scattered villages organized around kinship groups engaged in farming, stock-raising, and hunting. For political purposes the Chinese categorized the Jurchens of Manchuria into three groups: the Chien-chou, who occupied territory in the northeast to the west of the Yalu River; the Hai-hsi or Hun-lun confederation of the Hada, Yehe, Hoifa, and Ula, tribes whose land was in the west to the north of Mukden; and the more remote Yeh or "Wild" Jurchens, who lived in the forests further north. The first two groups had direct relations with China, the "Wild" Jurchens did not.

Throughout most of the Ming period, Jurchen tribes friendly with China were organized into approximately 200 small *wei-so* units, continuing an old Yüan policy. Theoretically, such units were part of a Ming military auxiliary, but, in reality, they were no more than an expedient political device designed to give the Chinese a simple structure by which they could maintain influence in the region and keep it out of Korean control. Unlike the native Chinese Han and T'ang dynasties, or the Mongol Yüan, the Ming dynasty did not directly rule territory outside of Liao-tung and parts of Liao-hsi. The large number of *wei-so* units undercut the authority of the Jurchen tribal confederations – an advantage to many local tribal leaders. Ming recognition entitled them to trade at the frontier and to visit Chinese cities on lucrative tribute missions by themselves. The Ming alliance also served as a buffer against the ambitions of the Mongol tribes that inhabited the steppes to the west.[21]

The ascent of the Jurchens began in the fashion of most frontier conflicts, bound up in tales of obscure killings and plots for revenge. Nurhachi (1559–1626), the founder of the Manchu state, was the son of a Chien-chou tribal chieftain who had died in one of the numerous wars between the Jurchen tribes. In 1585, he vowed to revenge his father's death by killing Nikan Wailan, the Chinese-supported khan who had led the enemy force. Nurhachi first attempted to get redress from the Chinese, but they refused to help because Nikan Wailan was their ally. Nurhachi then found that few of his own relatives were willing to take on a man with this powerful backing, so with only a small group of supporters (they could raise but thirteen sets of armor), he started his own campaign. To the surprise of everyone he successfully attacked all his neighbors to bring the Chien-chou under his command and within a year had succeeded in killing Nikan Wailan. His victory threw Jurchen politics into confusion.[22]

These were petty wars with opposing forces organized in groups of ten. According to Korean records, the "great chief" Nurhachi commanded only 150 troops until as late as 1596 and shared power with his brother, Shurhachi, the "little chief," who commanded 40 troops.[23] While it is reasonable to suppose that Nurhachi could have indirectly raised a larger number of troops by making alliances with other tribal leaders, it would have been difficult for any self-respecting bandit in China to gain much attention with a force this small. The importance of Nurhachi's early victory lies not in the numbers of men involved, but in the opportunity it gave him to reorganize the Jurchen tribes under a more centralized government. Military victories changed the character of Jurchen political organization, moving it successively from a petty tribal confederation into a complex border state. Nurhachi also set about securing his military power through a process of socio-economic development which provided him with a food surplus and the ability to produce his own weapons.

Early Manchu history under Nurhachi may be divided into two periods: a tribal phase lasting until 1619, and a border conquest phase that occupied him until his death in 1626. The first, and by far the longer period, involved his efforts to control and unite the Jurchen tribes. He employed the traditional tactics of wars, marriage alliances, and exploiting the Chinese tributary system to gain his ends. During this period he shared authority with his relatives. After he had united most of the tribes he centralized power and, in 1615, declared himself khan, although it was not until 1619 that he began to incorporate Chinese territory. During this second period he worked to create the rudiments of a true state, but he was handicapped by his own limited political vision. It was left to Nurhachi's son to create a true state and establish a real dynastic tradition.

Following the death of Nikan Wailan, Nurhachi's influence in the northeast rose considerably. He concluded two marriages in 1588, one with the granddaughter of the Hada chief and the other with the daughter of the recently deceased Yehe chief. These alliances were important because they connected him with the Hun-lun Jurchen. In 1590, Nurhachi went on a tributary mission to China and received a minor title. Tributary visits were of great value to Nurhachi. He had stolen about 500 Ming tributary patents which entitled the bearer to gifts and which enabled Nurhachi to reward his own followers. The minor title was a useful addition to his prestige in an area where Chinese influence carried weight in dealing with other tribes.

The rise of the young Nurhachi soon provoked opposition from the other tribal leaders. The chief of the Yehe, now Nurhachi's brother-in-law, demanded that certain lands be ceded to the Yehe. When Nurhachi refused, the Yehe, Hada, and Hoifa attacked and burned a few of his villages. In 1593, they organized an even larger attack which Nurhachi successfully defeated, and thereby greatly increased his power.

Nurhachi's power was based on more than military might. His territory, with its capital at Huluan Hada, controlled valuable resources including pearls, furs, ginseng, and silver. In addition, he pillaged neighboring regions for loot and captives, who were put to work bringing more agricultural land into production. At this time he also introduced Chinese methods of ironworking. It was probably this economic development and Nurhachi's growing domination of the Ming tributary system that incited other, more established, tribal leaders to move against him. His rising influence was recognized by the Ming court in 1595 when they granted him a grander title. Within a few years, Nurhachi felt powerful enough to initiate a policy of incorporating the important Jurchen tribes under his rule, conquering the Hada (1599–1601), the Hoifa (1607), and the Ula (1613). Only the Yehe temporarily kept him at bay.

This expansion was marked by a change of capitals, to Hetu Ala in 1603, and reorganization of his newly acquired kingdom. Blacksmiths were put to work making arms and a granary was established to provide Nurhachi more economic autonomy. He continued his strategy of raiding for Chinese captives in order to expand the amount of farmland in production. To finance his endeavors, Nurhachi did not rely on direct taxation, rather he followed an old tribal custom whereby each village was responsible for supporting ten families who produced for the government. Tribal groups, conquered or surrendered, were incorporated into the kingdom along kinship lines. They were organized into company units, known as "arrows," which followed local population divisions. Early records show that these arrows averaged only 150 families in Nurhachi's time, some containing as few as 100 families. Thus, the amount of change at the local level was minimal and well adapted to existing tribal and military units. Of the 400 arrow companies which existed in 1614, 308 were Jurchen-Mongol, 76 pure Mongol, and 16 Chinese.[24]

Nurhachi's major innovation was at the upper levels of organization where he created a supratribal army organized into "banners." To create these banners, arrow units were combined into groups of about 50 to form regiments, with five regiments to the banner. The eight banner units that eventually resulted were the core of Jurchen political and military organization. Arrow units might remain under indigenous leaders but they were subordinate to the larger imperial structure. The banner system, while incorporating tribal groups, superseded the older divisions and abolished previous lines of organization. As seen from the figures on arrow composition given above, the original eight Jurchen banners consisted of arrows with a surprisingly diverse ethnic composition and were never exclusively Jurchen. This lack of exclusivity helps explain the ease with which new allies were added by Nurhachi, and the difficulties facing scholars trying to determine the distinctions among different ethnic groups that were to make up the "Manchu" state under his successors.

At first, Nurhachi shared power with his brother, Shurhachi, and his oldest son, Chuyeng. This shared authority worked well when they ruled a few villages, but with the destruction of other Jurchen tribes Nurhachi became more protective of his senior position. Shurhachi was executed in 1611 after complaining about his brother's power. Two years later, while on campaign against the Ula and Yehe, Nurhachi entrusted the government to Chuyeng, but upon his return heard evidence that Chuyeng had plotted to seize power. Nurhachi arrested Chuyeng and had him executed in 1615.

Nurhachi consistently looked upon his immediate relatives as rivals for power, and it was the fear of rivals for the throne that appears to have stimulated the first great reorganization of the emerging Manchu state in 1615. It began when Nurhachi took the title of khan and declared himself sole leader of a new Chin dynasty. This put him at the head of a state, which was a major step beyond his previous claims as a tribal leader. At the same time, he doubled the number of banners to eight.

In 1601, at the beginning of his conquests, Nurhachi established four banners (the Yellow, Red, White, and Blue) and appointed his sons, Daishan, Manggultai, Hung Taiji (Abahai), and his nephew, Amin, to rule them. Nurhachi reduced their power in his 1615 reorganization by creating four new "bordered" banners and appointing four of his other sons to lead them. The original banner princes were thereafter recognized as the Senior *Beiles*, while the banner princes of the bordered banners became known as the Junior *Beiles*. The expansion created tension at the upper levels of government because the banner princes looked upon their troops as a personal estate. Therefore, to offset the power of the *beiles* as a group, Nurhachi chose five early supporters who were not blood relatives to become his closest advisors. They held the rank of *amban* and were further tied to Nurhachi by marriage alliances. This extrafamilial group wielded great power, even over Nurhachi's sons, the banner princes. They controlled access to Nurhachi's person and could exclude even the Senior *Beiles*. These *ambans* also acted as Nurhachi's agents within the individual banners.

From China's point of view, Nurhachi's proclamation of a Chin dynasty was his most important action. By traditional Chinese norms this was a ideological declaration of independence from Ming sovereignty and, after 1615, Nurhachi proved far more formidable to the Ming because they could no longer easily find allies among the Jurchen to oppose him. However, Nurhachi's choice of the Mongol title of khan showed that he was still firmly rooted in the world of tribal politics and did not see himself as a equal to the Ming emperor.

From a Jurchen point of view, the key events were structural rather than ideological. Nurhachi had rid himself of the vestiges of cooperative leadership and forced his relatives into subordinate positions. The steps he took were small but highly significant. Nurhachi and his successors were to be faced with the same problem throughout the dynasty's early history: the leader of the state could centralize power only by seizing it from his kinsmen who favored a weaker confederation with tribal autonomy.

The expansion of Nurhachi's kingdom brought economic problems in its wake. His original power base had been richly endowed with natural resources and he enlarged this base by engaging in trade with China. Raids for loot and captives had also increased his wealth. This approach to financing had two limitations. First, the productive land around Hetu Ala and the other villages controlled by the Jurchens was soon fully developed. After all available land was in production there was little value in capturing more people. Second, the Jurchen military structure was top heavy with under-productive soldiers and officials who were necessary for war but expensive to maintain in peace. As early as 1615, when the *beiles* wanted to fight the Mongols, Nurhachi had postponed action arguing, "We do not have enough food to feed ourselves. If we conquer them, how will we feed them?"[25]

Though militarily strong, the Jurchens' limited economic base often forced them to go on the offensive just to feed themselves. The Yehe were finally conquered in 1618, not because it was strategically advantageous, but because the Jurchens desperately needed to obtain their food. Nurhachi had to warn his Mongol allies not to seize any food as loot because it was necessary for his own winter survival. He later asked the Mongols to supply their own food on future campaigns. An attack on Ming frontier positions earlier that year had also been induced by economic problems induced by the Ming government's decision, in 1618, to respond to Jurchen raiding by cutting off trade. The Ming owed

Nurhachi a considerable amount of money for ginseng, so it was the Jurchens who were caught short. Since the dynasty also refused to recognize the stolen patents that had previously enriched Nurhachi's followers, he was forced for the first time to conquer the border city of Fu-shun in Liao-tung, located in Chinese territory, to recoup his losses.

In retrospect, these two conquests have been viewed as the beginning of a grand plan for Manchu expansion. In fact, both were moves made in desperation. They are evidence of a pattern that emerged in later campaigns in which the militarily powerful Jurchens were induced to attack, not because it was militarily advantageous, but because of their severe economic need. The great periods of Manchu expansion were largely the result of economic instability rather than strict military planning.

Although raiding along the frontier had become endemic, the Jurchen attack on Fu-shun was the first major conflict between Nurhachi and the Ming. The Ming responded by sending an expeditionary force of 80,000–90,000 troops to attack the Jurchens in 1619. Nurhachi defeated this force at Sar Hu and its destruction precipitated a string of surrenders by cities in Liao-tung so that by 1621 all areas of the peninsula east of the Liao River were in Jurchen hands. For the first time, Nurhachi was in control of a Ming provincial area and he had to accept the unfamiliar task of administering it. It was in this context that a dual form of governmental organization developed, not by plan but by a process of trial and error. The resulting structure resembled Mu-jung Hsien-pi or Khitan models of organization because those earlier Manchurian dynasties had faced similar problems and had found similar solutions when they moved to the Liao-tung region.

The conquest of Liao-tung did not meet with universal approval among the Jurchen nobility. Before 1619, Liao-tung was a frontier that was raided for slaves and loot. Since the banners were entitled to keep all the spoils they seized, they wanted a convenient place to raid. Although the incorporation of Liao-tung increased the size of the imperial Jurchen state, the territory now could not be raided and tax revenues went to the imperial government rather than to the banners. A second complaint concerned the non-tribal form of government employed by Nurhachi in Liao-tung. Traditionally, conquered subjects had been distributed among the banners as additional arrows, giving each banner increased manpower and each *beile* a stronger force. Nurhachi broke with this tradition by declaring that because Liao-tung was all Chinese, its residents would be treated as subjects of the state, with no relation to the tribal banners, and that Chinese administrators would be kept on to handle unfamiliar administrative tasks. This was a double blow to the *beiles*. They were denied the right to loot and acquire captives, which was a major source of wealth. Furthermore, the Chinese subjects and territory were to be under Nurhachi's control alone. By these means the Jurchen state created a form of dual organization in which non-Jurchen subjects were expected to be loyal to the Jurchen state, while not part of its tribal base.

Open opposition to the new policy surfaced when Nurhachi moved the capital south, out of tribal territory and into the Chinese Liao Basin. It was first transferred to Sar Hu, then to Liao-yang (Mukden), and Nurhachi demanded that the banners relocate themselves accordingly. His nephew Amin, Shurha-chi's son and one of the most troublesome *beiles*, defied Nurhachi by initially refusing to accept his assigned territory. Some of his sons schemed with sympathetic *ambans* to usurp the throne and return to the old ways. Nurhachi discovered the plots and acted quickly to maintain his authority. He executed some of his old advisors and, to reduce the power of the *beiles*, he took back many of the Chinese families he had assigned to them earlier. The banners' economic autonomy was reduced further in 1622, when Nurhachi declared that in the future any loot seized during raids would be distributed equally among all eight banners. This was designed to prevent any one banner from gaining too much power. To ensure compliance, *ambans* were ordered to oversee the distribution of goods personally and keep accurate records.

Nurhachi's policy toward his Chinese subjects initially followed the pattern he employed with the Jurchens. Although Chinese were not part of the banner system, Nurhachi needed their labor to increase his agricultural production. He attempted to entice farmers to emigrate from Ming-ruled Liao-hsi into Jurchen territory with promises of a better life: "If you go inside [China] your emperor being bad will not take care of you. If you go to Kuang-ning the Mongols will take you. Do they have grain or clothing? If you come to Liao-tung in the east I will give you land and treat you well. Come to Liao-tung."[26] This simple propaganda campaign failed both because conditions in Liao-tung were not really so good, and because the civil disorder in China had not yet generated enough of an incentive to leave. Previous large-scale defections to rulers of "barbarian" territories had occurred only when the Chinese government in power had completely collapsed. At those times foreign frontier states offered more safety from roving warlord armies and security from starvation. The state of affairs in Ming China had not yet come to such a crisis.

Nurhachi began his rule in Liao-tung expecting that the Liao-tung Chinese could be integrated into the Jurchen state, just as Jurchens, Mongols, and frontier Chinese had previously been absorbed. Indeed, after his troubles with the *beiles*, the Chinese must have appeared to Nurhachi as a useful counter-weight to tribal influence. But trouble broke out when Nurhachi ordered Jurchen and Chinese families along the border to live together within the same villages, a plan proposed by the Chinese in order to avoid deportation. While the Jurchens and Chinese were ordered to work the land together, the Jurchens treated the Chinese as servants rather than co-workers. The Liao-tung Chinese were quickly alienated by this attitude and, when the crops failed in 1623, they revolted. Although quickly suppressed, this rebellion badly frightened the Jurchens because the Chinese had employed the tactic of secretly poisoning their Jurchen neighbors. The poisonings convinced Nurhachi that his plans for assimilation were unworkable. He therefore instituted a policy of segregation designed to divide Jurchen and Chinese communities, establishing separate Jurchen villages and exclusive Jurchen quarters in cities. A letter sent to his banner officials outlining the new policy as it affected legal affairs gives a picture of Nurhachi's unvarnished style before it was retouched by later Ch'ing historians who, in Chinese accounts, sought to clean up his image as the founding ancestor of an important dynasty.

Let us make all our *beiles* and officials live happily. If I am now angry and spit in your faces, it is because your way of judging crimes is wrong. Why do you let Chinese in high positions be equal to you? If a Manchu has committed some crime, look to his merits. Ask what he has accomplished. If there is any little reason, use it as a pretext to pardon him. If a Chinese has committed some crime deserving of capital punishment, if he did not make an all-out effort as he should, or stole things, why not kill him and all his descendants and relatives instead of letting him get away with a beating? Judge the Chinese who have been with us since Fe Alan the same basis as the Jurchen. Once a sentence has been decided upon, you cannot change it again. It is like a mule that does not know how to go backwards. You eight *beiles* read this letter in secret to the *beiles* and officials of various banners. Do not let the people hear it. Do you not know that they [the Chinese] poisoned our women and children at Yao-chou after our troops left?[27]

The roots of the Manchu dual system of government, which separately administered Jurchens and Chinese, originated with their experiences in attempting to govern Liao-tung. The policy resulted from the failure of the old tribal model to work for administering the Chinese population in a Chinese province. Nurhachi had achieved the assimilation of small Jurchen and Mongol tribes as well as groups of frontier Chinese into his kingdom, but the large number of Chinese in Liao-tung and the danger of revolt made him keenly aware of the need for a new policy. The separation of the Jurchens and Chinese was not racially motivated, however, for the letter cited above reveals that the old frontier Chinese families who had been with the Jurchens since before the conquest of Liao-tung were considered equal to any Jurchen. Instead, it was a political strategy designed by a conquest minority concerned with maintaining its dominance over a much larger Chinese majority.

Under the new rules, Chinese and Mongols were forbidden to carry arms while Jurchens were obligated to. Separate quarters for Jurchens were established in towns. Chinese officials who had been granted offices to rule the Chinese population were demoted. This last measure infuriated many officials who had surrendered to the Jurchens with the understanding that they would retain their old ranks and duties. They had remained loyal in the 1623 revolt, which had been the work of the local Chinese peasants, but these new Jurchen restrictions prompted those Chinese officials to rebel in 1625. This revolt, like the first, was quickly suppressed by the Jurchens, who then removed many Chinese officials from office. The purge was tempered, however, by the Jurchens' need for Chinese experience in administration and Chinese labor for agriculture and war. When large numbers of Chinese fled following the 1625 rebellion, Nurhachi warned his commanders against wholesale killing. "If the Liao-tung people rebel and escape they are committing a crime. But why kill them? Take them as soldiers and let Chinese fight Chinese. It will be to the benefit of the Jurchen."[28] The Jurchens were learning the art of government, but slowly.

THE EARLY CH'ING STATE

Nurhachi died in 1626, following an unsuccessful attack on Liao-hsi during which Ming forces had employed cannons against the Jurchens. He left his small border kingdom still largely unorganized, baffled by the problems of a state grown too difficult to manage. He had been a brilliant manipulator of tribal politics to create the banner system and then clever enough to centralize power in order to maintain his control over it. However, his world view remained local rather than imperial. Even after declaring himself khan he was unable to separate the interests of the Jurchen state from the interests of the Jurchen tribes, except when his personal power was threatened. Hence, he was only marginally successful in organizing his Chinese conquests and keeping the banners in line. Although Nurhachi had moved to centralize his own power against all rivals, he was still firmly rooted to an ideal of shared tribal rule, for in his will he called for a cooperative confederation administered by a council with rotating leadership. Ironically, this recommendation displayed a nostalgia for the form of Manchurian clan government which Nurhachi had so violently rejected in his own lifetime. It was left to his successor, Hung Taiji, to see a greater potential and turn his father's Jurchen tribal khanate into the "Manchu" state capable of dealing with China.

Nurhachi's death opened a power struggle which laid bare the contradictions of Jurchen political organization. Throughout his life Nurhachi never lost his tribal orientation. He attempted to control the Jurchen tribes by breaking up the older tribal units and reorganizing them. However, this was done out of a need to preserve his own power and was not part of a plan to create a permanent centralized government. In his will Nurhachi proposed that the government be run by a council of the eight *beiles*, each in command of a banner. They were to meet together and reach collective decisions, with each *beile* rotating in turn as council leader. This council had been in existence since 1621 but, with Nurhachi firmly holding the reins of power, it had been of minor importance. The devolution of power onto a tribal council was quite popular with many of the *beiles* because it would return the government to the old tribal ways and give each *beile* more power and autonomy. These men would have gladly abandoned any imperial designs for the Jurchens as a whole to protect their own positions, just as they had done five years earlier, when they had opposed Nurhachi's occupation of Liao-tung. The immediate prospect was for a division of the khanate's territory, so that each banner leader could become an independent ruler.

Hung Taiji, the youngest of the Senior *Beiles*, was opposed to this devolution of power and he quickly seized supreme authority, taking advantage of divisions among the *beiles*. Under the terms of Nurhachi's will, the three sons of Empress Hsiao-lieh – Dorgon, Dodo, and Ajige – were each to receive a banner. The Senior *Beiles* feared that if these brothers acted in concert with their mother, who remained dowager empress, they would dominate the government. This fear was intensified by the rumor that Nurhachi had named Dorgon his heir. In response, the Senior *Beiles* forced Hsiao-lieh to commit suicide and gave banners only to Dorgon and Dodo. Hung Taiji took the extra banner for himself, thus giving him control of both the Plain and Bordered Yellow banners. He then enlisted (or coerced) the aid of Daishan, the most senior *beile*, who was leader of the Plain Red Banner, and Daishan's son Yoto, who led the Bordered Red Banner, to nominate him as khan. The eldest of Hsiao-lieh's sons, Ajige, was excluded from the competition for leadership because he had been denied a banner, while both Dodo and Daishan were too young to make effective use of their banners. This isolated Amin, Hung Taiji's cousin, who was willing to accept Hung Taiji as ruler only in exchange for the independence of his own Bordered Blue Banner. Unlike his father Nurhachi, Hung Taiji had a vision of imperial rule which he made clear in a letter rejecting Amin's plan to secede: "If I let him [Amin] go outside, then also the two red, the two white, and the Plain Blue Banner could all go across the border and live outside. Then I am without a country and whose emperor would I be? If I follow this suggestion the empire will fall apart."[29] Hung Taiji's election as khan was only the first step in the creation of a true imperial government in which the tribes were completely subordinate to the dynasty. His centralization of power rested on three policies: the removal of the other Senior *Beiles*, the increase in numbers and authority of a Chinese bureaucracy, and the reduction of banner autonomy.

If the Senior *Beiles* had acted in concert, they could have removed Hung Taiji from leadership. To prevent this, Hung Taiji rapidly purged the Senior *Beiles* from their banners after ending the policy of rotating council leadership in 1629. His first victim was Amin, Shurhachi's son. Amin had always proved the most insubordinate *beile* even in Nurhachi's time and as a cousin he commanded little support among Nurhachi's sons. After a particularly poor campaign against China in 1630, Hung Taiji took control of Amin's banner, a move which made him leader of three of the eight Jurchen banners. The next year he moved against his half-brother Manggultai, who was arrested and demoted, dying in prison two years later. Manggultai was posthumously charged with treason, which led to the arrest and execution of his family. The last of the Senior *Beiles*, Daishan, saved his own skin by suggesting that in the future Hung Taiji should be given precedence above everyone else. However, even Daishan did not entirely escape Hung Taiji's purge. He was charged with insubordination, but was pardoned. After this the Senior *Beiles* were either dead or thoroughly intimidated. When Hung Taiji formally declared himself emperor in 1636, there was no longer overt opposition to his rule among the tribal elite.

Hung Taiji did more than remove his opponents, however, he also altered the structure of government to permanently reduce the political influence of tribal leaders. To accomplish this, he turned to a growing group of Chinese officials who owed their loyalty to a new Manchu state and its leader, not to the *beiles*. They could prosper only if the Jurchen government became less tribal, with a more centralized bureaucracy. They were better versed in the mechanics of statecraft than their tribal rivals, and favored a model of government in which power was vested in an imperial leader. Hung Taiji realized that the Chinese could provide an important counterweight to the tribal banner officials and so increased both their governmental and military power. A Chinese banner was created in 1630, a second in 1637, four by 1639, and eight by 1642. Following the Manchu conquest of Inner Mongolia, Mongol banners were also organized. This had a profound impact on the importance of the original Jurchen banners, which were still tied to individual *beiles*. The new banners were attached directly to the imperial government and their leaders lacked the autonomy of Jurchen banner officials. Thus, they were tools of the government that could be used to keep Jurchen *beiles* in line.

The official declaration of the Ch'ing dynasty in 1636 marked both the greater ambition and organization of Hung Taiji's government. A year earlier he had proscribed the use of the terms "Jurchen" and "Chin" [dynasty]. Both appellations, he felt, harked back to the period of a small tribal people and a small dynasty. The "Great Ch'ing" dynasty of the newly renamed "Manchu" people aimed at a higher goal. Preparation for this change had begun in 1629 with the establishment of a Chinese-style Chancellery, the same year that rotation of *beiles* ended. New Chinese staff positions opened in 1631 when the Six Boards were instituted. Upon declaring his new dynasty, Hung Taiji created a Censorate to oversee the Six Boards and the *beiles*. Three courts were also created to handle records, personnel, and form a secretariat.

All of these administrative changes put power more directly into the hands of the emperor at the expense of the *beiles* and other Jurchen leaders. The Manchu banners were reduced to the role of vital supporters in a Manchu state of which they were a part, but which they no longer controlled. The dual organization that separated the Chinese population from the Manchus could also be employed by the emperor to exclude tribal leaders from independent sources of wealth, thus tying them to the court.

Hung Taiji's Chinese officials helped reduce the power of the banners by proposing reforms that centralized both political and economic power in the emperor's hands. In one proposal they aimed at the heart of banner autonomy: loot seized in border campaigns should no longer be divided equally among the banners, rather it should all be given directly to the khan to be distributed as he saw fit. Ironically Nurhachi had originally insisted on equal divisions among the eight Manchu banners to prevent the growth of any one, but now, a generation later, Hung Taiji moved to change this policy to make the banners more dependent on the throne and reduce banner autonomy. Hung Taiji's reliance on Chinese officials and Chinese-style institutions proved extremely useful in this process, but it is doubtful that much sinicization of the Manchu court took place at this time. For example while Chinese memorials occasionally waxed philosophical on the virtues of autocracy, they generally simplified the message for their tribal patron, warning, as one official put it, that "if ten sheep have nine shepherds . . . I feel that in a few years there will definitely be disorder and disunity and one cannot rule."[30]

Hung Taiji's wars were a reflection, on a larger scale, of Nurhachi's policy of funding the Manchu state and military by raiding and acquiring captives. The Ming defenses in the northeast, particularly at the strategic pass of Shan-hai-kuan, proved immovable. In order to raid China, the Manchus needed the cooperation of the Mongols from whose territory successful attacks could be mounted. Foreign relations were therefore critical to the success of the Manchu state. Hung Taiji's problem was that the Manchu army and government grew at a faster rate than did the available resources. Added to this burden was the perennial shortage of food necessary to buy the support of neighboring Mongol tribes. Manchu territories suffered famines in 1627–8 and 1635–6. Silver, which had been plentiful in Nurhachi's time, became scarce and members of the Manchu administration received bondservants in place of a regular salary. Thus, Manchu military strategy and timing was determined primarily by the need to acquire fresh resources, and not by a master plan to conquer and incorporate new territory. Short-term gains required to finance the Manchu state kept Hung Taiji lurching from one campaign to the next, in hopes that the Ming dynasty would collapse before the Ch'ing did.

Hung Taiji's first diplomatic effort after taking power was aimed at acquiring money. In 1627 he tried to negotiate a peace with the Ming in return for gold and silver. The Ming government, which had defeated the Manchus a year earlier, refused to consider the proposal. While the Ming had lost isolated Liao-tung, its defenses in the northeast were substantial. The Manchu's inability to overrun Ming frontier fortifications, compared with earlier Mongol successes, implies that Manchu forces were not exceptionally strong. Rejected by China, Hung Taiji invaded Korea. The King of Korea agreed to supply the Manchus with silver and cloth, enabling Hung Taiji to renew attacks on the Ming frontier later that year, but again he was repulsed.

Because direct assaults on Ming defenses in Liao-hsi had proved so unsuccessful, in 1629 Hung Taiji sought aid from his Mongol allies in order to use their territory as a base to attack China. This was the first of many invasions through Mongol territory and highlights the Mongols' strategic importance. As early as 1619, the Nurhachi had signed a treaty with the five Khalkha tribes of Inner Mongolia to create an offensive alliance against the Ming. Ten years later Hung Taiji signed a similar agreement with the Kharachin Mongols.[31] These treaties were critical for two reasons: the Manchus needed Mongol territory as a base from which to mount raids on China: and the Mongols were a threat to Manchu expansion. The Mongols flanked the Manchus and could attack them directly, or simply aid the Chinese by denying the Manchus horses and transit rights. Fortunately for Manchu interests, the Mongols were divided and the Ming court was too conservative to play tribal politics.

A Sino-Mongol alliance had been a real threat when Lighdan Khan (r. 1604–36) attempted to unify all the Mongol tribes under his banner beginning in the 1620s. Lighdan Khan was the leader of the Chahar Mongols, the grandson of Tümen Khaghan, and represented the most senior Chinggisid line in Mongolia. However, since the time of Altan Khan, the position of khaghan had lost its authority. Lighdan Khan attempted to reclaim the power of his ancestors by force to create a new steppe empire. This put him in opposition to the majority of Mongol tribal leaders who were satisfied with their political positions as beneficiaries of the Ming tributary system. The Chahars were the only major Mongol tribe to have refused to join the tributary system and had no vested interest in preserving it. The other steppe leaders viewed the Chahars as a threat to the status quo and actively resisted any movement toward Mongol unity, some tribes cooperating with the Manchus in opposition to Lighdan Khan.

Although the Chahars had been hostile to China, the Ming recognized the advantage of cultivating their friendship as a counterweight to the Manchus. After the fall of Liao-tung in 1618, the Ming actually concluded an alliance with Lighdan Khan. Such alliances with steppe nomads had preserved the Han and T'ang dynasties against rebels and frontier threats, but the Ming failed to exploit the possibilities inherent in aiding Lighdan Khan. For example, in 1621, Wang Hsieng-chien, an old frontier official, proposed that the Ming provide an annual payment of a million taels a year to create a Mongol buffer state outside Shan-hai-kuan, but this policy was rejected in favor of the reconquest of the region (though the Ming did continue to give subsidies to the Chahars). Lighdan depended on these subsidies from China to finance his bid for power, and, when they were cut off in 1628, the Chahars halted their wars on the steppe and resumed raiding China. Within a year Lighdan had lost control of the steppe, so that in 1629 the Manchus were able to use Mongol territory as a base for a large raid on China conducted with the aid of the Tümed and Kharachin. The Ming's short-sighted frontier policy had removed the only power capable of containing the Manchus.

The Manchus exploited the divisions among the Mongols by organizing an offensive alliance against the Chahars. In 1632, they caught the Chahars by surprise and routed them, forcing Lighdan to flee westward with his people. Two years later the Manchus again attacked the Chahars and defeated them. Lighdan Khan died of smallpox the next year (1635) and, with his death, the last resistance to the Manchus in southern Mongolia crumbled. All the Mongols along the frontier, from Manchuria to Kansu, were incorporated into the banner system. With their western flank now clear of opposition, and Hung Taiji firmly installed as emperor, the Manchus were free to concentrate on Ming China and to strike anywhere along the frontier.

Mongol unity had always been potentially fatal to Manchu plans. If a Mongol leader had created an organized force then the Manchus, hemmed in from the west and the south, would have fallen prey to an invasion or simply collapsed because they would have had no place to raid. Hung Taiji's Mongolian policy was therefore as important as any of his dealings with Ming China. This partly explains Manchu insolvency and the need to raid. Manchu territories might have supported the local population, but they could not supply the needs of the Mongol allies as well. Similarly, booty from China and silver from Korea was needed to pay for the expensive gifts which were offered to gain Mongol cooperation. The Manchus shouldered this burden both to prevent the Mongols from uniting under Lighdan and to preempt the Ming from turning the passive tributary agreements into an offensive alliance. The Manchus aided the Mongols even at the expense of their own subjects. Grain, always in short supply, went first to allied Mongol tribes in the west who provided the Manchus with horses and who agreed (for a price) to stop doing business with China. One document written soon after their alliance with the Mongols complained that: "Now [1633] the Manchu officials have completely sold all the grain to buy horses. Therefore there is nothing to eat and everyone has been suffering for several years."[32]

While the incorporation of the Mongols gave the Manchus greater military strength and a superior strategic position, they still proved unable to force the key Ming defenses at Shan-hai-kuan. Almost yearly invasions of China became routine, but these were for loot and not conquest. Korea was invaded again in 1638 to increase the amount of tribute it supplied and to provide grain to Manchuria. Expeditions to the north brought the wild and ill-organized tribes of the Manchurian forests under control. Yet these were all holding operations. Like other "vulture" dynasties, the Ch'ing strategy was to keep itself strong and well organized in order to take advantage of political turmoil in China. Their chance came in 1644, a year after Hung Taiji's death, with the sudden demise of the Ming dynasty and the consequent collapse of its frontier defense.

NOTES

1 The Chinese historical material about the steppe for this period is recorded in the *Ming Shih* (MS) chapters devoted to the nomads, particularly chapter 327 on the Mongols (Ta-tan) and chapter 328 on the Oirats (Wa-la). There are also Mongol chronicles for the post-Yüan era, notably the *Erdeni-yin tobchi* by Saghang-sechen (cf. Schmidt translation) and the *Altan-tobchi* by an unknown author (cf. Bawden translation). The historical account in this chapter is drawn largely from Pokotilov (*History of the Eastern Mongols During the Ming Dynasty*) with revisions by W. Franke in the same volume, and the extensive writings of Serruys, particularly 1959, 1967, 1975. Biographies of most of the nomad leaders and Ming frontier officials can be found in the *Dictionary of Ming Biography 1368–1644* (Goodrich and Fang, 1976).

2 Serruys, *The Mongols in China During the Hung-wu Period.*

3 The succession of these khans is too complex too deal with in a summary manner, Pelliot (*Notes critiques d'histoire kalmouke,* 2 vols) provides the most complete listing.

4 Serruys, *Mongols,* Appendix 3, pp. 286–93.

5 Dreyer, *Early Ming China,* pp. 65–172. Unlike most previous dynasties in China, Ming (and succeeding Ch'ing) emperors had only one "era name" by which they are generally known in most histories. Although technically a title, i.e. "The Yung-lo Emperor," because of their widespread use I have employed them as equivalent to personal names for ease of reference.

6 Farmer, *Early Ming Government – The Evolution of the Dual Capitals,* pp. 134–88.

7 Cf. Franke, "Yung-lo's Mongolei-Feldzüge."

8 Farquhar, "Oirat–Chinese tribute relations, 1408–1459," pp. 60–8.

9 Mote, "The T'u-mu incident," pp. 243–72.

10 MS 327:10b–11a; Pokotilov, *History of the Eastern Mongols,* pp. 70–1.

11 Wada, "A study of Dayan Khan"; Okada, "The life of Dayan Qaghan."

12 MS 173:18b; Pokotilov, *History of the Eastern Mongols,* pp. 85–6.

13 Goodrich and Fang, *Dictionary of Ming Biography,* pp. 17–20.

14 Serruys, *The Tribute System and the Diplomatic Missions (1400–1600),* pp. 64–93.

15 Ibid., p. 104.

16 Ibid., pp. 308–13.

17 MS 327:30a–b; Pokotilov, *History of the Eastern Mongols,* pp. 144–5.

18 Serruys, *Tribute System,* p. 68 n. 11.

19 Ibid., pp. 59–61.

20 Chan, *The Glory and Fall of the Ming Dynasty*, p. 197.
21 Michael (*Origin of Manchu Rule in China*) stresses the Ming precedents for Manchu organization, but the evidence that it followed the course of previous foreign dynasties is much stronger. In addition, the *wei-so* organization employed by the Ming was borrowed from the Yüan, cf. Farquhar "The origins of the Manchus' Mongolian Policy."
22 The Chinese records for this period make Nurhachi's rise to power and the creation of the Ch'ing state by Hung Taiji seem fairly smooth, but the original Manchu documents tell a much more revealing story of hardship and internal conflict. Gertraude Roth Li in her *The Rise of the Manchu State: A Portrait Drawn from Manchu Sources to 1636* provides the data from which this description is drawn. This work deserves to be more widely known, but many of its conclusions may be found in Roth, "The Manchu–Chinese relationship, 1618–1636" and "The rise of the Manchus" co-authored with Joseph Fletcher, in the *Cambridge History of China*, vol. 9, part 1 (forthcoming).
23 Li, *Rise of the Manchu State*, p. 15.
24 Ibid., p. 29.
25 Ibid., p. 34.
26 Ibid., pp. 38–9.
27 Roth, "The Manchu–Chinese relationship," p. 19.
28 Li, *Rise of the Manchu State*, pp. 111–12.
29 Ibid., p. 120.
30 Roth, "The Manchu–Chinese relationship," pp. 21–2.
31 Farquhar, "The origins of the Manchus' Mongolian policy."
32 Li, *Rise of the Manchu State*, pp. 171–2.

GLOSSARY OF KEY NAMES

MAIN TRIBES ON THE STEPPE FRONTIER

EASTERN MONGOLS
  Mongol tribes of northern and southern Mongolia
  represented Chinggisid line of descent
  Chahar and Tümed main sub-units
OIRATS (Western Mongols)
  Mongol tribes of Altai and Tien-shan region
  represented non-Chinggisid line of descent
URIYANGKHAI
  nomadic tribes along China's northeastern border
  composed of the Döen, Fu-yü, and T'ai-ning
JURCHEN
  forest tribes of northern Manchuria
  unify in early seventeenth century under Nurhachi

KEY TRIBAL FIGURES

ALTAN KHAN
  Tümed Mongol leader for forty years (1507–82)
  grandson of Dayan Khan
  established tributary relationship with Ming court
ARUGHTAI
  leader of the Eastern Mongols in early Ming period
  killed by the Oirats in 1434
DAYAN KHAN
  Eastern Mongol leader (r. 1488–1533)
  re-established Chinggisid authority in Mongolia
ESEN
  leader of the Oirats (r. 1439–55)
  united Mongolia, captured Ming emperor
HUNG TAIJI (Abahai)
  successor to Nurhachi (r. 1626–43)
  reorganized state structure and declared "Great Ch'ing" dynasty
  changed Jurchen name to Manchu
LIGHDAN KHAN
  leader of the Chahar Mongols (r. 1604–36)
  represented the most senior Chinggisid line in Mongolia
  failed to unify Mongols in opposition to Manchus
NURHACHI
  Jurchen tribal unifier (1559–1626)
  founding ancestor of Ch'ing dynasty

CHINESE DYNASTY

Ming (1368–1644)

KEY CHINESE FIGURES

HUNG-WU EMPEROR
  first Ming Emperor (r. 1368–98)
  expelled Mongols from China
YUNG-LO EMPEROR
  second Ming emperor (r. 1402–24)
  fought successful steppe campaigns against the Mongols
  moved capital to Peking

8

The Last of the Nomad Empires

The Ch'ing Incorporation of Mongolia and Zungharia

THE MANCHU CONQUEST OF CHINA

Ming China faced more problems than just Manchus and Mongols snapping at the frontier. Poor administration and increasingly higher taxes to finance government operations strained its internal resources. The most serious consequences were peasant rebellions, which broke out in the northwest following famines in the 1620s. Military campaigns were mounted against bandit armies there, and warfare soon caused as much damage to the region's economy as had the previous natural disasters. The northwest became a festering source of rebellion that imperial armies could contain but not eliminate. Li Tzu-ch'eng, known as One-eyed Li, became the leader of one of the most powerful of these rebel armies. He had established his base in Hunan in 1641 and his forces grew so quickly that the next year he scored a great victory by capturing the ancient capital city of K'ai-feng. His tactics were crude but effective: he diverted the Yellow River from its dykes to flood the city's defenders, killing hundreds of thousands of people and devastating the region. From there he marched north, surrounding or seizing all the strategic territory vital to the defense of the capital. The walled fortresses and border garrisons on the frontier were of no use against rebels from the south. The Ming emperor realized the capital would soon fall and, dispirited by the loss of his empire, committed suicide. Li Tzu-ch'eng entered Peking as the leader of the newly proclaimed Shun dynasty.[1]

Li's rule was short. The Shun administrative machinery consisted of little more than Li, his advisors, and military officers – none of whom had been responsible for administration during the fast-moving military campaigns. The rebel army was undisciplined and after a few weeks of calm they took to looting and killing the city's inhabitants. Li also faced a threat from the Ming frontier army at Shan-hai-kuan under the leadership of Wu San-kuei. Wu had been unable to dispatch his troops to Peking before the city fell, but his army was still intact. Li tried to induce a quick capitulation by offering money and later threatening the safety of Wu San-kuei's family. Neither ploy worked, so the Shun troops positioned themselves for an assault on Wu's garrison. Wu then struck a deal with the Manchus, joining them with his troops in exchange for a princely rank in the Ch'ing government. The Manchu army marched quickly through Shan-hai-kuan and arrived in time to aid Wu in a pitched battle with Li's troops. The Shun army fled, deserting Li, who was forced to abandon Peking. The Manchus entered the city on June 1, 1644, and declared the foundation of the Ch'ing dynasty. Disciplined Ch'ing troops restored order in the city. Many Chinese army units were reorganized and, with the aid of the banner troops, set to work conquering the rest of China in the name of the new dynasty. Although some Ming loyalists held out in the south, the Ch'ing conquest moved with remarkable rapidity and by 1652 all but the most southern parts of China were in Ch'ing hands. By 1660, all China was theirs, with Ming diehards holding only Formosa, although a number of southern areas were semi-autonomous dependencies in the hand of Chinese defectors like Wu San-kuei.

The Manchu conquest of China typifies the vulture strategy and demonstrates that Manchu strength was more organizational than military. Throughout Hung Taiji's reign the Manchus freely attacked China, but they had proved unable to hold cities outside of Liao-tung or to destroy the Ming forces guarding the capital. Li Tzu-ch'eng, by contrast, conquered whole provinces, seized key cities and fortresses, and easily defeated Ming armies in the field. It was he, and not the Manchus, who toppled the Ming dynasty. However, like many warlords who arose when the central government in China collapsed, Li had devoted his efforts almost exclusively to military affairs. When the Ming fell, the new Shun ruler was unable to restore order, the most basic task of government. The Manchus did not suffer from this fault. The struggle by Nurhachi, and more particularly by Hung Taiji, to subordinate the interests of the tribal military to an imperial state with a bureaucratic structure had left the Manchus with a more balanced organization. They had an organized military that obeyed orders, and a small but well-developed bureaucracy ready to administer Chinese territory. After Li Tzu-ch'eng had done the dirty work by actually destroying the Ming dynasty, the Manchus were able to rout him not because they had superior fighting ability, but because they were better organized. Their alliance with Wu San-kuei provided them with a corps of trained Chinese troops without whose aid they would not have been able to take the capital. After their first major defeat, the Shun army and leadership crumbled. It was an army easily led in victory but inexperienced at reorganizing after defeat.[2]

The Manchu conquest of Peking was immediately preceded by a dynastic succession problem, as Hung Taiji had died in 1643 without naming an heir. The Manchus had no regular policy of automatic succession and they fell back on a variety of conflicting customs that could justify support for a number of candidates. One was the Manchu tradition of selecting the ablest member of the imperial family by vote of a council. In his will Nurhachi had ordered such a council to be held after his death. This was not an open forum of debate, but the locus of a power struggle between well-known rivals where factions pushed their candidates.

Dorgon (1612–50) was the strongest contender. He was Nurhachi's four-teenth son, a forceful personality, and a great military leader. During the previous succession struggle he and his brothers (the sons of Empress Hsiao-lieh) had been victims of Hung Taiji's consolidation of power, but during his reign Dorgon had grown to become a powerful figure in the Manchu state. Hung Taiji's eldest son, Haoge, was the other major contender. His case rested on the fact that his father had been ruler and, as the eldest son, the throne should fall to him. Here again the problem that plagued so many Manchurian and steppe dynasties – rival claims of lateral versus lineal succession – split the Manchu elite. Both the Hsien-pi Mu-jung and the Khitans, as well as the Turks, had strong lateral traditions in which power rightfully moved from elder brother to younger brother until a generation was exhausted. The large number of Nurhachi's able sons made lateral succession an attractive possibility. This proposal was, of course, opposed by Haoge's supporters who declared that custom demanded that succession go to a son of the last ruler. In this thinking they were supported by Chinese officials who recognized only lineal succession as appropriate. Acceptance of this reasoning also implied an exclusive dynastic right that would give Hung Taiji and his descendants precedence over Nurhachi's other sons and their descendants. Hung Taiji's death, therefore, was of crucial political importance, for the course the Manchus followed laid down the rules for a dynasty that as yet had not established a firm tradition.

The struggle for succession was largely fought along Manchu banner lines. Although Hung Taiji had subordinated the banners to the imperial govern-ment, election to the throne was still a tribal affair. During an interregnum, banners became significant because each owed personal loyalty to its own leader. All the contenders for the throne, as well as other important political actors, controlled banners. In an extreme situation the number of banners which supported a contender determined his military potential to enforce his claim to rule. The meeting to choose Hung Taiji's successor, therefore, was potentially a prelude to civil war at a time when the Manchus most needed unity.

The conference was deadlocked from the start because Dorgon and Hoage controlled an approximately equal numbers of banners. A compromise was worked out by the other banner leaders by which a five-year-old son of Hung Taiji, Fu-lin, was named emperor, with Dorgon as regent and Jirgaleng (Amin's brother) as co-regent. To further assuage Dorgon, he was given a second banner that had been one of Hung Taiji's. In effect, Dorgon assumed command of the Manchu state in all but name. He personally controlled two banners, the same number as did the emperor. Hoage's faction won the battle restricting the succession to Hung Taiji's sons, but the settlement cost Hoage the throne. The Manchu elite was willing to make such a compromise in order to avoid a civil war and take advantage of the deteriorating situation in China. With these disputes at least temporarily resolved, Dorgon marched on Peking and sat Fu-lin on the throne as the Shun-chih Emperor.

While directing the war of conquest against the rest of China, Dorgon continued Hung Taiji's policy of centralization within the Manchu state by purging the vestiges of collegial rule favored by tribal leaders and by expanding the scope of the Chinese bureaucracy. Dorgon moved first against the weakest banner leader, his co-regent Jirgaleng. Like his brother Amin, Jirgaleng's kinship ties were the most distant from the other *beiles* and, in late 1644, Dorgon reduced him to assistant regent and then discharged him in 1647. Upon the death of his brother Dodo, whom he had appointed to replace Jirgaleng, Dorgon became sole regent and inherited direct control of a third banner. Dorgon arrested Hoage in 1648 and, like most arrested rivals to Manchu rulers, he died a year later. Dorgon was ruler in all but name and his power was clearly demonstrated by the distribution of conquered territory around Peking. He awarded his own White Banners the best land, although this meant ignoring the traditional order of precedence which gave primacy to the emperor's own Yellow Banners.

Like Hung Taiji, Dorgon increased the centralization of power at court, both to rule China and to be a counterweight to the banners. He retained most of the institutional practices of the Ming, even keeping minor bureaucrats of the old dynasty in office under the control of Ch'ing officials – mostly banner Chinese – in the provinces as well as at court. This policy, ironically, was attacked by both Chinese officials and Manchu bannermen. The Chinese protested that the Manchus monopolized the real power. The Manchu bannermen complained that Dorgon favored the Chinese.

The interests of the Manchu bannermen and the Ch'ing state were at odds from the beginning. The Manchu tribal elite looked for short-term gains and opposed all policies that reduced their autonomy, even though such policies had proved necessary for the empire to grow. It was they who had opposed Nurhachi's conquest of Liao-tung and his transfer of the capital south. It was they who had resisted Hung Taiji's creation of a Chinese-staffed bureaucracy and his addition of non-Manchu banners to the Ch'ing army. Every ruler, including Nurhachi, attempted to insulate the imperial government from tribal pressure. Dorgon's adoption of Ming institutions and officials was a logical progression along these lines. The tribal elite saw the Ch'ing government as a tool for the extension of their domination over China. The imperial leadership rejected this view and attempted to reduce the Manchu banners to tools of the dynasty. This distinction meant that the imperial government saw banner Chinese as loyal officials vital to the Ch'ing government. Indeed, to the Chinese population at large, these banner Chinese were Manchus and called such. To tribal Manchus, banner Chinese were interlopers who stole the spoils of victory from the "real" tribal Manchus. This is exactly what the Ch'ing government intended.

The Ch'ing dynasty sprang from the Manchus but it was determined to break the grip of the bannermen that limited imperial power. Adding Chinese officials as a counterweight to the tribal Manchus was their way of doing this. The adoption of so many Chinese institutions after the fall of Peking has sometimes been interpreted as the rapid sinicization of the Ch'ing dynasty. While much debate within the court centered in how much Chinese-style government could be adopted without weakening the Manchus, the partisans in this debate were less concerned with form than with power. Tribal customs favored the old Manchu elite and would preserve their importance in the new regime. Chinese institutions were designed to preserve an imperial autocracy that held no place for power-sharing, and their adoption freed the court from tribal control. The court leadership permanently severed itself from the aspirations of its tribal followers and strove to become an imperial dynasty, determined to rule both China and the Manchus.

The theme of autonomy versus centralization was most visible during succession crises, when members of the imperial elite were forced to seek support of the banners. However, once a leader was installed, he inevitably took up where his predecessor had left off, each time leaving the banners with less power. Nowhere was this more true than in the continuation of centralization following Dorgon's sudden death in 1650.

Dorgon's death opened a new struggle for power, for he had left no heir and his faction proved unable to hold power without him. Jirgaleng was initially named regent, but in 1653 he lost that post to a faction supporting the young Shun-chih Emperor's right to rule alone. Shun-chih's accession to power marked a major structural change in dynastic politics. Previous Manchu leaders had all been men of great experience, both in tribal affairs and warfare, who could legitimately claim to have fought their way to the top. They owed their positions as much to talent as to birth, fulfilling the requirements of the Manchurian tradition that the most talented leader of each generation should be chosen to rule. Shun-chih was the first Manchu ruler whose power was purely institutional. Chosen as the compromise candidate at Hung Taiji's death, Shun-chih was then a child with no demonstrated experience or proven ability, and Dorgon had been the real power behind the throne. When Shun-chih began to rule in his own name, the Ch'ing dynasty left behind its tribal tradition for a more complex government in which the emperor's authority derived almost exclusively from his office. The conquest elite was confronted by a Manchu emperor who held and maintained power by manipulating the forces of his office and the bureaucratic structure of the government.

In the eyes of the conquest elite Shun-chih's policies were notoriously pro-Chinese. He favored Chinese advisors and institutions and employed eunuchs. To many these actions appeared the work of a sinophile who had lost touch with his Manchu roots. Indeed, Shun-chih had little interest in such Manchu pastimes as hunting, riding, or archery. He was more interested in religion and his pleasure palaces. But he followed the route of his predecessors in attempting to force the Manchu conquest elite to abandon its autonomous power and make them subservient to the throne. The use of Ming administrative practices and Chinese officials was the easiest means to this end. Because he ruled by virtue of his imperial position, the autocratic structure of the Ming government had an obvious appeal.

Shun-chih's use of palace eunuchs in government is an example of this process. Upon the capture of Peking the Ch'ing had inherited a large number of eunuchs who had served the old dynasty. During late Ming times, many of these eunuchs had accumulated great power and wealth by acting as the emperor's secret police and personal aides. The Manchus (and many Chinese for that matter) blamed the fall of the Ming in part to their excesses. Dorgon had severely restricted the employment of eunuchs in the palace during his regency. After taking power in 1653, Shun-chih reversed that policy, creating a personal staff known as the Thirteen Offices, which was composed largely of eunuchs. This institution was designed to insulate the emperor from pressure by both the tribal banners and the regular bureaucracy. Shun-chih was harshly criticized after his death for reintroducing a corrupt Ming institution. Nevertheless, such an institution, purged of eunuchs, was to become one of the hallmarks of Ch'ing imperial rule because it was a very useful structural device for a palace-bound leader.

Shun-chih did not forget that in order to run a dual organization he could not solely rely on Chinese support. Even as he added more Chinese institutions to the court in order to centralize power, he defended the privileges of the Manchus. When the Chinese officials complained bitterly about harsh fugitive slave laws designed to ensure the return of escaped bondservants and proposed that these laws be eased in 1656, the "sinophile" emperor berated them. He claimed that the Chinese knew nothing of Manchu problems nor their duties in warfare that had entitled them to bondservants.

Therefore we have no choice but to establish very severe laws. This may work a hardship on the Chinese, but if we do not crack down, the concealers will become more brazen and the fugitives will multiply. Then who will be our servants? How will we survive? Is there no concern for Manchu hardship? Emperors of previous dynasties generally ruled only the Chinese, but I rule both Manchus and Chinese and must ensure that each group gets its due.[3]

"Decadent Chinese ways" was a popular gloss by which tribal Manchus could attack any policy of centralization that deprived them of their autonomy; and the sinocentric aspects of Shun-chih's reign were exaggerated by his opponents after his death in 1661. This became evident during the period known as the Oboi Regency (1661–9), when the banner elite made a last desperate effort to preserve and increase its role in the Ch'ing government under the guise of returning to traditional Manchu customs.

When Shun-chih died, the old empress dowager and her Manchu banner supporters published a forged will in which the emperor supposedly denounced his own policies as ill-conceived and dangerous to Manchu interests. A seven-year-old son (whose major virtue at the time was that he had survived smallpox) was named the K'ang-hsi Emperor and placed on the throne. The government was left in the hands of the empress dowager and four Manchu regents. Of these last, Oboi displayed the greatest ambition and skill. He quickly became the leading figure in the regency and soon was a virtual dictator, holding a position similar to Dorgon's a generation earlier. The regents represented a new generation of Manchu leadership. All had shown ability as junior commanders in the struggle to conquer China, but they had not been major figures. Deeply involved in banner politics, none of the regents was a member of the imperial clan, and it was this class of Manchus that suffered most directly from Dorgon's and Shun-chih's centralization policies. Under the guise of returning the government to Manchu values, Oboi attempted to restructure it in order to provide the Manchu banner elite with a permanent and dominant role in running China.[4]

The regents' first change was to abolish the Thirteen Offices, on the grounds that eunuchs had no place in a Manchu government. However, the regents were forced to concede that the emperor did need a personal staff, so they reverted to the old Manchu practice of employing bondservants to run palace business. Originally these bondservants had done agricultural and household labor for the nobility, but as early as 1638 bondservant companies had grown in importance and become assistants to the emperor, members of an institution known as the Imperial Household. The regents reinstated their role as the emperor's staff, thereby replacing eunuchs, in the hope that bondservants would remain a source of Manchu tribal tradition in the court.

The regents then attacked the use of Ming bureaucratic structures. They abolished Chinese dominated institutions, like the Grand Secretariat and Hanlin Academy, along with the examination system as a means of recruitment. In their place they recreated the Three Inner Courts, first instituted by Hung Taiji, which were packed with Manchu appointments. (Ironically, in his own day Hung Taiji had introduced the Three Inner Courts as a means to weaken the banners. At that time Manchu banner leaders had viewed this court system as Chinese, but with the passing generations Hung Taiji's innovations were regarded as traditional Manchu ways.)

The regents also transferred considerable power to a Council of Deliberative Officials. Formerly this had been an elite Manchu council, but it had long been on the decline, in part because it had been filled with non-Manchus loyal to the emperor. Under Oboi it was purged of non-Manchus and regained its key role in handling military affairs in order to preserve a Manchu monopoly on warfare. Like the use of bondservants in the Imperial Household, the Council of Deliberative Officials was designed as a permanent powerbase for the Manchu elite. To stress the importance of their Mongol allies, the regents returned the Court of Colonial Affairs to the prominence it had lost under Shun-chih.

All of these practices were defended as a return to native Manchu values that would save the Ch'ing dynasty from creeping Chinese decadence. In reality, it was an attempt to reintroduce the Manchu collegial tradition into Ch'ing government. The attempt failed, both because it was too late to revert to this long dead tradition, and because Oboi destroyed himself by abusing his power in an effort to settle old scores with other banner leaders.

Oboi was preoccupied with setting right a wrong done to his Bordered Yellow Banner by Dorgon after the conquest of Peking more than twenty years earlier. When Dorgon distributed the districts around the capital to the Manchu banners, he reversed the order of preference so that his own Plain White Banner received better land than the emperor's own Bordered Yellow Banner. Once in power, Oboi demanded that the lands be exchanged, over the objections of officials who pointed out the great hardship this would create. The land transfer took place in early 1667 and involved the transplantation of around 60,000 bannermen and an even greater number of Chinese who worked for them. The whole affair alienated other powerful banner leaders and they threw their support behind an anti-Oboi faction which favored the abolition of the regency. It was just this petty use of power that had always weakened the Manchu banners in the face of imperial power. While the Manchu banner elite supported the ideal of tribal participation of government, in practice they could not cooperate with one another. The K'ang-hsi Emperor would exploit the divisions created among the banners to wipe out all the institutional changes that Oboi had made.

K'ang-hsi assumed personal rule in the wake of the acrimonious land exchange in August 1667. In spite of the official end of the regency, Oboi continued his virtual dictatorship, appointing his allies to positions throughout the government. However, throughout this period the emperor was gaining strength and, in 1669, he denounced and arrested Oboi, who died in prison. Oboi's faction was removed from office and many were executed. K'ang-hsi purged much of the banner elite from crucial government positions and they never again held an autonomous role in future disputes over succession. Nevertheless, the tenacity of banner leaders in tribal politics was hard to eliminate completely, because they were still attached as personal retainers to imperial princes, and in this role played a part in the next succession in 1723. Not until the reign of the Ch'ien-lung emperor was this last tribal link cut, making all bannermen personally subject to the emperor.

K'ang-hsi continued the shift toward centralization and ushered in a period where government was firmly in the hands of the emperor. He destroyed the power of the banner leaders, though he retained the structure of some of the institutions that Oboi left him. For example, the Imperial Household continued to serve as an extra-bureaucratic institution under the personal control of the emperor but, far from being a center of tribal Manchu influence at court, it became the major imperial institution keeping Manchus and Chinese alike under the emperor's control. The critical issue was not staffing by eunuchs or bondsmen, but function. The bondservants were as closely tied to the emperor as any Ming eunuchs and never acted as representatives of tribal interests. K'ang-hsi also restored the Grand Secretariat and the other Ming institutions adopted by Dorgon that served the personal interests of the emperor. The Council of Deliberative Officials, which Oboi had intended as a bulwark to preserve the power of the tribal elite in government, was purged of his supporters and then relegated to meeting on only minor matters.

K'ang-hsi won the long battle between the imperial government and the banner elite, but this victory masked another potentially lethal threat to the dynasty. This was the existence of powerful Chinese warlords in south China. These men had defected to the Manchu cause at the fall of the Ming dynasty. They and their Chinese troops had been vital to the success of the Ch'ing conquest in the south which, for the first time in Chinese history, had given a Manchurian dynasty control of the entire country. In return, these warlords had been granted Ch'ing titles and given command of the southern provinces they helped conquer. While they were theoretically under the authority of the Ch'ing emperor, they had command of their own troops, collected taxes for themselves, and handled local administration. They also received large subsidies from the Ch'ing treasury, even though they often acted at cross-purposes with imperial appointees in their region.[5]

The most powerful Chinese warlord was Wu San-kuei, the former commander of Shan-hai-kuan who had helped the Manchus capture Peking. Following the conquest of Yunnan in 1659, Wu became firmly entrenched there and ruled almost all of southwestern China. K'ang-hsi attempted to resolve the problem of these warlords by refusing to let them pass on their positions to their descendants, and by transferring them to less strategic areas. Wu San-kuei refused to relinquish power and revolted in 1674. He was joined by the other regional warlords in the south, setting off the San-fan Rebellion, otherwise known as the War of the Three Feudatories. This rebellion encompassed all south China from the southeast coast, west to Szechwan, and north into Shansi. The Manchu preoccupation with corruption from within as a danger to the dynasty had blinded them to the more compelling possibility of destruction by invasion from the south. The Ch'ing capital of Peking was thrown into panic. Some Manchus even suggested that China be abandoned for a more secure refuge in Manchuria. To the historically minded, the situation could be compared rather ominously to the advance of the northern Sung in the eleventh century, which had left the Manchurian Khitans with only a toehold in China, or to the Ming expulsion of the Mongol Yüan dynasty in the fourteenth century. Since the end of the T'ang period, the south had been the center of population and production in China; now it lay in rebel hands.

K'ang-hsi took firm action, quieting the capital and organizing resistance, securing his flanks and other key areas to prevent a rebel drive north. Initially he employed Manchu commanders and banner troops led by members of the imperial family. They failed miserably, tarnishing the image of Manchu invincibility and proving to the emperor that he could not rely on them alone to preserve the dynasty. K'ang-hsi then turned to his Green Standard Troops, composed and led by Chinese loyal to the throne. They got the better of the rebel armies and eventually turned the tide. By 1677, the rebels were confined to the mountainous southwest, but final victory was not won until 1681, after Wu San-kuei died.

The termination of this eight-year struggle finally put the Ch'ing dynasty in direct control of all China with no internal rivals. The failure of the Manchu military leadership and the effective use of Green Standard troops also marked the consolidation of the Ch'ing government. Neither banner leaders nor old Chinese allies could consider themselves exempt from K'ang-hsi's authority. The Manchu bannermen in particular could no longer claim to be the military backbone of the empire after failing in their duty to the dynasty. From now on, these Manchus could only maintain their position by supporting the dynasty in hope of receiving imperial favor. K'ang-hsi was also free to employ Chinese in military or civil positions as he pleased. It was he who then reconciled the traditional Chinese bureaucracy to life under Manchu rule. The war also left K'ang-hsi with battle-hardened troops and a well-oiled military machine. For the first time since the fall of Peking, the Ch'ing turned its attention to Inner Asia.

CH'ING FRONTIER POLICY

Like other foreign dynasties the Manchus were skilled at frontier politics. Ch'ing policies reflected a firm understanding of the weaknesses in the tribal organization on the steppe and how to exploit them. The traditional Manchurian strategy was to keep the nomads of Mongolia in a state of anarchy so that they would be unable to organize and become a threat to north China. The Manchus elaborated this policy by keeping the nomads both divided and under a form of direct rule from China. This accomplishment had its roots in the ability of Manchurians to manipulate the steppe tribes and in the unusual political structure on the steppe at the close of the Ming period.

The Treaty of 1571 between Altan Khan and the Ming brought order to the steppe by funding a large number of petty princes who took part in the tributary system. These leaders were of Chinggisid lineage, the descendants of Dayan Khan, and each ruled over small parts of southern Mongolia. Earlier Chinese dynasties had funnelled aid through a single steppe ruler who monopolized its redistribution. Under such conditions minor tribal leaders were forced to play subordinate roles in a larger steppe political system. Altan Khan had not attempted to create such a monopoly, so each petty ruler established his own relationship with the Ming court. This effectively short-circuited the possibilities of political unity. Each local leader guarded his autonomy jealously and was unwilling to abandon direct links to China in return for a subordinate position in a unified steppe empire. The Ming employed this system in a passive manner, refusing tribute relations with Mongols who caused trouble.

Ch'ing policy toward the Mongols was more astute. They weaned the tribal elite away from the Ming by matching Ming tribute benefits and buying Mongol horses. The Manchus also arranged a web of marriage alliances that linked the Mongol and Manchu elites, something the Ming had never considered. Finally, the Manchus posed as the protectors of the Mongol princes against the expansionist plans of Lighdan Khan, who would have eliminated them. An alliance with the Manchus maintained the status quo for the Chinggisid elite and prevented the creation of a nomadic state along China's frontier. The culmination of these policies was the incorporation of the Inner Mongolian tribes into the Manchu state in 1634.

The Ch'ing government reorganized the tribes in southern Mongolia by incorporating them into the banner system. Banner units were organized along traditional tribal lines; in essence the old tribes became the new banners. Established Mongol leaders received positions of rank in the Ch'ing administration leading their own people, who were fixed to specific territories. The tribal population was apportioned out to these districts in units of fifty families. This policy reaffirmed the privileges of the conservative Chinggisid elite, who owed their continued power to the Manchus. At the same time, it lessened the opportunity for unrest by dividing the Mongols into tiny units whose members were forbidden to move away or seek new leadership. A schedule of heavy fines was promulgated, guaranteeing punishment to any leader who permitted his subjects to flee or who accepted such refugees. In 1662, these regulations were further tightened, making it a crime to leave the banner territory even on a hunt. By 1670, there were forty-nine banners in Inner Mongolia, each comprising some twenty-three arrows. Banner and arrow leaders were completely dependent on the Ch'ing dynasty for their continued survival. The Ch'ing court could, and did, fine, replace, or otherwise punish Mongol banner officials, further weakening the ties between the local tribesmen and their leaders. The aristocracy was tied to the court by marriage and other bonds that encouraged Mongol leaders to see themselves as part of a greater Ch'ing elite. By enforcing the rule of a conservative and unambitious nobility, the Manchus stymied the development of hostile political forces. Except for one Chahar leader, the southern Mongolians stayed loyal to the dynasty during the San-fan Rebellion.[6]

The arrow–banner system allowed the Ch'ing to control southern Mongolia at low cost with little direct intervention. However, they recognized that so much fragmentation made it difficult to use the Mongols militarily. Thus, when south China erupted in revolt in 1674, the Ch'ing reorganized the forty-nine Mongol banners into the Six Leagues. These leagues enabled military campaigns to be more easily organized, for each league was obligated to keep troops in readiness. Because the dynasty maintained firm control of the league heads, they never became autonomous political institutions. The Ch'ing derived maximum political benefit from this system, because the banner fragmentation weakened the southern Mongols while league organization provided the dynasty with a military reserve.

The incorporation of southern Mongolia was complete a decade before the Manchus took Peking. Northern Mongolia remained outside of Ch'ing control. Divided into a number of quarreling Khalkha khanates which were no threat to the dynasty, northern Mongolia nevertheless became an object of keen concern because of its weakness. The Ch'ing saw that region as vital to its own northern defense, and the dynasty's frontier policy was built around keeping the Khalkhas safely within the Manchu sphere of influence.

Four threats to Ch'ing control were to provoke a series of wars that continued off-and-on for the next century and led the dynasty to annex huge areas of Inner Asia in pursuit of frontier security.

1   Incessant conflict among the Khalkhas rendered them vulnerable to civil strife and subversion.
2   Russian expansion into Siberia and Manchuria put new pressure on the borders of Mongolia.
3   Tibetan Buddhism, with its church hierarchy and monasteries throughout the Mongol world, provided an alternative political structure and the locus of revolt for otherwise loyal Mongols.
4   The Zunghar tribes which bordered Mongolia were a direct military threat to the Khalkhas. They had the strength and the desire to incorporate northern Mongolia into a new steppe empire which would endanger Ch'ing control of southern Mongolia and put China's own frontier at risk.

These four threats became bound up in the long struggle for hegemony in Inner Asia between the Ch'ing and Zunghars, a struggle that was not concluded until 1755. Because China and Russia were to become the two exclusive powers in the heart of Asia, much attention has been devoted to their initial conflicts and treaties, leaving the impression that the Zunghars were only a minor irritant in a larger relationship. However, from the perspective of the Inner Asian frontier, the Zunghars were a major Ch'ing rival. Ch'ing expansion into Inner Asia and the dynasty's policy towards Russia were largely determined by the necessity of countering Zunghar threats. Only after the defeat of this last steppe empire did Inner Asian politics evolve into purely a Sino-Russian affair.

THE ZUNGHARS – LAST OF THE STEPPE EMPIRES

The Oirats largely disappeared from China's frontier history following Esen's death in the mid-fifteenth century, when the Eastern Mongols became dominant in southern Mongolia. However, Esen's failure did not lead to an immediate breakup of the Oirat confederation outside of this area. The Oirats continued to occupy northern Mongolia and Esen's son recouped some of his confederation's losses by attacking the Kazakhs in the west to bring the strategic Ili Valley under Oirat control. From here the Oirats dominated the oasis cities in eastern Turkestan and controlled trade through that region. This more remote but fairly stable empire, which lasted for about a century, ruled northern Mongolia until, after suffering a number of defeats at the hands of the Eastern Mongols, they lost Karakorum to Altan Khan in 1552. This forced an Oirat withdrawal into the Tarbaghatai region which had been their homeland. The movement of retreating tribes led to a breakdown of the confederation and its reorganization.

The steppe west of the Altai Mountains had long been the center of secondary nomadic empires. It had been the home territory of the Yüeh-chih and the Wu-sun during the time of the Hsiung-nu. It had been the center of the western Turkish khaghanate and later the home of the Qara Khitai. During the Mongol period it was the source of rebellions against Yüan rule on the steppe. Nomadic states west of the Altai Mountains took advantage of the caravan trade through Turkestan and exploited the resources of the small oasis cities to the south. Although rarely as rich or powerful as the states formed by nomads along the Chinese frontier, they had access to enough resources to remain stable. While they were often successful in expanding westward, such nomadic states rarely extended their control to the Chinese frontier in spite of great military victories. The difficulty was twofold. First, nomads in southern and northern Mongolia resisted incorporation by their western cousins and often sought Chinese aid to oppose them. Second, a leader from the west was so far from his home base that rebels could organize against him while he was gone. These problems had thwarted attempts by the western Turks and the Oirats to retain control of the Chinese frontier. However, the distance from China was also protective: even very powerful nomadic states based in Mongolia granted autonomy or independence to the area west of the Altai because the cost of incorporation outweighed the benefits.

After Esen's death the Dörben Oirat confederation consisted of four main tribes – the Choros, Dörbet, Khoshot, and Torghut. At the end of the sixteenth century they came under severe pressure from their neighbors. In the west they were hemmed in both by the Kazakh tribes and the Uzbeks, who, under the leadership of Shaybani Khan, were at the height of their influence. In the east they were bordered by the Eastern Mongols who, in the reign of Altan Khan, had driven them from Karakorum west to Khobdo. The Khalkhas later expelled them entirely from northern Mongolia between 1619 and 1621, and Khobdo became the core of the Altan or (Altyn) khanate. As a result, the Dörbet and Torghut retreated northeast into the upper Irtysh River region. These movements provoked warfare among the Oirat tribes in 1625, seriously weakening them. Pressured by the Choros, who had lost territory to the Khalkhas, the Torghut began a full-scale emigration in 1627–8, passing through Kazakh country until around 1632 they reached the lower Volga where they became known as the Kalmuks. The Khoshots relocated eastward, dominating Kokonor and eastern Tibet. The Choros took control of the Tarbaghatai region and brought the Dörbet with their Khoit clients into a new Zunghar confederation. The Zunghars were, in other words, a reconstituted Western Mongol state: the Choros, Dörbet, and Khoit leaders were all descendants of Esen.[7]

It was not until the reign of Ba'atur khungtaiji that the Zunghars became a major force in Inner Asia. Ba'atur's father, Khara Khula, had reorganized the confederation after the civil war in 1625. Upon his death in 1634, Ba'atur took power and began to expand the Zunghar territory. He renewed relations with the Russians, who were both enemies of the Kazakhs and his neighbors to the north. Immediately following this agreement, the Zunghars attacked and defeated the Kazakhs in 1635, taking many prisoners including the Kazakh khan's son, Jehangir. In 1638, Ba'atur aided the Khoshot khan Gushri in an invasion of Tibet which culminated in the toppling of the last Tibetan king in 1642 and placed the Dalai Lama at the head of the Tibetan church and state. Ba'atur defeated the Kazakhs again in 1643. In addition to his military campaigns, Ba'atur gained the cooperation of many Mongol tribes through the use of marriage alliances and peace agreements. The Zunghars also encouraged agriculture and craft production, which became more important after they constructed a city of stone on the Imil River, Kubakserai, to be their capital. This attempt at diversification was aided by diplomatic and trade relations with Moscow.

As early as 1616, envoys had been exchanged with the Moscovites, and a treaty was signed with some of the northwestern tribes in 1618. The Oirats wanted support in their battles with the Kazakhs and Khalkhas, while the Russians wished to protect their flank as they advanced into Siberia. As the Zunghars recovered their strength, this relationship grew more important. The 1635 treaty, the first formal agreement between the two states, provided the Zunghars with goldsmiths and other craftsmen, as well as gifts for Ba'atur. The only major difficulty between the Zunghars and the Russians was the status of certain border tribes which they both claimed. These disputes sometimes led to armed conflict (the Zunghars attacked Russian territory in 1649), but they were usually resolved by negotiation.[8]

While Siberia itself was of marginal value to the Zunghars, historically they had strong trade links there. Until the sixteenth century Siberia was ruled by Mongol khans who levied tribute in the form of furs and other forest products, much of which was exported south through Zunghar territory. The swift Moscovite expansion into Siberia had deposed these khans, and put the tributary collection of furs in their hands. Although the Moscovites had encountered little resistance in conquering Siberia, the territory would have been difficult to defend against the concerted and continual attacks like those the Zunghars conducted against their nomadic enemies. An agreement providing for friendly relations with the Zunghars was a necessity, particularly since during the seventeenth century the Moscovites had proved unable to subdue the nearby Kazakhs or the khanate of Khiva. In recognition of Zunghar interests, Moscovite expansion avoided the highland steppe area suitable for pastoralism. The Zunghars had few objections because their political interests lay elsewhere – in Tibet, in the eastern oases, along the Chinese frontier and on the Kazakh steppe.

By the 1630s the regional balance of power shifted in the Zunghars' favor because their neighbors were disorganized. Ming China was on the verge of collapse and preoccupied with internal rebellions. Most of the Eastern Mongols in southern Mongolia had been incorporated by the Manchus, isolating the Khalkhas, while Zunghar attacks in the west put the Kazakhs on the defensive. The Zunghars' political relations with Tibet also expanded their influence throughout the network of Buddhist monasteries which linked the Mongol world.

Ba'atur's imperial ambitions culminated in an international conference held in Zungharia that created a pan-Mongol confederation in 1640. With the exception of the Mongols under Ch'ing control, all the tribes attended, including the previously hostile Khalkhas and the far distant Kalmuks. At the conference they agreed to form a united Mongol confederation which would oppose attacks from outside powers and settle internal differences peacefully. Tibetan Buddhism was declared the official religion of the Mongols, while shamanistic practices were condemned. Although this alliance was short-lived, it demonstrated that the Zunghars had become the key nomadic power of Inner Asia. Far removed from the Chinese frontier, the Zunghars would provide formidable competition for the new Manchu rulers of China in the battle to dominate the heartland of Mongolia.[9]

When Ba'atur died in 1653 the Zunghars entered a period of political turmoil. Ba'atur's son Sengge inherited the throne, but he was actively opposed by his two half-brothers, Sechen tayiji and Jobta Ba'atur. They allied themselves with a disgruntled Khoshot leader and civil war nearly broke out in 1657. Sengge temporarily gained the upper hand in 1661 after the Khoshot faction opposing him was defeated. Externally, Sengge's major problem was a dispute with both the Russians in Siberia and the Altan khanate in Khobdo over the right to collect fur tax (*yasaq*) from the forest tribes. The Zunghars settled the question by conquering the Altan khanate in 1667, recovering the territory they had lost in northern Mongolia a half-century earlier. Sengge also attacked the Russian settlement of Krasnoyarsk the same year to enforce his right to tax tribes claimed by Moscow.

Table 8.1   Succession and dates of reigns of Zunghar rulers

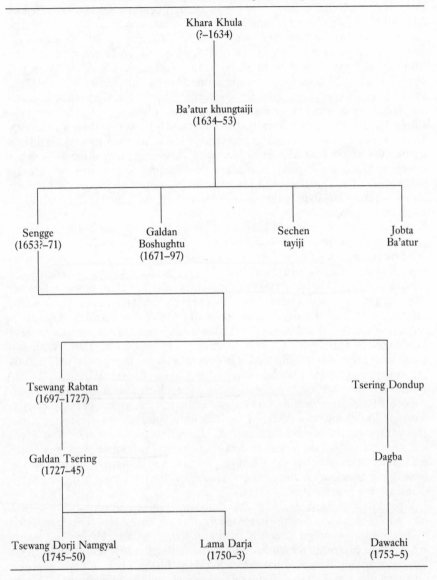

Sechen tayiji and Jobta Ba'atur attempted to seize power in 1671 by assassinating Sengge, but Sengge's younger brother, Galdan Boshughtu, killed them and took the throne himself. Galdan had previously been sent to Tibet to become a monk, and in the struggle with his half-brothers he was greatly aided by the endorsement of the Dalai Lama, as well as the support provided by Khoshot troops fighting on his behalf. Once firmly installed, Galdan turned on his erstwhile Khoshot allies and, in 1676, killed their khan to bring them and their territory in Koko-nor directly under his control. As a result, many Khoshots fled to Kansu where they caused no end of trouble for the Ch'ing government, which was already preoccupied by the San-fan Rebellion in south China. Immediately following his Khoshot victory, Galdan turned south to annex the Muslim oases. With the exception of the Torghut on the Volga, he had recreated the old Oirat confederation.

The Zunghar conquest of the Muslim oases hinged on exploiting civil strife in the area. The city-states of the region were under the nominal control of the old line of Chaghadayid khans, but the most influential political figures were the leaders of the two rival branches of the Makhdumzada family, a lineage of Nakhshbandi sufis, known as *khojas*, based in Kashghar and Yarkand. In 1677, the Chaghadayid khan Isma'il moved against them, forcing the Khoja Hazrat Afaq of Kashghar to flee. Hazrat Afaq sought the aid of Galdan, who seized the nearby oases of Hami and Turfan in 1679, and then captured Kashghar in 1680. Isma'il was imprisoned, thus ending the last vestige of Chinggisid rule in Turkestan, and Galdan appointed Hazrat Afaq ruler of a Zunghar protectorate in Kashgharia, which was soon extended to Yarkand.[10]

The Zunghar policy of indirect rule for administering the oases states had a long history. From Han times, nomads had exploited the resources of Turkestan through the manipulation of local rulers. While in some cases this control was based on the ability of the nomads to overwhelm the isolated oasis states, there was also a positive aspect. The overland trade with China was traditionally conducted by merchants from Turkestan who needed protection for their caravan routes as well as the protection of a powerful overlord in order to deal effectively with China. In Galdan's use of the Khojas as his instruments, the Zunghars followed this tradition. He gained the advantages of conquest – taxes, supplies, and trade – without the responsibilities of administration. Appointing Muslim clerics as intermediaries created a buffer between the Islamic inhabitants of Turkestan and the Buddhist Mongols of the northern steppe.

The expansion of the Zunghar empire under Galdan was not opposed by China because the Ch'ing dynasty was involved in a desperate struggle with Wu San-kuei in the San-fan war. However, while Kashgharia was outside the usual sphere of Chinese interests, the Zunghar conquest of Hami threatened the western approach to Kansu, previously invaded by those Khoshots fleeing Galdan. The rapid rise of a new steppe power on China's flank was an obvious threat to the Ch'ing. It could not have been lost on the historically minded Manchus that the last Jurchen dynasty in China fell to Mongol tribes who had been united under Chinggis Khan while the Chin dynasty was preoccupied by southern wars with the Sung.

Although Galdan's conquests were extensive, he still lacked control of the Mongol heartland, but Ch'ing government in this region was far from secure. Because their troops and attention were focused almost exclusively on the south, the Manchus were unable to provide a high level of supervision in Mongolia and lacked the military power to prevent revolts. When the Chahar prince Burni revolted and marched on Mukden in 1675, the Manchus were forced to field an army consisting of cooks and servants to oppose him.

Fortunately for the Ch'ing, this ragtag force defeated the Chahars.[11]

Six years later (1681) Galdan attempted to foment discontent among the Eastern Mongols by proposing an alliance with the Khorchin (the oldest of the Manchu allies). In a letter to them he asked, "Are we to become slaves of those whom we used to command? The empire is the heritage of our ancestors."[12] Although the Khorchin turned this message over to K'ang-hsi, the danger to Ch'ing interests was clear. Galdan also threatened Manchu control of Mongolia through the manipulation of his ties with the Tibetan religious hierarchy in Lhasa, which gave him influence among the Buddhist Mongols under Ch'ing control. Using military or religious/political means, Galdan could subvert the Eastern Mongols, particularly the Khalkha Mongols in the north.

In Galdan's time northern Mongolia was ruled by the Khalkhas who were divided into three autonomous khanates – the Jasaghtu khanate, Sechen khanate, and the Tushiyetu khanate (a fourth, the Altan khanate in Khobdo, had been reconquered by the Zunghars). In addition to these tribal regions, there was the Buddhist hierarchy under the influence of the Jebtsundamba Khutughtu, the most important religious figure in northern Mongolia. Since 1639 this position, filled by a line of recognized incarnations, had been endowed with considerable property and manpower. Its wealth and power constituted a force equal to any of the khanates, although it lacked a specific territory.

The expansion of the Zunghar, Ch'ing, and Moscovite empires had left the Khalkha khanates surrounded by aggressive neighbors. Because of their strategic importance, the Khalkhas became the focus of a struggle to control Inner Asia, with the Ch'ing attempting to exclude all rival powers. For the Manchus, Mongolia acted as a bulwark against invasion, providing China's northern frontier with protection. Zunghar domination of this area threatened the Ch'ing interests because from there the Zunghars could invade northern China and wean the southern Mongolian tribes away from Ch'ing control. Moscovite control of the region was also unacceptable to the Ch'ing, particularly after the Manchus discovered the inroads they had made into the Amur region. An autonomous northern Mongolia would have been acceptable to China, but the khanates were so divided that there was little chance they could fend off an invasion.

Galdan confronted the Ch'ing dynasty over Mongolia after a dispute broke out between the Jasaghtu Khan and the Tushiyetu Khan. The Ch'ing K'ang-hsi Emperor had attempted to resolve the dispute through negotiation in 1686 by organizing an intertribal conference, which included representatives of Galdan and the Dalai Lama. The Khalkhas agreed to bury their differences but, taking advantage of an incident in which the Jebtsundamba Khutughtu (the Tushiyetu Khan's brother) had insulted the Dalai Lama's representative by failing to follow accepted protocol, Galdan persuaded the weaker Jasaghtu Khan to reopen his dispute. In 1688, he sent his brother with a small number of Zunghars to aid the Jasaghtu Khan. The Tushiyetu Khan responded to this provocation by attacking the Jasaghtu Khan, killing both him and Galdan's brother. This brought on the full wrath of the Zunghars, who invaded Mongolia with 30,000 troops, quickly routing the Tushiyetu Khan, who fled to China along with the Jebtsundamba Khutughtu. The Zunghars then advanced to the Kerulen, seizing immense amounts of livestock and other wealth, and forcing the flight of tens of thousands of Khalkhas into the Manchu-ruled areas of southern Mongolia where K'ang-hsi provided them with food and money. The Zunghars now confronted the Manchus directly in a battle for control of Mongolia.

The Zunghar advance into Mongolia produced diplomatic problems for the Ch'ing in addition to the military threat. The Ch'ing feared that Galdan might create a military alliance between the Zunghars and the Russians against China. The Manchus had a history of conflict with Moscow over Cossack incursions into the Amur Basin. Open warfare between them had broken out during 1685 and 1686 when the Russians established a fort at Albazin, and the Ch'ing twice burnt it down. It is unclear whether the Russians would have been willing to provide the Zunghars with troops, but they could have supplied guns and powder (or craftsmen to make them). Although the Manchus had proved their military superiority over the Russians in the Amur, the Ch'ing government was willing to negotiate a treaty in order to forestall the possibility of a Russo-Zunghar alliance. Ch'ing envoys acted quickly to conclude an understanding with the Russians, signing the Treaty of Nerchinsk in 1689. In exchange for a promise of neutrality, the Manchus granted the Russians rights to trade and settled the border dispute over the Amur frontier. The strategy succeeded, for when Galdan tried to arrange an alliance with the Czar the next year, his overtures were rejected.[13]

K'ang-hsi's other diplomatic task was to gain the support, or at least the neutrality, of the Tibetan Buddhist hierarchy. The "Great Fifth" Dalai Lama had tremendous influence throughout the Mongol world and K'ang-hsi hoped to gain his support for a new peace conference. The negotiations were not forthcoming because the "Great Fifth" was dead, although this fact was covered up by his regent who ruled in his name, claiming that the Dalai Lama was in seclusion. The regent not only refused K'ang-hsi's request but, being a supporter of Galdan, asked the Ch'ing emperor to accept the Zunghar demands. While K'ang-hsi had outplayed Galdan to prevent a Russian alliance, Galdan had the support, at least in name, of the most important religious figure in the Buddhist Mongol world.

K'ang-hsi's final diplomatic concern was to bring the Khalkhas under direct Ch'ing control. The Khalkhas had remained apart under their own leadership until Galdan's invasion. The Jebtsundamba Khutughtu had initially considered seeking Moscovite support to counter the Zunghars, but in the end he followed the other Khalkha leaders into Ch'ing territory. Because of the frequent wars between the two, and the damage done by Galdan's invasion, the chances of a future Zunghar–Khalkha alliance were remote. Nevertheless, if the Zunghars consolidated their hold over northern Mongolia and extended overtures to the Khalkhas, this attitude might change. Taking advantage of the Khalkhas' miserable state, K'ang-hsi received them as refugees and, in 1691, incorporated them into the Mongolian banner system. The Khalkha leadership agreed to this in large part because they were terrified of Galdan. K'ang-hsi traveled to Dolonnor to formally receive their submission. The Khalkhas were divided into thirty-two banners based on the available population and following traditional tribal divisions. Unlike the Inner Mongolian banners, the Khalkhas had only one or two arrows per banner. The Khalkha elite, great and small, preserved its position of power in the new system by accepting appointments to lead banners and arrows under Ch'ing supervision.[14]

These diplomatic concerns illustrate the growing complexity of steppe politics in the seventeenth century. Previously, Manchurian dynasties were content merely to disrupt the steppe tribes. The forest regions of Siberia and the Amur never played a significant role in this interaction, nor had Tibet exerted much influence in Mongolia. The expansion of Muscovite power into Siberia and the integration of Mongolia into the Tibetan religious sphere of influence altered the old dynamics. Ch'ing frontier policy had to look beyond the borders of tribal Mongolia. To deal with Siberia, the Manchus had to come to terms with a distant government totally outside their cultural sphere of influence which refused to accept traditional Chinese forms of diplomatic usage. The compromises reached by the Ch'ing in dealing with the Russians were prompted by the need to outflank the Zunghars. Similarly, Ch'ing involvement in Tibetan politics was initiated because of the important role Tibetan Buddhism played in Mongolia. The Buddhist religious establishment was an alternative political organization that cross-cut tribal and regional ties. The religious hierarchy could be co-opted by tribal leaders like Galdan to extend their appeal to co-religionists along the Ch'ing frontier, or it might become a locus of rebellion for Mongols chafing under a harsh Ch'ing administration. In any event, Ch'ing frontier policy extended China more deeply into Inner Asia than at any other time, even more perhaps than during the period of Yüan rule.

The Ch'ing defense of Mongolia received its greatest aid from the Zunghars themselves when Galdan was confronted by a revolt led by his nephew Tsewang Rabtan, Sengge's son. This civil war, which occurred at the height of Zunghar power, was typical of problems that plagued so many other nomadic states over succession rights. Galdan had justified his succession to leadership in part on the principle that the office should be inherited laterally, from elder to younger brother. However, the Zunghars also commonly accepted direct succession, from father to son, so Sengge's sons posed a threat. Galdan murdered Sengge's eldest son in 1688, but the victim's younger brother, Tsewang Rabtan, fled with a small group of companions. While Galdan was campaigning in Mongolia, Tsewang Rabtan gained influence in Zungharia and revolted against his uncle. Galdan temporarily abandoned the invasion of northern Mongolia. He returned home to deal with his nephew in 1689, but was unable to dislodge him. This must have seemed a minor affair compared to the great Mongolian conquests, however, since Galdan resumed his war there the next year.

Galdan met little resistance during his 1690 campaign and spent the summer on the Kerulen. He then moved on southern Mongolia and advanced to within eighty leagues of Peking where he encountered the Ch'ing army, led by one of K'ang-hsi's brothers, at Ulaan Butung. The Manchus had cannons and anticipated a victory, but Galdan chose a good defensive location and sheltered his army behind camels armored with felt, which rendered the Manchu cannon ineffective (although it is not clear how many camels survived). The Ch'ing commander was eager to negotiate and arranged a truce whereby Galdan was permitted to withdraw unmolested with his loot. K'ang-hsi was furious at the fainthearted effort of his forces and demoted the officers in charge.

Despite his Mongolian victories, Galdan found himself with strategic difficulties. Tsewang Rabtan became more active in Zungharia, leaving Galdan isolated and without a firm territorial or tribal base. Such civil disorder in the midst of a campaign against China historically had proved fatal to other nomad leaders. At the same time, K'ang-hsi successfully brought the Khalkhas into the Ch'ing empire, foreclosed on Galdan's planned alliance with the Russians, and prepared to lead the Ch'ing armies personally against the Zunghars. Galdan withdrew west in order to rebuild his power in Zungharia. Not until 1694 did Galdan again advance on Mongolia, this time out of need, for it was reported that his territory suffered from famine. He again proposed an alliance with the Khorchin so that the Khalkhas could be attacked from two sides. The Khorchin passed the information on to K'ang-hsi, who laid a trap for Galdan by telling the Khorchin to agree to the Zunghar proposal.

Aware of Galdan's plans, K'ang-hsi organized a Ch'ing expeditionary force to combat the Zunghars. K'ang-hsi's attitude toward the northern steppe reflected his Manchurian heritage. He later criticized Chinese commanders for their willful ignorance about the conditions in Mongolia which had resulted in the defeat of so many armies.

The conditions of the northern areas can be understood only if you travel through them in person; and as you move you must pay attention closely to details of transport and supply. You can't just make guesses about them, as they did in the Ming dynasty – and even now, the Han Chinese officials don't know much about the region. Generals Boji and Sun Ssu-k'o thought in the 1696 campaign against Galdan, that it was enough to attend to military matters and left supplies to others. When I travelled from Pai-t'a northward the following year, I saw the remains of the bodies of troops who had died of hunger in their armies on that march, and ordered them buried by the roadside.[15]

Personal experience with conditions in Mongolia was rarely found among the Chinese military commanders under native dynasties because service at the border and knowledge of the nomads was culturally devalued. Insightful memorials about the nomads from knowledgeable frontier officials were usually ignored at court, and such officials rarely advanced to policy-making positions. When large-scale campaigns were organized, they were most often led by men with greater experience in court politics than with the complex problems of leading an army. With the exception of a few emperors, such as T'ang T'ai-tsung or Yung-lo, Chinese rulers viewed the land north of the border as *terra incognita*, the only region in East Asia that continually rejected Chinese conceptions of world order.

Foreign emperors understood the northern frontier peoples much better, in part because they actually liked visiting the region. K'ang-hsi thoroughly enjoyed his steppe campaigns as a wonderful change from court life and protocol in Peking.

It is when one is beyond the Great Wall that the air and soil refresh the spirit: one leaves the beaten road and strikes out into untamed country; the mountains are densely packed with woods, "green and thick as standing corn." As one moves further north the views open up, one's eyes travel hundreds of miles; instead of feeling hemmed in, there is a sense of freedom.[16]

In the spring of 1696, K'ang-hsi led the Ch'ing army north rapidly and made straight for Galdan, possibly aided by intelligence from Tsewang Rabtan who moved his forces east. Taken by surprise, Galdan fled the approach of one imperial column, only to be trapped by another at Jao Modo. Here Galdan's forces were destroyed, and many of the survivors joined Tsewang Rabtan. Galdan himself became a fugitive leading a small band of followers in the Altai region. K'ang-hsi pursued him there the next year. This expedition was more of a hunt than a war and ended with Galdan's suicide. Taking advantage of his presence in the region, K'ang-hsi seized control of Hami.

Galdan's defeat is often described as the end of the Zunghar empire. It was not. K'ang-hsi's success, while due in large measure to his good generalship, could not have been decisive without the aid of Tsewang Rabtan who had isolated Galdan and deprived him of Zunghar troops. Tsewang Rabtan's predominant position following Jao Modo also made it impossible for Galdan to recover from his defeat. From the Zunghar perspective, Tsewang Rabtan had manipulated the Manchus into aiding his civil war struggle with his uncle. The Zunghar empire was still intact and structurally sound. K'ang-hsi made no attempt to conquer it.

Following his uncle's death, Tsewang Rabtan was recognized as the undisputed leader of the Zunghars. In cooperating with the Manchus to bring about his uncle's fall, Tsewang Rabtan followed a policy similar to the "inner frontier" strategy whereby the weaker party in civil war on the steppe seeks a Chinese alliance to destroy his rival. In general, such alliances occurred when the weaker party was driven close to the Chinese frontier and involved making a formal submission to China in return for subsidies, trade, and sometimes military assistance. Such cooperation with China did not necessarily signify genuine submission, and the nomads often broke these ties after the civil war was over. Tsewang Rabtan never entered into a formal alliance with China but, like earlier nomad leaders, he used China's armed force to settle a civil war on the steppe. The price he paid for his victory was the loss of northern Mongolia east of the Altai to direct Ch'ing rule.

Even after K'ang-hsi's victories, the Zunghar threat to northern Mongolia remained a Ch'ing preoccupation, for the Manchus saw the territory as the key to their own defense. They forced the Khalkhas to man and patrol key border points, to keep troops in readiness, and to maintain a postal system of horse relays that conveyed news of the frontier quickly to Peking. Such precautions were not unwarranted, for Tsewang Rabtan had aims similar to Galdan's: he meant to retrieve northern Mongolia by creating the strategic conditions necessary to detach the Khalkhas from the Ch'ing empire.

The conflict between the Zunghars and the Ch'ing over northern Mongolia evolved into a struggle over position. The Zunghars tried to gain a strategic position so powerful that Mongolia would inevitably fall to them. Invasions, battles, and politics were all focused on controlling Mongolia, but there was little actual fighting in Mongolia itself. Events in Tibet, Turkestan, and Siberia became significant in so far as they affected Mongolia. The Ch'ing attempted to counter this threat by intervening far beyond the borders of Mongolia to prevent the Zunghars from ever achieving such a position. Like two chess-masters, Tsewang Rabtan and K'ang-hsi were often more concerned with the potential of an opponent's move than with its immediate result.

Tsewang Rabtan had a western as well as an eastern front to consider. His rivals there were the Kazakhs, a large confederation of nomads who had established themselves in the broad belt of steppe land from Lake Balkhash to the Ural River north of the Caspian Sea. In the late sixteenth century, the Kazakhs had advanced south to seize the cities of Tashkent and Turkistan from the more sedentary Uzbeks. Turkistan became the capital of the Kazakh Khan who was the head of three fairly autonomous groups. The Zunghar conflict with the Kazakhs had long centered on control of the Ili Valley which Tsewang Rabtan wanted for his capital. This territorial dispute was exacerbated by the sharp religious differences between the Buddhist Zunghars and the Muslim Kazakhs.

The Ch'ing defeat of Galdan was welcome news to the Kazakhs, who showed their contempt for the Zunghars by murdering their envoys and seizing trade caravans. In 1698, a year after taking power, Tsewang Rabtan responded to these challenges by inflicting a stinging defeat on the Kazakhs. Although the Zunghars continually defeated the Muslim Kazakhs in the west, as their Oirat ancestors had done from the time of Esen, they showed little interest in expanding in that direction. To a nomadic empire oriented toward China, western Turkestan always remained a secondary objective. When conquered, it invariably split off to form an autonomous unit as occurred during the first Turkish empire or after Chinggis Khan's death. Traditionally, Chinese-oriented empires rarely extended west of the Tien-shan or Pamir mountain chains. Only when the Kazakhs provoked them, or when the Chinese frontier was stalemated, did the Zunghars campaign in the west.

Following the Kazakh campaign, Tsewang Rabtan remained largely at peace with his neighbors. He did not have the military strength to engage in an open offensive against Mongolia, so his aims turned to increasing Zunghar political and economic power. According to Chinese reports, Tsewang Rabtan ruled over a nomadic population of 200,000 tents or about 600,000 people.[17] Their central geographic position allowed them to exploit the long-established cara-van trade with India, China, Tibet, and Russia. Most of the traders using this route were not Zunghars, but Muslim Turks from the oases whom the Russians generically labelled "Bukharans", although they were not necessarily from that city. Zunghar overlordship was a great advantage to these merchants. It protected them against abuse by other powers and entitled them to reduced taxes in their trade with Siberia, which consisted of furs, slaves, and salt. Merchants with Zunghar protection paid a tax of one-twentieth compared to the one-tenth the Russian government extracted from its own merchants; traders traveling in the name of the Zunghar khan paid no duty. Zunghar traders also supplied Chinese goods to Russia and other countries. Peaceful relations obviously facilitated the growth of this trade. By controlling access to it Tsewang Rabtan could grow rich without resorting to campaigns for booty.[18] Tsewang Rabtan enlarged the agricultural and artisan population on the steppe by transporting people from the oases in the south, in addition to taxing the existing city-states under Zunghar control. The artisans attached to the Zunghar settlements produced both cloth and iron, while agriculture expanded at the expense of pasture in the Ili valley. Russian envoys were impressed by the fields of wheat, millet, rice, and the wide variety of fruits they saw. Barriers to this type of development had always been more political than ecological. Investment in farms was vulnerable to nomadic raiding because, once destroyed, they were not easily replaced. However, when a strong central authority controlled the region, agriculture could thrive. The Zunghars also increased their ability to produce both iron and cloth.[19]

Tsewang Rabtan's anti-Ch'ing campaigns were based on the premise that a Zunghar conquest of Mongolia could be sustained against a Manchu counterattack only with the cooperation, or at least the neutrality, of the Mongol tribes there. This was because the Manchus depended largely on Mongol troops to defend their Inner Asian frontier, for they provided the Ch'ing with the cavalry necessary for effective fighting in wild and open steppe country. The Ch'ing court recognized this danger and gave special attention to controlling Mongol affairs through the banner system. For Tsewang Rabtan to succeed, he had to mount both an effective military campaign and a political offensive to gain the support of the tribes under Ch'ing control. The most effective means to acquire their support was through control of the Tibetan religious establishment which permeated the Mongol world.

The political importance of Buddhism as a link between Tibet and the Mongol world had begun as early as Yüan times, but it was not until the late Ming period that the religion made great inroads on the steppe. Politically, the most significant event in this process was the conversion of Altan Khan in 1578. He was a staunch supporter of the Dalai Lama and the teachings of the dGe-lugs-pa order (also known as the Yellow Church), helping them become preeminent in their rivalry with other Buddhist orders in Tibet. The dGe-lugs-pa order reciprocated the favor, and tied themselves more closely to the Mongols, when they recognized Altan Khan's great-grandson as the fourth Dalai Lama in 1601. The dGe-lug-pas reached the height of their influence under the leadership of the "Great Fifth" Dalai Lama (1617–82), who was installed as the supreme religious and secular ruler in 1642 after the Khoshots, led by their khan Gushri, deposed Tibet's last king. The administration of secular power rested largely with a regent who had broad powers and resided in Lhasa. Mongol wealth poured into Tibet as offerings to build monasteries and support the clergy. Buddhism became the dominant faith of the whole Mongol world. Tibetan texts were translated into Mongol and monasteries were established in many places, creating new centers of power that cross-cut tribal divisions. The Tibetan religious hierarchy played a key role in Mongol politics, just as Mongol wealth and military played a crucial role in Tibet.

During Galdan's reign the Zunghars and Manchus both lobbied strongly for the Dalai Lama's support. Galdan initially won this contest because of his closer ties with the religious establishment in Lhasa, but after his death K'ang-hsi moved to bring Tibet under a ruler friendly to China. He supported a coup by Khoshot Lajang Khan (Gushri's grandson), who seized power and deposed the regent in 1705, bringing Tibet nominally into an alliance with the Ch'ing court. Lajang Khan became embroiled in divisive religious politics after he ousted the Sixth Dalai Lama and replaced him with a young man rumored to be his own son. Because the Dalai Lama was the recognized incarnation of his predecessor, such a replacement was deemed illegitimate by most Tibetans. The Ch'ing court ordered the deposed Dalai Lama to exile in China, but he died en route. Opposition soon manifested itself in eastern Tibet where an infant was declared to be the rightful incarnation and successor to the dead Sixth Dalai Lama. Lajang Khan was put in a difficult spot, for the child's strongest supporters were the Khoshots of Koko-nor. They declared their open opposition to his rule and protected the newly recognized Dalai Lama by moving him to their territory in 1714. The Manchus intervened, demanding the child be sent to Peking, but the Khoshots refused. Fearful of a revolt and the possibility the Khoshots might invade Tibet, K'ang-hsi rushed troops to the area. No fighting broke out and as a compromise the boy was installed in Kumbum monastery under Manchu protection.[20]

This complex series of events gave Tsewang Rabtan a chance to upset Ch'ing frontier policy. Taking advantage of the divisions created by Lajang Khan in Tibet and among the Mongols, he planned to conquer Tibet and place the young Seventh Dalai Lama on the throne in Lhasa. This would then bring the Zunghars the support of both the Khoshots in Koko-nor and the Tibetan clergy. Once established in Tibet, the Zunghars would be free to attack northern Mongolia on two fronts and manipulate the Buddhist church against the Ch'ing.

Tsewang Rabtan began plotting as soon as the unrest among the Khoshots became known. Active hostilities broke out in 1715 with a Zunghar attack on Hami. They failed to take the city, due in no small part to the reinforcements K'ang-hsi had dispatched to the region when he feared a Khoshot revolt. This attack served the dual purpose of testing Manchu defenses at their most distant outposts and diverting attention away from Tibet, where the Zunghars planned to mount their main offensive. In 1717, after the important Tibetan monasteries agreed to support them against Lajang Khan, the Zunghars sent 6,000 men under the command of Tsering Dondup on a march from Khotan towards Lhasa. The choice of this difficult route through northwestern Tibet was designed to ensure surprise. The Zunghars also sent 300 horsemen to Kumbum monastery in order to recover the Seventh Dalai Lama and restore him to the throne in Lhasa.

The main force advanced smoothly through Tibet, but the raid on Kumbum failed. Tsering Dondup decided to proceed in spite of this setback. He won a series of battles, ending in an attack on Lhasa where Lajang Khan was killed. This victory was tempered by the displeasure of the Tibetans when they discovered that the Zunghars had not returned the Dalai Lama as promised. Tsering Dondup was soon forced to maintain his rule by force of arms. His

troops looted Lhasa and a number of monasteries with great loss of life.
The Manchus were alarmed by the fall of their client in Tibet. They
responded by attacking Zunghar territory in 1717 but with no great success.
The next year K'ang-hsi dispatched an army of 7,000 to attack the Zunghars in
Tibet. Tsering Dondup destroyed this force although he also suffered heavy
casualties. The Zunghars were faced with a second Ch'ing invasion in 1720
when K'ang-hsi ordered two armies, one from Szechwan and another from
Koko-nor, to advance west and north respectively. The Szechwan force
marched without opposition to occupy Lhasa as the Zunghars retreated south
to face the troops from Koko-nor. The Ch'ing army there consisted mostly of
Khoshots and other Mongols with some Manchu troops. K'ang-hsi had gained
their support by agreeing to restore the Seventh Dalai Lama to the throne in
Lhasa. Ironically, this gave the Ch'ing court the political advantage the Zunghars had originally sought. To keep the Zunghars from reinforcing Tsering
Dondup, two other armies were employed to attack Tsewang Rabtan. After a
running battle with the southern army, Tsering Dondup ordered a retreat and
the remnants of the Zunghar force went home. The Manchus entered Lhasa
with the Seventh Dalai Lama and established a protectorate over Tibet.

The Zunghar withdrawal from Tibet led to a period of watchful hostility in
Inner Asia as Tsewang Rabtan again waited for an opportune moment to strike
at the Ch'ing. Events on his Russian frontier opened up new possibilities. Peter
the Great had heard from his envoys that there were gold deposits in Yarkand
and, in 1715, he dispatched an armed expedition to find and exploit this wealth.
Unfortunately, the expedition blundered into Zungharia just as Tsewang
Rabtan had prepared his troops for attacks on the Ch'ing frontier and the
Russians were driven away. In 1719, a new expedition arrived to explore Lake
Iamysh. Galdan Tsering, Tsewang Rabtan's son, soundly defeated the Russians
there, in spite of the Russian force's superiority in firearms.

Tsewang Rabtan was not opposed to reaching some agreement with the
Czar. The strong Russian interest in gold mining could provide the basis for
mutual cooperation against China which would help regain Zunghar power lost
after their defeat in Tibet. After preliminary negotiations, a Zunghar envoy was
dispatched to the Czar in 1721 with a formal proposal. He offered free transit
for gold prospectors in exchange for an anti-Manchu alliance. Peter agreed in
principle to this proposal, offering troops and aid in return for Zunghar
submission and the right to mine gold in their territory. Tsewang Rabtan
needed such an alliance to block new Ch'ing advances in Turkestan, for in
1722 China occupied Urumchi. In spite of this threat, some Zunghars were
opposed to a Russian alliance on the grounds that the submission demanded by
the Czar was unacceptable. However, it is not clear that such a condition was
any more than a formality, and Rabtan certainly showed no signs that he was
prepared to relinquish his autonomy. Historically, in both China and Russia,
there was a tradition of requesting a formal submission from the nomads as a
prerequisite for diplomatic relations, even though no such condition existed in
reality. The Mongols, and earlier steppe peoples, were past masters at accepting the form and rejecting the content when this worked to their advantage.

The debate was rendered moot when word of K'ang-hsi's death reached the Zunghars.[21]

The death of the long-lived Manchu emperor in December 1722 changed the course of Inner Asian politics. The expected heir, Yin-ti, was leading the Zunghar campaign at the time, and being distant from the capital he lost the throne to his brother, who became the Yung-cheng Emperor. As a quasi-usurper, Yung-cheng had no desire to see his brother continue as a successful military commander backed by field-tested troops. He therefore made deals with Yin-ti's subordinates to factionalize the Ch'ing frontier army. He then recalled Yin-ti and withdrew Ch'ing troops from the area. The Khoshots took the opportunity to revolt. Ch'ing forces returned to mercilessly put down the uprising and Koko-nor was officially incorporated into the empire.

Tsewang Rabtan was unable to regain control of the Mongols in Koko-nor both because the rebellion there was not coordinated and because the Zunghars were preoccupied with a campaign against the Kazakhs in the west. In that campaign the Zunghars proved they were still a major Inner Asian power. They successfully attacked the cities of Tashkent and Turkistan and split the Kazakhs into three groups. Zunghar rule was extended into western Turkestan and on the steppe as far as Lake Barkol. A number of Kazakh chiefs of the Great and Middle hordes, as well as many Kirghiz, accepted Zunghar rule. The Ch'ing court was so preoccupied with internal disputes that it proposed a truce with the Zunghars which was signed in 1724. By this act the Chinese unwittingly forestalled the conclusion of a Russo-Zunghar alliance. With victory over the Kazakhs and a truce with China, the Zunghars had less interest in a deal with the Russians. The interest on the Russian side also disappeared after Peter the Great died in 1725.

Tsewang Rabtan died in 1727 and was succeeded by his son Galdan Tsering. The Ch'ing saw his death as a chance to reopen hostilities now that their own succession problems had been sorted out. Yung-cheng needed to neutralize the Russians, who had many unresolved complaints about the existing treaty, before going to war with the Zunghars. (It had been the declining value of the caravan trade and the difficulties in dealing with China that had encouraged Peter the Great to consider breaking with the Manchus in favor of the Zunghars.) By signing the wide-ranging Treaties of Kiakhta in 1728, the Ch'ing resolved these long-standing disputes and created the framework for Sino-Russian relations for the next hundred years. These treaties delineated the Mongolian frontier, organized diplomatic relations between the two empires, and set up regular trade. Like the Treaty of Nerchinsk, the new understanding was prompted by the Manchus' desire to isolate the Zunghars.[22]

In spite of opposition at court to more expensive frontier warfare, two armies were dispatched to fight the Zunghars. The northern route army was based in the Altai Mountain region while the southern route army was based in Hami. Raids and diplomatic exchanges began in 1730. The next year the northern route army was lured from its advance base in Khobdo by a small Zunghar attack. Falling victim to one of the oldest steppe tactics, the feigned retreat, the

Ch'ing commander unexpectedly found himself confronting the entire Zunghar nation. The nomads annihilated the northern route army, which lost four-fifths of its troops. Khobdo was evacuated and in the south Turfan was abandoned in fear of a Zunghar advance.[23]

This defeat destroyed the Ch'ing's northern shield, allowing the Zunghars to attack Mongolia directly. They crossed the Altai, pillaged the Khalkhas and destroyed Ch'ing forts. Because the Khalkhas had long been exploited to provide conscripts to guard the frontier, supply troops based in Mongolia, and provide horses to the Ch'ing war effort, their loyalty to the dynasty was in some doubt. Only the organized opposition of the Sayin Noyan Khan, Tsering, prevented the Zunghars from completely overrunning northern Mongolia. The Zunghars invaded Mongolia again in 1732, but in a fierce battle at Erdeni Juu, Tsering stopped their advance. The Zunghars retreated unmolested, however, because other Ch'ing commanders did nothing to oppose them. Nevertheless, the Manchus were to regain Uliasutai, and the war entered a period of stalemate in which envoys traded peace proposals. The war's expense and its rising unpopularity among the northern Mongols who bore the brunt of the fighting put pressure on the Ch'ing to seek a settlement. An agreement was not signed until 1739, however, at the start of the reign of the Ch'ien-lung Emperor. The treaty set the Altai Mountains and Lake Ubsa-nor as the boundary between the Zunghars and Khalkhas and brought twenty years of peace to the frontier.

Galdan Tsering died in 1745. Although his foreign adventures had failed, he left a viable Zunghar state, still powerful, prosperous, and able to fend off both Russian and Ch'ing advances. The most acute danger to the Zunghars, however, was internal strife which sapped their strength.

Galdan Tsering's successor was his second son, Tsewang Dorji Namgyal. He proved to be a spoiled and ineffective ruler who quickly alienated the Zunghar elite. He was deposed in 1750, blinded, and exiled in Aksu. The popular, but illegitimate, first son of Galdan Tsering, Lama Darja, was then named ruler. These events opened up the usual disputes about the rights of collateral descendants. Dawachi, the grandson of Tsering Dondup, made a bid for the throne in 1751 based on the claim that his grandfather was Tsewang Rabtan's brother. Lama Darja easily defeated Dawachi, forcing him to flee to the Kazakhs with the bulk of the Zunghar army hot on his heels. Among Dawachi's followers was a Khoyid chieftain Amursana, who escaped the defeat and then raised a thousand tribesmen with whose help he was able to advance on the Ili valley. In a surprise attack he killed Lama Darja, enabling Dawachi to return as ruler of the Zunghars.

These coups, civil wars, murders, and political intrigues broke the unity of the Zunghars. Like other steppe empires, the Zunghars were an imperial confederacy with a centralized court in charge of foreign relations, including trade, war, and internal security. At the local level, indigenous tribal leaders ruled their own people and were incorporated into the imperial hierarchy. Under normal conditions the imperial government kept these leaders in line, but when there was instability at the imperial level, the local leaders often acted individually, making their own deals unless or until imperial order was restored.

After the collapse of Zunghar central authority in 1750, local leaders acted in their own interest by refusing imperial commands or defecting to Ch'ing-controlled territory. Frontier commanders reported the arrival of important Zunghar leaders with their tribal followers. Even Amursana defected in 1754, along with 20,000 Khoshots, after an unsuccessful battle with Dawachi.

These defections and disorders within Zungharia provided the Ch'ien-lung emperor with an opportunity to complete his grandfather K'ang-hsi's conquests. In 1755 he prepared a new Zunghar campaign that employed defectors like Amursana in key roles. To gain further political support, Ch'ien-lung promised that each of the four major tribes would be resettled in its old territory under its own leaders. Unlike previous Ch'ing campaigns, this time the army advanced into Zungharia without facing serious military opposition because most Zunghars preferred surrender to fighting for Dawachi. He was captured and exiled to Peking where he was interned with princely honors. This easy conquest appeared to demonstrate that the Zunghars no longer constituted a serious danger to Ch'ing interests in Inner Asia. Ch'ien-lung quickly pulled most of his expeditionary force out of Zungharia and returned to China.

Dawachi's defeat was due less to Ch'ing power than to the politics of the Zunghar civil war. Amursana and the other defectors had no intention of giving up the empire. Following the inner frontier strategy, Amursana used Chinese wealth and military power to win a civil war, just as Tsewang Rabtan had done to destroy Galdan. As soon as the main Ch'ing force departed, Amursana demanded that he be recognized as supreme ruler of the Zunghars. When the Ch'ing court refused, Amursana revolted and organized his own confederation of Khoyids and Choros. Ch'ien-lung struck back in 1756. Renewing his promise that tribal leaders would maintain their positions, he dispatched large armies to reconquer the Ili region, forcing Amursana to flee to the Kazakhs. After restoring Ch'ing control, Ch'ien-lung again withdrew his armies, leaving only a small garrison to oversee the colonization of the Ili. The Zunghars revolted later in the same year, led by the very tribal leaders Ch'ien-lung had appointed. Amursana returned to take charge.

What had been planned as an opportunistic conquest turned into a tricky frontier problem for China. The withdrawal of Ch'ing troops had allowed the Zunghars to reorganize, yet to maintain a large force there threatened to provoke a revolt in Mongolia because of the expense of Inner Asian campaigns and their reliance on Khalkha troops and supplies. In order to begin his Zunghar war, Ch'ien-lung had requisitioned Khalkha livestock at well below its true value. The Khalkhas also had the responsibility of manning frontier defenses and providing troops. The unrest this provoked reached a crisis during the period of the last Zunghar wars. In 1756–7, when trouble in Ili was at its worst, Chinggunjab, a Khalkha leader, staged a rebellion against Ch'ing military and economic oppression. This revolt was not coordinated with Amursana, nor was it well led in Mongolia, where it was crushed. Nevertheless, the unsatisfactory policies of a quick evacuation of Ch'ing troops from Zunghar territory before it was militarily secured, and the attempts to rule indirectly through compliant Zunghar leaders, both stemmed from the need to bring the war to a close before more trouble erupted in Mongolia.[24]

A final campaign against the Zunghars was mounted in 1757. This time Ch'ing forces were aided both by tribal disorganization and, more importantly, by a smallpox epidemic which reportedly killed half the Zunghars. Amursana again fled to the Kazakhs, and then left them for Russian territory, where he too died of smallpox. The Ch'ing army instituted a policy of annihilation, supervised by their general, Chao-hui. He hunted down and killed most of the surviving Zunghars that could be found, while a few groups were deported to Manchuria. Those Zunghars that eventually remained were given grazing lands in the Ili under strict supervision. To finalize his victory, Ch'ien-lung proscribed the very name Zunghar.

The conquest of the Zunghars brings the history of nomadic empires to a close. From this time onward, conflicts in Inner Asia would be between the two remaining sedentary powers: Russia and China. A 2,000-year-old struggle had come to an end. It was not simply Ch'ing military power that had brought this about. A system that had in the past created and protected new nomadic states and ensured their survival had collapsed. A changing world economy, better transportation and communication, and the decline of the old imperial structure in China itself was rapidly putting an end to old patterns and relationships. The world of the steppe nomad was no longer his alone.

NOTES

1 Wakeman, "The Shun Interregnum of 1644."
2 Cf. Hsi, "Wu San-kuei in 1644: a reappraisal," pp. 443–53.
3 Kessler, *K'ang-hsi and the Consolidation of Ch'ing Rule, 1661–1684*, p. 17.
4 Oxnam, *Ruling from Horseback*, examines the Oboi regency in detail.
5 Kessler, *K'ang-hsi*, pp. 74–136.
6 Farquhar, *Ch'ing Administration of Mongolia*.
7 This following section on the Zunghars is based on Courant, *L'Asie centrale aux XVIIe et XVIIIe siècles: Empire kalmouk ou empire mantchou?*, which draws largely on Chinese records, supplemented by more recent Russian scholarship, the most complete being that of Zlatkin, *Istoriia Dzhungarskogo khanstva (1635–1758)*. The exact sequence of the early movements and the tribal composition of the Oirat/Zunghar confederation is still subject to considerable debate, cf. Zlatkin, *Istoriia*, pp. 31–4, 147–8.
8 Baddeley, *Russia, Mongolia, and China*.
9 Riazanovskii, *Fundamental Principles of Mongol Law*, pp. 46–52.
10 Akimushkin, "Le Turkestan oriental et les Oirats," also Akimushkin, *Shah-Mahmud ibn Mirza Fadil Churas: Khronika*, pp. 323–4.
11 Hummel, *Eminent Chinese of the Ch'ing Period*, I:305, II:784.
12 Courant, *L'Asie centrale*, p. 50.
13 Mancall, *Russia and China*, pp. 146–62.
14 Farquhar, *Ch'ing Administration of Mongolia*, pp. 71, 90.
15 Spence, *Emperor of China*, p. 13.
16 Ibid., p. 8.
17 Courant, *L'Asie centrale*.
18 Mancall, *Russia and China*, p. 210.

19 Courant, *L'Asie centrale*, p. 67.
20 Petech, *China and Tibet in the Eighteenth Century*, covers this whole period in great detail, drawing on both Chinese and Tibetan sources.
21 Mancall, *Russia and China*, pp. 211–15.
22 Ibid., pp. 249–55.
23 Cf. Parker, "Manchu relations with Turkestan," pp. 105–18.
24 Bawden, "The Mongol rebellion of 1756–57," pp. 1–31.

GLOSSARY OF KEY NAMES

MAIN TRIBES ON THE FRONTIER

CHAHAR
southern Mongolian tribe
represented senior Chinggisid line 16th–20th centuries
led resistance against early Manchu domination

KAZAKH
Muslim Turkish nomads
inhabited most of western Eurasian steppe 16th–20th centuries
often attacked by Zunghars

KHALKHA
Mongol tribes of northern Mongolia during Ch'ing dynasty
caught between Ch'ing and Zunghars

MANCHUS
renamed Jurchen forest tribes
core of Ch'ing dynasty conquest elite

TÜMED
southern Mongolian tribe of 16th–20th centuries
descendants of Altan Khan

ZUNGHAR
Western Mongols of Altai and Ili
descendants of Esen (Dörben Oirat confederation)
included Choros, Dörbet, Khoshot, and Torghut tribes
main nomad opposition to Ch'ing China
wiped out in mid-eighteenth century

KEY TRIBAL AND FOREIGN LEADERS AND RELIGIOUS FIGURES

DALAI LAMA
series of Buddhist incarnations in Tibet
led both the dGe-lugs-pa order and Tibetan government
"Great Fifth" (1617–82) key figure in Inner Asian politics

GALDAN BOSHUGHTU
Zunghar leader 1670
captures northern Mongolia
defeated by K'ang-hsi in series of steppe campaigns

GALDAN TSERING
  Zunghar ruler (1727–45)
  disintegration of empire began at his death
JEBTSUNDAMBA KHUTUGHTU
  highest Buddhist religious figure in northern Mongolia in Ch'ing times.
TSERING DONDUP
  Zunghar general who invaded Tibet in 1717
  brother of Tsewang Rabtan
TSEWANG RABTAN
  Zunghar ruler (1697–1727)
  seized leadership from uncle Galdan
  led fight with Ch'ing for control of Inner Asia

DYNASTY IN CHINA

Ch'ing (1644–1912)

KEY FIGURES IN CHINA

CHIEN-LUNG EMPEROR
  Manchu emperor of China (r. 1736–96)
  destroyed Zunghar state and people
  incorporated eastern Turkestan and Ili valley into China
DORGON
  Manchu leader of imperial line (1612–50)
  strongman responsible for conquest of China
K'ANG-HSI EMPEROR
  Manchu emperor of China (r. 1661–1722)
  incorporated northern Mongolia
  led fight against Galdan
  put down revolts in China
WU SAN-KUEI
  Ming frontier commander who defected to Manchus in 1644
  ruled much of southern China as vassal of Manchus
  failed revolt in 1674 almost toppled Ch'ing dynasty

9

Epilogue

On the Decline of the Mongols

Traditionally, the history of nomadic pastoralists in Inner Asia has been described as a case of unilineal development. The first 1,500 years is viewed as a period of ever-growing power in which one nomad empire followed another, culminating in the shattering conquests of the Mongols and their establishment of a nomadic state of unparalleled power and extent. With the collapse of the Mongol empire the steppe entered a period of unremitting decline, or decadence, for the next 500 years.[1] This period of decline is passed over quickly by most historians as a sad coda to the story of earlier nomadic greatness. The implication is that 1,500 years of carefully developed nomadic organization and power was squandered by wayward descendants in a half a millennium of degenerate living.

This view of steppe history is far from accurate. To view the Mongols as the product of a 1,500-year rise of the nomads ignores the sophistication of earlier steppe empires. The Hsiung-nu state developed the necessary structure and support for a nomadic empire in 200 BC. It was the most stable and long-lasting of any steppe empire. Stressing unilineal development also ignores the long periods of anarchy that followed the fall of both the Hsiung-nu and the Uighurs. For more than half of the pre-Mongol period, the steppe was weak and divided. Chinggis Khan's own struggle showed that the transition from anarchy to centralization could be exceptionally rapid. In less than a generation, nomads who lacked influence, strong organization, and security, even in their own homes, became masters of the world's largest empire. Although new empires often structurally resembled their predecessors, the nomads themselves were not conscious of the similarities because they had no memory of them. It was, ironically, the historical record of the literate Chinese, with their philosophy that the past should act as a mirror for the present, that stressed the continuity among nomadic states founded many centuries apart.

For a more accurate historical perspective it is necessary to examine the complex interaction between China, the steppe, and Manchuria, which created a regular cycle of development. The rise of powerful native dynasties in China and the unification of the steppe by nomadic empires was linked through the politics of trade and extortion. In this polarized world no autonomous border states could come into existence until China or the nomads lost their ability to control the frontier between them. Anarchy on the steppe and in China facilitated the conditions for the rise of Manchurian dynasties. These border dynasties moved out of the Liao River Basin area to conquer north China and keep the steppe in turmoil. The fall of these foreign dynasties to rebels in China opened the way for both the unification of China and the unification of the steppe. Far from being the logical culmination of developments in a long line of steppe empires, the Mongol empire was a unique hybrid that suppressed and overcame the usually fatal interference by a more sophisticated Manchurian state. Chinggis Khan combined a disciplined steppe nomad cavalry with a sophisticated technical corp, developed by Manchurians, into a single army. By linking nomadic mobility, striking power, and strategic thought with the ability to capture walled cities he produced a combination stronger than any other force previously known in Eurasia.

Following the collapse of the Mongol empire it is often assumed that the steppe nomads entered a period of steep decline, but this is an exaggeration. Later steppe rulers, of course, suffer by contrast to Chinggis Khan, but then few leaders of any kind fail to pale before such a comparison. However, this natural bias is compounded by the tendency in both Mongol and Chinese sources to focus on the Chinggisid line as the only legitimate source for steppe rulers and to minimize the importance of other groups. For example, Esen and the Oirats founded a fully functioning steppe empire that penetrated Ming defenses at will, destroyed an entire imperial army and captured an emperor, yet the Oirat empire has usually been treated as merely a minor interruption in the affairs of obscure Chinggisid leaders, who failed to measure up to their more famous ancestors. The supposed military weakness of the post-Yüan Mongols was certainly not apparent during Ming times. Throughout the Ming, not only the Oirats, but the Eastern Mongols under Dayan Khan and Altan Khan raided the Chinese frontier and even attacked Peking. In no other dynastic period was there as much continual frontier warfare with the nomads as in the Ming, demonstrating that the Mongols remained a major military threat centuries after their world empire had disappeared. Following the fall of the Ming, throughout the first century of Ch'ing rule the Eastern Mongols were that dynasty's military bulwark in Inner Asia against the expansion of the Zunghars.

Yet it is quite clear that by the nineteenth century there had been a great decline in both military power and economic prosperity on the steppe. Ch'ing records and accounts by western travelers paint a stark picture of poverty, exploitation, and political weakness in Mongolia. This state of decline in the last 150 years of the Ch'ing dynasty must be contrasted with the strength the Mongols displayed earlier. The traditional explanations of Mongol weakness in the Ch'ing period – the rise of monastic orders, a decadent aristocracy, and economic exploitation – were all results of Ch'ing policies that left the

Mongols far more vulnerable, once they were no longer needed to protect the dynasty from the Zunghars, to exploitation by both their own leadership and the Chinese.

Like other Manchurian dynasties, the Ch'ing was adept at dealing with tribal peoples. From a tribal background themselves, the Manchus understood the dynamics of steppe politics: marriage alliances, tensions between rival tribes or lineages, the necessity for nomad leaders to seek outside revenue, and the danger of rapid consolidation of nomadic power under able leaders. Previous Manchurian dynasties had met this threat by active campaigning on the steppe and by supporting rival tribes. Military campaigns and political interference were not designed to incorporate the steppe into China, but merely to keep it disorganized and to enable the ruling dynasty to crush any attempts at reunification. This policy is known in clearest detail from the history of the one time that it failed: when the Jurchen Chin dynasty pitted Mongols against Tatars, then Tatars against Mongols, and Naimans against Chinggis Khan. Chinggis's success at overcoming his enemies overshadowed the sophistication and effectiveness of a Manchurian policy that had previously served the T'o-pa Wei, the Khitan Liao, and the Jurchen Chin in good stead.

Ch'ing policy deviated from this usual Manchurian strategy. As a consequence of the Treaty of 1571 the Mongols remained divided into small tribal groups, the leaders of each having a personal tribute relationship with the Ming court. The structure of the Ming tributary system short-circuited attempts at unity because minor tribal leaders were fearful of losing autonomy and wealth if they became subordinates in a larger unified steppe empire. Division was further encouraged by a complex system of ranks and rewards that could be withdrawn for bad behavior. However, under Ming administration this system was passive. After the reign of the Yung-lo Emperor, Ming rulers did not try to employ the Mongol leaders, nor were the nomads part of a larger imperial structure. The Ming wanted to keep the nomads quiet and had simply recognized the status quo by giving aid to all tribal leaders, seemingly unaware that this would perpetuate division of the steppe. The Ming, unlike the T'ang, never seriously considered the use of nomads as allies: proposals to seek nomad aid against the Manchus or internal rebels were rejected at court.

The Manchus saw far more potential in this divided situation. At first, they merely replaced Ming subsidies with their own to buy Mongol support, but with the defeat of Lighdan Khan they initiated the banner system in southern Mongolia. The easy acceptance of this new organization was due in part to its use of a familiar tribal structure, for the banners and arrows were formed along traditional lines. It also succeeded because Ming aid had fragmented the steppe into small units, with petty leaders whose interests were preserved under the banner system. These leaders, from the conservative Chinggisid aristocracy, were confirmed in their traditional positions, granted new titles and subsidies, and given specifically defined territories with permanent control over a fixed group of subjects who were forbidden to leave their districts.

The Ch'ing turned the passive Ming approach into an active one by freezing in place a conservative nomadic leadership and making it part of the larger imperial hierarchy. Each petty ruler was tied to the court not just by tribute relations but by marriage alliances and offices in the Ch'ing government. Aggressive nomadic leaders could expend their energy expanding the Ch'ing imperium. The Mongol aristocracy saw its interests and those of the Ch'ing dynasty as one. The Manchus solved the problem of integrating the steppe by recognizing that it could not be ruled in a bureaucratic fashion. Rule in China was bureaucratic, rule on the steppe followed tribal lines, and both were integrated into the state at the imperial level. Unlike Han Chinese rulers, the Manchus did not see any need to use Chinese culture, institutions, or administrative structures on the steppe.

The greatest threat to this system was the Zunghars. They represented the old order of nomadic empires, an imperial confederacy capable of attacking over a huge frontier. They also posed a political danger. The banner system in Mongolia worked because of the cooperation of the Chinggisid aristocracy. It was they who gained the greatest benefits while their subjects lost both mobility and political freedom. A successful conquest of northern Mongolia would open the way to the destruction of this aristocracy by the non-Chinggisid Zunghars. This might well entice a majority of tribesmen to throw off Ch'ing rule if they thought they could get a better deal with the Zunghars, a fear illustrated by the defection of the Khalkha leaders to the Ch'ing following Galdan's attacks. The Ch'ing needed such leaders, but the Zunghars would have little use for them in a united steppe empire.

The Mongols acted both as a buffer for Ch'ing China and as their shock troops in Inner Asia. The Ch'ing relied on Mongol troops and supplies to fight the Zunghars, although leadership was largely in the hands of bannermen and members of the imperial clan. From the mid-seventeenth to mid-eighteenth centuries it was this traditional nomadic force, not firearms, which gave the dynasty its great Inner Asian conquests. Galdan had successfully fended off cannon with "armored" camels and K'ang-hsi was later forced to abandon his slow-moving artillery to keep pace with the retreating Zunghars. Cavalry remained the most important component of a steppe campaign. Without city walls or static defenses, slow-loading guns were not decisive. The Zunghar wars were fought along traditional lines.

The Zunghar defeat and the incorporation of their territory into the Ch'ing empire put an end to the usefulness of the Mongols as steppe fighters. The sharp decline of Mongol power began at this point, as elements which had been developing for fifty years suddenly accelerated. These included the decline of Mongol military readiness, the rise of monastic Buddhism, and economic exploitation which drained Mongolia of its wealth. These were all natural consequences of a Ch'ing administrative structure which had relegated the Mongols to a marginal position.

The Mongol armies had been organized into leagues in order to preserve their military readiness. Following the defeat of the Zunghars, the military importance of the leagues declined. While the Manchus may still have seen the Mongols as a military reserve, they allowed the previously rigorous system of inspections, annual reviews, and the quality of equipment to decline. In 1775, the Ch'ing court stopped sending representatives to view the troops and military reviews were held only once every three years. At the same time, the number of monasteries in Mongolia greatly expanded. The Ch'ing had kept close rein on the number of aristocratic Mongols and others who desired to become monks, in order not to sap military reserves. The rise in the number of monks corresponded with the declining need of the Ch'ing for Mongol troops. Ch'ing hegemony also established peace in Mongolia which allowed monasteries to be safely established in all parts of the steppe where they became centers for agriculture, trade, and learning. In some areas of Mongolia during the nineteenth century, between one-third and one-half of the male population became monks. Although the monks remained involved in the pastoral economy, sometimes even living at home, they were not liable for taxes or corvée labor. The monasteries themselves were endowed by gifts from the aristocracy and developed extensive livestock holdings in their own right.[2]

It has been argued that the Manchus deliberately fostered Buddhism in order to pacify the Mongols, but, in fact, they had adopted it under Altan Khan long before the Manchus arrived in Mongolia. Nor was Buddhism a sure cure for militarism, as neither the Eastern Mongols nor Zunghars stopped fighting after adopting the religion. If anything, the Manchus discouraged a strong desire by the Mongols to increase the number of monasteries and monks until after the Zunghars were defeated. After the Zunghar wars, when the barriers were lowered, it was Mongol money and support which created new monasteries. In this new context, the rise of monastic orders was not a threat to Ch'ing interests because the dynasty retained considerable influence over the Tibetan religious establishment through its representatives in Lhasa. Encouraging the Mongols to put their energy into religious endeavors instead of fighting was a natural, if unofficial, policy for a dynasty that was no longer militarily active in Inner Asia.

Ch'ing administration of Mongolia opened the steppe to direct economic exploitation by the Chinese for the first time. Previously it was the nomads who established the terms of trade for merchants who travelled in their territories, by setting prices or arranging barter exchanges. Nomads also went to frontier markets to trade. Ch'ing control of Mongolia gave Chinese merchants a chance to enter the steppe on their own by providing security for them and their property. Administrative posts and monasteries served as fixed bases from which these merchants could engage in long-term business. This expansion of Chinese merchants into Mongolia was opposed by the Ch'ing administration. The court issued decrees limiting both the duration of stay and the types of contracts Chinese merchants could have in Mongolia, but loopholes in the law and loose enforcement rendered these restrictions a dead letter. The Mongol economy suffered in a number of ways. Poor quality goods were delivered to the nomads in exchange for pastoral products which were deliberately undervalued by the merchants. However, the most damaging aspect of the trade was the introduction of credit and compound interest. Chinese merchants, mostly from Shansi, established large companies which extended money or goods on credit. Repayment at high rates of interest soon resulted in the interest charges bringing in far more revenue than the goods themselves. By means of compound interest, the wealth of Mongolia was drained into China, for there was no way for Mongols to rid themselves of the debts which over time amounted to most of a banner's assets. These debts were often secured by holding a whole banner financially responsible for the debts of its leaders, who were encouraged to import expensive luxury goods.[3]

These trading practices and wartime exactions were in part the cause of the revolt in northern Mongolia in 1756–7. Economic conditions worsened after this because when their need for frontier troops and baggage animals declined the Ch'ing dropped any serious attempts to restrict trade by Chinese merchants in Mongolia. The extreme poverty of Mongolia in the nineteenth century was due in large part to this exploitative structure of trade. Such a situation had not developed before because it could survive only under imperial protection. Before their incorporation into the Ch'ing banner system, nomad leaders who discovered the existence of sharp trade practices would seize a merchant's goods in punishment. Compound interest could only exist where there was a political structure to enforce debt repayments. When the nomads were autonomous they could simply move away and avoid payment. Traders would have to forgive debts that could not be repaid because of severe livestock losses if they wished to continue doing business. Under normal conditions merchants did not extend large amounts of credit to the nomads, but when they were regulated within the banner system it was possible to make large profits on paper and then collect them.

The Chinggisid aristocracy personally benefited from the system because they were extended almost unlimited credit in return for their banner's assets. After so many centuries of being on the Ming and Ch'ing payroll, they felt little responsibility for the plight of their nomad subjects, who were being squeezed. The defeat of the Zunghars removed the last threat that these aristocratic leaders might be superseded by more vigorous leadership. They became a class of tribute-extracting overseers at the edges of empire. Such was their alienation from ordinary Mongols that in southern Mongolia they sold tribal land to Chinese farmers for personal profit, destroying the very basis of the pastoral economy. Ch'ing political domination, with its numerous banners, restricted territories, appointed conservative tribal leaders, and corrupt imperial officials created an environment where merchants could exploit the Mongols with little danger of losing their assets.

Economic exploitation was also encouraged by the development of capitalism in China. Mongolia could now be drawn into a worldwide system of trade. The creation of railroads changed the relationship of the outer territories to the Chinese heartland. Goods could be transported cheaply by rail to urban centers from vast distances and Chinese settlers following the railhead took over ever larger tracts of Mongol land. Because the Russians had expanded into the steppe from the west, destroying the Kazakhs and Kirghiz in their wake, there was no autonomous territory to which the nomads could retreat.[4]

The collapse of the Ch'ing dynasty in China, and then the Czarist regime in Russia, brought about an end to the old system, but this did not lead to a re-emergence of nomadic power on the steppe. One of the oldest cycles of international relationships, long in decline, was dead. The traditional structure of trade and communications, war and politics, and of great deeds by men on horseback was no more.

NOTES

1 This assumption is quite apparent in bibliographical studies of Inner Asia. It is labeled "Period of Decadence" in Sinor's typology (*Introduction à l'étude de l'Eurasie centrale*) and followed by Schwarz for the most recent western bibliography of Mongolia, *Bibliotheca Mongolica*.

2 Farquhar, *Ch'ing Administration of Mongolia*, pp. 115–21, 148–9; cf. Miller, *Monasteries and Culture Change in Inner Mongolia*.

3 Bawden, *The Modern History of Mongolia*; Sandorj, *Manchu Chinese Colonial Rule in Northern Mongolia*.

4 Lattimore, *Studies in Frontier History*, pp. 134–59.

Bibliography

Aberle, David, *The Kinship System of the Kalmuk Mongols*. Albuquerque: University of New Mexico Press, 1953.

Akimushkin, O. F., "Le Turkestan oriental et les Oirats," *Études Mongoles*, 5 (1974): 157–63.

Akimushkin, O. F. (trans.), *Shah-Mahmud ibn Mirza Fadil Churas: Khronika*. Moscow: Nauka, 1976.

Allsen, Thomas, "The Yüan Dynasty and the Uighurs of Turfan in the 13th century," in *China among Equals*, Morris Rossabi (ed.), Berkeley: University of California Press, 1983, pp. 243–80.

Allsen, Thomas, "Guard and government in the reign of the Grand Qan Möngke, 1251–59," *Harvard Journal of Asiatic Studies*, 46 (1986): 523–50.

Andrews, P. A., "The white house of Khuransan: the felt tents of the Iranian Yomut and Goklen," *Journal of the British Institute of Iranian Studies*, 11 (1973): 93–110.

Bacon, Elizabeth, "Types of pastoral nomadism in Central and Southwest Asia," *Southwestern Journal of Anthropology*, 10 (1954): 44–68.

Baddeley, John, *Russia, Mongolia, and China*. New York: Macmillan, 1919.

Barfield, Thomas, "The Hsiung-nu Imperial Confederacy: organization and foreign policy," *The Journal of Asian Studies*, 41 (1981): 45–61.

Barth, Fredrik, "The land use patterns of migratory tribes of South Persia," *Norsk Geografisk Tidsskrift*, 17 (1960): 1–11.

Barthold, V. V., *Zwölf Vorlesungen über die Geschichte der Türken Mittelasiens*. Berlin: Deutsche Gesellschaft für Islamkunde, 1935.

Barthold, V. V., *Turkestan down to the Mongol Invasion*. London: Gibb Memorial Series, 1968.

Bawden, Charles (trans.), *The Mongol Chronicle Altan Tobci*. Wiesbaden: Harrassowitz, 1955.

Bawden, Charles, *The Modern History of Mongolia*. New York: Praeger, 1968.

Bawden, Charles, "The Mongol rebellion of 1756–57," *Journal of Asian History*, 2 (1968): 1–31.

Bielenstein, Hans, "The restoration of the Han dynasty," *Bulletin of the Museum of Far Eastern Antiquities*, 39 (1967): 92ff.

Bielenstein, Hans, "Chinese historical demography A.D. 2–1982," *Bulletin of the Museum of Far Eastern Antiquities*, 59 (1987).

Bingham, Woodbridge, *The Founding of the T'ang Dynasty*. Baltimore, Md: Waverley Press, 1941.

Boodberg, Peter A., "Two notes on the history of the Chinese frontier," *Harvard Journal of Asiatic Studies*, 1 (1936): 283–307.

Boyle, John A. (trans.), *The History of the World Conqueror*, 2 vols (Ata Malik Juvaini). Manchester: Manchester University Press, 1958.

Boyle, John A. (trans.), *The Successors of Genghis Khan (translated from the Persian of Rashid al-Din)*. New York: Columbia University Press, 1971.

Bulliet, Richard, *The Camel and the Wheel*. Cambridge, Mass.: Harvard University Press, 1975.

Burnham, Philip, "Spatial mobility and political centralization in pastoral societies," in *Pastoral Production and Society*, L'Équipe écologie et anthropologie des sociétés pastorales (ed.), Cambridge: Cambridge University Press, 1979.

Cambridge History of China: Sui and T'ang, 589–906, vol. 3, part 1, Denis Twitchett (ed.). Cambridge: Cambridge University Press, 1979.

Cambridge History of China, vol. 9, part 1. Cambridge: Cambridge University Press, (forthcoming).

Cambridge History of Iran: The Saljuq and Mongol Period, vol. 5, John Boyle (ed.). Cambridge: Cambridge University Press, 1968.

Chan, Albert, *The Glory and Fall of the Ming Dynasty*. Norman, OK.: University of Oklahoma Press, 1982.

Chan, Hok-lam, *Legitimation in Imperial China: Discussions under the Jurchen-Chin Dynasty (1115–1234)*. Seattle: University of Washington Press, 1984.

Chang, K. C., *Archaeology of Ancient China*. New Haven, Conn.: Yale University Press, 1977.

Cleaves, Francis (trans.), *The Secret History of the Mongols*. Cambridge, Mass.: Harvard University Press, 1982.

Courant, Maurice, *L'Asie centrale aux XVIIe et XVIIIe siècles: Empire kalmouk ou empire mantchou?* Lyon: 1912.

Crespigny, Ralph, *The Last of the Han*. Canberra: Australian National University, 1969.

Dardess, John, *Conquerors and Confucians: Aspects of Political Change in Late Yüan China*. New York: Columbia University Press, 1963.

Dardess, John, "From Mongol empire to Yüan dynasty: changing forms of imperial rule in Mongolia and central Asia," *Monumenta Serica*, 30 (1972–73): 117–65.

de Rachewiltz, Igor, "Yeh-lü Ch'ü-ts'ai (1189–1243): Buddhist idealist and Confucian statesman," in *Confucian Personalities*, A. F. Wright and Denis Twitchett (eds), Stanford, CA: Stanford University Press, 1962.

des Rotours, Robert, *Histoire de Ngan Lou-chan*. Paris: Presses Universitaires de France, 1962.

Downs, James, "The origin and spread of riding in the Near East and central Asia," *American Anthropologist*, 63 (1961): 1193–203.

Dreyer, Edward, *Early Ming China*. Stanford, CA: Stanford University Press, 1982.

Dubs, H. H., *The History of the Former Han Dynasty*, 3 vols. Baltimore, Md: Johns Hopkins University Press, 1938–55.

Eberhard, Wolfram, "Chronologische Übersicht über die Geschichte der Hunnen in der späteren Han-Zeit (25 n. Chr. – 220 n. Chr.)," *Türk Tarih Kurumu Belleten*, 4 (1940): 387–441.

Eberhard, Wolfram, *Das Toba-Reich Nord Chinas: eine soziologische Untersuchung*. Leiden: Brill, 1949.

Eberhard, Wolfram, *Conquerors and Rulers*. Leiden: Brill, 1970.

Ecsedy, Hilda, "Trade and war relations between the Turks and China in the second half of the 6th century," *Acta Orientalia Hungaricae*, 21 (1968): 131–80.

Ecsedy, Hilda, "Tribe and tribal society in the sixth century Turk empire," *Acta Orientalia Hungaricae* (B), 25 (1972): 245–62.

Endicott-West, Elizabeth, "Imperial governance in Yüan times," *Harvard Journal of Asiatic Studies*, 46 (1986): 495–522.

Fang, Achilles, *The Chronicle of the Three Kingdoms (220–265)*, 2 vols. Cambridge, Mass.: Harvard University Press, 1965.

Farmer, Edward, *Early Ming Government – The Evolution of the Two Capitals*. Cambridge, Mass.: Harvard University Press, 1976.

Farquhar, David, "Oirat–Chinese tribute relations, 1408–1459," in *Studia Altaica: Festschrift für Nikolaus Poppe*, Wiesbaden: Otto Harrassowitz, 1957, pp. 60–8.

Farquhar, David, "Ch'ing administration of Mongolia." Cambridge, Mass.: Harvard University thesis, 1960.

Farquhar, David, "The origins of the Manchus' Mongolian Policy," in *The Chinese World Order*, John Fairbank (ed.), Cambridge, Mass.: Harvard University Press, 1968, pp. 198–205.

Farquhar, D. M., "Structure and function in the Yüan imperial government," in *China Under Mongol Rule*, J. D. Langlois (ed.), Princeton, NJ: Princeton University Press, 1981, pp. 25–55.

Fletcher, Joseph, "The Mongols: ecological and social perspective," *Harvard Journal of Asiatic Studies*, 46 (1986): 11–50.

Franke, Herbert, "Chinese texts on the Jürchen. A translation of the Jürchen monograph in the San-ch'ao pei-meng hui-pien," *Zentralasiatische Studien*, 9 (1975): 119–86.

Franke, Wolfgang, "Yung-lo's Mongolei-Feldzüge," *Sinologische Arbeiten*, 3 (1945): 1–54.

Gardiner, K. H. J., "The Kung-sun warlords of Liao-tung 189–238," *Papers on Far Eastern History*, 5 (1972): 59–107; 6 (1972): 141–204.

Goodrich, Carrington, and Chaoying Fang, *Dictionary of Ming Biography 1368–1644*. New York: Columbia University Press, 1976.

Goody, Jack, *Succession to High Office*. Cambridge: Cambridge University Press, 1966.

Griffith, Samuel (trans.), *Sun Tzu: The Art of War*. Oxford: Oxford University Press, 1963.

Gryaznov, Mikhail, *The Ancient Civilization of Southern Siberia*. New York: Cowles, 1969.

Haloun, Gustav, "The Liang-chou rebellion, 184–221 AD," *Asia Major* n.s., 1 (1949): 119–38.

Hamilton, James R. *Les Ouïghours à l'époque des Cinq Dynasties d'après les documents chinois*. Paris: Bibliothèque de l'Institut des Hautes Études Chinoises, vol. 10, 1955.

Harmatta, J., "The dissolution of the Hun Empire," *Acta Archaeologica*, 2 (1952): 277–304.

Herodotus (trans. David Grene), *The History*. Chicago: University of Chicago Press, 1987.

Ho, Ping-ti, "An estimate of the total population of Sung-Chin China," in *Études Song en Memorium Etienne Balazs*, Françoise Aubin (ed.), Paris: 1970, pp. 3–53.

Holder, Preston, *The Hoe and the Horse on the Plains*. Lincoln, NB: University of Nebraska Press, 1970.

Holmgren, Jennifer, "The Empress Dowager Ling of the Northern Wei and the T'o-pa sinicization question," *Papers on Far Eastern History*, 18 (1978): 123–70.

Hsi, Angela, "Wu San-kuei in 1644: a reappraisal," *Journal of Asian Studies*, 34 (1975): 443–53.

Hsiao, Ch'i-ch'ing, *The Military Establishment of the Yüan Dynasty*. Cambridge, Mass.: Harvard East Asian Monograph Series no. 77, Harvard University Press, 1978.

Hsu, Cho-yun, *Ancient China in Transition: An Analysis of Social Mobility, 722–222 B.C.* Stanford, CA: Stanford University Press, 1965.

Hulsewé, A. F. P., *China in Central Asia, The Early Stage: 125 B.C.–A.D. 23.* Leiden: Brill, 1979.

Hummel, Arthur, *Eminent Chinese of the Ch'ing Period*. Washington, DC: US Government Printing Office, 1942–43.

Ikeuchi, Hiroshi, "A Study of the Fu-yü," *Memoirs of the Research Department of the Toyo Bunko*, 6 (1939): 23–60.

Irons, William, "Political stratification among pastoral nomads," in *Pastoral Production and Society*, L'Équipe écologie et anthropologie des sociétés pastorales (ed.), Cambridge: Cambridge University Press, 1979.

Jackson, Peter, "The dissolution of the Mongol Empire," *Central Asiatic Journal*, 22 (1978): 186–244.

Jenner, W. J. F., *Memories of Loyang*. Oxford: Oxford University Press, 1981.

Jettmar, Karl, *The Art of the Steppes*. New York: Crown, 1964.

Jou-jan tzu-liao chi-lu (Collection of historical source material on the Jou-jan). Peking, 1965.

Kessler, Lawrence, *K'ang-hsi and the Consolidation of Ch'ing Rule, 1661–1684*. Chicago: University of Chicago Press, 1976.

Khazanov, Anatoly, *Nomads and the Outside World*. Cambridge: Cambridge University Press, 1985.

Kierman, Frank, "Phases and modes of combat in early China," in *Chinese Ways in Warfare*, Frank Kierman and John Fairbank (eds), Cambridge, Mass.: Harvard University Press, 1974, pp. 27–66.

Kollautz, Arnauf, and Hisayuki, Miyakawa, *Geschichte und Kultur eines völkerwanderungszeitlichen Nomadenvolks: die Jou-jan der Mongolei und die Awaren in Mitteleuropa*, 2 vols. Klagenfurt: Rudolf Habelt Verlag, 1970.

Kostiner, Joseph and Khoury, Phillip (eds), *Tribe and State in the Middle East*. Princeton, NJ: Princeton University Press, forthcoming.

Krader, Lawrence, "The ecology of central Asian pastoralism," *Southwestern Journal of Anthropology*, 11 (1955): 301–26.

Krader, Lawrence, *Social Organization of the Mongol-Turkic Pastoral Nomads*. The Hague: Mouton, 1963.

Krader, Lawrence, "The origin of the state among nomads," in *Pastoral Production and Society*, L'Équipe écologie et anthropologie des sociétés pastorales (ed.), Cambridge: Cambridge University Press, 1975.

Langlois, J. D., *China Under Mongol Rule*. Princeton, NJ: Princeton University Press, 1981.

Lattimore, Owen, *Inner Asian Frontiers of China*. New York: American Geographical Society, 1940.

Lattimore, Owen, *Studies in Frontier History*. Oxford: Oxford University Press, 1962.

Le Strange, Guy, *The Lands of the Eastern Caliphate*. London: 1905.

Ledyard, Gari, "Yin and Yang in the China–Manchuria–Korea Triangle," in *China among Equals*, Morris Rossabi (ed.), Berkeley, CA: University of California Press, 1983.

Levy, Howard, *Biography of An Lu-shan*. Berkeley, CA: University of California Press, 1960.

Li, Gertraude Roth, "The rise of the Manchu state: a portrait drawn from Manchu sources to 1636." Cambridge, Mass.: Harvard University thesis, 1975.

Liddell-Hart, Basil, *Great Captains Unveiled*. London: 1928.

Lindholm, Charles, "Kinship structure and political authority: the Middle East and Central Asia," *Journal of Comparative History and Society*, 28 (1986): 334–55.

Liu, Mau-tsai, *Die chinesischen Nachrichten zur Geschichte der Ost-Türken (T'u-kue)*, 2 vols. Wiesbaden: Otto Harrassowitz, 1958.

Loewe, M. A. N., *Records of the Han Administration*, 2 vols. Cambridge: Cambridge University Press, 1967.

Loewe, M. A. N., "The campaigns of Han Wu-ti," in *Chinese Ways in Warfare*, Frank Kierman and John Fairbank (eds), Cambridge, Mass.: Harvard University Press, 1974.

Loewe, M. A. N., *Crisis and Conflict in Han China*. London: George Allen and Unwin, 1974.

Mackerras, Colin, "Sino-Uighur diplomatic and trade contacts (744 to 840)," *Central Asiatic Journal*, 13 (1969): 215–40.

Mackerras, Colin, *The Uighur Empire (744–840) According to the T'ang Dynastic Histories*. Columbia, SC: University of South Carolina Press, 1972.

Mancall, Mark, *Russia and China: Their Diplomatic Relations until 1728*. Cambridge, Mass.: Harvard University Press, 1971.

Martin, H. Desmond, *The Rise of Chinggis Khan and his Conquest of North China*. Baltimore, Md: Johns Hopkins University Press, 1950.

Michael, Franz, *Origin of Manchu Rule in China*. Baltimore, Md: Johns Hopkins Press, 1942.

Michaud, Paul, "The Yellow Turbans," *Monumenta Serica*, 17 (1958): 47–127.

Miller, Robert, *Monasteries and Culture Change in Inner Mongolia*. Wiesbaden: Otto Harrassowitz, 1959.

Minorski, V. "Tamim ibn Bahr's journey to the Uyghurs," *Bulletin of the School of Oriental and African Studies*, 12 (1948): 275–305.

Molè, Gabriella, *The T'u-yü-hun from the Northern Wei to the Time of the Five Dynasties*. Rome: 1970.

Mori, Masao, *Historical Studies of the Ancient Turkic Peoples*. [In Japanese]. Tokyo: Yamakawa Shuppansha, 1967.

Mori, Masao, "Reconsideration of the Hsiung-nu state – a response to Professor O. Pritsak's criticism," *Acta Asiatica*, 24 (1973): 20–34.

Mostaert, Antoine, *Sur quelques passages de l'Histoire secrète des Mongols*. Cambridge, Mass.: Harvard–Yenching Institute, 1953.

Mote, Frederick, "The T'u-mu Incident of 1449," in *Chinese Ways in Warfare*, Frank Kierman and John Fairbank (eds), Cambridge, Mass.: Harvard University Press, 1974, pp. 243–72.

Murazaev, Eduard, *Die mongolische Volksrepublik, physisch-geographische*. Gotha: Geographisch-Kartographische Anstalt, 1954.

Okada, Hidehiro, "The life of Dayan Qaghan," *Acta Asiatica*, 11 (1966): 46–55.

Oxnam, Robert, *Ruling from Horseback: Manchu Politics in the Oboi Regency, 1661–1669*. Chicago: University of Chicago Press, 1975.

Parker, Edward H., "Manchu relations with Turkestan," *China Review*, 16 (1887–88): 105–18.

Parker, Edward, "History of the Wu-wan or Wu-hwan Tunguses of the first century; followed by that of their kinsmen the Sien-pi," *China Review*, 20 (1892–93): 71–92.

Parker, Edward H., "The Turko-Scythian Tribes," *China Review*, 20 (1892–93): 1–24, 109–25.

Parker, Edward H., "The Turko-Scythian Tribes," *China Review*, 21 (1894–95): 100–19, 129–37, 253–67, 291–301.

Parker, Edward H., "The Early Turks," *China Review*, 24 (1899–1900): 120, 163, 170, 227.

Parker, Edward H., "The Early Turks," *China Review*, 25 (1900–01): 1–270.

Pelliot, Paul, *Notes critiques d'histoire kalmouke*. Paris: Librairie d'Amérique et l'Orient Adrien-Maisonneuve, 1960.

Petech, Luciano, *China and Tibet in the 18th Century*. Leiden: Brill, 1972.

Pinks, Elisabeth, *Die Uiguren von Kan-chou in der frühen Sung-Zeit (960–1028)*. Wiesbaden: Otto Harrassowitz, 1968.

Pokotilov, D., *History of the Eastern Mongols During the Ming Dynasty from 1368 to 1634*. Philadelphia: Porcupine Press, 1976.

Pritsak, Omeljan, "Die 24 Ta-ch'en, Studie zur Geschichte des Verwaltungsaufbaus der Hsiung-nu Reiche," *Oriens Extremus*, 1 (1954): 178–202.

Pritsak, Omeljan, *The Origin of Rus'*, vol. 1: *Old Scandinavian Sources other than the Sagas*. Cambridge, Mass.: Harvard University Press, 1981.

Prušek, Jaroslav, *Chinese Statelets and the Northern Barbarians in the Period 1400–300 BC*. Amsterdam: Reidel, 1971.

Pulleyblank, Edwin G., *The Background of the Rebellion of An Lu-shan*. London: London Oriental Series vol. 4, 1955.

Pulleyblank, Edwin G. "Some remarks on the Toquz-oghuz problem," *Ural-Altaische Jahrbücher*, 28 (1956): 35–42.

Radloff, Wilhelm, *Aus Siberien*, 2 vols. Leipzig: Weigal Nachfolger, 1983.

Riazanovskii, Valentin, *Fundamental Principles of Mongol Law*. Bloomington, Ind.: Ural and Altaic Series vol. 43, 1965 [1937].

Rogers, Michael, *The Chronicle of Fu Chien*. Berkeley, CA: Chinese Dynastic Histories Translation Series, 1968.

Roth, Gertraude, "The Manchu–Chinese relationship," in *From Ming to Ch'ing: Conquest, Region, and Continuity in Seventeenth Century China*, Jonathan Spence and John

Wills (eds), New Haven, Conn.: Yale University Press, 1979, pp. 1–38.

Rudenko, S. I., *Die Kultur der Hsiung-nu und die Hügelgräber von Noin Ula*. Bonn: Rudolf Habelt Verlag, 1969.

Rudenko, Sergei, *Frozen Tombs of Siberia: The Pazyryk Burials of Iron Age Horsemen*. London: Dent and Sons, 1970.

Sahlins, Marshall, "The segmentary lineage: an organization for predatory expansion," *American Anthropologist*, 63 (1960): 322–45.

Sahlins, Marshall, *Islands of History*. Chicago: University of Chicago Press, 1985.

Sandorj, M., *Manchu Chinese Colonial Rule in Northern Mongolia*. New York: St Martin's Press, 1980.

Schmidt, I. J., *Geschichte der Ost-Mongolen und ihres Fürstenhauses verfasst von Ssanang Ssetsen Chungtaidschi der Ordus*. The Hague: Mouton, 1961 [1829].

Schreiber, Gerhardt, "Das Volk der Hsien-pi zur Han-Zeit," *Monumenta Serica*, 12 (1947): 145–203.

Schreiber, Gerhardt, "The history of the former Yen dynasty," *Monumenta Serica*, 14 (1949–55): 374–480 and 15 (1956): 1–141.

Schurmann, Franz, *The Economic Structure of the Yüan Dynasty*. Cambridge, Mass.: Harvard University Press, 1956.

Schwarz, Henry, *Bibliotheca Mongolica*, part I: *Works in English, French and German*. Bellingham, WA: Western Washington, 1978.

Serruys, Henry, *Sino-Mongol Relations During the Ming*. 1: *The Mongols in China during the the Hung-wu Period*. Brussels: Institut Belge des Hautes Études Chinoises, 1959.

Serruys, Henry, *Sino-Mongol Relations During the Ming*. 2: *The Tribute System and the Diplomatic Missions*. Brussels: Institut Belge des Hautes Études Chinoises, 1967.

Serruys, Henry, *Sino-Mongol Relations During the Ming*. 3: *Trade Relations – The Horse Fairs*. Brussels: Institut Belge des Hautes Études Chinoises, 1975.

Shaughnessy, Edward, "Historical perspectives on the introduction of the chariot in China," *Harvard Journal of Asiatic Studies*, 48 (1988): 189–238.

Sinor, Denis, *Introduction à l'étude de l'Eurasie centrale*. Wiesbaden: Harrassowitz, 1963.

Smith, John, "Mongol and nomadic taxation," *Harvard Journal of Asiatic Studies*, 30 (1967): 46–85.

Spence, Johnathan, *Emperor of China: A Self-portrait of K'ang-hsi*. New York: Random House, 1974.

Spuler, Bertold, *History of the Mongols: Based on Eastern and Western Accounts of the Thirteenth and Fourteenth Centuries*. Berkeley, CA: University of California Press, 1972.

Stenning, Derrick, *Savannah Nomads*. Oxford: Oxford University Press, 1953.

Tao, Jing-shen, *The Jurchen in Twelfth Century China*. Seattle, WA: University of Washington Press, 1976.

Tao, Jing-shen, "Barbarians or Northerners: Northern Sung images of the Khitans," in *China among Equals*, Morris Rossabi (ed.), Berkeley, CA: University of California Press, 1983, pp. 66–88.

Tapper, Richard, "Your tribe or mine? Anthropologists, historians and tribespeople on the concept of tribe in the Middle East," in *Tribe and State in the Middle East*, Joseph Kostiner and Phillip Khoury (eds), Princeton, NJ: Princeton University Press, forthcoming.

Tekin, Talat, *A Grammar of Orkhon Turkic*. Bloomington: Indiana University Press, 1968.

Twitchett, Denis, "The composition of the T'ang ruling class," in *Perspectives on the T'ang*, Arthur Wright and Denis Twitchett (eds), New Haven, Conn.: Yale University Press, pp. 47–86.

Tzu Chih T'ung Chien (Comprehensive Mirror for Aid in Government), by Ssu-ma Kuang. Ku-chi ch'u-pan-she edition. Peking, 1956.

Vainshtein, Sevyan, *Nomads of South Siberia: The Pastoral Economies of Tuva*. Cambridge: Cambridge University Press, 1980.

Vladimirtsov, Boris I., *Le régime social des Mongols: le féodalisme nomade*. Paris: Adrien Maisonneuve, 1948.

Vladimirtsov, Boris I., *The Life of Genghis-khan*. Boston, Mass.: Houghton Mifflin, 1930.

Wada, Sei, "A study of Dayan Khan," *Memoirs of the Research Department of the Toyo Bunko*, 19 (1960): 1–42.

Wakeman, Frederic, "The Shun Interregnum of 1644," in *From Ming to Ch'ing*, Johnathan Spence and John Wills (eds), New Haven, Conn.: Yale University Press, 1979, pp. 39–88.

Wang, Gungwu, *Structure of Power in the Five Dynasties*. Stanford, CA: Stanford University Press, 1963.

Watson, Burton, *Records of the Grand Historian of China*, 2 vols. New York: Columbia University Press, 1961.

Wittfogel, Karl and Feng, Chia-sheng, *The History of Chinese Society: Liao (907–1125)*. Philadelphia: American Philosophical Society, 1949.

Wolf, Eric, *Europe and the People Without History*. Berkeley, CA: University of California Press, 1982.

Wright, Arthur, "Fu-t'u-teng: a biography," *Harvard Journal of Asiatic Studies*, 11 (1948): 321–3.

Wright, Arthur, *The Sui Dynasty*. New York: Knopf, 1978.

Wylie, A. (trans.), "History of the Heung-noo in their relations with China," *Journal of the Royal Anthropological Institute*, 3 (1874): 396–451 and 5 (1875): 41–80.

Yang, Lien-sheng, "Notes on the economic history of the Chin dynasty," *Harvard Journal of Asiatic Studies*, 9 (1946): 107–85.

Yang, Lien-sheng, "Historical notes on the Chinese world order," in *The Chinese World Order*, John Fairbank (ed.), Cambridge, Mass.: Harvard University Press, 1968, pp. 20–33.

Yü, Ying-shih, *Trade and Expansion in Han China: A Study in the Structure of Sino-Barbarian Economic Relations*. Berkeley, CA: University of California Press, 1967.

Zlatkin, I. Ia., *Istoriia Dzhungarskogo khanstva (1635–1758)*. Moscow: Nauka, 1964.

CHINESE SOURCES

The following lists the standard Chinese histories cited in the text in chronological order. All are *Po-na* editions, Shanghai, Commercial Press, 1937.

Shih-chi (Records of the Historian) of Ssu-ma Ch'ien.

Han-shu (History of the Former Han dynasty) by Pan Ku.
Hou Han-shu (History of the Later Han dynasty) by Fan Yeh.
San Kuo Chih (Chronicle of the Three Kingdoms) by Ch'en Shou.
Wei-shu (History of the [T'o-pa] Wei dynasty) by Wei Shou.
Chin-shu (History of the Chin Dynasty) by Fang Hsüan-ling.
Chou-shu (History of the Chou Dynasty) by Ling-hu Te-fen.
Peh-shi (Record of the Northern Dynasties) by Li Yen-shou.
Chiu T'ang-shu (Old T'ang History) by Liu Hsü.
Hsin T'ang-shu (New T'ang History) by Ou-yang Hsiu.
Liao-Shih (History of the [Khitan] Liao Dynasty) by Ou-yang Hsüan.
Wu-tai Shih-chi (History of the Five Dynasties) by Ou-yang Hsiu.
Chin-shu (History of the [Jurchen] Chin dynasty) by Ou-yang Hsüan.
Yüan-shih (History of the [Mongol] Yüan dynasty) by Sung Lien.
Ming-Shih (History of the Ming dynasty) by Chang T'ing-yü.

Index